THE FATE
OF NATIONS

THE FATE OF NATIONS

THE STORY OF THE FIRST WORLD WAR VOLUME TWO

G. J. MEYER

AMBERLEY

Dedicated to the memory of my parents,
Cornelia E. and Justin G. Meyer

First published 2018

Amberley Publishing
The Hill, Stroud
Gloucestershire, GL5 4EP

www.amberley-books.com

Copyright © G. J. Meyer 2006, 2018

The right of G. J. Meyer to be identified as
the Author of this work has been asserted
in accordance with the Copyrights,
Designs and Patents Act 1988.

ISBN 978 1 4456 8015 6 (print)
ISBN 978 1 4456 8016 3 (ebook)

British Library Cataloguing in
Publication Data.
A catalogue record for this book is
available from the British Library.

Maps by Jeffrey L. Ward.
Book design by Virginia Norey.
Origination by Amberley Publishing.
Printed in Great Britain.

Contents

List of Illustrations

Abbreviations for List of Illustrations

CNP   *Collier's New Photographic History of the World's War* (New York, 1918)

CPE   *Collier's Photographic History of the European War* (New York, 1918)

GW   *The Great World War: A History*, edited by Frank A. Mumby (Gresham Publishing Company, five volumes 1915–1917)

HW   *History of the World War* by Francis A. March (Philadelphia, 1918)

IWM   Imperial War Museum

NA   National Archives

NW   *The Nations at War* by Willis John Abbot (New York, 1917)

WW   *Liberty's Victorious Conflict: A Photographic History of the World War* (Woman's Weekly, Chicago, 1918)

List of Maps

Chronology

1916

January 8:   British complete evacuation of Gallipoli peninsula.

February 21:   Germans open offensive at Verdun.

March 18:   Russians attack German defenders at Lake Naroch.

May 5:   Beginning of Arab revolt against Ottoman Empire.

May 31:   The Battle of Jutland in the North Sea.

June 4:   Russians begin the Brusilov offensive in Austria and Poland.

July 1:   British and French begin the Battle of the Somme.

August 27:   Romania declares war on Austria-Hungary.

August 29:   Hindenburg replaces Falkenhayn as chief of German General Staff.

September 1:   Bulgaria declares war on Romania.

September 3:   German-Bulgarian-Turkish force invades Romania.

October 24:   French launch counteroffensive at Verdun.

November 23:   Provisional Greek government declares war on Germany and Bulgaria.

December 5:   David Lloyd George replaces H. H. Asquith as British prime minister.

December 6:   German troops enter Bucharest, Romania.

December 12:   Joseph Joffre is replaced by Robert Nivelle as commander of French forces on the Western Front.

1917

January 31:	Germany announces resumption of unrestricted submarine warfare.
February 3:	United States ends diplomatic relations with Germany.
February 23:	Germans begin withdrawal to Hindenburg Line on Western Front.
March 1:	Contents of Zimmermann telegram are made public.
March 15:	Tsar Nicholas II abdicates.
April 6:	United States declares war.
April 9:	British attack opens Battle of Arras.
April 16:	Nivelle offensive begins with French attack at the Chemin des Dames.
April 17:	First outbreak of mutiny among French troops on Western Front.
May 12:	John J. Pershing is appointed commander of American Expeditionary Force.
May 15:	Nivelle is replaced by Henri-Philippe Pétain as French commander in chief.
June 7:	British offensive at Messines Ridge in Flanders.
July 1:	Russians launch Kerensky offensive.
July 31:	British attack opens Third Battle of Ypres (Passchendaele).
October 24:	Austro-Hungarian forces open Battle of Caporetto on Italian front.
November 6:	Passchendaele falls to Canadian Corps, ending Third Battle of Ypres. Bolsheviks under Lenin and Trotsky overthrow Russian government.
November 20:	British attack with tanks at Cambrai.

1918

January 8:	Woodrow Wilson presents Fourteen Points peace program to Congress.
March 3:	Russians accept German peace terms at Brest-Litovsk.
March 21:	Germans launch Operation Michael on Western Front.

March 28: General Pershing invites Foch to use U.S. troops against German offensive.

April 9: Germans launch Operation Georgette.

April 14: Ferdinand Foch is named General in Chief of the Allied Armies.

May 27: Germans launch offensive at the Chemin des Dames and the River Aisne.

June 9: Germans attack at the River Matz.

July 15: Germans open final offensive in Champagne along the River Marne.

July 18: British and French counterattack to begin the Second Battle of the Marne, forcing German withdrawal.

August 8: British launch Amiens offensive, "the Black Day of the German Army."

August 21: Germans begin withdrawal back to Hindenburg Line.

September 8: Germans begin withdrawal from St. Mihiel salient.

September 15: Allied Army of the Orient moves out of Salonika against Bulgaria.

September 16: Americans launch Meuse-Argonne offensive north of Verdun.

September 30: Bulgaria agrees to an armistice—in effect a surrender.

October 1: Allied forces enter Damascus.

October 14: Italian offensive launches Battle of Vittorio Veneto.

October 26: Erich Ludendorff resigns as Quartermaster General of the German Army.

October 29: German sailors mutiny at Kiel naval base.

October 30: New Turkish government agrees to armistice.

November 4: Austro-Hungarian government agrees to armistice.

November 8: German delegation meets with Allied leaders in Compiègne to discuss armistice terms.

November 9: Kaiser Wilhelm II, having abdicated, goes into exile in Holland.

November 11: Armistice terms accepted by Germans become effective at eleven a.m.

Major Characters

Albert I. King of Belgium; commander of Belgian forces during the war

Alexandra. Tsarina of Russia; wife of Nicholas II

Alexeyev, Mikhail. Chief of staff to Nicholas II; commander in chief of Russian armies following the tsar's abdication

Asquith, Herbert Henry. British prime minister, 1908–16

Balfour, Arthur. British Conservative leader; succeeded Churchill as First Lord of the Admiralty in May 1915; succeeded Grey as foreign secretary December 1916

Below, Otto von. German general holding major commands on the Eastern, Western, and Italian Fronts and in the Balkans

Bernstorff, Johann von. German ambassador to the U.S. 1908–17

Bethmann Hollweg, Theobold von. Chancellor of Germany, 1909–17

Bonar Law, Andrew. British Conservative and Unionist leader; chancellor of the exchequer, 1916–18

Briand, Aristide. French politician; succeeded Viviani as premier, October 1915; headed government until March 1917

Bruchmüller, Georg. German artillerist; originator of brilliantly innovative offensive tactics

Brusilov, Alexei. Russian army and army group commander; leader of the 1916 offensive that bears his name

Byng, Julian. Commander of British Third Army in 1917 and 1918

Cadorna, Luigi. Chief of general staff of the Italian army, July 1914–November 1917

Caillaux, Joseph. Leader of French political opposition in 1914; arrested by Clemenceau government in 1918

Castelnau, Noël-Edouard de. French army and army group commander

Churchill, Winston. Britain's First Lord of the Admiralty, 1911–15; minister of munitions, 1917–18

Clemenceau, Georges. "The Tiger"; French premier from November 1917

Conrad von Hötzendorf, Franz. Austro-Hungarian field marshal; army chief of staff to March 1917

Currie, Arthur. Commander of Canadian army corps on the Western Front, 1917–18

Driant, Émile. French politician, writer, and lieutenant colonel; killed in opening fighting at Verdun

Enver Pasha. Turkish general; leading member of the Young Turks; minister of war 1914–18, commanding troops in the Caucasus and Middle East

Evert, Alexei. Commander of Russia's Western Army Group from September 1915

Falkenhayn, Erich von. Prussian war minister, 1913–15; army chief of staff, September 1914–August 1916

Foch, Ferdinand. French general; appointed Allied supreme commander, April 1918

Franchet d'Esperey, Louis. French army and army group commander on the Western Front and, from mid-1918, in Salonika and the Balkans

Franz Joseph. Emperor of Austria and King of Hungary, 1848–1916

Gallieni, Joseph. French general; key figure in First Battle of the Marne; minister of war, 1915–16

George V. King of Great Britain

Gough, Hubert. British division, corps, and army commander; removed after defeat of his Fifth Army in the German offensive of 1918

Grey, Edward. British foreign secretary, 1905–16

Gröner, Wilhelm. German staff officer and administrator; succeeded Ludendorff as Hindenburg's chief of staff, October 1918

Haig, Douglas. Senior general with British Expeditionary Force from August 1914; commander in chief from December 1915

Hertling, Georg von. German chancellor, November 1917–October 1918

Hindenburg, Paul von Beneckendorff und von. German field marshal; army chief of staff from August 1916

Hoffmann, Max. Key German military planner and leader on the Eastern Front

Holtzendorff, Henning von. Chief of staff of the German navy, 1915–18

Horne, Henry. Commander of British First Army, 1916–18

House, "Colonel" Edward. American president Woodrow Wilson's principal adviser on foreign affairs

Hutier, Oskar von. German corps and army commander on Eastern Front, 1915–17; introduced innovative offensive tactics that came to bear his name; commander of Eighteenth Army on the Western Front, 1918

Jagow, Gottlieb von. German foreign minister to March 1917

Jellicoe, John. Commander of Britain's High Seas Fleet, 1914–16; first sea lord, 1916–17

Joffre, Joseph. Chief of French general staff, 1911–16

Karl I. Emperor of Austria and King of Hungary from 1916

Kemal, Mustafa. Turkish division commander at Gallipoli; later served in the Caucasus and Middle East

Kerensky, Alexander. Russian social democratic leader; prime minister, July–November 1917

Kitchener, Horatio. British war minister, August 1914–June 1916

Kühlmann, Richard von. German foreign minister, August 1917–July 1918

Lansing, Robert. U.S. secretary of state, 1915–20

Lawrence, T. E. "Lawrence of Arabia"; planner and leader of Arab revolt, 1917–18

Lenin, Vladimir Ilyich. Leader of the Bolshevik faction of the Russian Communist Party; head of the government from late 1917

Lichnowsky, Karl Max. German ambassador to Britain

Lloyd George, David. British chancellor of the exchequer, 1908–15; minister of munitions, 1915–16; war minister, 1916; prime minister from December 1916

Ludendorff, Erich. German general; chief of staff to Hindenburg, August 1914–August 1916; quartermaster general of the German army, 1916–18; effectively dictator of Germany from mid-1917

Mackensen, August von. German field marshal holding important commands on the Eastern Front, 1914–18

Mangin, Charles. French general; prominent at Charleroi, Verdun, the Chemin des Dames, and the Second Battle of the Marne

Marwitz, Georg von der. Commander of the German Second Army at Cambrai in 1917 and in the 1918 offensive

Max of Baden, Prince. German chancellor, October–November 1918

Michaelis, Georg. German chancellor, July–October 1917

Milner, Alfred. Member of Lloyd George's War Council, 1916–18; minister of war from April 1918.

Moltke, Helmuth von. Chief of staff of German army, 1906–September 1914

Monash, John. Commander of Australian Army Corps on the Western Front from May 1918

Nicholas, Grand Duke. Cousin of Nicholas II; Russian general; commander in chief, August 1914–September 1915; then served in the Caucasus

Nicholas II. Tsar of Russia, 1894–1917; executed, 1918

Nivelle, Robert. Commander in chief of the French armies, December 1916–May 1917

Painlevé, Paul. French minister of war from March 1917; premier, September–November 1917

Paléologue, Maurice. French ambassador to Russia, 1914–17

Pershing, John J. Commander in chief of the American Expeditionary Force from May 1917

Pétain, Henri-Philippe. French general; army commander in chief from May 1917

Plumer, Herbert. British corps and army commander, responsible for sector around Ypres

Poincaré, Raymond. President of France, 1913–20

Polivanov, Alexei. Russian general; succeeded Sukhomlinov as war minister, June 1915; dismissed, March 1916

Rasputin, Grigori. Russian monk, mystic, and intimate of the tsar's family

Rawlinson, Henry. British general, serving primarily as commander of the Fourth Army

Robertson, William. British general; chief of the imperial general staff, December 1915–March 1918

Rupprecht, Crown Prince. Heir to the throne of Bavaria; commander of a German army from August 1914; of an army group from July 1916

Sanders, Otto Liman von. German general, commander of Turkish defenses at Gallipoli

Sarrail, Maurice. Commander of French Third Army, 1914–15; Army of the Orient at Salonika, 1916–17

Stürmer, Boris. Russian prime minister, February–November 1916; also served as interior minister and foreign minister

Tisza, István. Prime Minister of Hungary, 1913–17

Trotsky, Leon. Leading member of Bolsheviks; principal political adviser to Lenin; head of Russian delegation to Brest-Litovsk negotiations

Wilhelm, Crown Prince. Eldest son and heir of Wilhelm II; commander of the German Fifth Army from August 1914 and of an army group from September 1916

Wilhelm II. Emperor of Germany and King of Prussia, 1888–1918

Wilson, Henry. Britain's military liaison with France; chief of the imperial general staff from March 1918

Wilson, Woodrow. U.S. president, 1913–21

Zimmermann, Arthur. German deputy foreign minister

THE WAR IN THE WEST

BRITAIN

London
★
Thames

Southampton

Dover

English Channel

Seine Rouer

Brest

FRANCE

Atlantic Ocean

Loire Tours

Nantes

0 Miles 50 100

0 Kilometers 50 100

North Sea

NETHERLANDS

Amsterdam ✪

GERMANY

Bremen •

Rhine

Zeebrugge •
Ostend •
Calais •   Yser
ARTOIS   *FLANDERS*
Boulogne •   Ypres •
        Neuve-Chapelle •
        Loos • Lens •
        Vimy •
        Arras •
        Bapaume • Cambrai •
        Albert • Le Cateau •
        Péronne • St. Quentin •
Amiens •
PICARDY
        Mondidier • Noyon •
Compiègne •   Aisne
        Chantilly • Ourq
Paris ✪   Soissons •
        Seine   Reims •
                Marne
                Chateau- •
                Thierry
        Yonne   Seine

Orléans •

        Loire

Ghent •   BELGIUM
Antwerp •
✪ Brussels
Mons •   Namur •   Liège •
        Charleroi •   Meuse
Sambre

                ARDENNES
Cologne •

Koblenz •   Frankfurt •
        Mosel
        Rhine

✪ Luxembourg

CHEMIN
DES DAMES
ARGONNE   Sedan •
        Longwy •
        Meuse
        Verdun •   Metz •
CHAMPAGNE   Troyon •
        St. Mihiel •
                Nancy •   Strasbourg •
        LORRAINE   ALSACE
        Épinal •   Moselle
                        Rhine

        Saône

        Belfort •
                        Basel •

SWITZERLAND

© 2005 Jeffrey L. Ward

THE WAR IN THE EAST

NORWAY

Stockholm

SWEDEN

DENMARK

Copenhagen

Baltic Sea

North Sea

Königsberg

Danzig

EAST PRUSSIA

Amsterdam

NETHERLANDS

Elbe

Berlin

Oder

Posen

Tannenberg

Vistula

Brussels

BELGIUM

GERMANY

SILESIA

Lodz

POLAND

Luxembourg

Vistula

Krakow

WESTERN

FRANCE

Rhine

Danube

BAVARIA

Munich

Danube

Vienna

Budapest

SWITZERLAND

AUSTRIA-HUNGARY

TRENTINO

Trento

Piave

Caporetto

Isonzo

Milan

Vittorio Veneto

Trieste

Po

Venice

ITALY

Danube

BOSNIA-HERZEGOVINA

Belgrade

Sarajevo

Adriatic Sea

MONTENEGRO

Rome

ALBANIA

Mediterranean Sea

FINLAND

St. Petersburg

Tallinn

Moscow

Riga

LITHUANIA

Kovno
Stalluponen
Gumbinnen
Vilna
Lake Naroch

RUSSIA

Masurian Lakes

Baranovitchi

Bug

Warsaw
Brest-Litovsk

Lublin
*Pripet
Marshes*

San
Kiev

Tarnow
Gorlice
Przemysl
EASTERN GALICIA
Lemberg
(Lvov)

GALICIA

Carpathian Mountains
Czernowitz
Dniester

BUKOVINA

Dnieper

TRANSYLVANIA

ROMANIA
Bucharest

Danube
Black Sea

SERBIA
Sofia

BULGARIA

Constantinople

Salonika

TURKEY

GREECE

0   Miles   100   200
0   Kilometers   200

© 2005 Jeffrey L. Ward

Introduction

As 1916 began the Great War was seventeen months old, and the nations fighting it knew they were trapped in a disaster the likes of which the world had never seen. What no one could know was that the war, savage as it had already shown itself to be, was not yet half over – not nearly. And that the horrors already visited upon Europe and the Middle East and Africa and other places around the globe would be dwarfed by those that lay ahead.

Even less was it possible to foresee:

That far from clearing the way for the emergence of a new and better world order, far from being the war that (in David Lloyd George's words) would end all wars, the killing when it ended would leave much of the world morally brutalized, physically ruined, and teetering on the edge of chaos.

That even on the winning side, the war would come to be seen not as a triumph but (in the undisputed words of the American diplomat and historian George F. Kennan) as the twentieth century's "seminal catastrophe," the one out of which so many other catastrophes have grown and continue to grow today.

And that the sacrifices demanded by the war, crippling as they were, would produce heartbreakingly little in the way of positive results.

Even as it was being fought, the war was understood to be unique in history. Thus by 1916 it was already being called the first *world* war. This a quarter of a century before the arrival of its monstrous bastard offspring, the even uglier, even bloodier, even more global conflict of 1939–1945, would create the need to distinguish it as the *first* world war, part one of a two-part tragedy.

In intensity as well as in geographic reach, in sheer ferocity, this first of the whole world's wars was without precedent. It erupted when, for the first time, the wealth of the great powers and the advanced state of their technology made killing an industrial process, one that could be sustained for years on a massive scale. It also happened at a moment in history when the latest breakthroughs in weaponry gave the defense an almost insuperable advantage, making truly decisive battles nearly impossible. The generals of 1914 found that the arts of war had changed beyond recognition, and had to be learned anew. They saw to their shock that troops on horseback were useless, and attacks by massed infantry doomed, in the face of guns capable of firing five hundred rounds per minute. And that the answer to the machine gun -- if an answer was possible – remained to be discovered.

This set for the stage for slaughter on a scale that soldiers of the past could scarcely have imagined – and for slaughter without result. By the start of 1916 the war's costs in lives and treasure were already at horrifying levels, and were growing more horrible with each new month. Everyone professed to want the war to end, on both sides the leaders said it could not be ended short of victory, and though some claimed otherwise not one of them actually knew how to make that happen.

The nightmare was epitomized by the Western Front, the jagged and blood-drenched line of trenches that zigged and zagged from the French–Swiss border to Belgium's Channel coast. Frozen in place late in 1914, throughout 1915 it had been the scene of repeated convulsive attempts by both sides to break through their enemies' defenses and restore the kind of war of movement for which their armies had been trained. All these attempts ended in futility and failure – and in casualties totaling in the millions. The static character of this central theater of the Great War is evident in the names of its battles. Ultimately there would be a Second Battle of the Marne, a Third Battle of Artois, a Fourth Battle of Ypres. Each repetition was emblematic of the way the same ground had to be fought over again and again and again.

The situation was much the same elsewhere. The eighth day of 1916 brought a singularly bitter humiliation for the Entente: completion of the withdrawal from Turkey's Gallipoli Peninsula of a huge expeditionary force made up of British, French, Australian, New Zealand and Indian troops. Thus ended in ignominy a nine-month, brutally hard-fought campaign aimed at capturing

Constantinople, knocking the Ottoman Empire out of the war, and opening the way for an Entente drive into Central Europe via the Balkans. Here too nothing had been accomplished despite immense suffering and loss of life.

Only on the Eastern Front was there progress, and it was being achieved by the Germans. In August 1915, having earlier turned back the invasion of East Prussia with which Russia had opened the war, German troops captured and occupied Warsaw. From there they continued to pound away at the Russians, pushing them eastward at terrible cost to both sides.

Meanwhile the conflict continued to spread, rarely for the noblest of reasons. When Japan threw in with the Entente in 1914, she did so with the explicit understanding that when victory was achieved she would be rewarded with German colonial possessions in the Far East. In 1915 Italy essentially sold herself – and, as it turned out, the lives of half a million of her young men – to the Entente, accepting Britain's and France's secret promise that at war's end her borders would be advanced northward into the Alps. When Bulgaria declared war on Serbia and thereby aligned herself with the Central Powers, she made it all but inevitable that her neighbor and rival Romania would go the other way. Bulgaria, Romania and Serbia all wanted the same thing: to get bigger. They could do so only at each others' expense, and so were easily seduced into seeing the war as an opportunity for gain. And of course all of them, no less than the great powers whose pawns they were, insisted that their motives were pure, that they wanted nothing more than justice and lasting peace. They had no difficulty persuading themselves that they were innocent and their enemies evil, and that their ambitions had divine approval.

None of which brought the war closer to a conclusion of any kind. Anyone looking for evidence that a supreme being favored one side over the other would not have had an easy time. On the contrary, it could almost seem that some malign invisible hand was moving the pieces on the global chessboard in such a way as to keep the blood flowing and assure that neither side gained the upper hand. So many things could easily have turned out differently, tipping the scales decisively to one side or the other. If the Turks had not allowed themselves to be bullied into joining the Central Powers in 1914. If they had instead joined the Entente.

If Italy had not joined the Entente, thereby tying up millions of Austro-Hungarian troops in the Alps for the duration of the war. If Russia's vast armies had not been so badly trained and equipped and led at the start of the war, when the Germans had committed most of their armies to the drive on Paris and were outnumbered and vulnerable in the East.

Et cetera ad infinitum. Any one of a number of such things, if it had played out differently, might have brought the war to an earlier end, saving millions – many millions – of lives. Such an end would almost certainly have been handled in what had long been the traditional way, with the winners and losers seated at the same table, negotiating with each other, keeping the bitterness of the vanquished within manageable bounds. Even if the Central Powers had been the "winners," could the long-term consequences have been worse than they actually turned out to be after fifty months of total war? Worse than the replacement of the foolish and ineffectual Kaiser Wilhem with Adolf Hitler? Of Tsar Nicholas II with Stalin?

Even in the shortest of short terms, the costs of deadlock – and of efforts to break the deadlock – continued to be mind-bending. Nineteen-sixteen would be all of seven weeks old when the Germans launched the vast offensive that would develop into the Battle of Verdun and continue almost to the end of the year, claiming hundreds of thousands of lives and turning a wide area of eastern France into a moonscape. Less than five months later, on 1 July, an equally vast Entente offensive would open the Battle of the Somme and cause nearly twenty thousand British troops to perish in storms of machine gun fire on that one day. The Somme too would go on for months, devouring huge numbers of lives, gaining barely enough ground to show up on the maps of France and Belgium.

Then Romania would declare war on Austria-Hungary, and Greece would declare war on Germany and Bulgaria. The populations of the Central Powers would be reduced to starvation by the Entente's naval blockade. Britain would find herself on the verge of bankruptcy, barely able to scrape together the collateral needed to secure more of the American loans on which she and France had become utterly dependent. Russia would show signs of being on the point of collapse not only financially and militarily but as a nation, a civilized society.

And even after all this the war would remain deadlocked. It was beginning to seem possible that the destruction would go on until just one man was left standing, the rest of his generation having been wiped out. That what was happening was the suicide of a civilization.

Great questions loom over the second half of the war.

Why, as the horror continued to build, was there no serious effort by either side to find a way out through negotiations?

Can this failure be justified? If so, how? On what terms?

The naval blockade that brought malnutrition and death to untold numbers of civilians, the old and the very young especially ... the campaign of unrestricted submarine warfare that was Germany's response to the blockade ... the declaration of war that was Washington's response to the submarines ... and the crushing of Germany that could never have happened without American intervention ...

Were these things necessary? Can they be justified? Did their consequences have to be as disastrous as they turned out to be? These are among the biggest, hardest, most important questions about the Great War. Answers will perhaps be found among the established facts, or there may be no answers. And if there are no answers the war may make no sense except as a worldwide outbreak of madness.

Thus the following pages. Their purpose is to lay out the most pertinent and illuminating facts, help the reader to search for answers, and thereby extract meaning from one of the most epic and mysterious events in the history of our species.

G. J. Meyer
Mere, Wiltshire

PART ONE

1916

Bleeding to Death

With hot food and room to move about, these British troops are clearly on a break from the trenches.

Chapter 1

Verdun: Preparation

"The forces of France will bleed to death."
—Erich von Falkenhayn

Shortly after seven a.m. on February 21, 1916, the third consecutive clear morning after a week of snow and muddy cold, an eight-mile sector of the German lines a hundred and fifty miles east of Paris erupted in a blaze of artillery the likes of which the world had never seen. More than twelve hundred guns, among them thirty of the gigantic mortars that had destroyed the Belgian forts at the start of the war and naval cannon capable of firing two-thousand-pound projectiles twenty miles, suddenly began blasting away at French positions on the eastern bank of the River Meuse. All through the morning and most of the afternoon they sent up a hundred thousand rounds of high explosive, shrapnel, and gas per hour—12,500 shells hourly on each mile of front. French reconnaissance aircraft reported that it was impossible to identify specific enemy gun emplacements: a solid wall of flame was rising into the sky from the woods behind the German lines. The woods on the French side were being reduced to stumps and craters amid leaping fountains of earth. Observers on both sides found it difficult to believe that any of the troops huddled in those woods could possibly survive. "Thousands of projectiles are flying in all directions, some whistling, others howling, others moaning low, and all uniting in one infernal roar," a French officer wrote after sending one of his men to repair a severed cable. "From time to time an aerial torpedo passes, making a noise like a gigantic motor car. With a tremendous thud a giant shell bursts quite close to our observation post, breaking the telephone wire and interrupting all communication with our batteries. It seems quite impossible that he should escape in the rain of shell, which exceeds anything imaginable; there has never been such a bombardment in war. Our man seems to be enveloped in explosions, and shelters himself in the shell craters which honeycomb the ground; finally he reaches a less stormy spot, mends his wires, and then, as it would be madness to try to return, settles down in a crater and waits for the storm to pass."

After noon, just as abruptly as it had started, the "rain of shell" came to a stop. The fire from the Germans' long-range guns began probing deeper, while the short-range pieces fell silent. Thinking that the worst was over, expecting that as usual the barrage would be followed by an infantry assault, the French did exactly what the Germans wanted them to do. They came up out of their hiding places, showing their heads aboveground in order to survey the damage and watch for the coming attack. German spotters observed them and directed fire onto every point where the French had revealed themselves. The bombardment went on for hours more.

At four-forty-five p.m., with the sun already slipping below the horizon, the barrage again ended. This time German troops did appear, clambering out of holes in the ground and starting toward the French. Their advance was both surprisingly timed—infantry almost always opened new offensives in the morning—and surprisingly limited in comparison with the mayhem that had preceded it. Nine divisions came forward but did so tentatively, not in a mass but in clusters scattered across four and a half miles, making use of all the protection afforded by rough hill country. Their assignment was not to overrun the French but to feel them out, to see where and to what extent the first line of defenders had survived. Wherever they encountered resistance, they stopped. In places they pulled back. The mortar fire resumed, again lobbing explosives onto whatever French soldiers had shown themselves.

All along the cutting edge of the attack, German officers were reporting that the suspension of their advance was unnecessary, that the defenses, where not annihilated, were in serious disarray. The mortars fell silent yet again. An order went out from the headquarters of the German Fifth Army for the attackers to move forward in force and take possession of as much ground as possible. But the order came too late: the sun was down, the last of the light gone. When the Germans went to ground for the night, they did so, in most cases, along what had been the first and most thinly defended French line. Their long-range guns continued to pound away as here and there snow flurries blew across the ravaged terrain. The French had been given a reprieve: one long winter night in which to reassemble their stunned troops, shore up what remained of their entrenchments, and start bringing their own artillery forward.

And so began the Battle of Verdun, the longest battle of the Great War and one of the most terrible ever fought. It had its roots in the state of the Western Front as 1915 ended. Both sides, as they settled in for the war's second winter, had found reason to be satisfied but also many reasons for concern. The leaders of the Entente, especially, looked back on a year-long series of disappointments punctuated by disaster. Serbia had collapsed, and most of its army had been destroyed. Russia had lost Poland and Galicia. In the Gorlice-Tarnow campaign alone, a hundred and fifty thousand Russians had been killed, six hundred and eighty thousand wounded, and nearly nine hundred thousand taken prisoner. Erich von Falkenhayn told Kaiser Wilhelm that the tsar's army was "so weakened by the blows it has suffered that Russia need not be seriously considered a danger in the foreseeable future."

Though the French had been on the attack repeatedly during the year, they had accomplished essentially nothing and had done so at almost incredible cost. In the Champagne and Artois regions alone, three hundred and thirty-five thousand of their soldiers had been killed (though many were listed as missing rather than dead, their bodies lost in the chaos). This had brought to two million the number of French casualties since the start of the war. Some two hundred thousand British were dead—nearly twice the number with which the BEF had begun the war—out of total casualties of more than half a million.

Italy's entry into the war, an event that at first promised to be decisive, had simply produced another stalemate. Far off to the

East, in the Caucasus region between the Black and Caspian Seas, the Russians and Turks were colliding on yet another front where heavy loss of life was producing no results that mattered.

Still, there was optimism in Paris, in London, and even in Petrograd. The Entente's manpower advantage on the Western Front was greater than ever and growing. If the Italians had not achieved the hoped-for southern breakthrough, they had nonetheless brought many hundreds of thousands of troops into the struggle. Even if they could win no battles, those troops were tying up Austro-Hungarian divisions that otherwise would have been free to go elsewhere. Russia's military administration had been put under honest and competent leadership—a phenomenon that would prove to be short-lived—and its battered armies were being refitted and rebuilt. The little army with which Britain had begun the war was growing beyond recognition in spite of its heavy losses.

By the start of 1916 the British had nearly a million troops on the continent, and that number was increasing by almost one hundred thousand monthly. Every newly arrived battalion increased the price that the Germans were having to pay for their failed bet that by invading Belgium they could take France out of the war before Britain could get fully in. Britain's and France's armies were being steadily augmented by the arrival of troops from the colonies that both nations had around the world. The Germans and Austrians had no such resources to draw on and no possibility of moving troops by sea. The extent of London's commitment to the war was demonstrated in January 1916 with Parliament's passage of the Military Service Act. This measure, far from entirely popular even within the government (Prime Minister Asquith declined to take a position on it), was driven through the House of Commons by the steely will of David Lloyd George. It introduced conscription to Britain for the first time, ensuring that millions more men would be sent to the BEF despite a precipitous decline in enlistments. In all the nations of the Entente, the shell crisis was coming under control.

The British and French general staffs believed that their advantage was greater than it really was. Their intelligence analysts continued to assure them that the Germans were squandering troops at an unsustainable rate and soon would be exhausted. Actually, the opposite was true. The Germans had generally been far more careful than the British and French in husbanding their manpower, and their casualties through 1915 were only about half those of their enemies. Joffre and Haig, happy to accept the wishful thinking of their staffs, believed that the challenge for 1916 was simply to find the best way to overwhelm an enemy who lacked the means to respond. The answer seemed obvious: to stay on the offensive and go on killing Germans until Berlin could no longer keep its lines intact. Less obvious was where to do this, and when, but such questions do not appear to have troubled either commander very much. They concluded that their 1916 offensive, when it came, should take place *everywhere*. Determining exactly when mattered less than ensuring that all the armies attacked at the same time, making it impossible for the Germans to shift troops from one place to another to meet a sequence of threats. It was hard to imagine how, under such conditions, the Germans could avoid collapse.

The certainty that the Entente's numerical advantage could only increase with time was obvious in Berlin. Thus the Germans could find scant comfort in their successes on the Eastern Front and in fending off Joffre's offensives. They understood that the time available for bringing the war to a satisfactory conclusion was finite on their side—that regardless of how effectively they might fight a defensive war, remaining on the defensive would mean gradual exhaustion and defeat. They also understood, however, that as 1916 began they had enough troops in the west to compete effectively: ninety-four divisions on the line plus another twenty-six in reserve, versus ninety-one and fifty-nine respectively for the Entente. They understood that they needed to defeat someone somewhere while they were still capable of doing so. They had no way to decide on a specific course of action, however, without igniting the antagonism between Falkenhayn on one side and Hindenburg and Ludendorff on the other: the wearying argument about west versus east. Among the many questions for which there were no clear answers, two things seemed certain: Russia was crippled and likely to remain so for months; and the French could be depended on to continue their attacks no matter what the cost and how limited the potential gains.

The biggest strategic questions facing both sides were answered before the end of 1915. On December 6, at the great riverside château that was his headquarters in Chantilly, Joffre played host to a meeting of all the Entente's top army leaders. Britain, Russia, Belgium, Italy, and even Japan were represented. The assembled generals had no difficulty in agreeing that the Germans, fatally weakened, could be finished off with one great symphonic offensive involving all the major combatants on every major front. They agreed also that this tremendous climax should not take place until late summer. There seemed no need for hurry, and a half-year delay would give all the allies time to assemble overwhelming quantities of artillery and ammunition. It would provide time for Britain to continue the seasoning of its green new armies, and for the Russians to recover.

Later in the month Joffre and Haig met again to settle on the outlines of their part of the overall plan, the Western Front offensive. Joffre wanted it to take place in France, north of Paris, where the front was bisected by the River Somme. Haig preferred Belgium, farther north, where success could lead to the recapture of the lost Channel ports, a prime strategic prize. Joffre's Somme plan offered little chance of achieving any strategic objectives at all—nothing beyond a general pushing-back of the German line and the killing of more Germans. He prevailed nevertheless, in large part by virtue of owning a majority interest in the enterprise. Forty French divisions were to participate, while the British would contribute only twenty-five. An attack by sixty-five divisions promised to be unstoppable, especially with the Russians simultaneously launching a comparably massive offensive in the east and the Italians striking at the Austrians.

While the Entente commanders refined their plans, their German counterpart was putting together a scheme of his own. Working in his customary solitude, the secretive and deeply introverted Falkenhayn spent the first half of December ordering his thoughts. No option beyond the Western Front, he decided, could possibly produce results sufficient to Germany's need. Confident that "the Russian armies have not been completely overthrown but their offensive powers have been shattered," and believing that Russia was approaching revolution and collapse (in this he showed himself to be a man of sharp if premature insight), he thought it unwise to focus his limited resources on such an enfeebled foe. Ludendorff would have disagreed vigorously. But he was far off at the northern end of the Eastern Front, organizing the administration of conquered territories almost equal to France in size, and he was neither told anything nor asked for his opinion.

The war would never end, Falkenhayn had come to believe, until Britain was induced to give up on it. Playing artfully on Kaiser Wilhelm's resentment of his mother's homeland, he had been declaring as early as the autumn of 1915 that Britain had to be considered not just one of Germany's enemies but the archenemy, committed absolutely to the destruction of Germany. "She is staking everything on a war of exhaustion," he wrote. "We have not been able to shatter her belief that it will bring Germany to her knees. What we have to do is dispel that illusion."

But Britain herself, beyond the reach of the German army, was invulnerable. The only way to bring her to the peace table was to demonstrate that a continuation of hostilities would be pointless. Falkenhayn saw two ways of making this happen. One was a campaign of submarine warfare aimed at commercial shipping, at starving the British Isles. This was a momentous decision, as important as anything Falkenhayn did or decided to do during his tenure as chief of the general staff. He was an exception among German generals in his political sophistication—vastly more sophisticated than Ludendorff, for example—and in the aftermath of the sinking of the *Lusitania* he had sided with Chancellor Bethmann Hollweg in demanding an end to the first submarine campaign. Since then, however, his pessimism had deepened, and when their disaster at Gorlice-Tarnow failed to weaken the Russians' resolve, he had stopped hoping that anything could. When Admiral von Tirpitz assured him that the growing U-boat fleet could destroy Britain's ability to wage war within two months (other naval leaders said it would take four months—or six), he found the prospect irresistible. "There can be no justification or military grounds for refusing any further to employ what promises to be our most effective weapon," he declared. "We should ruthlessly employ every weapon that is suitable for striking against England on her home ground." His response to Bethmann's fears of American anger was that the United States "cannot intervene decisively in the war in time." This view echoed the dismissal of British intervention by the generals who had decided to invade Belgium.

The other thing Germany had to do, as Falkenhayn saw the situation, was to remove Britain's nearest and most important ally, France, from the war. Like France's Pétain, he had been convinced by the bitter disappointments of 1914 that victory in the west was not going to be achieved through a classic breakthrough and envelopment of the enemy. He understood, as Joffre and Haig did not, that such a thing was simply not possible in this new industrial kind of war, a kind of gigantic siege in which networks of railways made it possible to seal any break in the line by moving masses of troops quickly. The sole available alternative, he concluded, was to break France's *will* to fight. In reaching this conclusion he was influenced by what he knew—and his data were better than those available to the Entente's generals—of the disparity between French and German casualties. "France has arrived almost at the end of her military effort," he told the kaiser. "If her people can be made to understand clearly that in a military sense they have nothing more to hope for, the breaking point will be reached and England's best weapon knocked out of her hand." Falkenhayn entertained no dreams of defeating France outright on the field of battle, of sweeping her armies aside and entering Paris in triumph. His thoughts were focused on driving the French to despair and, once they came to terms, making Britain despair as well. These hopes underlay his strategy at Verdun.

Powerfully influenced by Joffre's evident willingness to pay almost any price in the pursuit of limited objectives, Falkenhayn devised a plan for luring the French into a German-built killing machine. His idea was to threaten some piece of ground that the French would do almost anything to hold, some piece of ground dominated by German artillery. Under such circumstances, he said, "the forces of France will bleed to death."

Deciding where to install his machine was not difficult. Verdun, the little city nestled at the center of a bristling network of fortresses, had held out against the German advance at the start of the war and had been left as a kind of spear point jutting into the German line. Strategically its importance had diminished considerably since 1914; the French no longer needed the kind of anchor it had provided during the Great Retreat, and withdrawing from it would have put nothing in jeopardy. But it had been a bone of contention between the Germans and the French for many years, and aside from Paris itself there was no place on the map to which the French people would be likely to attach more importance. That made it perfect for Falkenhayn's purposes.

Verdun had a further advantage too, at least where persuading the kaiser was concerned. It lay opposite the German Fifth Army, which was commanded by Crown Prince Wilhelm. Responsibility for executing Falkenhayn's plan would fall to the prince, and success would give the Hohenzollern family a particularly personal kind of triumph.

Falkenhayn spent several days in December in discussions with the crown prince and the Fifth Army's chief of staff, General Konstantin Schmidt von Knobelsdorf. He won their support but was less than forthright in doing so. By not being clear about what his objective actually was (to capture Verdun, or to draw the French army into destroying itself in a defense of Verdun?), he planted seeds of misunderstanding that would later bear bitter fruit. He then met with the kaiser at Potsdam, and Wilhelm approved everything. Preparations for the campaign began immediately and in the strictest secrecy. It was essential to take the French by surprise, and to do so before Joffre upset everything by launching an offensive of his own.

The French of course knew nothing of the plan. But neither did Falkenhayn know that, throughout the weeks when he was developing his ideas and getting them approved, Verdun was the centerpiece of a controversy involving not only the French military but the most senior levels of the government in Paris. The origins of the controversy reached back to the first days of the war, when Joffre, seeing the speed with which the Germans had destroyed the fortress networks at Liège and Namur, lost whatever faith he had once had in the value of such fortifications. Before the end of 1914, with the Germans trying to push westward out of Alsace and Lorraine, he had ordered the abandonment of Verdun. The senior French general in the region, the same Maurice Sarrail who now commanded the multinational force bottled up at Salonika, had disregarded this order and managed to hold on even as the Germans almost succeeded in encircling him. Unimpressed, Joffre in 1915 began stripping the Verdun salient of guns and men in order to add muscle to his offensives. The aged General Herr, upon becoming governor of the Fortified Region of Verdun in August,

warned that its defenses were deficient and asked for reinforcements. But his predecessor had been sacked for making exactly the
same complaint. Though Herr was not dismissed, he got little of
the help he requested.

Herr was not alone. Other generals both in Paris and in the
field shared his fears, as did a more junior officer, Émile Driant,
who though sixty years old and a mere lieutenant colonel had
more influence and, apparently, more political courage than most
of the others. Thirty years before the war, early in his career, Driant had been an aide to (and married the daughter of) a bizarre
character named General Georges Boulanger. A blustering, hapless, ultimately ludicrous figure, Boulanger rose to become minister of war and seemed in a moment of national hysteria in the
1880s to be on the verge of establishing a kind of Bonapartist dictatorship, but he failed to seize his opportunity at the moment of
crisis and ended by committing suicide on his mistress's grave.
Driant's association with Boulanger, and afterward with a militant right-wing faction called the Boulangists, had made him an
object of suspicion among the antiroyalist, anticlerical republicans who dominated the army at the turn of the century. When
he found himself at age fifty still a major and without hope of
promotion, Driant resigned his commission and turned to politics
and writing. He was elected to the National Assembly (a position
he retained even after returning to active duty at the start of the
war) and wrote a number of popular books calling for a revival of
national élan in preparation for the war with Germany that he regarded as inevitable. He wrote urgently of the need to strengthen
France's defenses along the eastern border, and among his works
was a treatise on fortress warfare.

Perhaps because of his age, perhaps also because the cloud that
had driven him out of the army still hung over his head, Driant
was assigned to an obscure staff position. This position happened
to be inside Verdun's central citadel. Throughout most of 1915
Verdun was practically out of the war, never seriously threatened. In time Driant managed to get himself transferred out of the
citadel and placed in command of two infantry battalions posted
at a hilly piece of woodland called the Bois des Caures, directly
opposite the German lines.

Driant was certain that Verdun would be attacked sooner or

later, and his trained eye saw how grossly unprepared it was. Unlike his superiors, he was not content to send his complaints up the chain of command and accept the lack of response. By August he was communicating with colleagues in the Assembly. "Should our front line be overrun in a massive attack," he wrote the Chamber's president, "our second line is inadequate and we're not managing to build it up: *not enough men to do the job,* and I add: *not enough barbed wire.*" Driant asked that his concerns be brought to the attention of General Gallieni, the unacknowledged hero of the Battle of the Marne who was now minister of war, and this was done. Gallieni, a strong-minded man though in precarious health, was himself by this time stewing with impatience at the conduct of the war and increasingly skeptical about Joffre's strategy. His frustration is apparent in what he wrote in his diary on December 16: "In the morning, Council of Ministers, discussion about Joffre and the trenches. Worry about the next German attack. At certain points, the defensive fortifications are not prepared. The matter is grave. Must do what is necessary towards Verdun."

Gallieni reacted quickly upon learning of Driant's warnings, dispatching an inspection team to Verdun. When the team issued a report that supported all of Driant's warnings, Gallieni passed it on to Joffre, requesting a response. Joffre, who was notoriously quick to see inquiries from the government as intolerable interference and skillful at giving no answers, responded in a kind of haughty and dismissive rage. "I consider that nothing justifies the fears you have expressed in the name of the government," he told Gallieni, claiming that the construction of "three or four successive defensive positions" was either "finished or on the road to completion." This was an outright lie, and in time it would contribute to Joffre's fall. At the end of 1915, however, he was still strong enough politically to feel free not only to lie to the government but to take the offensive against anyone who dared to challenge him. He demanded to know where Gallieni had been getting his information. In adding that "I cannot permit soldiers under my command to make their complaint or discontent about my orders known to the government through channels other than those which the military has established," and in referring to "officers serving at the front" and "politicians in uniform," he made it plain that he already knew. His failure to have Driant dismissed, transferred, or court-martialed may be explained by a reluctance to break with Gallieni, who had strong political allies and was not a man to be crossed.

Matters might have rested there except for mounting evidence of German activity opposite Verdun and rumors, reported by Entente agents in Berlin, that an offensive was coming. Rail traffic behind the German lines increased sharply, as did the use of aircraft to keep French scouts at a distance. Finally the pressure became too great for Joffre to ignore. On January 24 he sent General Noël-Edouard de Castelnau, who had recently returned to his staff after a year as an army commander, to Verdun to conduct an inspection. A Franco-Prussian War veteran who by this point had lost three sons in combat, Castelnau was alarmed by what he found. He ordered immediate steps to strengthen the defenses on the east bank of the Meuse—Herr had been concentrating his troops on the west bank—and ordered reinforcements to be brought in from other places. The first two divisions would not arrive until February 12—the day Falkenhayn had chosen for the start of his attack.

A kind of blind race now began in which both sides hurried with their preparations and neither knew what the other was doing. That the French now regarded the situation as an emergency was signaled when not only President Poincaré but even Joffre himself, perhaps eager to cover up his long neglect, paid brief visits to Verdun and some of its outlying forts. Everything possible was done to make the best of available resources, which included far too little artillery, and to bring in more men and guns. On the east bank of the Meuse, where the Germans were massing a hundred and fifty thousand men and more than eight hundred guns, Herr was able to place only about thirty-five thousand troops. Though he had more than nine hundred pieces of artillery, more than half were light field guns and many were semiobsolete models without rapid-fire recoil mechanisms. At the center of the preparations, exactly where any German attack was likely to strike first, were Driant and the thirteen hundred men under his command. They were hastily constructing concrete strongpoints in the Bois des Caures.

The Germans meanwhile were accomplishing prodigious feats

in getting everything in place. Helped by the hilly, wooded countryside and the cloudy winter weather of the Verdun region, they were doing an astonishingly good job of keeping the French from learning what they intended to do, or when, or even exactly where. No fewer than five new railway lines were constructed across the German-held portion of the Woëvre plateau immediately to the east of the Verdun hills. In a seven-week period between late December and early February, thirteen hundred trains—not railcars but entire *trains*—hauled in 2.5 million shells. Earth-moving equipment, construction machinery, and everything required to prepare the offensive and support three hundred thousand troops in winter came rolling up to Verdun. The guns were positioned in the woods and covered with camouflage—a new development in warfare, made necessary by air reconnaissance. Underground chambers capable of holding as many as five hundred men each were excavated opposite the French lines and lined with steel and concrete. In the sky above all this was the greatest concentration of aircraft yet seen on any front, one hundred and fifty aircraft, a German umbrella so impenetrable that, even on the rare days when visibility was good, the French pilots were unable to get a close look at what was happening.

By the second week of February everything was in place for an offensive with the potential to change the course of the war. One thing, however, was missing: a clear and shared understanding of how to take full advantage of all the force the Germans had assembled. The worst of the tactical problems began with the strange ambiguities of Falkenhayn's plan—a plan aimed not at capturing Verdun but at bringing the French army within range of the German artillery and, in the general's words, bleeding it white. His goal at the start of the campaign was simply to mass his artillery in the hills north of the city, force the French to try to drive those guns away, and blow them to pieces as they did. The core idea was to maximize French casualties while keeping the German infantry out of the fight to the fullest possible extent. In itself this objective was entirely commendable. But it led to Falkenhayn's decision to limit the first day's attack to only four and a half miles of front, to wait until the end of the day to send the infantry in, and to advance on the east bank of the Meuse only.

There were many problems with this decision, but the most

serious was also the most obvious: it would leave the French artillery on the west bank unthreatened and free to blast away across the river. The crown prince and his chief of staff, Schmidt von Knobelsdorf, battled Falkenhayn on this point, insisting that ample manpower was available for an offensive on both banks and demanding a broadening of the campaign. They were joined by the best-informed of the Fifth Army's corps commanders, General Hans von Zwehl, who before the war had participated in three war-game simulations of an attack on Verdun. Every one of those exercises had demonstrated that a move on the east bank only would be doomed to failure. The crown prince, Knobelsdorf, and Zwehl even had the implicit support of the famous French general De Rivière, who in the 1880s had directed an expansion of the Verdun defensive system. Upon completing his task, De Rivière had ruefully concluded that Verdun continued to be vulnerable at one point: the *west* bank. Falkenhayn was unpersuaded. He continued to insist that the initial infantry attack be severely limited, that the reserves necessary for exploiting success be kept well to the rear, and that those reserves be not under the crown prince's control but his own.

Falkenhayn said he simply did not have enough troops to attack on both sides of the river. His subordinates, with three hundred thousand men at their disposal, could not understand what he meant. Falkenhayn explained that troops had to be held back for use in responding to whatever counteroffensives the French or British might launch at other points along the front. His subordinates, rightly convinced that neither the French nor the British were ready to attack in force anywhere, once again were baffled. What they didn't know, because Falkenhayn didn't tell them, was that he didn't really care whether Verdun was captured or not. In all likelihood, he secretly preferred that Verdun *not* be captured—at least not quickly. He appears to have feared that a quick capture of Verdun might cause the French to withdraw and disengage, thereby spoiling his plan. One wonders if it ever occurred to him that, had he seized the city at the start of the campaign, the French would be practically certain to attack him and his massed artillery. *Not* taking Verdun, on the other hand, would leave the French in their defenses and require the Germans—assuming that Falkenhayn wanted the battle to continue—to attack again and again and again. He was relinquishing the opportunity to make one lightning strike and then fight on the defensive.

What Falkenhayn ordered, in the end, was "an offensive in the direction of Verdun." These were words of art, intended to deceive. The crown prince and Knobelsdorf, understandably, interpreted them as an order to *capture* Verdun. Literally interpreted, however, they merely meant that the German forces were to move in that direction.

All was in readiness for the attack to begin on February 12. The night before, it began to snow, and snow was still falling heavily when morning came. Visibility was zero, which meant the artillery was blind and everything had to be suspended. Conditions remained terrible for a week, but on February 19 the skies finally cleared. The next day was even better—not only sunny but warm, with the mud beginning to dry. By then the element of surprise was lost: the French knew that an attack was imminent, and they had a good idea of where it would come. That night Driant slept as usual in a house some distance from where his battalions were dug in at the Bois des Caures. He rose before dawn on February 21, gave his wedding ring and a letter addressed to his wife to his manservant, and departed for the front. He was already there when the German artillery opened fire. All that day he and his men were under bombardment, their strongpoints blasted apart one by one. Late in the day the survivors, Driant among them, were attacked by German infantry, but the attackers came in less than overwhelming numbers and the poilus held their ground. When night fell, nothing was left of Driant's battalions but Driant himself, seven lieutenants—every one of whom was wounded—and about a hundred troops still capable of fighting. But they were still in possession of the Bois des Caures.

OLD WOUNDS UNHEALED

JULIUS CAESAR WOULD NOT BE SURPRISED TO learn that a great battle took place at Verdun two millennia after his conquest of Gaul. The place was well known to the Romans, who recognized its inherent military importance. They named it, in fact—called it Verodunum, "strong fort." As the name suggests, the Romans made it a military center as their empire grew. It was a base from which they could move against still-unconquered tribes, and a refuge to which they could withdraw when barbarian hordes came plundering.

Verdun had almost certainly been a stronghold long before Roman times. Its importance grew out of its position on the River Meuse, which snakes northward from headwaters in the French Alps into Belgium and Holland on its way to the North Sea. Any geographer could have predicted that a town would emerge where Verdun did in fact appear: it was the only point on a long stretch of the Meuse where even Bronze Age travelers could cross the river with comparative ease. From earliest times it was a gateway connecting the Rhineland with central France and the two little river islands where Paris would be born. Any mass of warriors on the rampage in western Europe was likely to find itself drawn to Verdun.

Thus Verdun's whole history has been written in blood. Even Attila the Hun sacked and burned the place. When the quarreling grandsons of Charlemagne met in 843 to divide the Frankish empire, they did so at Verdun. Their agreement, the Treaty of Verdun, created three new realms. In the west was the Kingdom of the West Franks, which would evolve over the centuries into France. The Kingdom of the East Franks became Germany (and gradually broke into hundreds of fragments). Between the two was a long and vulnerable strip-kingdom, called Lotharingia (the root of the name Lorraine) for the unfortunate grandson, Lothair, who received it as his share. It ran from what is now Holland south through the old kingdom of Alsatia (thus Alsace) all the way to Rome. It became a battleground between its neighbors and soon disappeared from history.

It is not much of an exaggeration, in light of this history, to say that not only France and Germany but also their twelve hundred years of struggle over the territories between the Meuse and the Rhine all were born at Verdun.

For a while Verdun belonged to the western kingdom. In 923, at a time when France was feeble and the Holy Roman Empire strong, the Germans took it. Verdun and the territories around it, Alsace and Lorraine included, remained German for more than six hundred years, which might have been expected to settle the question of its cultural identity. But by the sixteenth century the balance of power had shifted. France was centralizing under the king at Paris and growing stronger, while the Holy Roman Empire was almost too fractured to defend itself. Verdun was plucked away by Henry II of France. In the seventeenth century Cardinal Richelieu, chief minister to Louis XIV, seized Alsace and Lorraine as well, shifting the border between France and Germany eastward to the Rhine.

Louis XIV, the Sun King, had in his service possibly the greatest military engineer in history, Sébastien Le Prestre de Vauban. When Vauban installed a great chain of frontier fortresses west of the Rhine, he made Verdun its northern anchor. He transformed it from a fort into a network of forts spread across the rugged, wooded hills at the center of which the town sits like a plum in the bottom of a bowl. Until advances in artillery and siege warfare overtook Vauban's work, Verdun remained impregnable.

Every war drew armies to Verdun. It withstood a siege during the Thirty Years War and fell to the Prussians in 1792, when the monarchies of eastern Europe were making war on Revolutionary France. The French soon got it back, but the idea of retaking and keeping Alsace and Lorraine became a key element in the German nationalism that Napoleon's wars had ignited.

Verdun held out longer than all of France's other eastern fortresses in the Franco-Prussian War of 1870. The Germans returned it to France as part of the settlement of that war, but they kept Alsace and a substantial part of Lorraine—five thousand square miles in all. Now the recovery of the two provinces became a *French* dream, their loss a wound so painful as to destroy any possibility of reconciliation with Germany. In Paris's Place de la Concorde, a statue representing Strasbourg, principal city of the lost territories, was permanently draped in black.

The latest, westward shift of the border had left the French with no major defenses between Verdun and Germany. Verdun became, therefore, part of France's first line of defense. In the final years of the nineteenth century, it and a line of fortress cities to its south (Toul, Épinal, and Belfort) were further expanded and strengthened. Observing this work, Alfred von Schlieffen concluded that the only feasible way to take the offensive against France was to go through Belgium.

Just a few years before the Great War, the largest of the Verdun strongpoints, Forts Douaumont and Vaux, were covered with protective shells that not even the biggest guns could destroy. By the outbreak of the war, the word *Verdun* signified a ten-mile-wide military region bisected by the Meuse and including a dozen major fortresses, eight smaller strongpoints, and forty additional redoubts that, though smaller still, also bristled with guns.

Verdun proved crucial to France's survival in the opening weeks of the war. It remained the anchor that Vauban had intended it to be, allowing the French armies to maintain an unbroken line as they fell back toward the Marne. Almost but never quite cut off, by October 1914 it was the hard nucleus of a salient protruding into the German line. Early in 1915, the Germans tried to pinch it off but failed. Thereafter that sector of the front became quiet, and Joffre began stripping Verdun of its firepower. Ultimately 80 percent of its artillery was sent off for use in offensives elsewhere. Its manpower was reduced to levels that every commander on the scene found to be cause for alarm.

Alsace and Lorraine by this time had been invaded by the French and retaken by the Germans, but their status remained unsettled. The population of the two provinces was largely German-speaking and German in culture—even today their architecture and place names are more German than French. But loyalties were mixed. The region had been French at the time of the Revolution and had remained French long enough to become republican in its sympathies and unaffected by the rise of nationalist sentiment inside Germany proper. After the Franco-Prussian War it had been put directly under the governance of Berlin, rather than being given the kind of semiautonomy enjoyed by other German states. Its people had little liking for the Prussians, who moved in like an occupying force. On the other hand, most of the Alsace-Lorrainers were Catholic, and the militant anticlericalism of the French government in the decade before the war (a prejudice so potent that it put even senior French army officers under a cloud of suspicion) made many of them wary of Paris.

The behavior of the Prussians seemed almost calculated to push Alsace and Lorraine into the arms of France. In 1913 a young Prussian lieutenant insulted the people of the town of Zabern and injured a protesting civilian with his sword, but Berlin took no disciplinary action and offered no apology. Anti-Berlin feeling became inflamed, and the overreaction of the authorities quickly made things worse. In August 1914, when mobilization was not greeted with universal enthusiasm, the German military authorities felt confirmed in their disdain.

Mobilization went smoothly enough, though in all of Alsace and Lorraine only eight thousand men volunteered and a fourth of the sixteen thousand conscripted men living abroad reported for duty as ordered. Many of those who did report were deemed to be of questionable loyalty, and when it became clear that disproportionate numbers of them were being sent to the Eastern Front, they naturally grew resentful. More than seventeen thousand Alsace-Lorrainers, meanwhile, were slipping across the border to volunteer in France.

Ultimately, three hundred and eighty thousand men from Alsace and Lorraine served in the German army during the war. Their desertion rate was eighty out of every ten thousand, compared with one in ten thousand for other German troops. The high command responded with increased distrust and even harsher treatment both of the provinces themselves and of the soldiers who had come from them, and the sense of alienation deepened. It widened beyond possibility of repair when the government's postwar plans for the provinces became public knowledge. Rather than being granted autonomy as one of the German states, they were to be punished: Alsace was to be given to Bavaria, Lorraine to Prussia.

Thus did Germany, through its own actions, lose Alsace and Lorraine long before France took them back.

Chapter 2

Verdun: Execution

"It wouldn't take anything, just a slightly harder blow, for everything to collapse."

—Anonymous French soldier

Anyone inclined to believe that some dark force beyond human comprehension intervened again and again to make the Great War long and ruinous would have no difficulty in finding evidence to support such a thesis. There is no better example than the Battle of Verdun, which in its length and cost and brutality and finally in its sheer pointlessness has always and rightly been seen as a perfect microcosm of the war itself.

Nothing at all was inevitable about the battle. Though Falkenhayn may have been right in thinking that Germany had to take the offensive somewhere early in 1916, he had other targets to choose from, even on the Western Front. Ludendorff, if given the chance, could have argued persuasively for action in the east.

And if Verdun was in fact the right choice, Falkenhayn's tactics were questionable at best. They stripped his troops of the opportunity that his artillery had created to capture the heart of Verdun's defenses. They gave the French, who by midday on February 21 were in no condition to withstand an attack in force, time to pull themselves together.

The French for their part had little real need to hold Verdun. Their front was firm at all points at the start of 1916, and historians have argued that they would have been wiser to abandon Verdun, fall back on the hill country to the southwest, and oblige the Germans to settle for a symbolic victory of minor strategic value. But the fates decreed otherwise. The defense of Verdun fell to men who were not willing to consider even an advantageous retreat. And so it continued.

The second day began with a German bombardment as shattering as that of February 21. The French could do nothing but curl up at the bottom of whatever bunkers or holes they could still find amid the rubble and pray not to be vaporized or buried alive. This time the Germans began their advance at the end of morning, and they came forward in far greater numbers. They found the French forward positions even more obliterated than on the previous afternoon, and they had hours of daylight in which to keep moving.

The courage of the French troops in the face of all this defies belief. On the first day they had held their ground first with rifle and machine-gun fire, then with grenades, and finally, even in the face of that horrific new weapon the flamethrower, with gun-butts and stones. Now they somehow managed, even before the lifting of the barrage, to launch small, scattered, and uncoordinated counterattacks. It was, once again, the French doctrine of attacking whenever possible and trying immediately to recapture any lost ground. It confused and slowed the Germans, but it also led the French into exactly the kind of slaughter upon which Falkenhayn had built his hopes.

An entire German division was sent to the Bois des Caures, still held by the surviving members of Émile Driant's battalions, with orders to take it at all costs. During the first day's bombardment an estimated eighty thousand shells had fallen on the Bois des Caures, an area measuring five hundred by one thousand yards. Now, on the second morning, thousands more had come screaming down. Driant lost still more of his men, most of his bunkers were unrecognizable, and his position was nearly surrounded. Coolly, he burned his papers and ordered a withdrawal during which he was killed—shot in the forehead, according to men who were with him.

When the day ended, the Germans had again pushed the French back, but their gains were again less than spectacular. Casualties on the German side were as light as Falkenhayn could have hoped: the two infantry divisions on the cutting edge of the

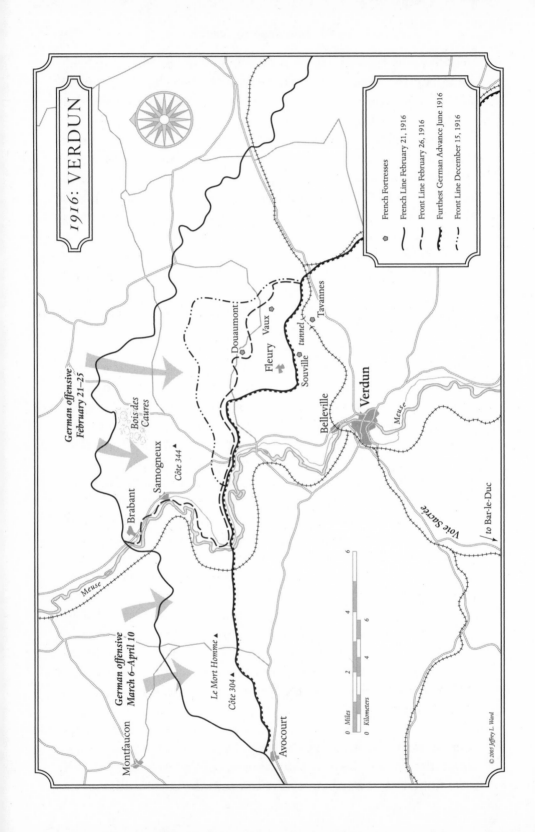

1916: VERDUN

French Fortresses
French Line February 21, 1916
French Line February 26, 1916
Front Line February 26, 1916
Furthest German Advance June 1916
Front Line December 15, 1916

German offensive
February 21–25

Bois des Caures

Brabant

Samogneux
Côte 344 ▲

Montfaucon

German offensive
March 6–April 10

Meuse

Le Mort Homme ▲
Côte 304 ▲

Avocourt

Douaumont

Vaux

Fleury

Souville

tunnel

Tavannes

Belleville

Verdun

Meuse

Voie Sacrée

to Bar-le-Duc

0 Miles   2   4   6
0 Kilometers   4   6

© 2005 Jeffrey L. Ward

attack would report fewer than two thousand men killed or missing in the first *month* of the battle. By contrast, French deaths exceeded twenty-three thousand in the first five days. Of this total, nearly twenty thousand were listed as "missing," which meant they had been taken prisoner or, more commonly, that their bodies had been destroyed or buried by the shelling. It was a rare case—extremely rare for the Western Front—of defenders suffering substantially heavier losses than their attackers. Three-fifths of the troops with which the French began the battle became casualties within two weeks.

On the third day, after a night of intense cold that deepened the misery of the troops on both sides and ended the lives of hundreds of the wounded scattered across the landscape, the situation appeared to stabilize. The French troops continued to display an astonishing willingness to die rather than surrender or retreat, and they were inspired by the arrival of reinforcements from the rear and by increasing artillery support. The Germans again advanced, but their gains again were modest. The situation appeared to be moving toward a restoration of the old and familiar stalemate.

But suddenly on the fourth day, February 24, the French line began to fall apart. The day was a series of disasters for the defenders, and the first occurred hours before dawn. The Germans had been threatening the town of Samogneux on the right bank of the Meuse some four miles southeast of the Bois des Caures. On the night of February 23 a unit of French troops outside Samogneux broke in the face of an attack. After fleeing through the town, these soldiers told everyone they encountered, wrongly if understandably, that Samogneux had been lost. In fact it was still in French hands, but the commanders in the rear were sent reports of its fall. One general ordered a counterattack. Another directed artillery fire onto the town. At fifteen minutes after midnight French shells began falling both on the French in Samogneux and on those hurrying to retake it. By four a.m. the Germans were in possession.

The German artillery continued to blast away, and when dawn came and the infantry returned to the offensive, it quickly broke through a new line of defense that Castelnau had ordered to be put in place during his visit to Verdun late in January. With the breaching of this line, which had proved to be a powerful obstacle until it was overrun, French resistance seemed to dissolve. When the

Germans attacked the next line in their path, the French ran. The Germans gained more ground on this day than on the first three days of the battle. They advanced three and a half miles, stopping only when the great bastions of Fort Douaumont and Fort Vaux, the two strongest points on the east side of the Meuse, blocked their way. French reinforcements continued to arrive, but as they did so they were sent off to whatever points appeared to be in greatest trouble without being concentrated or coordinated. They were quickly shot up without achieving anything. "It wouldn't take anything, just a slightly harder blow," said a French ambulance driver observing the situation, "for everything to collapse."

The French general with overall responsibility for the Verdun region, Fernand de Langle de Cary, telephoned Joffre to say that he wanted to withdraw from the Woëvre plain, the expanse of gently sloping farmland several miles east of the city. This was an astonishing proposal: the Germans had not even attacked on the Woëvre. Withdrawal there would gravely compromise the French army's ability to threaten the Germans' great salient at St. Mihiel, south of Verdun. It would imply eventual abandonment of the entire east bank. Joffre, however, responded with the preternatural calm for which he was by now famous. Telling Langle de Cary to do as he thought best, he returned to his supper. Langle de Cary went ahead with the withdrawal. Almost as soon as he did so, German troops moved in from the north to fill the vacuum. It was another part of the spreading French collapse.

Shortly after Joffre finished his meal, Castlenau arrived to tell him of the deteriorating situation. He recommended that the French Second Army, commanded by General Henri-Philippe Pétain and currently being rested at the town of Noailles in Normandy, be sent to the west bank at Verdun. Joffre agreed and retired for the night. At eleven p.m., having received alarming reports of fresh reverses, Castelnau was again at Joffre's door. When a frightened aide reminded him that the commander in chief's rest was not to be disturbed, Castelnau swept past him. Joffre, roused from his sleep, listened impassively to the latest news. He remained confident that the attack at Verdun was not a serious threat—his intelligence staff had assured him that it was a diversion in advance of a bigger German offensive planned for Champagne. When Castelnau asked permission to proceed to

Verdun with authority to do there whatever he found to be necessary, Joffre again assented. He returned to bed and Castelanau
departed by automobile.

At Noailles, meanwhile, another little drama was being played
out. Castelnau's telegram ordering the Second Army to Verdun
had been delivered to Pétain's headquarters, but Pétain himself
was not there. He had left earlier in the day without telling anyone
his destination. His aide, Bernard de Serrigny, knew his chief well.
He summoned a car and set out through the dark countryside for
Paris. It was almost three a.m. when he entered the sleeping city
and directed his driver to the hotel at the Gare du Nord. There he
roused the night manager. When she insisted that no General Pétain was on the premises, he refused to believe her. A search of the
upper floors proved him right. Outside the door to one of the guest
rooms stood a pair of army boots of yellowish leather—Pétain's
boots. Next to them—all suspicions confirmed—was a dainty pair
of ladies' slippers.

When he answered the knock on his door and saw who was
there, Pétain stepped into the hall in his nightclothes. Serrigny
briefed him, displaying the message instructing him to meet with
Joffre at Chantilly at eight that morning. From inside the dark
room came the sound of a woman weeping. Pétain, as calm as
Joffre had been, told Serrigny to take a room, get some sleep, and

General Noël de Castelnau
Rushed to Verdun at start of battle.

meet him in the lobby at seven. Four hours later the two were speeding northward out of the city toward Chantilly.

At about the same time, miles to the east, Castelnau was arriving at Verdun, where the sun was rising over an icy landscape and the German Fifth Army was beginning the fifth day of its offensive. The French were in such disarray, and so demoralized, that they almost certainly would have been routed if hit with sufficient force. The crown prince and Knobelsdorf saw the opportunity and were eager to exploit it, but their meager reserves had already been committed. The main German reserve force was still under the control of Falkenhayn, who refused to release it. He thereby wasted his second chance to take Verdun. He was sticking with his plan and in so doing was fatally outsmarting himself.

All that day Castelnau traveled from place to place, bringing order out of confusion and quietly taking stock. As he did so, stunning news reached him. Mighty Fort Douaumont, the centerpiece of the Verdun defensive system, a stronghold built to be impregnable, and impregnable in fact when properly defended, had been captured by the Germans. This was not supposed to happen.

The story of how it happened is like something out of Kafka. The Germans had brought to bear upon Douaumont the same monster howitzers with which they had destroyed the Belgian forts a year and a half earlier, but this time their bombardment failed. The latest improvements had covered Douaumont's interior with alternating layers of reinforced concrete and loose rock and earth, a shock-absorbing dome that no shell could penetrate. The fort remained intact through explosion after explosion, the men inside badly rattled but unhurt.

Those men, however, numbered only sixty. Most of the fort's garrison, along with every piece of artillery that could be moved, had been sent away months before. On February 25 the troops who remained were huddled deep in the interior, as far as possible from the mayhem above. Three little parties of Germans— one of them consisting of a solitary sergeant—crept up on the fort at different points and met no resistance. Each party, unaware of the others, found an undefended entrance. Once inside they wandered unchallenged through empty chambers and passageways. After much confused exploring during which the solitary sergeant discovered a commissary and paused to gorge on hard-boiled eggs, they eventually and half-accidentally took the French by surprise, capturing them and the fort itself. German reinforcements were quicker than the French to rush forward, so that one of the anchors of Verdun fell into German hands without a shot being fired by either side.

In spite of the disasters occurring all around him, Castelnau decided that Verdun could be held. Being a firm adherent of the doctrine that when unable to attack the French should never give ground, he did exactly what Falkenhayn would have wanted him to do: he resolved that Verdun *must* be held.

Meanwhile not everything was going well for the Germans. For reasons that will never be known because every witness was instantly reduced to his constituent molecules, an enormous German ammunition dump at the village of Spincourt suddenly blew up. Four hundred and fifty thousand shells disappeared in an explosion that seemed to rend the heavens, leaving the Germans instantly and gravely short of ammunition. And from the west bank of the Meuse, a haven for French artillery because of Falkenhayn's refusal to include it in his offensive, long-range guns were methodically putting the big German howitzers out of action one by one.

At three-thirty in the afternoon Castelnau telephoned Joffre and told him of his decision to stand and fight. He announced another decision as well: all the other senior generals in the area having been found wanting, Pétain should be given command not just of the west bank but of the entire theater. When Pétain arrived near midnight, at the end of a day that had included a pro forma meeting with the sphinxlike Joffre and long hours on crowded wintry roads, he was coming down with what appeared to be a bad cold. Castelnau briefed him, gave him handwritten orders to take command and to hold the east bank at all costs, and departed. Pétain slept for a few hours in an armchair in an unheated room, and when he awoke he was burning with fever. A doctor was called in, and after a hurried examination he declared that the general had double pneumonia. This condition was debilitating and potentially lethal in the days before antibiotics, especially for a man of sixty. Pétain would have been amply justified in declaring himself unable to continue. Instead, issuing strict orders that his illness be kept secret, he organized a system in which members of his staff would serve as his eyes, ears, and voice, and he himself would rarely have to leave his room. For most of the next week he reorganized the defense of Verdun from a sickbed. During part of that week his life hung in the balance.

The appointment of Pétain put Verdun in the hands of a man who, probably more than any other in the French army, was capable of organizing an effective defense while at the same time protecting his troops from unnecessary destruction. Pétain was an infantryman who had taken the trouble, in the course of his long career, to make himself expert in the science of artillery. At a time and in a place that put nearly unendurable pressure on France's common soldiers, he was unique in his ability to understand the troops under his command: in his unwillingness to throw their lives away, and in his willingness to share their dangers. He was a leader, and the poilus responded to him. His was a remarkable case of the right man being in the right place at the right time.

From his first day in command, too weak to stay on his feet, Pétain began moving men and guns back into the strongholds that Joffre had all but abandoned. He ordered an end to hopeless attacks on lost positions, Fort Douaumont included. He installed a so-called "line of panic" where the French could gather for a last stand if the Germans broke through. He took charge both of the artillery and of the system by which Verdun was supplied. The guns were positioned, and their fire coordinated, to inflict maximum damage on the German assault troops as they came forward through the gullies between the hills. This turned the tables on Falkenhayn. Now the Germans were advancing not just against battered infantry but into a concentrated barrage. The French soldiers were soon aware of the change, and their morale rose swiftly.

Though still concealed behind his wall of secrecy, Pétain saw that Verdun's greatest vulnerability was its tenuous line of supply. Because it was a salient, a bulge in the line left exposed by the Germans' 1914 advances to the east and south, the city had only one connection to the rear: a road that ran northward from the ancient hill town of Bar-le-Duc, forty miles to the south. Everything needed to sustain the fight—men, guns, ammunition, food—had to travel along this road. It had been widened in 1915, providing barely

Generals Ferdinand Foch (*left*) and Henri-Philippe Pétain

enough room for two trucks side by side. Never in history had an embattled army the size of Pétain's been supported for an extended period through such a thin line.

Pétain's staff could find only seven hundred trucks. All of France was searched for more, so that ultimately thirty-five hundred would be streaming north and south day and night. At the peak of the conflict, trucks arrived in Verdun at a rate of one every fourteen seconds. Any vehicle that broke down was rolled into the ditches that lined the road, and at any given time as many as fifteen thousand men were at work keeping the roadbed in usable condition. Upon unloading, the trucks would be filled with men—not with the wounded only, but with soldiers being sent away for recuperation from the horror of an unending artillery barrage—and returned to Bar-le-Duc. This too was part of Pétain's plan: he ordered a constant rotation of units into and out of the combat zone, so that relatively fresh troops were always arriving and the men under fire had something more to look forward to than remaining under fire until they were dead. In time three-fourths of the entire French army—125 divisions—would be rotated through Verdun, so that it more than any other battle of the war became a shared national experience. The French writer and politician Maurice Barrès would call the Bar-le-Duc road the Voie Sacrée, the Sacred Way, and it has been remembered by that name ever since.

The actions taken by Pétain, coupled with the Germans' lack of reserves, changed the character of the fight. On February 27, barely forty-eight hours after standing on the brink of taking the city, the Germans for the first time captured no new ground at all during a full day of combat. Kaiser Wilhelm, after days of waiting at his son's headquarters to enter Verdun in triumph, gave up and left the area.

February 28 brought a thaw, melting the ice and snow and turning frozen earth to mud—and threatening to make the Bar-le-Duc road impassable. Thousands more men were assigned to shoveling gravel and scrap metal and whatever else was available onto and into the mud, and the trucks kept moving. Between February 24 and March 6 twenty-five thousand tons of supplies and a hundred and ninety thousand men were carried into Verdun.

For the Germans, the thaw was a disaster. Their roads had been severely damaged by French artillery fire, and as they softened into a quagmire, the movement of guns and shells became nearly impossible. Howitzers in forward positions remained short of ammunition and under fire. Forward units of German infantry found themselves under a barrage little less deadly than the one that had descended on the French a week earlier. Much of this fire was coming from a long ridge west of the Meuse that for centuries had borne the ominous and suddenly prophetic name of Le Mort Homme, the Dead Man. With every new day the Germans were paying a higher price for Falkenhayn's refusal to include the west bank in his offensive.

Even at this juncture, one way remained open for the Germans to deliver a mortal blow without expending infantry. They could have directed artillery fire onto the Bar-le-Duc road, the Verdun lifeline, which was jammed to capacity around the clock and in constantly deteriorating condition. In preparation for his offensive, Falkenhayn had sent batteries of long-range naval guns to Verdun; the road was within their range. The Germans also had almost total control of the air over Verdun at this early stage; with bombing and strafing their aircraft could have reduced the road to chaos. Somehow—another of the war's many mysteries—the Germans failed to make use of these opportunities. They continued to allow men and equipment to pour into Verdun even as movement of their own forces became all but impossible.

On the last day of the month, February 29, the crown prince and Knobelsdorf met with Falkenhayn to decide the biggest possible question: whether the offensive, which had obviously come to nothing, should be continued. There was much to be said for stopping, with German losses not yet at all painful by Great War standards. The capture of Douaumont alone was sufficient for propaganda purposes. The assembled generals surely were mindful of the reasons for stopping: among military strategists it has long been a truism that prolonging an unsuccessful offensive invariably proves futile.

The crown prince, however, appears to have been seduced by visions of what might have been achieved if his ideas rather than Falkenhayn's had been allowed to shape the attack of Feb-

German troops struggling to move a piece of light field artillery

ruary 21. He and Knobelsdorf declared themselves in favor of continuing if three conditions were met. The offensive must be widened to include the hills west of the Meuse, the French artillery positions around Le Mort Homme especially. The reserves held back by Falkenhayn must be brought forward and used. Finally, this widening of the fight and raising of the stakes must not be open-ended. The entire operation had to be called off, the crown prince said, as soon as it became clear that the Germans were losing as many men as the French. Falkenhayn agreed. His goal remained what it had been all along: "not to defeat but to annihilate France."

And so the Germans, having in the space of a week thrown away two opportunities to capture Verdun, cast aside the chance to get out cheaply.

THE LIVING DEAD

BY 1916 THE ARMIES OF BRITAIN, FRANCE, AND
Germany were being diminished not just by the numbers of men
killed and wounded but by something so new to human experience
that the English had to coin a name for it: *shell shock.* By the thousands and then the tens of thousands, soldiers on the Western Front
were being turned into zombies and freaks without suffering physical
injuries of any kind.

The phenomenon appeared in 1914, and at first no one knew
what to make of it. The medical services on both sides found themselves confronted with bizarre symptoms: men in a trancelike state,
men shaking uncontrollably, men frozen in weird postures, or partly
paralyzed, or (though unwounded) unable to see or hear or speak.
By December British doctors were reporting that between 3 and 4
percent of the BEF's enlisted men and up to 10 percent of its officers
were displaying symptoms of this kind. Their German counterparts
would record almost twelve thousand such cases in the first year of
the war.

The victims got little sympathy. Career officers were accustomed
to separating soldiers into four groups: the healthy, the sick, the
wounded, and the cowards. They were predisposed to put men with
nervous and mental disorders into the last category, to order them
back to duty, and to mete out harsh punishment to any who failed to
obey. But the number of men unable to obey became too big to be
ignored or to be put in front of firing squads; it has been estimated
that twenty-four thousand had been sent home to Britain by 1916.

The army's career physicians agreed with their generals: this was
not illness but malingering, and the solution was punishment. Any
who failed to agree were met with contempt. But doctors who had
been brought out of private practice with mobilization looked for
medical explanations. Theories were offered. An early favorite was
that the soldiers' nervous systems were being damaged in some

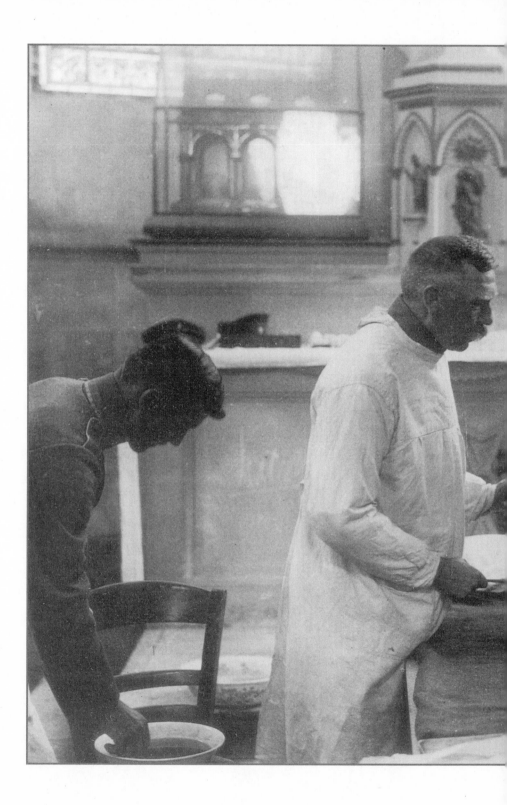

mysterious way by shock waves from high explosives. Thus the term *shell shock* came into general, even diagnostic, use.

Gradually it became clear that the words did not fit the facts. Many of the victims had not been shelled—at least had not been exposed to shellfire shortly before breaking down. More oddly, *none* of the victims had been physically injured. By 1916 a more sophisticated understanding was emerging. Charles Myers, a young English psychiatrist, decided after making a close study of the subject that *shell shock* was "a singularly ill-chosen term." The condition, he said, had nothing to do with the physics of shellfire or with physical damage to nerves. It rose out of the peculiar conditions of trench warfare, an experience beyond anything the human psyche was built to endure. The troops were cracking because they could not absorb what was happening to them, because they knew themselves to be utterly powerless (bravery had little survival value when one was on the receiving end of a bombardment), and because they had no confidence that the generals who had put them in danger knew what they were doing. Men whose courage was beyond challenge could and did break down if subjected to enough strain of this kind. Conversely, many shell shock victims recovered sufficiently to be returned to action, and some performed heroically after doing so.

Myers's analysis of the relationship between trench warfare and breakdown—which came to be called *hysteria* when the victims behaved manically, *neurasthenia* when they sank into depression—was confirmed as the war continued. Observers noticed that breakdowns had been least frequent in the opening months of the war, before the Western Front became rigid (and later that their frequency declined when the deadlock was broken and the armies again began to move). Further confirmation came in the fact that one in six victims was an officer, although the BEF had only one officer for every thirty men. Junior officers on the front lines not only bore heavier responsibilities than the men they commanded but were more often exposed to enemy fire.

By trial and error, it was discovered that soldiers who broke down were most likely to recover when treated almost immediately, at casualty clearing stations behind the lines, rather than being sent to hospitals. Various treatments were tried—hypnosis, electric shock,

Previous pages: Surgery in a French church

simple and often bullying forms of talk therapy—and several proved to be at least somewhat effective. Treatment was often indistinguishable from punishment. Men unable to talk were given electric shocks until they screamed in pain, at which point they were declared to have recovered. Always the objective was not to "cure" the victim, to identify and deal with the underlying causes of his symptoms, but to get him back into action. The British created two categories of cases: men who had broken when actually under fire, and those who had not been under fire. Only those in the first category were entitled to wear on their sleeves the stripe awarded to men wounded in action, and only they, if they did not recover, were entitled to disability compensation. It remained inadmissible for physicians to suggest that a loss of the will to fight could ever be justified. The few who dared to suggest that it might be rational for a man to disobey an order that could not possibly lead to anything except sudden death—an order to climb out of a hole into blanketing gunfire, for example—were likely to be dismissed. Any nonmedical officer who seriously challenged such orders was dismissed or worse.

The problem remained immense. This is an area in which data are scarce—little is known about the incidence or treatment of shell shock among the Austrians and Russians, though the continued fluidity of the Eastern Front may have limited the problem there. But by the end of the war, two hundred thousand shell shock cases entered the medical records in Germany, eighty thousand in Britain. Sixteen thousand cases were reported by the British just in the second half of 1916, and this total included only those men in the first category, the ones whose problems were judged to be less dishonorable. Fifteen percent of all the British soldiers who received disability pensions—one hundred and twenty thousand men in all—would do so for psychiatric reasons. In 1922, four years after the war's end, some six thousand British veterans would remain in insane asylums.

Chapter 3

Verdun Metastasizes

"Verdun was the mill on the Meuse that ground to powder the hearts as well as the bodies of our soldiers."
—Crown Prince Wilhelm

On March 6, after a week when the artillery on both sides continued to pound away but infantry operations were limited to attacks and counterattacks of little consequence, the Germans attempted to restart their stalled offensive. In keeping with the conditions that the crown prince had set in agreeing to continue, they did so with many more troops this time (Falkenhayn had released a corps of reserves) and on a much broader front. They again attacked in the craggy wooded hills east of the Meuse, but now they also made a complementary move on the west or left bank. There the main objective was Le Mort Homme, the ridge from which French gunners had been sending fire across the river. The battle remained above all an artillery contest. As on February 21, the Germans began by trying to use their firepower to obliterate the defenders. Once again men died by the hundreds without seeing or being seen by the men who killed them.

The balance had shifted, however. The French had hurried two hundred thousand troops up the Voie Sacrée from Bar-le-Duc, and the long-range guns that they had positioned all through the region were wrecking the Germans' howitzers. Pétain, anticipating a German advance on the west bank, had positioned four divisions of infantry there—something on the order of sixty thousand troops—with a fifth in reserve. Though not fully recovered from pneumonia, he was back on his feet and directing everything.

Conceivably, if he had been free to make his own decisions, Pétain might have elected to withdraw from Verdun. He understood that he would have sacrificed nothing of strategic importance in doing so, and he would have left the Germans in a difficult position from which to proceed. But he knew too that President Poincaré, for reasons of national morale, had demanded that the city be held, and that if he proposed anything different he would likely be dismissed. Fortunately for him, the Falkenhayn plan had by this point lost all coherence. The dynamics of the situation were drawing the Germans into a nearly obsessive willingness to attack and attack again regardless of cost, and to attack not only with guns but with troops. Blindness, loss of perspective, had become a more serious affliction on the German side than on the French.

On the ravaged ground of the east bank, after again throwing masses of infantry against reinforced French defenses and murderous artillery fire, the Germans found themselves reeling under the magnitude of their losses and unable to advance. On the new battleground west of the river too, the center of the attack was quickly stopped. Only on the left flank of the west bank offensive, the flank directly adjacent to the Meuse, was the story different. There the attackers made rapid and substantial progress, managing to blast the French out of village after village, capturing the first and then the second lines of defense along four miles of front, taking thousands of prisoners. The situation became so desperate, the danger of a general collapse so great, that the sector's French commander issued a warning to his troops. If they tried to withdraw, he would order his own artillery and machine guns to fire on them.

The Battle of Verdun began to settle down into stalemate. On March 7 the Germans' drive on the west bank brought them up against a woodland called the Bois des Corbeaux, one of several points protecting the approaches to Le Mort Homme. Artillery wiped out many of the defenders, put the survivors to flight, and allowed the Germans to take possession of the woods. Early the next morning the French returned in a wildly courageous counterattack that should have been a disaster but through sheer audacity panicked the Germans and sent them running. But the next day, when a blast of artillery blew off both legs of the dashing colonel who had led the counterattack carrying only a walking stick, the Germans yet again captured the Bois. This time they held it. But the victory was little more than pyrrhic. It left the Germans exhausted and pinned down. Not only Le Mort Homme but the high points nearest it remained in French hands, bristling with artillery and machine guns, guarded by entrenched riflemen. Further movement was out of the question.

The crown prince's attack on two sides of the river had miscarried as badly as Falkenhayn's on one. If the French were being bled white, so were the Germans. The two sides were draining each other in a fight so huge and costly, so rich in drama, that it had captured the imagination of the world. Verdun had been elevated to such colossal symbolic importance that France needed only to hold on in order to claim a momentous victory. Falkenhayn, originally indifferent to whether Verdun fell or not, now desperately needed to take it. The trap that he had wanted to construct for the French now held him firmly in its grip.

As a direct result of Verdun, the war in the east flared back into life. Late in 1915, when the Entente's senior commanders met to make plans, the Russians had complained about what they saw as their allies' failure to help when the Germans were hammering them out of Poland. General Mikhail Alexeyev, sent to Chantilly as the tsar's new chief of staff, demanded an agreement that whenever one front was threatened, an offensive would be launched on the other to relieve the pressure. The Battle of Verdun was only days old when the French reminded Petrograd of this commitment. The Russians responded with yet another expression of their almost touching readiness to try to come to the rescue whenever asked—an eagerness that contrasted sharply with the cynicism and contempt that so often tainted relations between the British and the French. It is difficult to imagine Joffre or Haig responding as the Russians did if the situation had been reversed.

Only the tsar was really eager. When the Russian general staff gathered at his headquarters on the third day of fighting at Verdun, the army group commanders argued that they were not ready for an offensive and attacking now could only spoil their chances of doing so successfully later. They pointed out that the spring thaw was approaching and that the resulting floods would usher in the annual "roadless period," during which movement of men and guns became all but impossible. Tsar Nicholas decided otherwise. He ordered not only that an attack be launched but that it take place in advance of the thaw. The only remaining question was where to hit the Germans.

The Russians appeared to have good options from which to choose. The loss of Poland had enormously shortened their lines, increasing the number of troops available for each mile of front. In the north, in the sector commanded by Hindenburg and Ludendorff on the German side, the Russians had three hundred thousand troops to the Germans' one hundred and eighty thousand. In the center the Russian advantage was even greater: seven hundred thousand men facing three hundred and sixty thousand Germans. In the south, where the front slanted eastward toward the Balkans, things were more evenly balanced, with half a million men on each side. Here, however, the enemy troops were mainly Austro-Hungarian rather than German and therefore considerably less intimidating. That the Russian troops were largely half-trained recruits and deplorably ill equipped (tens of thousands remained without rifles) seems to have caused little more concern than the questionable quality of their leadership. Though the whole vast Russian army was a sorry mess by the standards of the Germans, French, and British, War Minister Alexei Polivanov was improving training and supply. Recent events gave cause for encouragement. Grand Duke Nicholas had launched an offensive in the Caucasus in January and within a week had won a major victory over the Turks at Koprukov. On February 16 his forces had captured Erzerum, the Ottoman Empire's most important northern stronghold. Obviously Russian armies were capable of winning.

It was decided that the new offensive should take place in the northwest, at Lake Naroch near the Lithuanian capital of Vilna, and should include the northern and central army groups. Together they could provide ten corps, more than twenty divisions, enough to outnumber the Germans by what promised to be a decisive margin. They were commanded by two of the most senior Russian generals, Alexei Evert and Alexei Kuropatkin.

After a series of delays that gave the Germans ample foreknowledge of what was coming, the Russians kicked off their attack on

March 18. The dreaded thaw had begun the day before, covering the terrain with knee-deep slush, but success seemed certain nevertheless. Of all the Russian armies, those commanded by Evert and Kuropatkin were richest in guns and ammunition. They began Verdun-style, in eight hours firing thirty thousand three-inch shells and nine thousand heavier projectiles at the entrenchments of the German Tenth Army. When the Russian infantry moved forward—four corps on a front of twelve miles—it did so against a defending force that was barely one-fifth its size, and in short order it overran the Germans' first two lines. In less than a week, however, the attack broke down completely, with the Russians trying and failing to take the high ground beyond the positions they had captured.

There are several explanations for this failure. Bad weather and inadequate air reconnaissance had left the Russian artillery almost blind, so that much of the barrage fell harmlessly on unoccupied ground. Even when the gunners had the opportunity to support their infantry, they often failed to do so. The end of winter, with the snow cover melting and then freezing hard and melting again, made conditions terrible for the infantry. The quality of the troops was low on the Russian side, high on the German, and the sixty-eight-year-old Kuropatkin was a deplorable product of the Russian autocracy's tendency to keep mediocrities in important positions long after their unfitness had been demonstrated beyond doubt. A favorite at court, he had served as minister of war from 1898 to 1904 and then was given command of all Russian ground forces in the Russo-Japanese War. Though he had been replaced after causing a disastrous defeat at Mukden, his connections got him returned to senior command. He again performed clumsily early in the Great War but had nevertheless been made commander of the Northern Army Group in 1915. Now, at Lake Naroch, he failed to support the cautious Evert in much the same way that Rennenkampf had failed Samsonov at Tannenberg, and with equally painful results. Evert's men, trying to advance in deep ice-melt against an enemy firing down on them from defenses that Ludendorff had been strengthening all winter, were massacred. Twelve thousand unwounded Russians, still flimsily dressed after a year and a half of war, froze to death when temperatures plunged overnight. The offensive ended so quickly, at so little cost to the Germans, that it had no impact on Verdun. Outnumbered as they were, the Germans had required no reinforcements.

At this same time there departed from the stage possibly the best leader, almost certainly the best man, in the French military establishment. Joseph Gallieni, whose interventions as a sidelined general had led to the victory at the Marne in 1914 and as minister of war had helped to save Verdun in February 1916, resigned in March in preparation for surgery needed to save his life. Worn down by the demands of office, told that he should wait six months to recover his strength before undergoing the operation, he refused. He hoped to be able to return to duty quickly (although, disgusted by politics, he vowed that upon recovering he would serve wherever he was wanted *except* as a member of the cabinet). But the doctors' warnings proved accurate: he did not survive the surgery, dying on March 27. He was still a comparatively obscure figure at his death, his greatest contributions to the war effort unknown to the public. In 1921, posthumously, he would be made a Marshal of France.

Gallieni was not the only major figure to depart the stage in 1916. The year became a kind of parade of personalities, with high generals, admirals, and government leaders falling from power in all the combatant countries and being succeeded by new faces. Great changes in the French command structure began early in April with the arrival at Verdun of General Robert Nivelle, the dashing figure who in 1914, as a colonel in command of field artillery, had won fame by breaking up one of the last attacks by German forces advancing on Paris. A passionate adherent to the cult of the offensive, Nivelle in the year and a half following the Marne had become a favorite of Joffre's, rising almost as rapidly as Pétain. Upon reporting at Verdun, he became commander of a corps on the east bank of the Meuse. That part of the battleground was, at the time, almost inactive. The Germans were focused on the west bank, pouring steel and flesh into their increasingly desperate, increasingly bloody efforts to drive the French from Le Mort Homme. "One must have lived through these hours in order to get an idea of it," a French chaplain said of life in one of the fortresses blocking approaches to the hill. "It seems as though we are living under a steam hammer . . . You receive something like a blow in the hollow of the stomach. But what a blow! . . . Each explosion knocks us to the ground. After a few hours one becomes somewhat dumbfounded." He wrote of badly wounded men left unattended for eight days, "lying down, dying of hunger, suffering thirst to the extent that they were compelled to drink their urine."

Pétain's artillery too was taking a fearsome toll, but literally foot by foot the attackers were clawing their way forward in what was by now a war of attrition of the rawest and most savage kind. Though the French defenses were once again firm—the Pétain system of rotating troops into and out of the battle was making the nightmare less intolerable for the French than for the Germans—the pressure on them remained intense.

And the losses were mounting: eighty-nine thousand French and eighty-one thousand Germans dead or wounded by the end of March. Nivelle, however, was intent on attacking. He began to do so repeatedly in spite of Pétain's disapproval, blithely and with unshakable confidence shrugging off one costly failure after another. He had the enthusiastic support of a man who had come with him to Verdun: General Charles Mangin, now commander of the crack Fifth Division, known to his own men as "the Butcher" for his indifference to casualties. The aggressiveness of this pair won them Joffre's admiration. Pétain, by contrast, was sinking into disfavor. Joffre was impatient with his stubborn unwillingness to go on the offensive and stay there, his repeated efforts to keep Nivelle and Mangin in check. Pétain regarded himself as fortunate to be able to stand his ground in the face of the onslaught on the west bank, and he was content to hold back and make the Germans pay the price of their persistence. But Joffre was always quick to remove officers who failed to do as he wished.

On April 8, blind or indifferent to the fact that only one day before the east bank had erupted in a German assault that pushed back the French front line, Joffre sent a telegram urging Pétain to launch "a vigorous and powerful offensive to be executed with only the briefest delay." This was nonsense under the circumstances, and it was rendered moot by what followed the next day: an enormous, convulsive renewal of the German offensive on both banks simultaneously. The intensity of this new attack rivaled that of February 21; before sending their infantry into action, the Germans fired off seven trainloads of artillery shells. Only the guns that Pétain had concentrated on the west bank prevented a breakthrough. Then it began to rain, and the rain continued for twelve days, bogging everyone down and saving the French from being overrun.

For the Germans this newest failure was crushing. It led Crown Prince Wilhelm to conclude that the entire campaign was a failure, that continuing could no longer possibly produce results commensurate with the costs. (After the war, in his memoirs, he would write that "Verdun was the mill on the Meuse that ground to powder the hearts as well as the bodies of our soldiers.") It would deepen the divisions within the German general staff and lead to a change of command. In the near term, however, only Pétain's fate was sealed. Joffre could see nothing except that Pétain was still on the defensive, still not attacking. But Pétain was now a national hero in his own right, known to the public as the savior of Verdun and therefore safe from being sacked. Joffre's solution was to kick Pétain upstairs. He dismissed Langle de Cary, hero to no one and savior of nothing, as commander of Army Group Center, which included Pétain's Second Army. Pétain became Langle de Cary's successor. The French Second Army, and with it responsibility for conducting the Battle of Verdun, were given to Nivelle, who soon discontinued Pétain's system for allowing no division to remain under fire for more than a week at a time. This system had contributed immeasurably to French morale. But its end pleased Joffre, who had always regarded it as an unnecessary complication as he tried to prepare for an offensive on the Somme.

German and French gunners continued to blast away at each other on the west bank, and slowly the Germans inched forward. By April 21 there was hand-to-hand fighting for control of the Mort Homme crest.

It can only be mentioned here that intense but fruitless fighting was in process all around Ypres:

That on Monday, April 23, the city of Dublin exploded in an Easter Rebellion that British troops needed a week to suppress;

That the Russians and Turks were continuing their war in the Caucasus and around the Black Sea;

And that in Berlin the German government was once again engaged in a bitter struggle over whether to restrict the operations of its growing fleet of U-boats.

In the far South Atlantic the explorer Sir Ernest Shackleton arrived at a whaling station on South Georgia Island at the end of a horrendous year and a half stranded with his men amid the ice floes fringing the Antarctic continent. It had been 1914, the fighting in its earliest stages, when Shackleton lost contact with the outside world.

"Tell me," he asked the first man he encountered. "When was the war over?"

"The war is not over," he was told. "Millions are being killed. Europe is mad. The world is mad."

The Eastern Front had fallen quiet in the aftermath of Lake Naroch, but there too important changes were taking place. On the day Nivelle arrived at Verdun, Tsar Nicholas peremptorily discharged Alexei Polivanov as minister of war, thereby removing a man who, in the months since his appointment, had been achieving near-miracles. Polivanov had been fearless in flushing corruption and incompetence out of the administration of the Russian war effort and in repairing the damage done to the tsar's armies in 1915. He was dismissed not because of the defeat at Lake Naroch, in which he had no role, but because Tsarina Alexandra hated him and had long wanted him put out of the way. As a reformer, Polivanov was despised by the court's inner circle; he was willing to work cooperatively with the national legislature that the tsar had been forced to create in the bloody turbulence following the Russo-Japanese War; and he had tried to dissuade Nicholas from assuming command of the army in 1915. All these things, in Alexandra's small and rigid mind, made him an enemy of the autocracy that she was pathologically committed to preserving for her son. His final offense, the one that finished him, was to intervene when he learned that four of the war ministry's fastest automobiles had been handed over to Rasputin to enable him to escape police agents. Polivanov departed in official disgrace and without a word of thanks. With Nicholas II away at army headquarters, the government was essentially under the control of the tsarina. And she was essentially under the control of the mysterious Rasputin. "I shall sleep in peace," she told her husband upon learning that Polivanov was gone.

There followed the appointment, as commander on Russia's southwestern front, of a still-obscure general named Alexei Brusilov. It happened—perhaps for no better reason than that even a blind hog finds an acorn once in a while—that this appointment put into a crucial position at a crucial time the most talented Russian field commander of the Great War. A member of a military family of noble origins (his own father had been a general), Brusilov had performed brilliantly at the start of the war, leading the forces that drove the Austro-Hungarians out of Galicia and back into the passes of the Carpathians. Later his army absorbed the German Carpathian offensive of May 1915, preventing a calamity bigger than Tannenberg. Brusilov had directed a two-hundred-mile fighting retreat, striking out at the advancing Germans night after night, disrupting their movements, and saving the Russian forces from being encircled. His appointment gave him the opportunity to transform the war in the east, and he would not be slow to seize it.

Just days after Brusilov took up his new command, with Joffre demanding that the Russians do something more helpful than the

General Alexei Brusilov
*Turned the war around
on the Eastern Front.*

Lake Naroch debacle, the tsar's staff and front commanders met to decide what to do next. New as he was to such august assemblies, Brusilov showed himself to be the only general willing to commit to a new offensive. Thus he dominated the proceedings, proposing a joint attack by his four armies and the larger forces commanded by Evert and Kuropatkin to his north. In this way, he said, the Germans could be pinned down at every point on the front. They would be unable to shift their forces to wherever the danger was greatest. Evert and Kuropatkin, careful men under the best of circumstances and stunned by the failure at Lake Naroch, were unwilling to agree. They were overruled by the tsar's chief of staff, General Alexeyev, an able strategist who had been Brusilov's superior in 1914 and had personal experience of his capacities. Alexeyev decreed that all the front commanders should prepare for a joint offensive to take place in July. Brusilov was warned (perhaps because his group was the only one that did not greatly outnumber the enemies facing it) that he must expect no reinforcements. He returned to his headquarters and got to work. Evert and Kuropatkin did essentially nothing.

On April 28, after waiting more than a month for the ground to firm up, Hindenburg and Ludendorff launched a counterattack at Lake Naroch. It was as spectacular a success as the original Russian attack had been a failure, recapturing in a day everything that the Russians had managed to take in a week in March. The ease with which the Germans swept back over their lost ground was in part the result of an innovation introduced by the commander of their artillery, a lieutenant colonel of retirement age named Georg Bruchmüller. This was the *Feuerwalz,* or dance of fire. (The British would give it the more prosaic name "creeping barrage" when they adopted it later in the year.) It replaced days of shelling with a shorter, shockingly intense bombardment that, when the infantry advanced, moved ahead of it into enemy territory like a protective wall. Its effectiveness lay in the way it gave defenders no time to adapt, and attackers the sense that they were being literally shielded from the enemy as they advanced. It was, implicitly, a rejection of the artillery tactics being used by both sides on the Western Front. Ultimately it would prove to be one of the war's most important tactical innovations. Ludendorff's strategist Max Hoffmann recognized its brilliance in bestowing on its inventor the nickname Durchbruchmüller—Breakthroughmüller.

In the two fights at Lake Naroch the Russians had suffered at least one hundred thousand battlefield casualties, a total that excludes the twelve thousand troops who froze to death. German losses totaled twenty thousand. But it was not the direct results of the battle (neither side gained any ground) that made it important. Lake Naroch changed the course of the war in the east by persuading Evert and Kuropatkin that further offensives could not succeed regardless of how many men, guns, and shells the Russians used.

AIRSHIPS AND LANDSHIPS

THE GREAT WAR DID NOT GIVE BIRTH TO AVIATION; the Wright brothers made their first flight at Kitty Hawk eleven years before the war began. It did not even give birth to *combat* aviation; the Italians had used nine primitive airplanes in snatching Libya away from the Ottoman Empire in 1911 and 1912.

But the war transformed aviation with dazzling speed. In a matter of months it changed the airplane from a novelty of uncertain value—"a useless and expensive fad," Britain's top general said as late as 1911—to an essential element in the arsenal of every nation.

The Great War *did* give birth to the tank, which would not have been invented nearly as early as it was if not for the stalemate on the Western Front.

Both phenomena, air *forces* as opposed to mere airplanes and tanks as an antidote to trenches and machine guns and barbed wire, made their first appearance in 1916.

It is sometimes claimed, falsely, that Europe's military leaders remained almost entirely blind to the potential of the airplane during the decade before the war. Skepticism was indeed widespread, and sometimes it was absurd: Ferdinand Foch, when he was commandant of the French War College, had declared the new flying machines "good for sport but not for war." But in 1909, when Louis Blériot crossed the English Channel in a plane he had designed and built himself, more than a few British leaders understood that their island nation was suddenly no longer as safe as it always had been. When the French began using aircraft effectively in their annual military exercises, the Germans understood that their fledgling aviation industry and its inferior products had better catch up—and fast.

France (not America, despite the Wright brothers) was the leader in heavier-than-air flight throughout the prewar years. Though both France and Germany began the war with more than two hundred airplanes in military service, those of the French were distinctly superior. The British lagged behind with fewer than a hundred aircraft, only forty-four of which were sent to the continent with the BEF. The Russians, though they had acquired substantial numbers, were entirely dependent on foreign sources for their planes. Few and simple as they were, however, airplanes quickly proved their value. Weeks after French fliers confirmed the shift of the German First Army away from Paris, setting the stage for the Battle of the Marne, the British began using their aircraft as artillery spotters. When the Western Front became static and cavalry were rendered useless, aircraft became essential in reconnaissance. Aerial photography reached a high level of sophistication as early as 1915.

Air combat followed as the fliers on both sides began trying to knock each other out of the sky. French and German pilots (often enlisted men at first—mere chauffeurs) went aloft carrying passengers who fired at each other with rifles and shotguns. Somebody got the idea of mounting a Hotchkiss light machine gun at the front of France's Morane Saulnier monoplane, which with a top speed of a hundred miles per hour was the best of the war's first aircraft. Another innovation soon followed: steel plating on the back side of the propeller blades, to spare pilots the indignity of shooting themselves down. So armed, the French began destroying their adversaries in numbers that mattered. The Germans, who until then had been spending most of their aviation budget on massive lighter-than-air Zeppelin dirigibles, again had to scramble to catch up. There began a game of technological leapfrog that continued through the war, with first one side and then the other gaining temporary advantage. The rudimentary technology of the time made the game a fast one. As the British aviation pioneer T.O.M. Sopwith said, "We literally thought of and designed and flew the airplanes in a space of about six or eight weeks."

A major advance came in the form of a new German plane designed by the Dutch engineer Anthony Fokker. In most respects this Fokker Eindecker, introduced in 1915, was little more than a copy of a captured Morane Saulnier. But in one respect it was revolutionary: Fokker equipped it with an interrupter gear (an idea he got from a Swiss engineer) that permitted its two machine guns to fire through the propeller without hitting the blades. This innovation completed the integration of piloting and killing. It turned airplanes into true weapons—flying gun platforms built for attack. With it the Germans dominated the air by late 1915. They were able to establish a virtually impenetrable umbrella over Verdun, keeping their preparations for the attack there a secret from the French. Even so, the Eindeckers needed half an hour to climb to ten thousand feet and had a top speed of only eighty-seven miles per hour.

The French and British regained the lead with three new and distinctly superior models: the Nieuport and Spad biplanes, and a Sopwith triplane that was a marvel of climbing power and maneuverability. The Entente armies assembled hundreds of these aircraft in preparation for their offensive on the Somme. The Germans, inevitably, responded with even more potent new aircraft that were ready for service by the fall of 1916. The race would go on from there.

The war's great fighter aces have since become romantic legends—the Red Baron and his kind, knights on flying horses—but there was more to air combat than chivalry. Before the war was a month old, the Germans were dropping bombs on Antwerp from their Zeppelins. In 1915 Zeppelin raids over southern England became almost commonplace, killing and wounding hundreds. As airplanes became more capable, they also became specialized: scout planes, fighters, and aircraft equipped for strafing troops on the ground. The vulnerable Zeppelins were replaced with increasingly heavy bombers, making the war terrible in a wider variety of ways. February 1916 brought the first sinking of a ship, a British merchantman, by bombardment from the air. In July a French raid on the city of Karlsruhe inadvertently bombed a circus, killing 154 children.

The tank, unlike the airplane, came out of nowhere. In fact there was no such thing as a tank when the war began; only a few obscure visionaries had even imagined such a weapon, and none might have been built by the war's end if not for Winston Churchill. As early as 1914, impressed by the effectiveness of armed and armored cars in the early weeks of fighting (they would become useless as soon as the war of mobility ended), Churchill was asking the naval designers at the Admiralty to see if they could turn such vehicles into some kind of "trench-spanning" machine. Such a machine proved impracticable, there being no way to drive wheeled vehicles across trenches, but by January 1915 Churchill had found a different approach. Convinced that human flesh and bone were never going to be a match for artillery and machine guns, and encouraged by military engineers, Churchill sent a memorandum to Prime Minister Asquith proposing the development of "steam tractors with small armored shelters, in which men and machine guns could be placed, which would be bullet-proof" and would "enable trenches to be crossed quite easily." Asquith passed the suggestion along to Kitchener, who was not enthusiastic but ordered that design work should begin. After another month, dissatisfied with the pace at which the war ministry was proceeding, Churchill assembled his own design team and funded it out of the Royal Navy's budget. By the time he was replaced as First Lord of the Admiralty, contracts had been let for the construction of eighteen prototype "landships."

The project slowed down drastically after Churchill was dismissed, and it probably would have died if he had not intervened to persuade his successor of its potential. In January 1916 a first working prototype—it would be nicknamed "Mother"—was ready for testing. It was a mother indeed, thirty-three feet long and eight feet wide and high. It carried a crew of eight with two machine guns and two cannon firing six-pound shells. It weighed twenty-eight tons and under optimum conditions could achieve a top speed of four miles per hour. It moved not on wheels but on caterpillar-type steel tracks capable of crossing trenches and crushing any barbed-wire barricades in its path.

As the first of the new vehicles came off the production line, the project was shrouded in deepest secrecy. Anticipating the questions that would be provoked by huge, strangely shaped objects concealed under tarpaulins, officials at the war office decided to say that they were special water carriers—mobile *tanks*—bound for Russia. That was the name that stuck. Among the names rejected were *landship* (too descriptive), *reservoir,* and *cistern.*

In the summer of 1916, when Churchill learned that Britain's (and the world's) first forty-nine tanks were being sent to France for use on the Somme, he was horrified. He thought it essential that the new weapon be kept out of action and unknown to the Germans until sufficient numbers could be assembled to produce a decisive breakthrough. He appealed first to Lloyd George and then to the prime minister. Asquith agreed that delay seemed advisable, but when he suggested it to Haig, he was politely ignored.

Chapter 4

Maelstrom

*"These were the happiest days of my life,
and my joy was shared by all of Russia."*
—General Alexei Brusilov

B y the end of April casualties at Verdun totaled one hundred and thirty-three thousand for the French, one hundred and twenty thousand for the Germans. And the slaughter continued. The Germans were still doing most of the attacking, forcing their way onto the slopes of Le Mort Homme, taking part of the crest at one point but unable to hold on. General Max von Gallwitz, a skillful artillery commander and a veteran of the conquest of Serbia, arrived to take command on the west bank. Upon getting a look at the situation he declared that Le Mort Homme must indeed be taken, but that it never would be until the guns protecting it were cleared from an adjacent ridge called Côte 304. To that purpose he assembled more than five hundred heavy guns along a single mile of front, an even greater concentration of firepower than the Germans had mustered for their earlier attacks, and on May 3 he opened fire. The idea was the usual one—to blow the French away, so that the infantry could then move forward almost unopposed. As usual it didn't quite work.

Gallwitz's barrage continued through all the first day and all of the night that followed and another entire day beyond that. But though it reduced thousands of the defenders to body parts and buried many others alive, and though neither food nor water could be got through to the French troops cowering in the depths

of their ruined bunkers and trenches, those troops were not annihilated and the ones who survived did not run. (The mystery
of how men could hold their ground under such circumstances
is explained in part by what awaited them in the rear: their own
sergeants and junior officers, ready to shoot them on the spot if
they tried to escape.)

The Germans captured Côte 304 in the end, taking possession
of ten thousand rotting French corpses with it (the victors got
double rations of tobacco as an escape from the smell), but they
had needed three terrible days of fighting at close quarters to do
so. They had broken off another important piece of the Verdun
defensive system, taking another step toward gaining control of
the west bank, but they had paid dearly for their success. What
was worse, Le Mort Homme still stood unconquered in front of
them, its guns still in action. But again the attackers were ordered
to push on.

The Germans' nightmare deepened on May 8, before anyone
had an opportunity to celebrate the conquest of Côte 304, when
Fort Douaumont suddenly blew up. No one lived to explain what
had happened, but there had been complaints that ammunition
was not being handled properly as it was moved into and out of
the fort. The prevailing theory, based on evidence collected after
the disaster, is that it began when a group of Bavarian soldiers
sheltering inside Douaumont opened a hand grenade to get a few
thimblefuls of explosive for use in heating coffee. The resulting
fire is believed to have ignited a cache of grenades, which in turn
set off some flamethrower fuel tanks, which in turn started a chain
reaction among stacked artillery shells. Whatever the cause, some
six hundred and fifty German soldiers were killed. The few survivors, emerging from the depths of the fort with faces blackened by
the blast, were immediately shot by German troops who had no
idea what had happened inside and assumed that the fort had been
overrun by French colonial units from Africa.

Spirits were not high, understandably, when the staff of the
German Fifth Army met at the crown prince's headquarters on
May 13 to discuss an east bank offensive that had been repeatedly delayed because of weather, the disruptive though otherwise unsuccessful attacks being launched repeatedly by Nivelle
and Mangin, and ongoing artillery fire from Le Mort Homme.

The crown prince, having given up on Verdun, was urging both Falkenhayn and the kaiser to call off not only the new offensive but the entire campaign. In doing so he was putting himself at odds with Knobelsdorf, who before the war had been his tutor in tactics, since August 1914 had been his chief of staff and mentor, and remained convinced that Verdun could be taken. He and Falkenhayn were encouraged by the false belief (mirrored by equally wrong French estimates of German casualties) that their enemies had by now lost well over two hundred thousand men.

A surprising unanimity emerged. Even Knobelsdorf conceded that enough was enough. He promised, in fact, to visit Falkenhayn that same day and try to persuade him to bring Verdun to an end. What happened next has never been explained. When he reached Falkenhayn's headquarters, Knobelsdorf did the opposite of what he had promised. He told Falkenhayn that the French guns at Le Mort Homme would soon be silenced and that the east bank offensive could then be safely resumed. Getting agreement from Falkenhayn, who by now had staked his place in history on Verdun, is not likely to have been difficult. No doubt Falkenhayn was mindful of the fact that the leading pessimists—the crown prince, Gallwitz, and others—all had opposed his elevation to commander in chief after the fall of Moltke. The crown prince, when he learned of Knobelsdorf's betrayal, could do nothing. Though heir to the imperial throne, he had been treated with disdain by the kaiser all his life. Even now, after a year and a half as an increasingly competent and serious-minded army commander, during which time he had gradually acquired the confidence to stand up to the iron-willed Knobelsdorf, he was kept at a distance from his father.

And so the carnage would continue. It would be accelerated, in fact, as Knobelsdorf hurried with Falkenhayn's encouragement to complete the capture of Verdun before Joffre and the British were ready with the offensive that they were obviously preparing along the Somme. The crown prince could only complain that "if Main Headquarters order it, I must not disobey, but I will not do it on my own responsibility."

The hopes of the optimists were about to be upended by the man who supposedly was their one great military ally, the Austrian Conrad. In the course of his career Conrad had been obliged to watch the new Kingdom of Italy encroach on the Austro-Hungarian territories to its north, and he had developed a nearly pathological hatred and contempt for the Italians. ("Dago dogs," he called them.) Since late 1915 he had been badgering Falkenhayn for help in mounting an offensive southward out of the Alps, a campaign that would destroy Italy's ability to wage war and restore Vienna to possession of the north Italian plain. Falkenhayn, his armies outnumbered on every front and his attention focused on Verdun, had brushed these appeals aside. He pointed out that while conquests in Italy might bring pleasure to Vienna, they could contribute little to the winning of the war. He had done so with unnecessary brusqueness. An outwardly cold figure, Falkenhayn had no close friends even among his fellow Junkers, and he disliked and distrusted Conrad. He demolished whatever possibility remained of a constructive working relationship with Conrad by keeping him in the dark. The Verdun offensive had come as more of a surprise to the Austrians than to the French. And though Falkenhayn's secretiveness had not been directed exclusively at Conrad (for valid reasons he had drawn such a curtain of security over his preparations that not even the commanders of the German armies west and south of Verdun knew exactly what was coming), the Austrian was deeply offended. He decided not only to proceed with an Italian campaign but to tell the Germans nothing of what he was doing.

His plan was to attack not at the Isonzo, already the scene of four battles and still the place where the Italians were concentrating most of their forces, but farther west, in the mountainous Trentino region northeast of Lake Garda. He began by sending more than a dozen of his best remaining divisions to an assembly point just north of the passes leading into Italy. From there they would be able to descend upon the farmlands and cities of Lombardy, lands and cities that in Conrad's view rightfully belonged to Vienna. Once in open country, the Austrians could wheel around and take the Italians on the Isonzo in the rear. Not for the first time and not for the last, Conrad smelled triumph. Six of the divisions committed to the Trentino were taken from Galicia, where he saw no possibility of trouble. The Russians had been thoroughly thrashed in Galicia in late 1915 (though mainly by German troops that Falkenhayn had since sent to Verdun), and their numerical advantage was smaller there than at any other point on the Eastern Front. If Conrad was even aware of the appointment of Alexei Brusilov as commander of Russia's southwestern front, he could not have regarded it as significant. He secured pro forma approval of his plan from the Hapsburg archduke who was his official commander in chief and assumed personal command of operations in Italy.

Conrad consistently asked his troops to do things that were beyond their capacity. If he was the strategic genius that some historians have called him, he was also less than a realist. He would venture forth not just to meet and fight his enemies but to crush them, to destroy them even when he was terribly outnumbered. And there was a pattern to his campaigns. They would begin thrillingly, with spectacular gains, and they never failed to end in disaster except when the Germans came to his rescue. Their cumulative result, by early 1916, was the loss of so many troops (more than two million casualties in 1915 alone, including seven hundred and seventy thousand men taken prisoner) that the Austro-Hungarian military was at the end of its ability to mount independent operations. Perhaps this accounts for Conrad's eagerness to invade Italy. Perhaps even he had lost confidence in his ability to accomplish anything on the more challenging Russian front.

In taking charge of the Trentino campaign, Conrad did not move his headquarters to or even near the places where the invasion force was being assembled. He did not even pay them a visit. He remained in Silesia, six hundred miles to the north, where he had happily settled with a new wife and all the comforts of prewar aristocratic life. He perfected his isolation by keeping all communications on a one-way basis, and by sending out detailed instructions as to exactly what the Austrian divisions in the Trentino were to do, and when and where, while ignoring questions and suggestions. He drew marks on maps showing which objectives each division was supposed to reach each day, and as far as he was concerned that was that. If following his instructions required the troops to climb through deep snow over a mountain crest when they could have reached the same objective by moving downhill through a valley, that too was that. No discussion was wanted or tolerated. When the chief of staff of the army group being formed in the Trentino requested permission to travel to Silesia and confer with Conrad, he was refused.

Conrad had wanted his offensive to begin almost immediately, in April, but on this point he had to bend to reality. Neither his troops nor their supply trains could get into position that quickly at that time of year, though hundreds froze to death or were buried in avalanches in the attempt. When the Austrians finally attacked on May 15, they were one hundred and fifty-seven thousand strong. The one hundred and seventeen thousand Italians standing in their path were rather easily pushed back. True to the Conrad pattern, the Austrians made progress for three weeks, sweeping southward on a broad front. By the end of May they had captured four thousand prisoners and 380 guns. The tsar, accustomed by now to urgent appeals from Joffre, found himself being begged for assistance by the King of Italy as well.

There were good reasons for Nicholas to pay heed, and they went beyond Verdun and the Austrian invasion of Italy. Everything seemed to be working in favor of the Central Powers. North of Paris, a German attack intended mainly to disrupt French and British preparations for their summer offensive had shocked Joffre by driving the British out of positions from which they had been preparing to take Vimy Ridge, an immense strongpoint dominating the plain of Artois to the west. The French had sacrificed mightily in establishing those positions, and had regarded them as secure when, in March, they handed them over to the British. Haig, though humiliated by the loss, was unable to organize a counterattack because so many of his resources were now being concentrated at the Somme.

At Verdun on May 22, "Butcher" Mangin, dreaming his dreams of glory and confident of success, opened an attack aimed at retaking Fort Douaumont. The bitterness of the struggle was becoming unnatural, almost psychotic. "Even the wounded refuse to abandon the struggle," a French staff officer would recall. "As though possessed by devils, they fight on until they fall senseless from loss of blood. A surgeon in a front-line post told me that, in a redoubt at the south part of the fort, of 200 French dead, fully half had more than two wounds. Those he was able to treat seemed utterly insane. They kept shouting war cries and their eyes blazed, and, strangest of all, they appeared indifferent to pain.

At one moment anesthetics ran out owing to the impossibility of bringing forward fresh supplies through the bombardment. Arms, even legs, were amputated without a groan, and even afterward the men seemed not to have felt the shock. They asked for a cigarette or inquired how the battle was going."

In the five days preceding the start of his attack, Mangin's three hundred heavy guns had fired a thousand tons of explosives onto the quarter of a square mile centered on the fort, and the assault that followed broke into the fort's inner chambers. The Germans regrouped, however, and after days of hellish close-quarters underground combat drove the attackers out. The failure had been so complete and the costs so high—more than fifty-five hundred troops and 130 officers killed or wounded out of twelve thousand French attackers, another thousand taken prisoner—that Mangin was relieved of command. "You did your duty and I cannot blame you," Pétain told him resignedly. "You would not be the man you are if you had not acted in the way you did." Meanwhile, in almost equally intense fighting nearby, the Germans were forcing their way closer to Le Mort Homme.

By this time General Mikhail Alexeyev, still in place as the tsar's chief of staff in spite of having been the fallen Polivanov's partner in reform (he had survived, probably, by virtue of being at army headquarters and therefore remote from the intrigues of Petrograd), was asking his sector commanders when they could attack. Evert said predictably that he was able to do nothing. Brusilov surprised even Alexeyev by answering that his preparations were essentially complete, his four armies ready to go. It was decided that Brusilov would attack at the beginning of June. Evert, directly to his north, was coaxed into agreeing that he would send his immensely larger forces into action on June 13. He was reluctant in spite of having a million men under his command and two-thirds of Russia's heavy artillery.

On May 26 Joffre met with Haig, at the insistence of Pétain, and asked him to move up the date of the Somme offensive from mid-August. Haig disliked the idea, but when Joffre told him that if he waited another two and a half months "the French army could cease to exist," he yielded.

On May 31, for the first and last time in the war, the dreadnoughts of the British Grand Fleet and Germany's High Seas

Fleet met in battle. The German commander, having concocted a plan to lure Britain's battle cruiser force southward away from the protection of dreadnoughts, had steamed into the North Sea the previous day with a mighty array of ships: sixteen dreadnoughts, six older battleships, five battle cruisers, eleven light cruisers, and sixty-one destroyers. Unknown to him, the British, having intercepted and decoded his radio messages, were coming at him with a hundred and fifty ships that outnumbered him in every category.

They met near Jutland, a peninsula on the Danish coast, and what followed was the greatest sea battle in history until the Second World War. It was a complex and confused affair, unfolding in five distinct stages as the fleets separated and converged and changed directions again and again, and it was marked by serious mistakes and much ingenuity on both sides. The Germans lost one battleship, one battle cruiser, four light cruisers, five destroyers, and twenty-five hundred men before withdrawing to home ports from which they would never again venture.

The British losses were heavier: three battle cruisers, three cruisers, and eight destroyers, sixty-two hundred men. Technically the battle was a draw, and strategically it changed nothing. The British had been outgunned and outmaneuvered. Though the public was told of a glorious victory, and British fleet commander John Jellicoe was celebrated as a hero, the Admiralty knew better.

At about the same time the Germans took possession of Le Mort Homme at last, eliminating the artillery threat from that quarter. Now they were free to shift over to the defensive on the west bank and start the climactic east bank offensive that was going, according to Knobelsdorf, to carry them into Verdun. By June 1, with the main force for the new offensive still being put in place, German units making an exploratory attack fought their way up to the final approaches to Fort Vaux. This fortress, smaller than Douaumont but formidable nevertheless, was now the last major strongpoint standing between the Germans and the city. Everything needed for the capture of Verdun appeared to be falling into place.

One blow after another was falling on the Entente. The Austrians were out of the Alps and on open ground. They appeared to be positioned to encircle the Italians retreating before them.

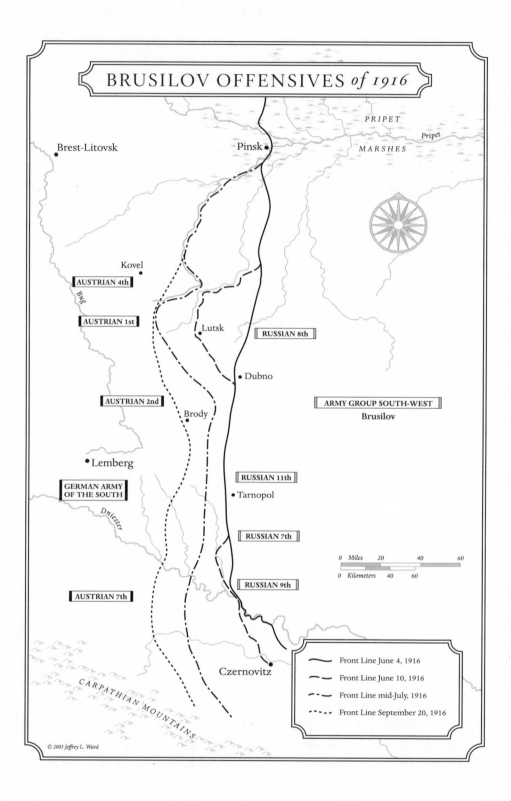

BRUSILOV OFFENSIVES *of 1916*

PRIPET

Pinsk

Pripet

MARSHES

Brest-Litovsk

Kovel

AUSTRIAN 4th

Bug

AUSTRIAN 1st

Lutsk

RUSSIAN 8th

Dubno

AUSTRIAN 2nd

ARMY GROUP SOUTH-WEST
Brusilov

Brody

Lemberg

RUSSIAN 11th

GERMAN ARMY
OF THE SOUTH

Tarnopol

Dniester

RUSSIAN 7th

0	Miles	20		40		60
0	Kilometers		40	60		

AUSTRIAN 7th

RUSSIAN 9th

Czernovitz

——— Front Line June 4, 1916

— — — Front Line June 10, 1916

—·—·— Front Line mid-July, 1916

········· Front Line September 20, 1916

CARPATHIAN MOUNTAINS

© 2005 Jeffrey L. Ward

In Flanders the Germans captured a piece of high ground called Mont Sorel two and a half miles south of the heaps of broken stone that once had been the beautiful city of Ypres.

But then it was June 4, and Brusilov ordered his guns to open fire. Brusilov's preparations had been imaginative and aggressive, with everything focused on taking the Austrians by surprise across such a broad front that they would find it impossible to react effectively. His use of air and ground reconnaissance to identify enemy weak points was without precedent in Russian military operations, and his efforts to deceive the Austrians had gone so far as to include the painting of phantom trenches on the ground behind his lines. His barrage lasted only one day, its purpose not to obliterate the Austrians' defenses but to neutralize their artillery and clear away their barbed wire. It did both things. His infantry, when it attacked on June 5, found the Austrians in confusion. Its advance stunned them with its scope, extending as it did along a line of more than two hundred and fifty miles. Brusilov's idea was that by attacking everywhere, he was sure to find holes somewhere, and he had moved his reserves (scant though they were) close enough to the front that they could exploit opportunities as soon as any appeared. On point after point—the brevity of his bombardment, his refusal even in the face of appeals from Alexeyev to mass his troops on a narrow piece of the front, his willingness to attack forces equal to his own in numbers—he ignored what had become by now the tactical orthodoxy of the Great War. And the result was, from the first hour, a success of almost incredible magnitude. The Austro-Hungarian Fourth Army disintegrated when hit; seventy-one thousand of its men, more than half of the army were killed, wounded, or captured. The Seventh was wrecked even more completely, losing one hundred and thirty-three thousand men. It was the same almost everywhere; after three days Brusilov found himself in possession of three hundred thousand prisoners. Before the end of the first week, more than half of the Austrian defenders had become casualties.

The remnants (most of them Slavs, the more trusted Austrian units having been sent off to Italy) fled back toward the Carpathians. They were incapable of restoring their lines both because they had no reserves—what could have been their reserve

force was south of the Alps—and because their senior commanders were absent. They were at a Hapsburg castle in the faraway
town of Teschen, partying with Conrad.

June 4 was, by what turned out to be a singular stroke of bad
luck for the Austrians, the birthday of the nonentity who was
titular commander in chief of all the Austro-Hungarian armies.
This was Archduke Frederick, a nephew of Emperor Franz Joseph and one of the several Hapsburg grandees holding ceremo-
nial posts in the upper reaches of the army. A great celebration
had been arranged in honor of the occasion, and Conrad, confident that the impending conquest of Italy would give the empire
and its dynasty much to celebrate, had attended not only with
senior members of his own staff but also with generals from Galicia. The festivities were still in progress when word arrived that
the Russians had suddenly become active on their southern front.
Conrad serenely assured all present that there was no reason for
concern.

It did not take long for him to learn otherwise. Two days after
the party the Italian commander in chief, General Cadorna, used
troops taken from his fifth (and brief and unsuccessful) Isonzo offensive to counterattack the Austrians who had descended out of
the Trentino. He was successful this time and Conrad's Italian
campaign came to its end. In Galicia, Brusilov had shattered the
Austro-Hungarian forces on his flanks and was positioned to encircle the center. Only one thing was stopping him: he lacked the
necessary manpower. Many times the number of troops needed
to do the job were with Evert in the northwest, but Evert remained unwilling either to attack or to let go of any of his divisions. June 13, the day on which Evert had pledged himself to an
attack, came and went without action. This was a mortal failure.
Max Hoffmann wrote afterward that if Evert had attacked, "the
crisis would probably have developed into the complete defeat
of the Austro-Hungarian Army." Instead, the Germans opposite
Evert's army group remained unengaged and free to shift southward against Brusilov.

Even without Evert's assistance, a conclusive defeat of Austria-
Hungary seemed inevitable. Conrad, thoroughly alarmed, hurried by train not to the front but to Berlin, where he reported
the end of his Italian adventure and begged Falkenhayn for help.

General Luigi Cadorna (right)
Launched attack after attack at River Isonzo.

Falkenhayn responded even more coldly than usual, promising nothing. But the German Army of the South was still in Galicia, and now it hit the Russian Eighth Army at exactly the point where the Brusilov offensive was achieving its deepest penetration. Brusilov, his troops exhausted and the Russian supply system failing him in its usual fashion, had to halt to regroup.

He had achieved tremendous things. He had destroyed two Austro-Hungarian armies and all but wrecked others, delivering a deeply damaging blow to the shaky morale of Vienna's armies. His hordes of prisoners included thousands of officers, and he had captured hundreds of machine guns and pieces of artillery. The ground taken by his troops was not crucially important when measured against the vastness of the eastern theater, but with his enemies in such disarray he faced rich opportunities for further conquest. He had redeemed every pledge that Russia had ever made to its allies. If he had not stopped the Austro-Hungarian descent upon Italy—Cadorna had seen to that—he had made certain that the Austrians could not reinforce the Trentino campaign.

No less important was the sense of confidence that he had restored to the armies of the tsar. "This town today is a veritable maelstrom of war," a British correspondent wrote of the entry of Brusilov's troops into newly conquered Lutsk. "From not many miles away, by night and day, comes an almost uninterrupted roar of heavy gunfire, and all day long the main street is filled with the rumble and clatter of caissons, guns, and transports going forward on one side, while on the other side is an unending line of empty caissons returning, mingled with wounded coming back in every conceivable form of vehicle, and in among these at breakneck speed dart motorcycles carrying dispatches from the front. The weather is dry and hot, and the lines of the road are visible for miles by the clouds of dust from the plodding feet of the soldiery and the transport. As the retreat from Warsaw was a review of the Russian armies in reverse, so is Lutsk today a similar spectacle of the Muscovite armies advancing; but now all filled with high hopes and their morale is at the highest pitch."

Perhaps most important of all, Brusilov had suddenly and terribly complicated Falkenhayn's manpower problems at a point when the Germans seemed once again on the brink of forcing their way into Verdun. Knowing that an Entente offensive on the Somme was drawing near, Falkenhayn had been planning a preemptive attack. Now, thanks to Brusilov, that plan had to be abandoned. As scornful as he was of Conrad, as reluctant as he was to use scarce resources to pull Conrad's chestnuts out of a fire that Conrad himself had made possible, Falkenhayn had no choice but to start transferring troops—eighteen divisions, ultimately—away from the Western Front.

But Brusilov too was in a difficult position. He had paid a great price for his victory: three hundred thousand men lost, huge stores of ammunition expended, and other supplies depleted to the point of exhaustion. And Brusilov, more than any of his enemies, more even than the Austro-Hungarians, lacked any hope of making good his losses. With the war ministry in the hands of

an inoffensive but superannuated general whose only qualifica-
tion was his unquestioning loyalty to the Romanov family, the
Russian military administration was barely functioning except for
the benefit of profiteers. In a real sense Russia's collapse and the
revolution that followed stemmed directly from Petrograd's inability to resupply Brusilov and from Evert's failure to give him
support. Balancing the Russian calamity was Ludendorff's refusal
to send troops from his base in the north to help either Falkenhayn at Verdun or Conrad in Galicia. It can be said in Ludendorff's defense that he continued to be faced with Russian armies
that outnumbered his and had to be expected to attack.

As events on four fronts—Verdun, the Somme, Galicia, and
Italy—began to interlock, the strain was intense everywhere. The
Italian government fell as controversy erupted over Cadorna's
handling of the Trentino offensive. For the first time in the war
the French National Assembly was forced to meet in secret session, the opposition demanding answers about Joffre's strategy.

The whole month of June was a time of terrible and sometimes
weird events. The British were shocked to learn that a cruiser
bound for Russia had struck a mine near the coast of Scotland,
and that among those lost was Earl Kitchener of Khartoum. The
ever-amazing Conrad, many of his armies barely functional, proposed to an incredulous Falkenhayn a giant offensive aimed at surrounding and destroying Brusilov's army group. He was not just ignored but laughed at; even his Austrian colleagues were learning to
despise him. And as if there were not enough active fronts already,
an Arab revolt was breaking out with British support in the desert wastes at the southern end of the Ottoman Empire, while at
Salonika French General Sarrail was nearly ready to take his force
northward into the Balkans.

Fort Vaux, the all-but-final obstacle on the Germans' long and
bloody road down the east bank of the Meuse to Verdun, surrendered after days of bitter and brutal combat. Its defense had been
so heroic that the French commander, who had given up at last
only because his men were literally dying of thirst, was honored
personally by the crown prince, who gave him a sword to replace
one lost in the fight. The captive Major Raynal returned the favor
by noting that young Wilhelm Hohenzollern was "not the monkey that our caricaturists have made him out to be." The fall of

Fort Vaux left only one final small strongpoint, Fort Souville, between the Germans and the city. It cleared the way for the climactic offensive that Knobelsdorf had been hungering for since April.

The last of Falkenhayn's reserves went into this attack: thirty thousand men on a front of just three miles against an objective that, if taken, would leave them only two and a half miles from the central citadel at Verdun. Knobelsdorf was so confident of success that he invited the kaiser to join him. June 22 was reserved for the artillery barrage, which was as savage as ever and ended with the firing of shells containing a new kind of gas, phosgene, that killed every living thing, even plants and insects. "Our heads are buzzing, we have had enough," a French lieutenant somehow was able to write in his journal while this attack was in process. "Myself, Agnel, and my orderly are squashed in a hole, protecting ourselves from splinters with our packs. Numb and dazed, without saying a word, and with our hearts pounding, we await the shell that will destroy us. The wounded are increasing in numbers around us. These poor devils not knowing where to go come to us, believing that they will be helped. What can we do? There are clouds of smoke, the air is unbreathable. There's death everywhere. At our feet, the wounded groan in a pool of blood; two of them, more seriously hit are breathing their last. One, a machine-gunner, has been blinded, with one eye hanging out of its socket and the other torn out: in addition he has lost a leg. The second has no face, an arm blown off, and a horrible wound in the stomach. Moaning and suffering atrociously one begs me, 'Lieutenant, don't let me die. Lieutenant, I'm suffering, help me.' The other, perhaps more gravely wounded and nearer death, implores me to kill him with these words, 'Lieutenant, if you don't want to, give me your revolver!' Frightful, terrible moments, while the cannons harry us and we are splattered with mud and earth by the shells. For hours, these groans and supplications continue until, at 6 p.m., they die before our eyes without anyone being able to help them."

The infantry attacked at five a.m. on June 23, breaking through the center of the French lines. Pétain, learning of this, decided that in order to save hundreds of artillery pieces from capture he was going to have to abandon the east bank. Trenches were being dug, and barricades erected, in the streets of Verdun.

But the Germans were paying the price of advancing on a narrow front: they were exposed to murderous fire on both flanks while aircraft strafed them from above. The forward edge of the advance got to within twelve hundred yards of the crest of the last ridge before Verdun, but that was as far as it could go. At the end of two days of horror for the men on both sides, the Germans had to give up. This failure too came down to a shortage of troops. Just days before, faced with telegram after telegram detailing the emergency in the southeast, Falkenhayn had decided that he had no choice but to begin pulling divisions out of Verdun and getting them onto trains bound for Galicia. Just one of those divisions, if thrown into the final lunge at Souville, might have swung the balance. That no division was available has to be considered part of Brusilov's achievement.

The French, at the climax, had appeared to have no chance of holding on. Joffre's view of the situation is clear in his decision to dispatch to Verdun four of the divisions he had been saving for the Somme. Everywhere there was panic and an almost frenzied shuttling of troops. Conrad ordered the transfer of eight divisions from Italy to Galicia, and a desperate Aristide Briand, Premier of France, traveled to Haig's headquarters to beg him to begin his offensive on the Somme. He must have been powerfully persuasive: Haig began his bombardment that afternoon. Pétain, when he telephoned Joffre to report that he was removing his artillery from the east bank, was told of the start of action on the Somme and ordered to stand fast. He did so, and with what must have seemed miraculous speed the pressure lifted.

The fight for Verdun—a prize that would have cost the French little if they had lost it and done the Germans little good if they had won it—was at an end. Falkenhayn diverted still more troops and guns to the east.

For the French, at least where Verdun was concerned, the worst was over. But a nightmare of a different kind, the Battle of the Somme, had just begun.

THE JEWS OF GERMANY

THE MIDPOINT OF THE WAR BROUGHT A GREAT turning point in the long history of Jews in Germany. Until 1916 that history had been largely a striving for acceptance, for integration, for official and popular recognition that a Jew could be as good a citizen as any Christian and deserved to be treated accordingly. After 1916 many Jews abandoned such hopes.

What precipitated the change was less the war itself, during which more than a hundred thousand German Jews became soldiers (German cemeteries along the Western Front are studded with markers bearing the Star of David), than the government's attitude toward its Jewish troops. Specifically, it was the Prussian minister of war's October order of a census to determine how many Jews were in every army unit, how many had not yet been called up, and how many had been released from service or found to be unfit.

News of this census came as a shock to the Jewish community. It gave rise everywhere to a painful question: *Why?* Jewish volunteers had rallied to the colors at the start of the war. Jews were putting millions of marks into war bonds, and Jewish industrialists and scientists were making important contributions to Germany's ability to fight. Why were *they* being singled out for investigation? The answer, for many, was that their loyalty counted for nothing, and that it was folly to expect anything else.

To say that Germany at the start of the war was a culture steeped in anti-Semitism is to say nothing that sets it apart from the other countries of Europe. The whole Western world was so anti-Semitic that its prejudice was taken for granted: it was simply assumed, at every level of society, that Jews were not only different but different in ways that made them a problem. Germany was not the worst in this regard. That distinction belongs to Russia, which barred almost all Jews from citizenship, regarded its Jewish population as a threat to security, and continued to single the Jews out for atrocious mistreatment after the start of the war. France was not nearly that bad, Britain was a paragon of tolerance by comparison, but in every country to be a Jew was to be an alien to a greater or lesser extent. In all of them there were outbreaks of violence against Jews during the course of the war.

The German situation had always been particularly complicated and particularly marked with hypocrisy. As early as 1812, at the climax of the Napoleonic wars, the Kingdom of Prussia had issued an Emancipation Edict granting citizenship to Jews. In its way and for its time this edict was modestly progressive, but only within narrow limits. It excluded Jews from serving as military officers—that was the preserve of the Junkers—and from the government bureaucracy, including the judicial system. The rationale was that the Christian citizens of a Christian nation should not have to take orders from Jews.

In 1869, with Germany midway through its wars of unification, another new law guaranteed that all government appointments would be made without regard to religion. Formally, this meant that every career, including the army, was open to every qualified candidate. In reality, it meant almost nothing. Whenever a Jew applied for a position, reasons were found for selecting someone else. It meant even less after the creation of the German Empire, when exclusion became unofficial policy.

The intensity of the problem is explained by the peculiar nature of the Prussian state, and by the Junkers' belief that the state belonged to *them*. Anyone who was not a Junker was an outsider, and in the last decades of the nineteenth century Berlin launched campaigns of persecution against the Catholics who made up a third of the Reich's population, against Social Democrats with their demands for democracy, and against ethnic Poles. And of course, against the Jews. All these groups were systematically excluded. Even to have a Social Democratic relative was enough to close the doors of advancement to an able and ambitious young man.

Jews, meanwhile, were distinguishing themselves in every field that was open to them: the professions, industry, banking, science, journalism, and the arts. With every generation their prosperity improved. In Prussia more than five hundred out of every ten thousand Jewish boys became university students; the corresponding numbers were fifty-eight for Protestants and thirty-three for Catholics. Some Jews became rich, others prominent. But their very success bred trouble. When the economy declined or things went badly for Berlin on the international stage, "the Jews" were commonly blamed.

From 1885 to 1914 not one Jew was given a commission in the Prussian army. (The same was not true in Catholic Bavaria, which maintained a separate army.) Again the problem was the Junker mentality. The expansion of the military establishment during the prewar arms race made it impossible to fill the officer corps with sons of the landed aristocracy—there weren't enough of them. Others had to be admitted. Increasingly if grudgingly, the offspring of the new urban middle class were deemed to be acceptable—assuming that their families were sufficiently respectable and unimpeachably Lutheran. Jews continued to be unacceptable. They applied for commissions, they were often superlatively well qualified in terms of education and other criteria, the law said that religion was not to be taken into account—and without exception, decade after decade, every candidate was turned away.

This exclusion became a major symbolic issue for Germany's Jews, especially for those most determined to win acceptance by the community at large. Abandoning the hope that the regular army might ever accept Jews, they focused on the reserves. And with good reason. Reserve commissions carried extraordinarily high prestige in Prussia. They provided access to the best society and could be essential for advancement in civilian careers. They, more than anything else, represented inclusion.

Jewish leaders complained, petitioned, and tried to use their influence. They found support in liberal non-Jewish groups, and the question was debated repeatedly in the Reichstag. But one war minister after another refused to acknowledge that a problem existed. Whenever a particular case was offered as proof of flagrant discrimination, whoever was war minister at the time would order an investigation (which meant nothing more than asking local military officials to decide if they themselves had broken the law) and report that, regrettably, the candidate in question had proved to be unfit.

August 1914 seemed to change everything. Kaiser Wilhelm, who before the war had called the Jews "the curse of my country," proclaimed the dawn of *Burgfrieden,* a new era in which all Germans were accepted fully and all would join together to save Germany from her foes. There were six hundred thousand Jews in Germany at the time, about 1 percent of the population, and with no important exceptions they embraced the war. Even the small Zionist minority accepted it as a means of liberating the Jews of Poland and giving the

Russians a lesson. This, Jewish leaders said, was the hour they had been waiting for. And there seemed to be reason for hope. Jews were made officers—though they were not to be promoted to any rank higher than captain.

From the start, the conservatives were not happy with *Burgfrieden.* They had always sought national unity through the exclusion of anyone not regarded as a real German, and they warned that the changes brought by the war would lead to the end of Germany as a truly German state. But early in the war the people holding such views were often prevented from publishing or speaking in public—the first suppression of anti-Semitic propaganda in German history. Again the Jews were encouraged, but the new era proved to be a short one. As the war dragged on and life became difficult and the hope of victory faded, the inevitable search for scapegoats began. Capitalism was to blame for Germany's predicament, and the capitalists were Jews. Or socialism was to blame, and the socialists were Jews. Jewish profiteers were draining the nation's lifeblood, Jewish liberals were contaminating the young with democratic ideas, Jews who cared more about Jews than about Germany were trying to turn the Fatherland into a refuge for undesirables from Poland.

Disillusionment set in, affecting Jews at the front no less than those at home. They had gone to war filled with expectations that by sharing in the national sacrifice, they would dissolve the barriers that had so long kept them apart from other Germans. What they found, more often than not, was an unbridgeable cultural gulf between themselves and the Gentile soldiers. What they did not find, usually, was acceptance as *German* troops.

This was the climate in which War Minister Adolf Wild von Hohenborn ordered his census. It was supposed to be secret, but it soon became known everywhere and aroused an angry Jewish reaction. Within the army it was widely misinterpreted; officers who received it sometimes reacted by sending all their Jewish soldiers immediately to the front. Hohenborn's motives, ironically, appear not to have been malign. He was responding to a rising chorus of complaints that the Jews were shirking, using their notorious wiles to avoid doing their share. He could simply have joined the chorus—plenty of other officials, the kaiser included, were doing exactly that. Instead he decided to establish, in coldly objective terms, what the facts were. And the facts turned out to be very different from the complaints: the Jews were doing their share and more. By the time these findings were disclosed, Hohenborn was no longer war minister. His successor, trying to quiet the furor, stated rather obscurely that "the behavior of Jewish soldiers and fellow citizens during the war gave no cause for the order by my predecessor, and thus cannot be connected with it."

But there was no apology, nobody in a position of authority said anything about the Jews who were fighting and dying, and much damage had been done. The Jewish troops continued to do their duty—twelve thousand would be killed—but the dream of 1914 was dead. In its place was fear of what Germany would be like after the war was over.

"A war after the war stands before us," said the newspaper of the Central Association of German Citizens of Jewish Faith, long an optimistic voice for full Jewish integration into German life. "When the weapons are laid to rest, the war's storm will not have ended for us."

Chapter 5

The Somme

"When we started to fire we just had to load
and reload. They went down in their hundreds.
We didn't have to aim, we just fired into them."
—German machine-gunner

I f it had been possible to win the war in the west by sheer force, by overpowering the enemy with manpower and firepower, the Battle of the Somme would have done the job. The British and French attacked a German army that they outnumbered by an enormous margin. They had an equal advantage in artillery and total control of the air. They were backed by all the resources that modern industrial economies could put at the disposal of their soldiers.

First conceived in the closing days of 1915 as one part of a great combination of attacks by Britain and France and Russia and Italy on every one of Europe's many fronts, the battle was long in the making. The whole first half of 1916 was devoted to building up great masses of armaments, to bringing forward the green new armies that Kitchener had recruited in 1914, to literally laying the groundwork (in the form of new roads and railways and lines of communication) for a success so complete that the enemy would be crushed and stalemate would be transformed into sudden, final, total victory.

As originally planned, the offensive was to be a French show primarily, with forty of Joffre's divisions providing most of its weight and the British in a secondary role. But the unexpected upheavals of the first half of 1916—Verdun first, then Lake Na-roch, and finally Conrad's offensive in Italy and Brusilov's in Gali-cia—disrupted everything on all sides. As Verdun went on and on, most of the French army was run through Falkenhayn's kill-ing machine. As unit after unit was chewed up, Joffre gradually (and resentfully) found himself unable to assemble even half the number of troops he had originally wanted for the Somme. Lake Naroch meanwhile paralyzed the will of the men commanding Russia's central and northern fronts; Conrad's Trentino campaign rendered Italy incapable of a summer offensive; and the Brusilov offensive (undertaken, it should be remembered, in response to French appeals for help) had a similar impact on the Russians in the south.

The British alone were untouched. Of all the Entente com-manders, only Haig remained free to proceed almost as if no battles were happening anywhere. And Haig cannot be accused of failing to make use of his great gift of time. He devoted the first half of 1916 to two things: to preparing for a fresh offensive in Flanders, where he hoped to join with the Royal Navy in retak-ing Belgium's Channel ports, and to getting ready (reluctantly at first) for the offensive that Joffre was determined to launch on the Somme. As the so-called "Kitchener's armies" arrived on the continent, they were alternated between routine line duty on quiet sectors of the front and training that included mock assaults on simulated enemy trenches. By June Haig had half a million men on and behind the Somme front. New guns were arriving as well, along with mountains of the shells being bought from America and produced by Lloyd George's ministry of munitions. Along with them came all the bewildering panoply of equipment and supplies required by a modern army readying itself for ac-tion. Seven thousand miles of telephone lines were buried to keep them from being cut by German artillery, and 120 miles of pipe were laid to get water to the assembling troops. Ten squadrons of aircraft—185 planes—were brought in to drive off the sudden-ly outclassed German Fokkers and serve as spotters for the gun crews as they registered on their assigned targets. Tunnelers were digging out cavities under the German lines and packing them with explosives. It was a massive undertaking, all done as efficiently as anyone could have expected, and ultimately Haig was responsible for every bit of it.

The planning of the attack was his responsibility too, and there lay the rub. Haig had eighteen divisions on the Somme by early summer, and two-thirds of them were used to form a new Fourth Army under General Sir Henry Rawlinson, who had been with the BEF from the start of the war. Rawlinson was a career infantryman—the only British army commander on the Somme not, like Haig, from the cavalry—and his ideas about how to conduct the coming offensive differed sharply from those of his chief. Haig wanted a breakthrough. He was confident that his artillery could not merely weaken but annihilate the German front line, that the infantry would be able to push through almost unopposed, and that this would clear the way for tens of thousands of cavalry to reach open country, turn northward, and throw the whole German defensive system into terminal disorder.

Rawlinson, by contrast, had drawn the same lessons as Falkenhayn from a year and a half of stalemate. He thought breakthrough impossible, and that trying to achieve it could only result in painful and unnecessary losses. He opted for a battle of attrition, one intended less to conquer territory (there being no important strategic targets anywhere near the Somme front, actually) than to kill as many Germans as possible. To this end he favored "bite and hold" tactics similar to those with which Falkenhayn had begun at Verdun. Such tactics involved settling for a limited objective with each attack, capturing just enough ground to spark a counterattack, and then using artillery to obliterate the enemy's troops as they advanced. Rawlinson and Haig never resolved their differences; rather, they opened the battle without coming to an understanding on what they were trying to do or how it should be done.

The men of the Fourth Army were as new to war as they were eager for it after eighteen months of training. Haig was untroubled by their lack of experience. In this regard it was he who was like Falkenhayn at the start of Verdun. He had fifteen hundred pieces of artillery, one for every seventeen yards of the eighteen miles of curving front along which the BEF would be attacking. Between them the British and French had 1,655 light, 933 medium, and 393 heavy guns. The corresponding numbers on the German side were

454, 372, and 18. Haig's confidence that his batteries could para-
lyze the German defenses before his infantry climbed out of its
trenches was communicated down the chain of command. "You
will be able to go over the top with a walking stick, you will not
need rifles," one officer told his troops. "When you get to Thiepval
[a village that was one of the first day's objectives] you will find the
Germans all dead. Not even a rat will have survived."

Every part of the attack was planned to the minute. Every unit
was told what points it would reach in the first hour and exactly
where it would be at the end of the day. And though in the end
Haig did not have quite as many weeks to prepare as he wanted—
the emergency at Verdun made that impossible—the tightening
of the schedule still left him with time to do everything needed.
It had no effect on the conduct of the campaign, or on his serene
confidence that the machine gun, "a much-overrated weapon,"
could be overcome by men on horseback. He was ready enough
by June 24, when French Premier Briand came to implore him for
help, to begin his artillery barrage.

The French had one corps of Ferdinand Foch's Army of the
North positioned on the north bank of the Somme, immediately
south of Rawlinson, and five others arrayed along an eight-mile
line extending southward from the river. They were even better
equipped than the British with artillery, especially heavy artillery, a
weapon in which France had been deficient at the start of the war.
Their assignment was a holding attack intended to make it impossible for the Germans opposite to shift their reserves (of which they
had virtually none) northward to stop Rawlinson's advance.

Facing them all, bracing for the attack that was all too obviously coming, was a stripped-down German Second Army under
General Fritz von Below. Below had only seven divisions along
the entire front, five north of the river and two to the south. Because they were so few, all of them were up on the front line—a
dangerous arrangement, but an unavoidable one in light of how
badly the Germans were outnumbered. The particular thinness
of the German line opposite the French was Falkenhayn's doing:
confident that Verdun had left the French incapable of attacking
anywhere else, he had instructed Below to deploy his troops accordingly. But the German preparations had been superb, and
Falkenhayn was responsible for that too. Under his instructions

Field Marshal Sir Douglas Haig
Commander of the British
Expeditionary Force
*Attacked often—and continued
his attacks too long.*

the Germans had been doing much more than merely digging trenches. The infrastructure they had put in place was a marvel of engineering, designed so that all the strongpoints protected each other and any enemy penetration could be quickly isolated. Beneath and behind the trenches, thirty feet and more deep in the chalk that underlay the rich topsoil of Picardy, the Germans had created what was almost an underground city, a long chain of chambers and passageways reinforced with concrete and steel. This human beehive was equipped with electric lighting, running water, and ventilation and was impervious to all but the most powerful artillery. Above it, slowly crumbling under Haig's barrage but still largely ready for use when the time came, were three (and in some places more) lines of trenches that together formed a defensive zone up to five miles deep.

Haig's plan called for five days of bombardment, but when rain began to fall on June 26 and continued into June 28 a two-day postponement had to be ordered to allow the ground to dry. The intensity of the barrage was reduced so that the supply of shells would not run too low. Still, it remained a staggering display of power. By the time the troops went over the top on July 1, more than 1.5 million shells had descended upon the Ger-

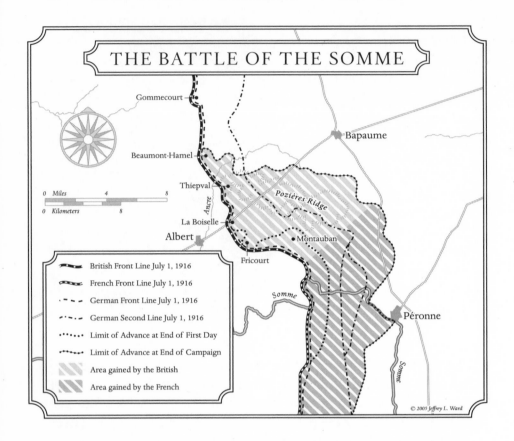

man lines—a quarter of a million on the morning of the attack alone. A ton of munitions had been dropped on every square yard of German front line with the same spirit-crushing results that both sides had been experiencing at Verdun for more than four months. "Shall I live till morning?" one of Below's soldiers wrote in his diary. "Haven't we had enough of this frightful horror? Five days and five nights now this hell concert has lasted. One's head is like a madman's; the tongue sticks to the roof of the mouth. Almost nothing to eat and nothing to drink. No sleep. All contact with the outer world cut off. No sign of life from home nor can we send any news to our loved ones. What anxiety they must feel about us. How long is this going to last?"

The Tommies and poilus looked on happily, rejoicing in the thought that nothing could survive such an inferno. And indeed the Germans were hurt, and badly. Nearly seven thousand of them died under the shellfire, and many of their guns were destroyed. Even for the survivors, the underground city became a chamber of horrors in which they could only cower in the dark, unable to bury the dead bodies around them, waiting for death. But tens of thousands survived, especially opposite the British lines. Somehow they remained sane, watching through periscopes for signs of movement on the other side. Their artillery was likewise invisible. Weeks before, the German gunners had taken the range of the British and French trenches and likely lines of advance. Then they too had gone underground, their weapons concealed in woods and covered with camouflage. Their unbroken silence made it seem certain that they too had been destroyed.

The attack, when it came, could scarcely have been less of a surprise. The area through which the front snaked is open, rolling farmland. Though the landscape was studded with woods, there were none in no-man's-land, which was clear at almost every point, open to view. Late on the afternoon of June 30 the British units chosen to lead the assault were mustered out of the villages where they had been waiting and started toward the front. As they filled the roads, they became obvious to German observers on high points behind the front. Great columns of cavalry came forward as well. It took no Napoleon to perceive the meaning of it all. As the Germans settled in for another night of agony, they did so knowing that the hour of truth was at hand.

Midsummer nights are short in the north of Europe, and in July in Picardy the sky is dimly alight by five a.m. This is also a region of predawn mists and low-lying fog. Haig could have kicked off his offensive in the early light; had he done so, his troops might have crossed no-man's-land almost unseen. But the French had insisted on a later start, and Haig found it necessary to comply. At exactly 6:25 a.m., as on all the days preceding, the British ended their usual early-morning cease-fire and started blasting away as usual. They had established this routine as a way of lulling the Germans into thinking that July 1 was going to be just another day. But this was an unlikely conclusion for them to reach, considering what they had seen the evening before.

Ten minutes before the start of the attack, at 7:20 a.m., the British detonated a huge mine that they had excavated under a German redoubt at Hawthorne Ridge, near the village of Beaumont-Hamel. "The ground where I stood gave a mighty

convulsion," a distant British observer reported. "It rocked and swayed . . . Then, for all the world like a gigantic sponge, the earth rose in the air to a height of hundreds of feet. Higher and higher it rose, and with a horrible grinding roar the earth fell back on itself, leaving in its place a mountain of smoke." Terrifying and deadly as the explosion was, it was too limited in its effects to justify the final alert that it sent to the Germans up and down the line. And now it was the turn of the British to receive a signal—a chilling one. The supposedly extinct German artillery suddenly opened up, its fire falling with stunning accuracy on the trenches in which the British soldiers waited. Obviously the Germans were still out there. Obviously they still had guns, and obviously those guns were registered for maximum effect. Ten remaining British mines, none of them as big as the one at Hawthorne Ridge, went off at 7:28. Two minutes later whistles blew and scores of thousands of British troops hauled themselves up onto exposed ground and started toward what every one of them must have hoped was nothing more than the dirt tombs of their enemies.

At this same moment the British artillery, which on every previous morning had continued until 7:45, was lifted off the German front line and shifted to more distant targets. There was supposed to be a creeping barrage for the infantry to advance behind, but it was badly managed and moved too quickly. In short order most of the British shells were falling in the German rear. The shift provided the defenders with yet another alert. As soon as they saw—felt, heard—that the barrage had moved beyond them, they scrambled up out of their hidden chambers, took their positions, and unlimbered their machine guns.

Even up on the surface, the extent of artillery damage turned out to be astonishingly limited. What seemed most inexplicable, the German barbed wire and the wooden posts from which it was strung remained in place almost everywhere. It provided the defenders, as wire always did where it was left uncut, with a nearly impenetrable protective barrier.

For the attackers, who were forced to converge wherever they could find openings, it was a death trap. At this point certain hard

Previous pages: British troops amid the mined landscape of the Western Front

truths about the fantastic British bombardment became apparent. Huge numbers of shells—as many as a third by some estimates, almost certainly hundreds of thousands—had been duds that failed to detonate. Too many of the shells that did explode contained shrapnel rather than high explosives, and more than half of the others were too small to penetrate the German dugouts. Even the fuses had turned out to be defective. Part of the problem was a collapse of quality control as Lloyd George rushed the British factories, many of them employing unskilled workers, to increase shell production. Another was Haig's decision to keep many of his heaviest guns in Flanders, where he continued to hope for a coastal offensive. What turned these misfortunes into a scandal was the refusal of senior British commanders, in spite of repeated warnings from observers up on the front lines, to believe that the wire had not been destroyed.

The Tommies knew nothing of this as they set out. Their inexperience and ignorance of what lay ahead helped to keep their enthusiasm high. They had also been fortified—steadied, dulled— by extra rations of rum. (In some units the men were given as much as they would drink.) To the extent that further motivation was required, it was provided by warnings that any man who failed to advance would be shot by his sergeants. Such practices were common and often backed up with action, though the orders were never put into writing. Nor were any officers foolish enough to put into writing the orders they issued with respect to the taking of prisoners. For a number of the units attacking at the Somme, these orders were simple beyond possibility of misunderstanding: no quarter was to be given. Any Germans attempting to surrender were to be dispatched forthwith.

The Germans were astonished by what they saw. Instead of coming forward in a rush, instead of ducking and dodging and making use of whatever cover the terrain offered, the British were lined up shoulder to shoulder in plain view. Instead of running, they were walking almost slowly, as if to demonstrate their skill at close-order drill. Rifles and bayonets at the ready, they were like a vision out of the era of flintlock musketry. If this was little short of insane, it was also exactly what had been ordered: a high-precision advance by soldiers in tidy rows. This was Rawlinson's idea. He thought that his troops, inexperienced as they were, would be incapable of advancing in any other way. "The attack must be made in waves," he said, "with men at fairly close interval in order to give them confidence." This would have made perfect sense if the Germans had in fact been wiped out. Each row was to proceed at a pace of exactly one hundred yards every two minutes, with everything timed to the second and all of it made tolerable by a creeping barrage that turned out not to be there.

According to the immensely detailed British plan of the day, the advancing soldiers were not to break into a run until within twenty yards of the enemy. Running would in any case have been nearly impossible: every man in the first wave carried some seventy pounds of weaponry, ammunition, and gear, so that even getting out of the trenches had been a challenge. The men in the later waves were more heavily burdened still. Their assignment was to consolidate the ground taken by the men ahead of them, and they had been equipped accordingly. They carried all the same things as the first wave plus everything needed to construct a new defensive line: boards, rolls of barbed wire, bundles of stakes, machine guns. If ordered to run, they would have been unable to do so, especially over ground that the bombardment had turned into an obstacle course. "Fancy advancing against heavy fire," one survivor would recall, "carrying a heavy roll of barbed wire on your shoulder!"

No-man's-land was a mile across at some points, a few hundred yards at others. The ground sloped downward toward the Germans in some places, more commonly upward, but everywhere it left the advancing troops as exposed as tin figures in a shooting gallery. Wherever they found themselves approaching uncut wire, as happened to unit after unit, they had no choice but to search out gaps and try to crowd through. Thus their slow-moving lines, or the parts of them that reached the wire, had to jam together in clusters barely able to move at all.

The Germans simply pointed their machine guns at these knots of flesh and cut them down in swaths. "We were surprised to see them walking," said a German machine-gunner. "We had never seen that before . . . When we started to fire we just had to load and reload. They went down in their hundreds. We didn't have to aim, we just fired into them."

"The infantry rushed forward with fixed bayonets," another

of the German defenders remembered. "The noise of battle became indescribable. The shouting of orders and the shrill British cheers as they charged forward, could be heard above the violent and intense fusillade of machine guns and rifles and the bursting bombs, and above the deep thunderings of the artillery and the shell explosions. With all this were mingled the moans and groans of the wounded, the cries for help and the last screams of death. Again and again the extended lines of British infantry broke against the German defense like waves against a cliff, only to be beaten back. It was an amazing spectacle of unexampled gallantry, courage and bulldog determination on both sides."

Of the sixty-six thousand men in the first wave, few got close to the German line. More than half were killed or wounded, including three-quarters of the officers. Some did make progress: the Thirty-fourth Division captured all of twenty acres, losing three of four men in the process. At Beaumont-Hamel nine out of every ten members of a Newfoundland battalion advancing toward the Hawthorne Ridge crater were shot down in forty minutes. Injured men streamed back to their own lines, throwing the later waves into deeper disorder, but as the day went on still more long rows of troops were sent forward one after another.

At day's end perhaps a third of all the units involved in the attack had reached what were supposed to be their objectives for the first hour. Few had gone farther. Not one of the five villages that were supposed to be taken in an hour had fallen. The units at the British center and left had accomplished nearly nothing. Three divisions of cavalry, having stood poised for action throughout the day, were still blocked and idle when the light failed. The number of casualties had reached sixty thousand, and almost twenty thousand of them were dead. It was the worst day in the history of British warfare. (England's casualties at Waterloo a century earlier had totaled eighty-four hundred. A generation later, at the Normandy invasion, the British and Americans together would be in combat for twenty days before their dead, wounded, and missing totaled twenty thousand.) German losses for the first day on the Somme totaled approximately eight thousand, including two thousand men taken prisoner—not by Rawlinson's army.

Before it was over the German gunners, at points in the center where the carnage had been most terrible, found themselves unwilling to continue firing. Shutting down their guns, they watched in silence as the British departed with whatever wounded they were able to take with them. Later, though, when some of the wounded left behind began to shoot from where they lay, the Germans too resumed firing.

There had been two successes, neither of them expected. South of the river, what was supposed to have been a holding action by units of Foch's battle-hardened "Iron Corps" turned into exactly the kind of breakthrough that Haig had planned for his own line. It had torn open the defenses, capturing several villages and losing only two thousand men. This happened in part because German troops were so sparse in the area, in part as a result of an effective creeping barrage. It happened mainly, however, because of what Great War historian Cyril Falls would call the "speed, dash, and tactical brains" of the French infantry. Foch and his generals made none of the British mistakes. Their poilus, when they advanced, were allowed to leave behind everything not required for the day's fighting. They were able to run and were encouraged to do so. They advanced not in marching lines but helter-skelter, platoon by platoon, darting from one shell hole to another, encircling the German machine guns rather than hurling themselves frontally against them. Foch was unable to use his gains to swing around and help out farther north, however. He was blocked by the Somme and its marshy banks.

The French corps north of the river, using the same tactics, made almost equal gains. Its advance shielded the flank of the southernmost British unit, a corps commanded by General Sir Walter Congreve, enabling it to drive northward two thousand yards and reach its objective, the village of Montauban. This was a startling achievement in comparison with what was happening elsewhere on the British line. It led, however, only to more frustration. Beyond Montauban, the countryside was open and undefended—ripe for the taking. But Rawlinson, in keeping with his bite-and-hold approach, had told his commanders that "no serious advance is to be made until preparations have been completed for entering the next phase of the operations." Congreve reported his success, requesting permission to resume his advance, but he received no answer. The French on his right were then likewise unable to advance farther, because doing so alone would have exposed their flank. Congreve had opened a path through which Haig's cavalry could, that very afternoon, have charged unobstructed into the German rear. But Haig and Rawlinson were fighting different wars, and the opportunity was lost.

When darkness finally descended, the Battle of the Somme was already deadlocked. Verdun remained deadlocked too. So did the Italian front, and the east.

FAREWELLS, AND AN ARRIVAL AT THE TOP

THE EMPEROR OF AUSTRIA AND APOSTOLIC KING of Hungary developed a cough. Soon he had a fever that went up and down and up again. Franz Joseph was eighty-six years old in November 1916, and the sixty-ninth anniversary of his coronation lay just weeks ahead. Among all the monarchs in European history, only Louis XIV of France had had a longer reign.

Narrow and backward-looking and rigid though he was (he refused to use the telephone or ride in automobiles), Franz Joseph was in many ways a good and simple man. All his life he had done his best to be faithful to the code in which his strong-willed mother had raised him. Every night he got down on his knees to pray before retiring, and every morning he knelt down again as soon as he was out of bed. His dedication to what he saw as his duty almost surpasses understanding, especially in light of how little benefit he had derived from being so faithful. Even now, aged and coughing and fevered, he had himself awakened at three-thirty in the morning and was at his desk long before sunrise. With brief interruptions he would stay at that desk until after nightfall, struggling to manage the empire that his ancestors had built up over a thousand years and that was falling in around him.

A cloud of doom hung over once-gay Vienna. Franz Joseph's great palace of Schönbrunn, so long the scene of so much Hapsburg splendor, had grown dark and somber. His prime minister had recently been shot to death by a socialist.

As his illness worsened, the old man refused to rest. He would put his head down on his desk and let his pen fall to the floor but then recover himself and return to his papers or his next official visitor. When he was put to bed for the last time, he had to be carried there against his will. "I still have work to do," he complained. "Wake me tomorrow at half past three." That night he was given the last rites, lost consciousness, and quietly died.

His was one of the good deaths of 1916; it is impossible not to feel grateful that Franz Joseph did not live to see what the rest of the war would bring. Something similar can be said of the passing of Kitchener in June. He too was getting on, and by the time of his drowning he was clearly a failure as minister of war. His autocratic ways had been totally unsuited to cabinet government, and only his stature as a public hero kept him in his job. He had been free to accept the tsar's invitation to visit Russia because nobody really wanted him in London. The sinking of his ship gave him a kind of warrior's death that he might have welcomed. His future, like the Austrian emperor's, would likely have been laden with disappointment.

December 29 would bring a different kind of death. Late that night the monk Rasputin made a visit to the palace of Prince Felix Youssopov, husband of the tsar's niece Irina and heir to a fortune bigger than that of the Romanovs. This young nobleman was a degenerate who had spent his life in the pursuit of every kind of sensual excess. As early as 1915 he had become obsessively committed to the notion that Rasputin was a threat to the survival of the regime of which he and his family were such spectacularly conspicuous beneficiaries. Rasputin, he decided, must die. Slowly, hesitantly, he assembled a little circle of conspirators, among whom was the young Grand Duke Dmitri Romanov, cousin to the tsar.

It is alleged, though some say otherwise, that what drew Rasputin to the palace that night was Youssopov's hint that the beautiful Irina would be made available to him there. This might explain why the customarily foul monk arrived in a new silk blouse, his boots polished and his person heavily perfumed. It is also said that after his arrival he was given wine and candies heavily laced with potassium cyanide, but other accounts say that whoever was responsible for providing the poison lost his nerve and used cooking powder instead. The poison story is particularly questionable: nothing Rasputin ate or drank that night appeared to have any effect beyond helping to keep him drunk. After a long period of music and dancing, with Rasputin not only failing to expire but suggesting a visit to Petrograd's brothels, Youssopov directed his attention to a silver and crystal crucifix displayed in a nearby cabinet. When the monk went to look, Youssopov pulled out a revolver and shot him in the back. Rasputin fell to the floor, apparently dead.

Youssopov's accomplices, who had been waiting in concealment upstairs, joined him in nervous celebration. Sometime later Rasputin

Grigori Rasputin with some of his many female admirers

opened his eyes. Then he was on his feet, lunging at Youssopov. The prince broke free and ran up the stairs, Rasputin close behind. When Youssopov escaped through a door and locked it behind him, Rasputin left the palace. He was on his way to the gate when one of Youssopov's accomplices began firing at him with a pistol. The first two shots missed, but the third brought Rasputin down. The gunman drew nearer and fired yet again, believing that this time he had shot his prey in the head. Youssopov came running out of the palace with a club in his hand. After several hard blows Rasputin sank into the snow, again apparently dead. His body was wrapped in a curtain, bound with rope, and dumped into the icy waters of the canal outside the gate. Later, when the corpse was fished out of the ice, police investigators found that before dying Rasputin had worked free of his bindings. An autopsy determined that the cause of his death was drowning. He had still been alive when thrown into the water and was not yet out of fight.

The mystery of Rasputin is impenetrable. That he was a singularly low character is beyond question, but if he did not also have strange powers he was singularly successful at seeming to do so. Among his effects was a letter written days before his death. It was addressed to "the Russian people, to Papa [his name for the tsar], to the Russian Mother and to the Children, to the land of Russia." In it he predicted that he would not live to see the new year, which was only days away when he wrote, and offered a warning. "Tsar of the land of Russia," he wrote, "if you hear the sound of the bell which will tell you that Grigori has been killed, you must know this: if it was your relations who have wrought my death then no one of your family, that is to say none of your children or relations, will remain alive for more than two years. They will all be killed by the Russian people."

The news of Rasputin's murder caused public jubilation. Youssopov and his accomplices, though they denied involvement, were acclaimed as heroes. Rasputin was buried in Romanov parkland, his funeral secret and attended by scarcely a handful of people. Among that handful, however, were the tsar and tsarina and their children. Whether anything would have turned out differently if Rasputin had died a year or two earlier, there is no way of knowing. By the time it came, his death was too late to change anything.

At almost exactly the same time, at the end of an almost indescribably complex struggle that split Britain's major parties into a jumble of disconnected fragments, Herbert Henry Asquith was displaced as prime minister. What broke Asquith in the end was not any failure on his part (through more than two years of war he had been a skillful if cautious leader, first of the Liberal government, then of the coalition that replaced it) but the demands of David Lloyd George for an ever-larger role in the management of the war. Finally those demands grew to a point where Asquith felt he could not accede to them without becoming a mere figurehead. A showdown was inevitable, and it came at a time when Asquith, absorbing the shock of his son's death in the Battle of the Somme, was unable to keep himself focused. ("Whatever pride I had in the past and whatever hope I had for the future—by far the largest part was invested in him," Asquith wrote after learning of this death. "Now all that is gone.") When Asquith misplayed his hand, Lloyd George unseated and replaced him.

The new prime minister had had the kind of career that causes people on the western side of the Atlantic to say "Only in America!" Born into exceedingly humble circumstances, orphaned at an early age and raised in Wales by a shoemaker uncle, he began as a law clerk, struggled to gain admission to the bar, married a farmer's daughter, and won election to Parliament at the age of twenty-seven.

A firebrand reformer, a champion of progressive legislation and of industrial and agricultural workers, he rose fast in the Liberal party and by 1908, at forty-five, was chancellor of the exchequer. Along the way he built a record of opposing military spending and overseas adventures, favoring domestic programs instead. He paid a political price for doing so and learned to be careful not to alienate the Conservatives too much.

In July 1914 Lloyd George was a leading figure among the Liberal ministers resisting the slide into war. When the German invasion of Belgium radically changed public opinion, he quickly and adroitly moved with it. From then on he was not only a supporter of the war but a tireless agitator for total British commitment, controversial at times for his absolute rejection of any possible settlement short of victory. He more than anyone else was the force behind Britain's conscription laws, and it was he who created and then took charge of the ministry of munitions in response to the shell crisis of 1915, giving up his post at the treasury to do so.

In the summer of 1916, when Kitchener drowned, Lloyd George bullied where necessary and maneuvered where possible to get himself named secretary of state for war. In that position he soon became more powerful and effective than Kitchener ever had been. His rise to prime minister at the end of the year ensured that, however long the war lasted, Britain would have strong and capable and unwaveringly determined political leadership. It also ensured that that leadership would often be bitterly at odds with the leading British generals—with Robertson, the chief of the imperial general staff, and with Haig at the BEF.

Chapter 6

Exhaustion

*"It is not surprising if the effect on some
intelligent men was a bitter conviction that
they were being uselessly sacrificed."*
—Official Australian history of
the Battle of the Somme

Throughout the second half of 1916, great irruptions of violence followed one after another as the forces set in motion
earlier in the year overflowed into places previously untouched
and finally played themselves out in failure and despair. The Battle of the Somme, after its terrible first day, contracted immediately though not permanently into a more limited conflict. On
July 2 Haig, aware by now of the extent of his losses, sent only
three divisions into attacks—barely more than a fifth of the number that had gone into action the preceding day. Not one of those
divisions, strangely, was sent to exploit Congreve's breakthrough
at Montauban, and Congreve himself was again not allowed to
move. Along much of the front, action was limited to gruesome
nighttime forays into no-man's-land for the purpose of finding
those still alive among the heaps of corpses. At Beaumont-
Hamel, where the number of dead and wounded was unmanage-
ably large, German soldiers slipped out of their trenches after dark
and, without a word being exchanged, helped the British rescue
parties with the work of retrieval.

Also on July 2, at Baranovitchi in the northern reaches of the
Eastern Front, Russian General Evert at last launched the offensive that he had promised weeks earlier in support of Brusilov.

Evert had a thousand guns, each of which fired a thousand rounds in advance of the assault, and he had more than twenty-six divisions to send against two Austrian divisions backed by six German divisions in reserve. The result was a disaster almost equal to Lake Naroch in its magnitude. Though one of the Austrian divisions collapsed, the other held its ground, and when the Germans came forward, they inflicted eighty thousand casualties on the attackers, losing only sixteen thousand men themselves. This ended any possibility of further Russian initiatives in the north.

For the first time the Brusilov offensive was given first priority by the tsar's headquarters. All available troops found themselves headed toward his theater of operations. Brusilov resumed his campaign even before the Baranovitchi fight was over, and in short order he was again producing stunning victories. In four days he took forty thousand prisoners and captured three hundred and thirty guns. He began moving his armies, which now outnumbered those facing him by two to one, northward toward the Austro-Hungarian stronghold at Kovel.

On July 10, in a final lunge at glory, Knobelsdorf sent off a cobbled-together force roughly equivalent to three divisions in another attempt to take Verdun. A handful of these troops reached Fort Souville and stood briefly atop its protective shell waving flags. But Knobelsdorf had no reserves with which to follow up, and they were soon blown away by French artillery. The attack was suspended with a speed that was merciful to the troops on both sides. It was the Germans' last spasm at Verdun, though by no means the end of the killing. It was also the end of Knobelsdorf's part in the drama; on the orders of the kaiser, who had been driven by mounting disappointment to begin listening to his son, he was sent off to command a corps on the Eastern Front. Falkenhayn, harried by the crises on the Somme and in the southeast, increased the number of troops being transferred to both places.

At the Somme, meanwhile, the British continued to pound away with their artillery at the German defenses. One German soldier, after being taken prisoner, described for an English journalist the experience of having to take turns huddling in overcrowded bunkers under a barrage so intense that supplies could not get through. "Those who went outside were killed or wounded," he said. "Some of them had their heads blown off, and some of them had both their legs torn off, and some of them their arms. But we went on taking turns in the hole, although those who went outside knew that it was their turn to die, most likely. At last some of those who came into the hole were wounded, some of them badly, so that we lay in blood."

Sir Henry Rawlinson was slowly and with difficulty winning Haig's approval for another attack on the Somme. His plan this time was to send four divisions (with others guarding their flanks) across no-man's-land in the middle of the night, pause while the artillery pounded the Germans for only five minutes, and attack in the earliest predawn light. The French, judging the dangers of being caught on open ground after sunrise to be unacceptably great, refused to join in. But when the attack went off on July 14, it was a complete success—at first. There were only four battalions of defenders, and the British quickly overran their first line and broke through parts of the second. This time (and for the first time since 1914) the British cavalry did get into action, but it had been positioned so far behind the lines that it needed nine hours to reach the point of breakthrough. By the time it arrived, the Germans had been able to rush forward reserves to block the hole. Men and horses were mowed down by machine guns, and by the end of the day the Germans were once again in control of their second line. It had been a near thing, however. Although Haig by now had given up on achieving and exploiting a breakthrough, this latest attack persuaded him that the Germans really were at the end of their manpower. He decided that the Somme was worth continuing as an attrition battle. Encouraged by his staff's exaggerations of German losses, he approved Rawlinson's plan for yet another assault later in the month.

Across Europe it went on and on, new offensives coming one after another like waves on a sea of blood. At Verdun, a day after Rawlinson's July 14 offensive, Mangin the Butcher, lifted out of disfavor by Nivelle and promoted to command of a corps, sent a division to capture the village of Fleury. This was such a total failure, costing the French so many men, that Pétain intervened. He ordered that there were to be no more attacks without his specific approval, and he made it clear that he would approve no actions that had not been properly prepared. Mangin and his chief,

Nivelle, began laying plans for an even bigger assault of a kind that Pétain would have to approve.

On July 23 Rawlinson launched his next attack. The troops of the Anzac Corps, many of them veterans of Gallipoli, took possession of part of Pozières Ridge, their assigned objective. But that was the only thing gained in another round of heavy losses, and the fight dragged on fruitlessly for another two months. "Although most Australian soldiers were optimists, and many were opposed on principle to voicing—or even harboring—grievances, it is not surprising if the effect on some intelligent men was a bitter conviction that they were being uselessly sacrificed," the official Australian history of the battle later observed.

On July 25 a Russian general nearly as talented as Brusilov, Nikolai Yudenich, commander of an army that had been winning victory after victory in the Caucasus, found that masses of Turks were converging on him from two directions. He struck at the Turkish Third Army and shattered it, killing or wounding seventeen thousand of its men and capturing another seventeen thousand while causing thousands of others to desert. He then turned to meet the Turkish Second Army, which continued to bear down on him and included among its corps commanders Mustafa Kemal, the hero of Gallipoli.

As the month ended, Brusilov continued his drive on the transportation center at Kovel, doing further damage to what remained of the Austro-Hungarian army. But he was being slowed down by an all-too-familiar problem: inadequate transport, supplies, and reinforcements. What was new and worse, German divisions were arriving in significant numbers from the west. This was a potentially mortal danger, but Brusilov could take pride in the fact that it was happening. Three months earlier the Germans had 125 divisions in the west, forty-seven in the east. But the ratio had been changing steadily ever since in response to the crisis that Brusilov had created, and by August it was 119 west, sixty-four east. Hundreds of thousands of German troops who could have made a critical difference at Verdun were in Galicia instead, or on their way there.

Though the year was unfolding in nothing like the way envisioned at Chantilly in December, by August it was beginning to appear possible that Joffre's objectives would still be achieved.

The Germans were outnumbered and on the defensive at Verdun and on the Somme, and the same was true of the combined German-Austrian force in the southeast. The Austrians were on the defensive in Italy (where the Sixth Battle of the Isonzo began on August 6, generating more than a hundred thousand casualties before petering out after twelve days), and Turkey too was an empire in extremis, tormented by Yudenich's Caucasus campaign and the revolt in the Arabian desert. To complete the picture, French General Sarrail was preparing to move his quarter of a million men—twenty-three British, French, Italian, and Serbian divisions—northward out of Salonika. There seemed good reason to expect that, if all this pressure could be maintained, Germany would crack as Austria-Hungary had already done. This belief—that the Germans couldn't possibly still have enough men and guns to keep their defensive wall intact—persuaded Haig to keep hammering away at the Somme.

At this juncture, however, two things happened to turn everything upside down again. The Brusilov crisis forced Vienna to consent to putting almost all its armies under unified German command. Conrad howled in protest, but no one now cared what Conrad thought; undoubtedly he would have been dismissed if his many critics had been able to agree on a successor. Almost the whole Eastern Front was placed under the command of Hindenburg, which meant under Ludendorff, who could emerge at last from his isolation in the Baltic wastes. As soon as he had authority over the southeast, Ludendorff stopped insisting that none of the divisions he had been hoarding in the northeast could be spared for duty elsewhere. Hundreds of trainloads of his troops, guns, and supplies began pouring toward Galicia. As they took up positions, Brusilov's chances of restarting his campaign rapidly grew smaller.

Romania chose this moment, after months of hesitation, to throw in with the Entente. This decision was taken in spite of the fact that Romania's royal family was a junior, Catholic branch of the Hohenzollerns. It was precipitated by Brusilov's successes, especially his occupation of the Bukovina, a Hapsburg province on the northern border of Transylvania. This little conquest, of modest importance by every other measure, mattered because the Romanians hungered to annex Transylvania, which not only included many Romanians in its mixed population but had been part of Romania until seized by the Austrians in 1868. The Romanians feared that if they failed to act now, Transylvania would fall permanently to the Russians.

On August 17 Romania signed a secret agreement under which it joined the Entente and was promised Transylvania in return. It was assured of protection from its neighbor Bulgaria (now on the side of the Central Powers and eager to recoup what it had lost in the Second Balkan War) by the army that Sarrail was bringing up from Salonika. On that same day, ironically, a mainly Bulgarian force under German General Mackenson hit Sarrail's army at the village of Florina in Greece. Sarrail was forced into a retreat that would continue for more than three weeks. The die was cast, however.

On August 27 Romania issued a declaration of war, and that night it sent four hundred thousand troops, twenty-three divisions, through the mountain passes separating it from Transylvania. On the other side of those passes were only thirty-one thousand Austro-Hungarian soldiers. A quick and almost painless conquest seemed certain.

The addition to the Entente of Romania with its army of more than half a million men was one of those Great War triumphs that turned out to be less than met the eye—infinitely less, in this case. It was controversial before it happened, with Britain's David Lloyd George and Russia's General Alexeyev among those opposed. Alexeyev warned that the Romanian army was useless in spite of its size, and that Russia would find itself forced to protect hundreds of miles that had until now required no protection because of Romania's neutrality. He argued, in short, that Russia would be worse off with Romania as an ally than if Romania stayed out of the war. The tsar ignored Alexeyev. He listened instead to Boris Stürmer, the craven, conniving, and inept courtier who (to the shock of everyone, including Petrograd's conservative old guard) had been appointed prime minister in February and in July, after Sergei Sazonov was dismissed, had taken on the additional duties of foreign minister. Stürmer, who had absolutely no experience in such matters and was despised by nearly everyone who knew him, told Tsar Nicholas that the Romanians would sweep across Transylvania and into Hungary. He effortlessly carried the day.

Romania's declaration of war seemed a disaster to the Germans, and for Falkenhayn it was. He had been assuring Kaiser Wilhelm that if Romania entered the war at all, it couldn't possibly do so before late September, after the harvest was brought in. Chancellor Bethmann Hollweg, who had wanted Falkenhayn's dismissal since the two split over unrestricted submarine warfare, seemed suddenly justified. The coup de grâce was delivered when Hindenburg, prodded by Ludendorff and Hoffmann, threatened to resign if he was not made commander in chief. Kaiser Wilhelm, deeply discouraged about the state of the war and too weak politically to face down Hindenburg, gave up. On August 29 he sent a message inviting Hindenburg and Ludendorff to meet with him in Potsdam. When Falkenhayn, reading the signs, offered his resignation, it was accepted without discussion. Falkenhayn then made a final effort to save himself, warning Wilhelm that Hindenburg's appointment would mean the end of his, the kaiser's, ability to command the army or the nation. His power would be usurped not by Hindenburg, who scarcely mattered except as a symbol adored by the public, but by Ludendorff. Much as he resented Hindenburg and despised Ludendorff as a ruffian upstart, Wilhelm could see no alternative. The next day Hindenburg accepted Falkenhayn's job. Falkenhayn, offered appointment as ambassador to Constantinople, asked for a military position instead. Soon—perhaps it was Ludendorff's idea of a joke, or of ironic revenge—he was given the job of subduing Romania.

Ludendorff, explicitly given joint authority with Hindenburg over the German armies, was no longer satisfied with being chief of staff. He had the title of Quartermaster General of the German Army conferred on himself instead. He then departed by train for Verdun, taking Hindenburg with him. After getting a brief and appalling look at the situation there (the entire region was a blasted waste, its landscape described by a French aviator as like "the humid skin of a monstrous toad"), he made the inevitable official, decreeing that there would be no more German attacks.

The Romanian army, meanwhile, was showing itself to be even more hopeless than Alexeyev had warned. It was untrained and disorganized, so ill equipped that most of its divisions didn't possess a single machine gun, with an officer corps so bizarre that its senior commanders had issued an order permitting only those

above major in rank to wear makeup. The divisions entering Transylvania should, by sheer force of numbers, have been able to push
the Austrians out. Instead they proceeded with excruciating slow-
ness, waiting for Russian help that wasn't coming. Alexeyev was
disgusted by the entire enterprise, certain that Romania could not
be defended, and unwilling to add to the small number of Russian
troops already there.

The timidity of the Romanians in Transylvania, coupled with
a period of quiet at Verdun and the Somme (where the French
and British were not yet ready for their next attacks), gave the
Germans precious time. Whole armies were being hurried across
Hungary—fifteen hundred trainloads of men and equipment during September alone—while Mackensen, having stopped Sarrail, began shifting the bulk of his Bulgarian force northward out
of Greece. Only now did the full extent of Romania's unreadi-
ness begin to make itself felt, turning war into low farce. Planning nothing more than a feint, Mackensen sent a smallish force
to threaten the Romanian fortress of Turtukai on the Danube.
The commander of this fortress, whose garrison greatly outnumbered the troops sent by Mackensen, declared boldly that
"this will be our Verdun." One day later, upon being attacked,
80 percent of the Romanians at Turtukai surrendered almost
without a fight. Those who did not surrender ran away, so that
three Romanian divisions essentially evaporated. Mackensen then
crossed the Danube into the province of Dobruja on the edge of
the Black Sea. His arrival sparked celebrations: Dobruja had been
taken by Romania in the Second Balkan War, and most of its population was Bulgarian.

At almost every point where they encountered enemies, the
Romanian units simply collapsed. In their haste and confusion
some of them attempted to surrender to one of the few Russian
units in Dobruja—their own allies, who were distinctly un-
amused. The local Russian commander, ordered by Alexeyev to
try to organize a joint defense, replied that trying to turn the Romanians into a disciplined force was like trying to get a donkey
to dance a minuet. Greece too had by this time been drawn into
the Entente (temporarily, as it would turn out, and as the result of
indescribably complicated political machinations), and it too was
putting troops in the field. But those troops saw no more reason

to fight than the Romanians did. An entire corps surrendered to Mackensen without a shot being fired and was happily sent off by train to Silesia, where it would pass the rest of the war in the safety of internment camps. When Romania's commanders responded to the Dobruja crisis by shifting troops from the west, the only result was to thin their inert force in Transylvania.

In mid-September Falkenhayn arrived in Transylvania and took command of a new German Ninth Army, which was being assembled out of the many troops now arriving in the region. He was a man with something to prove—giving him an army to command rather than an army group had been an insult—and one day after taking up his new duties he started his forces toward the mountain passes leading to Romania. Meanwhile new convulsions erupted from France to the Caucasus. A September 15 assault by eight British divisions on the Somme included the battlefield debut of the tank. Only sixty of the new machines were in France at the time; of them only thirty-two were able to go into action, and only nine got far enough to help in temporarily pushing back the German line. (Ultimately the attack was another failure.) Churchill, who had wanted to keep the new weapon secret until enough could be assembled for a major surprise, was in anguish. "My poor 'land battleships' have been let off prematurely and on a petty scale," he wrote. "In that idea rested one real victory." Haig, who had insisted on not waiting, was not discouraged. He told the war office that he wanted a thousand more tanks as soon as possible. The French and the Germans got to work on tank programs of their own.

In the Caucasus Yudenich and Kemal, determined and able and well matched, struck at each other again and again, capturing towns and then having to give them up. In Greece Sarrail stopped his retreat with a counterattack against the Bulgarians and again began trying to push toward the north.

Three of the disasters of this period were particularly pointless. The Italians started the Seventh Battle of the Isonzo, which like its predecessors lasted only a few days, generated thousands of casualties, and accomplished nothing. On Brusilov's front, Tsar Nicholas sent an elite army of Imperial Guard units that were nominally under his personal command (he didn't go with them, however) to join in the advance on Kovel, now largely defended by Germans. The Guards, a hundred and thirty-four thousand of the best infantry and cavalry remaining to Russia, outnumbered the defenders and were better supplied with guns and shells. But their commander, a Romanov grand duke handpicked for the job by the tsar, ignored the lessons of the Brusilov offensive. Regarding flank attacks as unworthy of a force as superb as his, he sent the Guards in frontal assaults straight at the guns of the Germans. He sent them seventeen times—they found themselves trying to advance through waist-deep water while being strafed by aircraft—and every attempt ended in slaughter. Brusilov, who was not even consulted, could only read the reports and grieve. When the enterprise was called off at last, fifty-five thousand Guardsmen were casualties. As news of this disaster spread among the troops and into the civilian population, anger and resentment boiled to the surface. The heads of generals rolled, but the damage had been irretrievable.

At Verdun, which otherwise remained quiet by Verdun standards, the French on September 4 experienced a disaster that uncannily mirrored the earlier German explosion inside Fort Douaumont. In a fourteen-hundred-foot railroad tunnel that was being used by Nivelle's troops as a barracks, communications channel, storage depot, medical treatment center, and refuge, a fire somehow broke out where rockets were being moved by mule. It spread to a chamber where grenades had been stockpiled, then to the fuel for the tunnel's generators. It burned out of control for three days, trapping and killing more than five hundred men. The poilus too were finding reason to grumble.

September 25 brought another British thrust on the Somme. Again Haig used his tanks—only 30 percent got as far as no-man's-land before breaking down—and as usual the Tommies paid a high price in lives for gains that included the village of Thiepval, which had been a prime objective back on July 1 and now fell at last after two days of hard fighting. Thereafter the weather failed, the onset of autumn rains making further movement impossible.

Falkenhayn, at the same time, was clearing Transylvania. Late in September he delivered a thrashing to a Romanian force at Hermannstadt. (As the name of this town indicates, Transylvania had a substantial German population, one eager to help Falkenhayn's army with intelligence and in all other possible ways.)

The Romanians fell back to the so-called Transylvanian Alps and prepared to make a stand in the passes. They were reinforced by two hundred thousand of their countrymen sent from the Danube. Their numbers, and the fact that they were on high ground protected on both sides by mountains, appeared to make them secure. Falkenhayn desperately needed to get past them and link up with Mackensen. His whole plan depended on that. But with winter approaching in the high country, time was running out. If this thrust were not to degenerate into another stalemate, he had to force the Romanians out of the passes before the snows came.

Early October brought a three-day Eighth Battle of the Isonzo, which cost many lives but otherwise had no results, and preparations for a new French attack at Verdun. On October 19, satisfied that this was not going to be another squandering of lives, Pétain allowed Nivelle to begin bombarding the Germans with six hundred and fifty pieces of artillery (among them new siege guns bigger than the German Big Berthas) and fifteen thousand tons of shells assembled for the purpose. It was February in reverse: for four days the French blasted away at demoralized German troops who, huddled under an intermittent freezing rain, saw their defenses blown apart around them. On October 22 Nivelle played a trick. Suddenly all his guns fell silent, after which, by prearrangement, the thousands of French troops positioned along the front line sent up a great cheer—always until now a sure sign of an attack. Thoroughly fooled, the Germans uncovered the artillery that they had kept concealed until now and opened fire, thereby disclosing their positions. This was what Nivelle had wanted. There followed not an infantry attack but another day and a half of French shelling, during which sixty-eight of the Germans' 158 batteries were destroyed. Many of those that remained were so worn out by almost a year of heavy use as to be no longer accurate. The new French guns slowly began to break Fort Douaumont apart, setting its interior afire. The German garrison was pulled out, leaving the fort undefended.

The assault force was commanded by Mangin. When it attacked on the morning of October 24, its soldiers were concealed in mist, shielded by a creeping barrage, and thoroughly prepared. (At least partly to satisfy Pétain, a full-scale model of Douaumont had been constructed behind the French lines, and one French unit after an-

other had captured it in mock assaults.) The attack was a total success. In one day the French retook positions on the east bank of
the Meuse that the Germans had spent four and a half months and
tens of thousands of men capturing. The retaking of Douaumont
sparked national jubilation. When Fort Vaux fell nine days later (it
too was abandoned by the Germans and captured almost without
a fight), France was prepared to believe that at Verdun its army
had won one of history's great victories. Nivelle, almost overnight,
became the nation's new hero, the man who had "the formula"
(so he himself declared) for turning the tide. Few wanted to notice
that the Germans still held all their gains on the west bank, so that
their artillery could block further advances on the other side of the
river. Nor did it seem to matter that though the Germans were giving ground, they were doing so slowly and in good order. The hills
retaken by the French were without strategic value, and nothing
remotely like a breakthrough had been achieved. But Nivelle and
Mangin were eager to strike again.

Nor was Haig quite finished (or the Italians, who on November 1 began a three-day Ninth Battle of the Isonzo that brought
to almost one hundred and forty thousand the number of casualties suffered by both sides on that little front during 1916). On
November 13 the British detonated a mine that their tunnelers
had dug under a German redoubt on the blood-soaked ground of
Beaumont-Hamel, and the subsequent attack by seven divisions
captured both the redoubt and twelve hundred German soldiers.
This fight went on for six days. Then on November 18 a blizzard
brought it to an end. The Battle of the Somme was at an end as
well. Absurdly, in their final forward plunge the British commanders had pushed their line downhill from a freshly captured ridge
to the low ground beyond. The only result was that thousands of
troops would, for no good reason, spend a miserable winter entrenched in cold, deep mud dominated by enemy guns.

Casualties on the Somme totaled half a million British and
more than two hundred thousand French. Though the British
and French originally estimated German casualties at above six
hundred and fifty thousand and this number was long accepted
by historians, it cannot be accurate. Official German sources place
their Somme casualties at two hundred and thirty-seven thousand, a total that corresponds approximately to the calculations

of Australia's official historian. The extent to which the British and French exaggerated is clear in the various governments' official (and credible) tabulations of total deaths on all sectors of the Western Front in all of 1916: one hundred and fifty thousand British, two hundred sixty-eight thousand French, and one hundred forty-three thousand German.

Whatever the numbers, many of Kitchener's armies were now not only battle-seasoned but seriously reduced. German losses, though far from outlandish in comparison with those of their enemies, had been higher than necessary. The reason was that Fritz von Below, commander of the Second Army at the Somme, had threatened to court-martial any officer who allowed his men to withdraw and later launched hundreds of useless counterattacks. Ultimately Falkenhayn was responsible. "The first principle in position warfare," he had decreed, "must be to yield not one foot of ground; and if it be lost to retake it by immediate counterattack, even to the use of the last man." Ludendorff, upon making his first visit to Verdun, ordered an end to such practices and began the introduction of more flexible, less costly tactics.

Just ahead of heavy snows that might have kept them blocked all winter, Falkenhayn's divisions now forced their way through four mountain passes. The Romanians, virtually out of ammunition, were unable to resist. Mackensen began moving toward Falkenhayn from Dobruja, which he had thoroughly subdued. The Romanian commander divided his force to strike simultaneously at Falkenhayn and Mackensen, trying to keep them apart. It was a bold move but completely beyond the capabilities of the army that attempted it. It might have had a chance of success with Russian support, and by now Alexeyev had relented. In response to the threat that Romania's collapse was beginning to pose for Russia itself, he did what he had feared from the start that Romania's entry into the war would force him to do. He told Brusilov to extend his line more than two hundred miles to the east and south. This ended the danger of a German move into Russia, but it so dispersed Brusilov's troops as to render him incapable of continuing his offensive. Alexeyev was trying to send troops into Dobruja from the east, but he had acted too late in a theater that was without adequate railroads. Sarrail, meanwhile, was again trying to come to the rescue from the south. He raised hopes by capturing the city of Monastir in southern Serbia, but thereafter his advance stalled.

At the start of December Falkenhayn and Mackensen came together and finished the destruction of the Romanian army in the Battle of Arges. Since their government's declaration of war, two hundred thousand Romanians had been killed or wounded (half the dead were victims of disease, actually) and one hundred and fifty thousand had been taken prisoner. Those able to flee went northward into Russia. The Germans, Bulgarians, and Austrians (plus some Arab units contributed by the Turks) had lost about sixty thousand men. On December 6 they crowned their victory by taking possession of the capital city of Bucharest. The forces that Alexeyev had been trying to send against them were able to do nothing more than block Mackensen from advancing northward out of Dobruja along the shore of the Black Sea.

The consequences of the Romanian campaign transcended the numbers of men lost and the propaganda benefits reaped by the victors. Over the next year and a half the Central Powers would remove from Romania more than two million tons of grain, one million tons of oil, two hundred thousand tons of timber, and three hundred thousand head of livestock. To a considerable extent, Romania fueled Germany's ability to stay in the war.

All the battles were now over except the oldest, the one at Verdun. On December 13 the political ice under Joseph Joffre broke at last. Questions about his leadership, above all about his failure to prepare at Verdun, had finally generated more pressure than his defenders were able to withstand. The hero of the Marne, the revered savior of France, was moved into an empty position as adviser to the war cabinet. To satisfy his supporters, to keep them and Joffre himself from resisting or protesting, he was made a Marshal of France. His successor as commander in chief was not his able deputy Castelnau (too aristocratic and Catholic to be acceptable to the republicans who dominated the government), not the demonstrably effective Foch (also too Catholic—he was a member of a lay religious order, and one of his brothers was a Jesuit priest), and not the supremely competent and sensible Pétain (too chronically contemptuous of politicians and his fellow generals to be digestible by either the government or the army). The new chief was France's new darling, Robert Nivelle, the self-styled genius credited with changing Verdun from a tragedy into a national triumph.

Two days after Nivelle's promotion, his man Mangin attacked for the last time at Verdun. This was another success, at least from Mangin's perspective. It resulted in the capture of eleven thousand Germans and 115 of their guns. But it lacked any real importance—by the third day the Germans were successfully counterattacking—and by the time it was brought to a halt the number of French casualties since the end of the German offensive had risen to forty-seven thousand.

Verdun was over at last. For months the battle had been little more than a struggle over a symbol. No one seemed capable of asking why the French were attacking or the Germans were bothering to defend. The crown prince, in his postwar memoir, offered the German rationale. To have walked away from ground over which so much blood had been spilled, he wrote, would have been politically impossible—would have caused explosions at home. The French in the end were fighting for nothing more substantial than glory—not France's so much as Mangin's glory.

Meaningless as it was, the last assault of 1916 brought an ominous if largely unnoticed foreshadowing of the year that lay ahead. As they moved forward to the trenches from which they would once again have to throw their flesh against machine guns, the French troops began to bleat like sheep. The sound echoed all around. *Baaaa, baaaa*—the one pathetic form of protest available to men condemned to die. More than the fighting, more than any piece of ground won or lost, this was the sign of what was coming next.

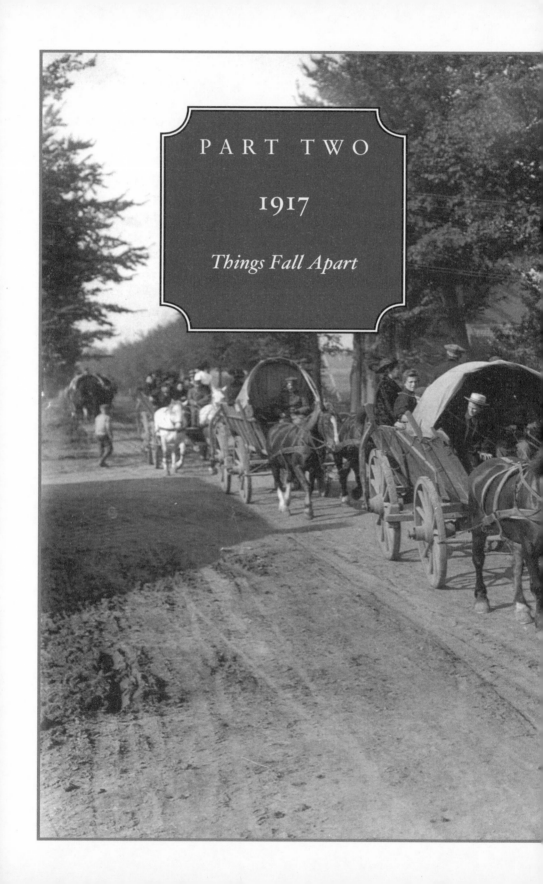

PART TWO

1917

Things Fall Apart

Innocent, but not bystanders: these French refugees join the countless millions of civilians whose lives were turned upside down by the world's first total war.

Chapter 7

Turnips and Submarines

"I could not advise His Majesty to do other than to accept the opinion of his military advisers."

—Theobald von Bethmann Hollweg

By the winter of 1916–17 the Central Powers had more reason than ever to want the war brought to a swift conclusion. Their military situation was far grimmer than it had been a year earlier: the Austro-Hungarian armies broken beyond hope of repair, the Germans exhausted by Verdun and the Somme and the scramble to cope with the Brusilov offensive, and the Ottoman Empire unraveling north and south. On the home front things were even worse. Germany and Austria alike were beginning to die from within, their cities sinking into want and despair, their children literally starving.

As early as October 1916 Germany's Chancellor Bethmann Hollweg was seeking to get the American president to interject himself as a mediator between the warring sides. This proved infeasible, Woodrow Wilson being embroiled in an election that he was by no means certain of winning. So Bethmann sent a diplomatic note to Europe's neutral nations, declaring that Germany was prepared to enter into negotiations. He offered no concessions but also set no conditions, rather grandly making note of recent German successes including the conquest of Romania. In spite of support from the pope, within days this initiative was rejected by all the members of the Entente. The Russian Duma passed a resolution stating that peace would be possible only after "victory over the military powers of Germany." The tsar, in a message to his troops, scornfully characterized Bethmann's offer as evidence of German desperation. In London, David Lloyd George said the British would "put our trust rather in an unbroken army than in broken faith." The Entente's leaders pointed to Bethmann's failure to say anything about Belgium—a particularly serious issue for the British, for whom permanent German domination of Belgium would be an intolerable security threat. Bethmann himself had recognized that in not addressing this question he was reducing his chances of accomplishing anything, but divisions within the German leadership had forced him to keep silent. Generals and admirals too powerful to be ignored were insisting that Belgium must at the war's end remain a German dependency or even be absorbed into the Reich. Ludendorff was typical in this regard: Belgium's postwar dependence on Germany, he said, must be "economic, military and political."

President Wilson, once he was safely reelected on a campaign slogan of "He kept us out of war," set out eagerly to become the world's peacemaker. He issued a diplomatic note in which he proposed an international peace conference. To establish a basis for discussion, he asked all the belligerents to state their war aims—to explain what they hoped to accomplish in continuing the struggle. Germany reacted first, endorsing the idea of negotiations and making lofty affirmations of its innocence and its willingness not only to talk but to participate in the creation of a new international system to prevent wars. It said nothing specific, however, about what Berlin would regard as an acceptable settlement concerning Belgium or any other question. This was the best Bethmann could do; putting the Ludendorff position in writing would have ended any possibility of negotiations.

Bethmann's reticence did not help. The Entente dismissed the German position as empty posturing and repeated its demand for a withdrawal from Belgium and France. On January 10 the Entente's leaders amplified their reply, complaining that Wilson had implied "a likeness between the two belligerent groups" when, in their view, Germany and its allies were solely responsible for the war. They outlined an array of demands that began with the "restoration" of Belgium, Serbia, and Montenegro and the payment of reparations by the Central Powers. Most ominously from the per-

President Woodrow Wilson
"He kept us out of war."

spective of the Central Powers, they called for "the reorganization of Europe." They wanted not only the return of Alsace and Lorraine to France but the dismemberment of the Austro-Hungarian and Ottoman Empires.

This was followed by recriminations from both sides, and all hope of substantive discussion evaporated. We have no certain way of knowing whether the Entente really was unwilling to consider anything short of victory or was simply attempting to begin discussions on the strongest possible footing. What is certain is that both sides were afraid to say anything that might be interpreted as weakness either by their enemies or by their own people, and that powerful factions in both camps were determined to win the war. Lloyd George, for one, was mindful that his position as prime minister was dependent on the support of the Conservatives, who would have rebelled if he had displayed any willingness to compromise with the Germans. On the other side, the contempt with which the Entente had responded not only to Bethmann's but to Wilson's notes made Germany's conservatives feel justified in opposing further attempts to make peace.

It had become easier than ever to argue that Berlin had no option but the military one. But its military prospects seemed bleak.

Ludendorff, in the weeks since taking charge of the high command, had been reviewing the situation on the Western Front. After two years in the east, he brought a fresh eye to the deadlock—and he did not like what he saw. "Our position was extremely difficult, and it seemed impossible to find a way out," he would write later. "We ourselves were not in a position to attack, and we dared not hope that any one of our enemies would collapse. If the war continued for any length of time, defeat seemed inevitable." What was definitely inevitable was that the Entente would be launching new offensives on both fronts in 1917, and Ludendorff believed that Falkenhayn's defensive system was sacrificing too many troops by holding doggedly to ground of little value. In any case, Germany clearly could not survive indefinitely, much less win the war, by standing on the defensive. The challenge, as Ludendorff saw it, was twofold: to find a less costly defensive doctrine and to arrive at some way of seizing the initiative, of carrying the war to the enemy. The search for a new defense brought out the best in the German general staff. The search for a way to widen the war, for a kind of new front where Germany could have the advantage, led to a reopening of the long-festering dispute over submarine warfare.

By 1917 the war was affecting civilian populations throughout Europe, but the naval blockade had raised suffering in Germany and Austria-Hungary to a uniquely high level. The French, from the beginning of the war to the end, had to sacrifice less than any of their enemies or allies. The Paris government never imposed effective controls on food production or distribution for the simple reason that it never had to: consumption actually increased throughout the war. This fact—astonishing in light of what was happening elsewhere—was made possible by shippers' nearly unimpeded access to France's Atlantic and Mediterranean ports, and by the high priority that the Paris government gave to food imports, at least partly as a way of limiting popular discontent with the war. Almost the only general inconvenience was a shortage of coal resulting from German occupation of France's prime coal-producing region, but even this was eventually made good. Problems had arisen, inevitably, from the 1914 induction of fully one-fourth of France's farmers and agricultural workers, from the military's requisitioning of thousands of horses, and from the diversion of rail facilities to military use. But these problems too proved to be manageable. By 1917 butter was still almost as plentiful and inexpensive as it had been at the start of the war—this at a time when, in Germany and Austria, butter was virtually unobtainable at any price and only expectant mothers and the smallest children were allowed even a meager ration of milk.

The situation was worse in Britain, which in the years before the war had been importing 60 percent of the calories consumed by its population, but there too things were short of desperate. With its centralized administration and strong executive—all the stronger after Lloyd George became prime minister—Britain was able to impose controls on all aspects of the system by which its people were fed. Nevertheless there had been food shortages in 1916 (as much because of the year's bad harvest as because of the U-boats), and early in 1917 Lloyd George took measures to increase agricultural production. Voluntary rationing was tried, and when it proved ineffective, it was followed by mandatory

Planting time in France
Across Europe, with men and animals gone to war,
women took on new labors.

controls on the distribution of the staples that were in shortest supply. A decline in nutrition manifested itself in a 25 percent increase in deaths from tuberculosis in England and Wales, and in rising infant mortality. Civilian health care deteriorated: hundreds of doctors were with the BEF on the continent, and hospitals throughout the British Isles were flooded with sick and wounded soldiers.

American agriculture boomed as exports to Britain and France increased; more and more land was put into production. Skyrocketing demand, however, caused prices to rise on the U.S. domestic market. Paradoxically, in the midst of abundance and the prosperity that came with it, there were food riots in several eastern U.S. cities during the winter of 1916–17.

In the management of food as in so many other areas, Tsarist Russia was a dismal failure. It had ample capacity to feed its population, and throughout the war it produced more than enough food to do so. Millions of tons of surplus grain were on ships in Black Sea ports, ready for export but unable to get through the Dardanelles. Russia was increasingly unsuccessful, meanwhile, in getting food and fuel to its cities, which were crowded with refugees, including the millions of Jews whom the Russians themselves had driven out of Poland in 1915. Much of the nation's railway system had been given over to the military, and much of what remained was in disarray. In the large cities, the price of food increased much faster than wages. The infant mortality rate doubled in Petrograd from 1914 to 1916, and by 1917 women working ten-hour days in factories were also spending forty hours weekly standing in line to get food and fuel for their children. Riots and strikes began to break out—six hundred seventy-six thousand workers struck in Petrograd in January and February 1917—and even in 1916 troops sent to suppress disturbances had refused to do so. By early 1917 the capital had only a few days' supply of grain in reserve and was a tinderbox ready to ignite.

On the other side of the Eastern Front, inside Germany and Austria-Hungary, the situation was equally grim if not quite so explosive. Here it was not only the urban centers that were in trouble. The problem was not just bad management—though there was enough of that—but a true, protracted, and by 1917 pervasive absence of the necessities of life. Neither empire had done anything to prepare for a long war, let alone for what amounted to a years-long siege, and both had begun experiencing shortages of food when the war was only a few months old. As early as October 1914 ten thousand horses were slaughtered in Vienna. The following spring, when German farmers defied a ban on feeding grain and potatoes to livestock, the Berlin bureaucracy ordered the mass butchering of all hogs. Nine million animals perished in this *Schweinemord,* and the consequences were uniformly unfortunate. After a brief collapse, pork prices rose sharply and permanently, and there was no longer enough breeding stock to replenish the supply.

A number of factors contributed to making the naval blockade as devastating as it was. The jerry-built political structures of the German and Austro-Hungarian Empires made consistent central control and even coordination practically impossible; Bavaria blocked the removal of its produce to other parts of Germany, while Hungary began selling its agricultural surplus to Germany rather than sharing it with Austria. Before the war Germany had been importing two million tons of nitrate and phosphate fertilizers per year, plus six million tons of grain for fodder and a million seasonal agricultural workers. As this input dwindled, agricultural productivity fell; grain production declined by half between 1914 and 1917. Inevitably, the needs of the armies were given first priority, and these were colossal and inexorable: seventeen million pounds of meat, sixty million pounds of bread, and one hundred thirty million pounds of potatoes every week. The first food riots erupted in Vienna in May 1915, in Berlin five months later. Food prices rose 130 percent in Berlin during the first year of war, 600 percent in two years. Even for industrial workers wages did not come close to keeping pace, climbing only 78 percent for men employed in German war plants from 1914 to 1917 (women were paid substantially less) and 52 percent for men in nonmilitary factories. Profiteering was widespread, creating new millionaires whose conspicuous prosperity made them objects of popular hatred.

Heavy rains, early frost, and shortages of fertilizer and labor made the 1916 harvest a disastrous failure, and outright famine became widespread. The potato crop, increasingly essential as meat and dairy products became nearly unobtainable, fell by half in Germany and more than that in Austria-Hungary. Scores of thousands of people were lining up at soup kitchens every day. Textiles were being manufactured from paper and plant fiber, shoes from paper and wood, coffee from tree bark. Destitute war widows—Germany already had tens of thousands—spent their days waiting in long lines with their children for pathetically tiny rations. The diet of adult Germans consisted of a grotesque black "war bread" containing little real grain, fatless sausage, and a weekly allowance of three pounds of potatoes and one egg. Germans increasingly relied, for sheer survival, on one of the least appealing vegetables known to man, the humble turnip.

The bad harvest was followed by the long, cold winter of 1916–17, remembered ever after as "the turnip winter." The chief physician at one of Berlin's principal hospitals reported that eighty thousand children had died of starvation in 1916. In Austria families were allowed to heat only one room of their houses, which led to an epidemic of frozen and burst pipes. People were using dogs to pull their carts through the streets of Vienna—until it became necessary to eat the dogs. Even in Hungary, once rich in agricultural output, people were eating horses and dogs. German schools were closed for want of heating fuel. The average daily adult intake of calories, estimated at thirty-four hundred before the war, fell to twelve hundred. Deaths from lung disease increased from fourteen to nearly twenty-three per 100,000 women. Rickets, a deformation of bones and joints caused by malnutrition, became widespread among children.

"One of the most terrible of our sufferings was having to sit in the dark," a German woman wrote of life during the blockade. "It became dark at four in winter. It was not light until eight. Even the children could not sleep all that time. One had to amuse them as best one could, fretful and pining as they were from under-feeding. And when they had gone to bed we were left shivering with the chill which comes from semi-starvation and which no additional clothing seems to alleviate, to sit thinking, thinking." A German who was a schoolboy during the war would recall that "everybody seemed to be keeping rabbits because of the shortage of meat. They took us out in whole classes and sent us into the country to help the farmers. We liked that, but it meant we didn't get much teaching. All the teachers were out as soldiers anyway, and generally the whole life of the country was becoming grimmer. There was a strong sense of people saying, 'This war is lasting too long.' Some became quite outspoken. The feeling was that the war was lasting too long and that Germany didn't have much chance of winning it, because the conditions within the country were getting so very difficult."

Even the expected bounty from the conquest of Romania made little difference, increasing the amount of grain available in Germany and Austria by barely 6 percent. In both countries once-prosperous city-dwellers were venturing out into the countryside to trade jewelry and prewar clothing made of authentic wool and cotton for whatever food they could find. In Vienna tens of thousands of women were trying to survive through prostitution. As governments repeatedly expanded the work week to increase factory output, strikes by workers not earning enough to feed their families grew in frequency, size, and violence. Mobs of women looted stores and government food depots.

This is the dark background against which, on the ninth day of 1917, Germany's leaders met for a showdown over the question of submarine warfare. The kaiser was there, of course, still his empire's All-High Warlord though increasingly passive and incapable of asserting himself. Hindenburg and Ludendorff were there as well, recently back from their inspection of the Western Front and freshly convinced that continued stalemate was the best Germany could hope for there in the coming year. Also present were the navy's leaders, most notably Henning von Holtzendorff, chief of the navy's general staff and a passionate advocate of the submarine as the only way of bringing Britain to its knees. Finally—last to arrive, because not invited until almost too late—was Chancellor Bethmann Hollweg.

In response to pressure from the United States, Germany had been keeping its submarine fleet in check since September 1915, when unrestricted operations were brought to an end. Bethmann had insisted on this measure, and though the kaiser supported him, most of the generals and admirals were furious at him for refusing to lift restrictions. Their estimates of what a renewed campaign could accomplish, however, had changed with the passage of time. At the beginning of 1915, in urging the removal of all restrictions, the admirals had said that such a step would put Britain in serious trouble within six weeks. Now, with the submarine fleet considerably expanded, Holtzendorff was saying that the job could be done in six months. Bethmann was horrified. He remained certain that what Holtzendorff was proposing would bring the United States into the war, and he dreaded the consequences. The kaiser asked Holtzendorff for his view. "I will give Your Majesty my word as an officer," the admiral replied, "that not one American will land on the Continent."

Ludendorff's views on the subject were no secret to anyone. Two weeks earlier he had sent Bethmann a telegram stating that a U-boat campaign was "the only means of carrying the war to a rapid conclusion," and that "the military position does not allow us to postpone." Though Kaiser Wilhelm shared Bethmann's fears, a far stronger ruler than he would have found it difficult to resist the demands of his officers. Virtually the entire German nation was clamoring for an end to restrictions on U-boat operations. Industry, the armed forces, the population at large—all were experiencing the ruinous effects of the blockade, and all had come to see submarine warfare not only as justified morally and legally but as absolutely necessary in practical terms. The Reichstag passed a series of resolutions opposing the limits that Bethmann was now nearly alone in trying to maintain.

The issue was quickly settled. Bethmann dutifully restated his reasons for opposing any change. But then, having done so, he withdrew his opposition. "I declared myself incompetent to criticize the judgment of the military experts who insisted that the war could not be won on land alone," he wrote later. "In view of these facts and of the declared readiness of Headquarters to risk war with the United States, I could not advise His Majesty to do other than to accept the opinion of his military advisers." In yielding as he did, Bethmann removed whatever basis the kaiser might still have had for resisting. He surrendered the last barrier to an unrestricted submarine campaign—very nearly the last barrier to America's entry into the war. More than one fateful page was turned. Control of German policy passed conclusively out of the hands of the kaiser, out of the hands of the kaiser's government, and into those of Erich Ludendorff.

The ultimate tragedy, from the German perspective, is that

the decision taken on January 9 arose out of profoundly mistaken assumptions. Holtzendorff was wrong in his appraisal of the submarines' effects, and of America's military potential; this would become clear soon enough. Ludendorff was equally wrong in believing that Russia remained capable of offensive operations on the Eastern Front. If the U-boat decision had been deferred by just a few months, the truth about Russia's collapse would have made it unnecessary. Washington's principal grievance against Germany would have been removed.

The decision having been made, the Germans had no time to waste. It seemed essential, in order to demonstrate that if the war continued the British would starve as Germany was starving, to cut off British imports before the 1917 harvest was brought in. This meant before August 1, which in turn meant—Holtzendorff having predicted that the U-boats would need six months—starting by February 1. These calculations were as sound as they were simple, but the conclusions drawn from them were pure wishful thinking. Holtzendorff estimated that the submarines could sink six hundred thousand tons of shipping monthly from February through May, four hundred thousand monthly thereafter. He believed that losses of this magnitude would discourage many neutral shippers from trying to reach Britain, whose ability to continue the war would thereby come to an end.

These forecasts were accurate enough in the near term. Even in January, while still allowing American merchantmen to pass by unharmed, the U-boats would sink numerous ships totaling more than three hundred thousand tons. The lifting of restrictions became effective on February 1, and in that month five hundred and forty thousand tons would be sunk—well over half of them British. This total was followed by five hundred and ninety-three thousand tons in March, eight hundred and eighty-one thousand in April, five hundred and ninety-six thousand in May, and six hundred and eighty-seven thousand in June.

The German public rejoiced over the start of the campaign and the deliverance that it seemed to offer. But there was no deliverance. Life became more difficult in Britain but never nearly as difficult as in Germany and Austria. The flow of imports slowed for a time but never came close to stopping. The British and Americans put into service many of the German freighters that they had

Homeward bound
U-boats returning to port at the end of a North Atlantic hunting expedition.

impounded in ports around the world at the outbreak of the war. As they became more adept both at sinking German submarines and at eluding them, it became obvious that the U-boats were going to deliver none of the things that Holtzendorff had promised, and that American entry into the war was going to be anything but unimportant.

Holtzendorff, who had been so terribly wrong, would nevertheless keep his job. Ludendorff, who had supported Holtzendorff with every political weapon at his disposal, not only kept his job but became de facto autocrat of Germany. Only Bethmann Hollweg would be purged.

CONSUMING THE FUTURE

UNDER PRODDING FROM ERICH LUDENDORFF, THE Reichstag late in 1916 approved an Auxiliary Service Law that carried the concept of total war to a level previously unimagined. It put every German male between the ages of seventeen and sixty at the government's disposal. Anyone not sent to the war could be assigned to a munitions factory, to agricultural labor, to a desk in the bureaucracy—to whatever the war ministry decided. Once in an assignment, no one could quit without permission. Those who disobeyed could be jailed for a year and fined.

At the same time, presumably because the law had made cheap labor plentiful, the government ordered massive increases in the manufacture of war matériel. Gunpowder and light artillery production quotas were doubled to twelve thousand tons and three thousand barrels per month respectively. The target for machine guns was tripled to seven thousand per month, and rifle production was boosted to one hundred and twenty-five thousand monthly.

The service law did not go as far as Ludendorff had wanted. He had proposed applying it to women, particularly to all the childless war widows who were, or so he complained, idling away their days. He had wanted to close the schools and universities. He had proposed these things in spite of the fact that unemployed women far outnumbered the available jobs, and every youth of sufficient age and fitness was already in uniform. But even in the limited form accepted by the Reichstag, the measure proved to be unenforceable, a bureaucratic nightmare that angered the workers and their unions while accomplishing little. It was soon abandoned.

The new production quotas likewise were often not met. But they were typical of what all the belligerent countries were trying to do as the war entered its third year. They were throwing everything they had—their people, their production capabilities, all the wealth accumulated over generations of industrial development—into the effort to destroy one another. The longer the war continued, the deeper they were willing to dig. Even as they weakened physically, with able-bodied men growing scarce and essential commodities even scarcer, their commitment to fighting on grew stronger. Almost no plausible measure was regarded as too extreme.

Which gives rise to a rather elemental question: where did the money come from? How did Germany and Austria-Hungary and Turkey and Bulgaria on one hand, Britain and France and Russia and Italy on the other, pay for such an immense and protracted struggle?

The answer, in a nutshell, is that they didn't. None of them even tried. In addition to being the greatest bloodbath in the history of western Europe and the greatest in eastern Europe until the Second World War, the Great War was a process by which all the great powers, victors and vanquished alike, transformed themselves from bastions of prosperity into sinkholes of poverty and debt. Financially as in so many other ways, the war was a road to ruin.

This development was not unforeseen. As technological progress accelerated in the nineteenth century and fueled tremendous military expansion, the question of how much a general war would cost became one of the great imponderables facing the governments of Europe. In 1898 a Russian named Ivan Bloch produced a six-volume study, *Future War,* in which he postulated that armed conflict between the great powers would mean "not fighting, but famine, not the slaying of men but the bankruptcy of nations and the break-up of the whole social organization." He predicted that any such war would be short because financially insupportable. Twelve years later a book titled *The Great Illusion,* by the Englishman Norman Angell, became an international best-seller by predicting that not even the winners could possibly benefit from a major war. Military power, Angell said, had become "socially and economically futile, and can have no relationship to the prosperity of the people exercising it." Such a warning seemed credible: when Angell's book appeared, all the great powers were spending scores and even hundreds of millions of dollars annually on their armies and navies. Such spending continued to increase through the last four years of peace, and much of the increase was made possible by borrowing. Only Britain, wealthiest of the European powers and the one with the smallest army, was balancing its budget.

What was not foreseen was the ability of the industrialized nations to go on fighting year after year even while devouring themselves financially. As astute an economist as John Maynard Keynes was a year into the Great War before he understood that total war would not cause total financial collapse. "As long as there are goods and labor in the country the government can buy them with banknotes," he wrote in September 1915, "and if the people try to spend the notes, an increase in their real consumption is immediately checked by a corresponding rise of prices." The truth, he concluded, was that bankruptcy would never force the great powers to stop fighting. They could be stopped only by the exhaustion of their manpower, their physical resources, or their will to continue. The next few years showed him to be entirely right.

With the start of the war, every one of the nations involved cast aside any semblance of financial restraint. As early as October 1914 Chancellor of the Exchequer David Lloyd George was admonishing the British war office not to come to him for approval before ordering whatever it thought it needed. It was the same in every capital: governments worried not about how much they were spending but about whether their military leaders were doing everything possible (which often meant *buying* everything possible) to outmatch the enemy. Budgets ceased to matter.

Great nations found themselves unable not only to pay their bills but even, in some cases, to pay the interest on what they were borrowing. By 1917 the German government's expenditures amounted to 76 percent of net national product; they had been 18 percent just before the war. Tax revenues were covering only 8 percent of the spending. That same year Britain's military spending was 70 percent of national output, and revenues were about a fourth of expenses. France's military budget, thanks to heavy borrowing, was equal to or even more than total output.

The strategies adopted by the various countries for maintaining sources of credit varied greatly and were almost indescribably complicated. The problems were greatest for the least developed nations, Russia and Austria-Hungary in particular. The solution in both cases was reliance on stronger senior partners. Russia began borrowing from its allies as early as October 1914. Eventually it borrowed £568 million from London and three and a half billion francs from Paris— colossal sums for the time, equivalent to billions of dollars. Germany

On the home front
A French couple with what remains of their home.

found it necessary to be similarly generous to Austria-Hungary, and later to Turkey and Bulgaria as well. The Russians had compounded their difficulties by shutting down the state monopoly on alcohol early in the war as a gesture of austerity, patriotism, and willingness to sacrifice. This accomplished nothing except cutting off a fourth of Petrograd's revenues, creating a huge black market in vodka, and worsening inflation.

Not one country attempted to meet its expenses or even reduce its deficits through increased taxes. Where taxes were increased, the purpose was either to inhibit inflation by soaking up some of the wages flowing to workers or to maintain a flow of revenue sufficient to satisfy the credit markets. New taxes were sometimes imposed on profiteers, but more to maintain public morale (damaged everywhere by the spectacle of tycoons reaping fortunes while everyone else suffered) than to increase revenue. Tax systems became less rather than more progressive. Governments tried to limit the amounts of money available to working people for the pursuit of increasingly scarce goods while simultaneously helping the wealthy to retain their assets for investment in postwar rebuilding.

The situation first became serious for the Central Powers, which virtually from the first day of the war had lost their merchant fleets and access both to their own overseas investments and to global sources of credit. They had to do nearly all their borrowing internally, through loans from domestic financial institutions and the sale of bonds. They were surprisingly successful. Germany issued war bonds twice annually. The many marks raised in this way covered two-thirds of its war costs.

The British and French were far more able than the Germans to repatriate money they had invested overseas, and because of the naval blockade only the Entente was able to buy and borrow from the United States. But gradually, inexorably, their treasuries were depleted. Questions arose in New York and Washington about their ability to make good on their debt. In November 1916 the U.S. Federal Reserve Board warned its member banks against continuing to buy foreign—which meant British and French—treasury bills. The result was a near-panic in which London retaliated by briefly ceasing to place orders in the United States and urged France to do likewise. By April 1917 the British were spending $75 million a week in the United States, were overdrawn on their American accounts by $358 million, and had only $490 million in securities and $87 million in gold to draw on to make good their debt. In short, they were only weeks away from insolvency.

But this was a crisis for the United States too. American manufacturers and farmers had become dependent on sales to the Entente, and American banks were owed immense amounts. A British and French financial collapse—never mind the outright defeat of the two nations—would have been a disaster for the U.S. economy. Thus the German submarines were not Washington's only reason for wanting to save the Entente. In purely practical business terms, it became dangerous for the United States *not* to enter the war.

It is estimated that the war ultimately cost $208 billion—this at a time when skilled workers were paid a few dollars a day. The final bill was $43.8 billion for Britain, $28.2 billion for France, and $47 billion for Germany. In each case, the result was the same. The wealth of all the belligerent countries was drastically reduced.

The ultimate result is expressed in the word *disinvestment.* All the European powers stopped making the kinds of investments required for real economic growth. Everything, even the future, went into the flaming cauldron of the war. Britain, that paragon of affluence and commercial success in 1914, ended the war sunk in debt, its civil infrastructure a shambles. The Europeans had begun the war at the pinnacle of the world's economic and financial hierarchy, and they ended it as wrecks. Ivan Bloch had been wrong about the feasibility of keeping such a war going. About the consequences, however, he had turned out to be dead right.

Chapter 8

A New Defense, and a New Offensive

*"This is a plan for the army of
the Duchess of Gerolstein."*

—Louis Lyautey

O n February 24 British troops near the French city of Arras
reported something exceedingly strange. The German lines
opposite them were being shelled—by *German* artillery. Scouting
parties sent out to investigate discovered something even strang-
er: the enemy's trenches had been abandoned. The men who had
occupied them were nowhere to be seen. The purpose of the shelling, clearly, was to destroy what the departing soldiers had left behind.

One of the most remarkable tactical moves of the Great War,
in its improbable way one of the boldest, was in process. After
two and a half years of Western Front combat in which both
sides had clung desperately to every yard of barren turf, the Germans were pulling back. Though the extent of the withdrawal
remained for a time not at all apparent—at Arras the line shifted
just a short distance, so that the British thought they were witnessing nothing more than a minor adjustment—over a period
of several weeks the Germans would withdraw twenty miles
along seventy miles of front between Arras and St. Quentin. Quietly, voluntarily, they would give up a thousand square miles
of conquered French territory. They would turn their backs on
ground soaked with their own blood, on positions that Erich von

Falkenhayn, when he was head of the high command, had ordered held at all costs.

The withdrawal was Ludendorff's doing, and it was fraught with risk. If the British and French had attacked while the Germans were abandoning their old line and before they were settled into new positions, the results could have been disastrous. It was also a task of almost unbelievable magnitude; Ludendorff's plan was not only to shift to a new line but to make that line immeasurably stronger than the one being given up. Three hundred and seventy thousand men (German reserves and civilians, Russian prisoners of war) worked for four months on the construction of the new defenses, digging trenches and subterranean chambers for the concealment of men and equipment, building fortifications of concrete reinforced with steel, and erecting huge barricades of razor-edged concertina wire. Farther east another hundred and seventy thousand workers assembled the necessary materials and sent them forward to the construction crews. More than twelve hundred trains were assigned to the project, hauling steel and concrete and everything else that was needed. And aside from that mystifying bombardment at Arras, most of it was accomplished in secret.

The withdrawal was code-named Alberich, after a maliciously tricky dwarf king in German (and Wagnerian) mythology. The new wall of defense that it created was named the Siegfried-Stellung Line by the Germans, but the Entente would call it the Hindenburg Line. The decision to construct it was among those taken by Ludendorff after he and Hindenburg replaced Falkenhayn as joint commanders in chief, and it showed once again Ludendorff's ability to think and to act on a grand scale. It grew out of the conclusions he had drawn after an inspection of the Western Front in the aftermath of Verdun and the Somme: that his armies were no longer capable of taking the offensive, that too many of Germany's diminishing manpower resources had been squandered, and that the defensive doctrine currently in use had to be scrapped.

"The decision to retreat was not reached without a painful struggle," Ludendorff would write later. "It implied a confession of weakness bound to raise the morale of the enemy and lower our own. But as it was necessary for military reasons, we had no choice." The decision was made possible by the enormous power that Hindenburg and Ludendorff together exercised in Berlin. They were the conquerors of the east, the people looked to them as saviors, and no one in the civil government, not even the kaiser, was prepared to stand against them. Again and again, in crisis after crisis, they almost always got their way—by threatening to resign if not by other means. Late in 1916, when Ludendorff demanded the mobilization of Germany's entire civilian population for the war effort, he did not get everything he wanted, but he got a great deal. Sectors of German industry that had not already converted to the production of war matériel now did so. The army itself was restructured: Ludendorff created thirty-one new divisions in the fall of 1916 and thirteen more in January 1917, mainly by making each existing division smaller while giving it more machine guns and artillery. Boys born in 1899 were drafted ahead of schedule—though they proved, upon reporting for training, to be alarmingly malnourished.

The benefits of the withdrawal, if it could be pulled off, promised to be substantial. The front as it ran southward from Arras to Soissons and the area of the Chemin des Dames ("the Ladies' Road," so named because it had been a favorite bridle path of the daughters of King Louis XV) was a great ninety-mile bulge curving westward to include the city of Noyon, only a few days' march from Paris. The Hindenburg Line would be twenty-five miles shorter, freeing thirteen divisions and fifty batteries of heavy artillery (roughly the equivalent of an entire army) for use elsewhere. This was a crucial consideration, because the German manpower situation had been difficult since mid-1916. At the start of 1917 the Germans had two and a half million men, 134 divisions, on the Western Front. Facing them were nearly four million Entente troops organized into 175 divisions (a total expected to rise substantially by year end as the BEF continued to expand). The danger that Germany would be numerically overwhelmed seemed to be increasing with every new month.

The creation of the new line would also enable Ludendorff to install, from scratch, the kind of physical infrastructure needed for a new kind of defense. Under his new approach, there was no longer to be a German front line in the traditional sense. The now-customary continuous line was replaced by small, mutually supportive steel-and-concrete camouflaged blockhouses laid out in a checkerboard pattern and manned by machine-gun crews. Wherever possible, these blockhouses were positioned on the forward slopes of hills, from which they would look down on attacking troops. They would be shielded by high rows of razor wire configured so as to channel attackers into narrow, lethal passages as had happened more or less inadvertently at the Somme. The men in the blockhouses, rather than standing their ground and fighting to the death, were to fall back when they had done what they reasonably could to slow the enemy's advance. The old, brutal system, in which troops were packed together in the forward trenches in an effort to create an immovable mass and were expected to die at their posts, became obsolete. In its place was something intended to be significantly more flexible and much less costly in terms of lives.

The first true defensive line, in the new system, would be far to the rear—as much as a mile behind the blockhouses, beyond the reach of enemy mortars and light artillery. Another line would be another mile back, and the reserves would be positioned even farther in the rear than that, safe from most artillery but ready to counterattack as soon as an opportunity appeared. The result would be an elastic defensive network designed to draw the enemy into a miles-deep killing zone, one in which the reserves were no longer reserves at all in the traditional sense but a strike force poised to throw the enemy back at that point of maximum vulnerability where his initial thrust had exhausted its energy.

This was Ludendorff's vision for the Western Front in 1917. It had everything to recommend it except for the short-term risk—the possibility that an Entente offensive (and one was sure to come before long, possibly early in the year) might catch the Germans midway through their withdrawal and between their old and new lines. This risk seemed so great that even Ludendorff hesitated—until fate intervened.

At the beginning of February the Germans intercepted and decoded a message sent from the Italian foreign office in Rome to Petrograd. It contained bad but not surprising news: the British and French were preparing an attack on the Western Front. It was to be yet another massive offensive, bigger even than the Somme, involving some one hundred divisions. But there was good news too, and it was very good indeed. The attack would not be coming until April—two months or more in the future. The Germans would have time enough to complete and man their new line. They would have time to school the troops in the execution of the new system. On February 4 Ludendorff ordered work to proceed, and it was fully under way five days later.

The Hindenburg Line, as it took shape, proved far too formidable for the humble term *trench warfare* to remain appropriate. It began with a trench, but one that was to remain unoccupied. This trench was almost ten feet deep and twelve feet across—a trap for tanks, and an equally forbidding obstacle for men advancing on foot. Behind it, one after another, were five or more rows of barbed and razor wire, each row twelve feet deep and twice a man's height, each twenty yards distant from the next. Then came the blockhouses, with two machine guns in each. Beyond them—dangerously far beyond, for enemy infantry trying to advance under fire—lay the first true line, a largely underground beehive of chambers and passageways covered with up to eight yards of earth and impregnable to artillery and bombs. Farther back still, also down below the surface and positioned wherever possible on a reverse slope so as to be almost unreachable by artillery, were two lines of guns. This was defensive warfare raised to a new plane. It appeared to be invulnerable. It was the work of a commander of immense vision, energy, and ambition—a man prepared to bend the entire German Empire to his purposes.

And it was made possible by the fact that the British and French would not be attacking until April.

Entente planning for 1917 had begun in much the same way as the preparations for 1916: with a gathering of the high commanders at Joffre's château in Chantilly, and with all the assembled generals eager to get back onto the offensive and finish off the Germans. This meeting took place on November 15, and the British, French, Italians, and Russians had no difficulty in agreeing once again that they would all attack simultaneously. They agreed also that they would wait until May, so that snow would not be a problem on the Eastern Front or for Italians pushing into the Alps. French General Robert Nivelle, now popular in Paris as the supposed hero of the final stages of the Battle of Verdun, presented a plan for a February attack on the Chemin des Dames, but it was set aside.

The assembled commanders even repeated themselves in failing once again to agree on where, exactly, the British should attack. As usual, Haig wanted to strike in Flanders, on the old Ypres battleground, with the old objective (dear to the Royal Navy, and of unquestionable strategic value) of capturing the Belgian ports. Once again Joffre wanted the British to be concentrated farther south, near if not actually on the old Somme line, and once again he was able to argue that his wishes should prevail because the French would be providing most of the troops. This point of disagreement was a mere detail, however. The generals more or less cheerfully left it to be decided later. Even Haig was optimistic. David Lloyd George, then still minister of war, arrived at Chantilly late in the discussions, after the decisions had been made. Though he had long since evolved into one of Britain's most determined advocates of victory at whatever cost, he was also appalled by the Western Front's casualties and not at all satisfied that they had been necessary or worthwhile. He was infuriated when he discovered that the military men had once again shown themselves to be incapable of coming up with anything better than a continuation of what was, in his view, their "legacy of inevitable disaster." But there was nothing he could do—at the time.

During the six weeks remaining until the end of the year, the earth shifted under all their feet. Lloyd George became Prime Minister of England. Joffre fell from power and was replaced by Robert Nivelle. Suddenly the agreements reached at Chantilly mattered hardly at all.

The new year began with a January 5 conference of Entente leaders at Rome. Neither Haig nor Nivelle attended. They were separately engaged in developing their plans for the next offensive, the former still focusing his hopes on Flanders, the latter on a Chemin des Dames attack that would leave little room for action in Flanders. Lloyd George used the occasion to try to reduce the bloodletting on the Western Front. To the surprise and annoyance of General Robertson, who had accompanied him to Rome as chief of the imperial general staff, he proposed giving first priority in 1917 to a reinforced strike out of Italy aimed at destroying the remains of the Austro-Hungarian armies and taking

Vienna out of the war. This idea had been conceived originally by Luigi Cadorna, the Italian commander in chief, and it had strategic merit. For Lloyd George it had the attraction of making another Somme or Ypres almost impossible in the near term. It would also take precedence over Nivelle's Chemin des Dames campaign and a supporting British attack that Nivelle wanted at Arras. It would involve Italian infantry, mainly; the principal British and French contribution would be enormous quantities of artillery.

Cadorna, when he saw how hostile the British generals were to his idea, began to backpedal. The French premier, Aristide Briand, also was unethusiastic, perhaps because he knew that Nivelle would never agree. Having so recently participated in the displacement of Joffre, Briand would be in an awkward position if he disregarded the wishes of the man to whom he had entrusted the armies of France. Lloyd George, despite his recent elevation, had no leverage with which to impose his will on the others. He had become prime minister in spite of having few real friends in positions of power anywhere. Many members of his own Liberal Party resented him for having colluded in the fall of Asquith, the Conservatives had long and with good reason regarded him as a foe, and it was widely expected that his government could not last more than a few months. His hopes for an Italian offensive having died for want of support, he departed Rome a thwarted and disgruntled man.

Lloyd George stopped in Paris on his way home, and upon arrival he was met by Nivelle, who greeted him with a smart, flatteringly respectful salute. By all accounts Nivelle was a man of extraordinary charm. His ability to make political friends had contributed at least as much as his aggressiveness and dash to his startlingly rapid rise. He now worked his wiles on Lloyd George, who, accustomed to the disdain of his own country's generals (Haig had called him a "cur," though not to his face), must have been delighted. Nivelle brought unique advantages to his meeting with the Welsh Lloyd George. He was not only not Catholic but Protestant, and not only a Protestant but one who did not hesitate to display contempt for the faith of his Catholic countrymen. This had made him attractive to the French republicans, and now it made him attractive to the British. He spoke perfect

David Lloyd George
Weary of the generals'
"legacy of inevitable disaster."

English without an accent (his mother was English-born), which again made him exceptional among France's senior commanders. And—no small matter, as it turned out—he had a pleasing skull. Lloyd George was a believer in phrenology, the then-popular pseudoscientific discipline based on the idea that character and destiny are revealed in the shape of one's head. He considered the contours of Nivelle's head and saw victory there.

Nivelle explained his plan for the Chemin des Dames. It would involve a multipronged attack on the German line west of Reims, and he proclaimed with invincible confidence that it would decide the war in twenty-four to forty-eight hours. It would be a French attack primarily (Lloyd George had to be pleased to hear that), supported by a complementary British offensive. It would use the same tactics that had produced such supposedly glorious results in the final weeks at Verdun. (Lloyd George was unaware that those results were achieved only after the Germans had given up on Verdun, and that the operation that produced them was on a comparatively tiny scale.) The death blow would be delivered by a strike force (Nivelle called it his Mass of Maneuver) made up of twenty-seven divisions of French infantry and cavalry. Best of all, Nivelle offered assurances that the offensive not only would not but *could* not turn into another Verdun or Somme. He promised that if somehow the impossible happened and it did not succeed within two days, he would bring it to a stop.

Lloyd George was won over. He invited Nivelle to travel to London and meet with the British war cabinet on January 15. There again Nivelle proved irresistible, winning over British politicians who had been steeped in skepticism by the failures of 1915 and 1916. The only difficulty was the question of timing. Nivelle wanted to start quickly—as early as February. Haig, not happy about what amounted to a rejection of his Flanders offensive, was suggesting May. The result was compromise: what would go down in history as the Nivelle offensive was approved for April 1. It was only two weeks later that Ludendorff learned of it and ordered completion of the Hindenburg Line to proceed.

When the Entente leaders met again at Calais on February 26, they made it clear to Haig that he was expected to be ready at the beginning of April, and that he was to cooperate fully with Nivelle. In letters written after the conference, Haig referred to a proposal that Lloyd George had rejected out of hand. "The French put forward a terrible scheme for putting the British under a French commander in chief," he wrote in a letter to a friend. "Thank God even Lloyd George thought it went too far." This incident requires note because of Haig's later claim, made after the war and long widely believed, that Lloyd George had himself suggested putting the BEF under Nivelle and had been stopped only by the threat of Haig, Robertson, and other British generals to resign or face courts-martial rather than agree. Though required to attack at Arras rather than in Flanders, in all matters tactical Haig retained control of the BEF. He was explicitly given the right, if in disagreement with Nivelle, to appeal directly to London. He left Calais with the further assurance that Nivelle's campaign would be ended if it did not lead quickly to a breakthrough, and that the BEF would then be free to resume preparations for an offensive in Flanders.

Nivelle remained supremely confident. He moved his headquarters to a magnificent château that had once been the property of Marie Antoinette. He took his wine cellar with him—took all the appointments appropriate to a generalissimo, along with the favorites ("Butcher" Mangin prominent among them) who had been with him at Verdun. Those he did not favor found themselves sidelined. Foch was banished to the dormant front near Switzerland. Pétain, Castelnau, and others found that they too no longer mattered. No one mattered but Nivelle. In his lofty and splendid isolation, he proceeded with arrangements for a Napoleonic stroke that was now just weeks in the future.

But a problem emerged: several of France's most proven commanders were convinced that the Nivelle plan had no chance of success. The reluctance of Haig and his generals might be written off as sour grapes, but Pétain, Foch, Franchet d'Esperey, and even General Alfred Micheler (who had been given command of Nivelle's Mass of Maneuver) all were soon arguing that Nivelle was preparing to do the wrong thing in the wrong place and was headed for disaster. No one wanted to listen: not Lloyd George, not the president or premier of France.

Late in 1916 France's most brilliant colonial soldier, a onetime protégé of Gallieni's named Louis Lyautey, had been brought back from Morocco for what would prove to be a short tour of duty as minister of war. When he learned what Nivelle was planning, this future Marshal of France was incredulous. "This is a plan for the army of the Duchess of Gerolstein," he exclaimed, making reference to a popular operetta. But still no one would listen. When in March Paul Painlevé became minister of war (the Briand government had fallen because Lyautey refused to share military secrets with other members of the government), he tried strenuously to persuade Nivelle to make his attack more limited, less ambitious, less risky. No one in a position to make a difference would listen.

HEARTS AND MINDS

BY 1917 MORALE HAD BECOME A CRITICAL PROBLEM both in the armies of the great powers and among their home-front populations. As the level of sacrifice being demanded of people in and out of uniform came to seem almost insupportable, and as the death and deprivation seemed to be achieving practically nothing, the enthusiasm that had marked the beginning of the war fell ever closer to the vanishing point. Soldiers wanted to go home and wanted to know why they couldn't. Their families wanted them home and wondered what their sons were dying for. All of them wanted a return to what had been lost.

Governments responded in a variety of ways. They became harsher in suppressing dissent. They increased their emphasis on propaganda, on bolstering the loyalty of people whose suffering had not yet turned them into dissenters. The control and manipulation of information that all the warring nations had been practicing since August 1914 became more systematic, more sophisticated, and farther-reaching. It came to be an essential function of government.

Inevitably, to the extent that the propaganda was effective, it made an end to the fighting more difficult to achieve. "However the world pretends to divide itself," the English writer Rudyard Kipling declared in a London newspaper, "there are only two divisions in the world today—human beings and Germans." Similar things were being said about the British by writers in Berlin. People everywhere were being told that this war was no continuation of politics by other means, no traditional struggle for limited objectives. It was a fight to the death with the forces of evil, and the stakes were survival and civilization itself. It is no simple thing to make people believe such things and later persuade them to accept a settlement based on compromise.

Control of public opinion was made possible by the same economic and technological developments that had made Europe capable of fighting such a war. In all the belligerent countries, the most developed of them especially, industrialization had drawn millions of people from traditional, predominantly rural ways of life into fast-growing urban centers. It created a need for the education of these people—for a literate workforce—while slashing the cost of producing newspapers. Both an enormous new reading public and new means of reaching that public came into existence. London alone had sixteen daily papers by 1914, and the largest were selling nearly a million copies a day. Germany had four thousand newspapers—half of them dailies—with a huge total circulation.

If the readers of these newspapers were not necessarily well informed, they were certainly receiving information of a kind that their ancestors had rarely seen. The strains and pressures and opportunities of modern life were politicizing them as never before. People understood that they had a stake in the issues of the day, they formed opinions on those issues, and increasingly they felt entitled to express themselves and be heard. As the war made their lives darker and harder, governments found it increasingly necessary to persuade them to endure.

The war's first propaganda fell into place almost effortlessly. As invariably happens at the start of a war, people everywhere were swept up into ecstasies of patriotism. Almost everything they heard and read assured them that their glorious armies would soon be victorious, that their cause was a noble one, and that the enemy was wicked in ways rarely seen in history. Formal censorship of the press was scarcely necessary; many newspaper owners were themselves caught up in the general frenzy, and few of those who had doubts found it convenient to express them. There were exceptions in all countries—the *Manchester Guardian* said Britain was entering "a war in which we risk everything of which we are proud, and in which we stand to gain nothing"—but they rapidly grew rare.

British public opinion had been particularly well prepared for the conflict. Throughout the two decades leading up to the war, Germany's growing economic strength and emergence as a naval power provoked cries of alarm in many of the most influential newspapers. The Rupert Murdoch of the day, Alfred Harmsworth (more famous as Lord Northcliffe after he was elevated to the peerage), owned a number of important papers aimed at different segments of the public. He used all of them to alert his readers to what he saw as the German menace, fostering, one of his competitors complained, "an anti-German frame of mind that takes no account of the facts." When war came and no correspondents were allowed near the front, neither Northcliffe nor his competitors complained about having to depend on official sources for information about what was happening there. Nor did they see reason for complaint. Many saw it as their mission not to inform the public (which long remained ignorant of the realities of the war) but to do their bit to keep morale high.

A Press Bureau was established in August 1914 (by Winston Churchill, ready as always to take the broadest possible view of his responsibilities) to determine what should and should not be published. Soon thereafter a Defense of the Realm Act made it unlawful to print anything "of such a nature as is calculated to be or might be directly or indirectly useful to the enemy." At about the same time a new Secret War Propaganda Bureau was given responsibility for assisting the foreign office in wooing neutral nations. Where the home front was concerned, the propaganda machinery remained fairly primitive. It placed less emphasis on actively manipulating public opinion than on preventing the publication of anything that might limit confidence in the success or heroism of the BEF. The task was simplified by a general absence of people prepared to publicly question the cause.

The French government began by leaving the management of war news in the hands of General Joffre and his staff. Throughout the first half of the war this simple system worked about as well as Britain's, and for similar reasons: the newspapers tended to be content to get their information from the military, and few people with a voice in public life wished to question or complain. The Germans entered the war with probably the world's most fully developed information-and-propaganda system, but it was directed not at the home front but at other countries—the United States especially—and was crippled when the British navy cut the only cable connecting Germany with the Western Hemisphere. From the beginning, the Berlin government was even less sophisticated than the British and the French in trying to shape the opinions of its own people. Like so many other problems that would grow worse for the Germans as the war dragged on, this one arose at least in part from the peculiarities of German society. The Junker elite loathed and feared the urban masses, wanted nothing from them but acquiescence and obedience, and was loath to do anything to indicate that public opinion mattered.

For two years all three countries relied primarily on a strict but easily maintained press censorship (often banning publications that refused to cooperate), on assuring their populations that the war was being won, and on depicting the enemy as evil incarnate. Their methods were predictable and in retrospect sometimes seem ridiculous. The German story line was that the Reich was fighting a defensive war against a cabal of unscrupulous enemies determined to destroy it. The British and French followed an exactly opposite script, one in which they were defending civilization against Huns who wanted to rule the world. Even the atrocity stories that were staples in the newspapers of the Entente were mirrored in those of the Central Powers. The Germans were reported to be cutting off the hands of French boys so they could never become soldiers, to be raping children and bayoneting infants. The German public was told that the Russians were poisoning the lakes of East Prussia and cutting off the limbs of captured German soldiers, and that the French and Belgians made a specialty of gouging out prisoners' eyes. Lying was epidemic—newspapers ran old photographs of Russian pogroms against Jews as evidence of Germany's "rape of Belgium"—and officials with access to the facts were not immune. David Lloyd George, long before he became prime minister, was declaring in public that "the new philosophy of Germany is to destroy Christianity."

This state of affairs began to change, and to change in ominous ways, as the war entered its third year. The British government, alarmed by spreading strikes and protests, singled out pacifists and conscientious objectors for blame. Pacifist leaders (many of them socialists who had remained silent earlier) were arrested if they attempted to address assemblies of workers. As labor unrest became commonplace everywhere (British munitions production was briefly brought almost to a stop in May 1917), the governments of Britain, France, and Germany all tried to ignore the real causes: rising living costs, long hours working under harsh conditions, and shortages of food. In all three countries strikers were accused of treason, and governments increased their efforts to make the public agree.

Nineteen-seventeen was the turning point. In February of that year Lloyd George established a Department of Information to tighten control over what the public was told. Four months later he created a National War Aims Committee, with former prime minister Asquith as its president. Despite its name, the committee's purpose was not to articulate the nation's war aims (which were intentionally kept vague so as not to bring political divisions to the surface), not to respond to German propaganda, but to neutralize domestic dissent. The unprecedented sum of £240,000 was appropriated to finance its activities, which were focused on blanketing areas of labor unrest with gruesome (and generally fabricated) tales of German atrocities. The committee's aim was to persuade workers that there could be no negotiated peace with such a barbaric foe.

France created a new propaganda agency, a Maison de la Presse that was part of the ministry of foreign affairs but aimed at the home front. It too focused on atrocity stories, on the war as a crusade to save justice and liberty, and on what it depicted as the essentially spiritual character of the struggle. Ludendorff followed suit by starting a program of "patriotic instruction." Its purpose, inevitably, was to remind an increasingly disheartened German public that it was involved in a struggle to save civilization. "Good propaganda must keep well ahead of actual political events," said Ludendorff. "It must act as pacemaker to policy and mold public opinion without appearing to do so. Before political aims are translated into action, the world has to be convinced of their necessity and moral justification." He was becoming a thoroughly modern general, an innovator not just in battlefield tactics but in the uses of PR.

The results of all the propaganda would be tragic. By raising the stakes of the war beyond the limits of reason, the propagandists ensured that whichever side lost would feel terribly, irredeemably wronged. And that whichever side won would find it difficult to deal rationally with the populations it had defeated.

Chapter 9

Revolution and Intervention

*"All this is really no business of mine but
something must be done. And if I don't do it
nothing will be done."*

—Erich Ludendorff

The six weeks leading up to the Nivelle offensive brought
two of the most world-changing events since the French
Revolution. The Romanov dynasty that had ruled Russia for
three centuries came to an end, and the United States entered the
Great War.

Like many of history's great upheavals, the end of the Romanovs was both a long time coming and shockingly sudden. In
military terms, Russia's situation had seemed mildly promising
as 1917 began. The Brusilov offensive, in spite of its costs, had
been one of the war's most brilliantly successful campaigns and
had given the Russian commanders new confidence. The winter
had provided the army with months in which to regroup, Austria-Hungary was obviously no longer dangerous, and France and
Britain were sending huge amounts of equipment—artillery and
shells in particular, but other weapons and essential matériel as
well—to the Eastern Front. Even Germany, its forces stretched
thin, no longer seemed as intimidating as before. As Churchill
would write after the war, to emerge victorious Russia had only,
from 1917 on, to maintain an intact front. Its generals thought
they could do more than that. When Joffre originally proposed
a multifront offensive for 1917, they showed no reluctance to

join in. When Joffre fell and was succeeded by Nivelle, and when Nivelle's plan for the Chemin des Dames became the Entente's Western Front plan for 1917, the Russians said they would have seventy divisions ready for action when Nivelle attacked. Those divisions would be equipped with tens of thousands of machine guns and pieces of artillery. Such numbers made even generals as cautious as Evert, whose timidity in 1916 had saved the Germans from ruin, willing to attack.

These promising developments would mean nothing in the end, however, because the Russian home front was slipping into chaos. The winter of 1916–17 was exceptionally hard, with extraordinarily deep snows and temperatures so low that more than a thousand steam locomotives froze up and exploded. The railway system, never more than satisfactory, became barely capable of functioning. Throughout most of Russia the situation remained manageable, but the flow of food and fuel into the largest cities slowed to a trickle. The problem was especially serious in Petrograd—which in addition to being the capital was Russia's most important industrial center—because of its remoteness from the interior. By early in the new year factories were shutting down for lack of fuel. The workers were left with nothing to do but roam the streets, cold and hungry, frightened and angry. The bakeries that had flour could not make bread because they could not heat their ovens; the women of the city, unable to get their usual scant rations even by waiting in line for hours, began to loot. The tens of thousands of troops stationed in Petrograd, many of them untrained and bewildered recruits, were harangued by wandering agitators calling for revolution and an end to the war.

Almost everyone by now was demanding change, especially the appointment of a "responsible" Council of Ministers—one willing and able to carry out the duties for which the tsar's cabinet was supposed to be responsible. But nothing changed, and the expectation of a final crisis came to be almost universal. That any such crisis would almost certainly topple the regime seemed obvious, and outbursts of hostility toward the tsar and tsarina became commonplace even in privileged circles. General Sir Henry Wilson, a senior member of the British general staff, visited Russia and reported that "everyone—officers, merchants, ladies—talks openly of the absolute necessity of doing away with them." When the young

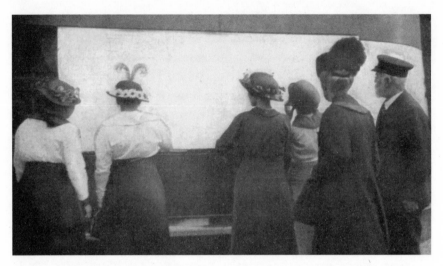

Russian women reading the latest list of deaths on the front

democratic socialist Alexander Kerensky told the Duma that Nicholas and Alexandra must be deposed "by terrorist methods if there is no other way," he was cheered and promised protection. Though his words were suppressed by the newspapers, they spread through the capital and were everywhere applauded. On February 23 the Duma's president, ending a meeting with the tsar, said he thought they would not meet again because revolution was imminent. Nicholas, who had retreated deep within himself by now, did not respond. Among the civil authorities, however, an uprising was regarded as so nearly inevitable that the police were issued machine guns.

Nicholas was weary, isolated, impervious to advice, incapable of action, possibly aware of what lay ahead and internally preparing himself for it. He had spent much of the winter secluded with his wife and children in their palace at Tsarskoe Selo near the capital. Almost everyone who had access to him—Alexandra excepted—was begging him to appoint a new cabinet, but he did nothing. The tsarina, a majority of one, was urging him to rule autonomously and ruthlessly. "Lovy, be firm, because the Russians need you to be," she wrote him after he left home for army headquarters. "At every turn you show love & kindness—now let them feel your fist, as they themselves ask. So many of late have told, that we need the knout. It's strange, but that is the Slav nature." But even to her

Alexander Kerensky
*His fatal error: trying to keep
Russia in the war.*

appeals Nicholas made almost no response. People who met with him would remember how distant and detached he had become, seemingly untouched by what was happening. He would listen patiently to repeated appeals for action, smile vacantly, and say and do nothing. The only official in whom either Nicholas or Alexandra placed any confidence was the ludicrously incapable Alexander Protopopov, who gave less attention to his duties as minister of the interior (which duties were supposed to include getting essential supplies into the cities) than to the séances at which he assisted the tsarina in trying to establish contact with the late Rasputin. Protopopov was a singularly manipulative fool: in the presence of the tsarina he would fall to his knees and declare in tones of wonder that he had seen the figure of Jesus standing behind her.

On Wednesday, March 7, Nicholas raised the hopes of every reasonable member of the government by abruptly announcing that on the following day he would go to the Duma and declare his intention to appoint a new cabinet. That same evening, however, he made a second announcement—that he was leaving immediately for army headquarters, that there would be no visit to the Duma, that he was, in short, breaking his promise. Within hours he was gone from the capital. It is likely that he departed both at the insistence of his wife, who thought Nicholas was being intolerably weak if he so much as acknowledged the existence of the

Duma, and to escape from her constant instructions and appeals. He had no particular need to be at army headquarters, with the Eastern Front still locked in winter. That may be precisely why he went—to escape from everything. He was perhaps in a depression, perhaps simply resigned. As soon as he was gone, events began to unfold rapidly.

On Thursday street demonstrations in Petrograd turned as before into riots and looting. Cossack troops, the cavalry traditionally used by the tsars to control unruly or merely disfavored civilian populations, were sent into the streets to restore order. These Cossacks, however, were mainly young, inexperienced, and half-trained; those of their elder brothers who had not by now died in the war were off at the front. Significantly, they did not carry with them the whips with which Cossacks customarily subdued crowds. Instead of attacking the rioters, most of whom were women, they mingled with them and assured them that they were in no danger.

On Friday the crowds were even larger than before, the rioting more violent. The leaders of the capital's most radical leftist groups, suddenly bold after years of ferocious repression, called for a general strike.

On Saturday the crowds and the Cossack horsemen were once again out in force. The latter, ordered to fire on the demonstrators, turned their guns on the police instead. This almost unimaginably shocking turn of events, the end of generations of Cossack loyalty to the regime, sent the cabinet into a panic. Members sent a telegram to the tsar offering their resignations and asking him to return to Petrograd and form a new government. The reply that he sent was magnificently absurd in its irrelevance to the situation: "I order that the disorders in the capital, intolerable during these difficult times of war with Germany and Austria, be ended tomorrow."

That tomorrow, Sunday, March 11, was in fact comparatively quiet, the streets almost empty. Before leaving the capital Nicholas had given his newest prime minister, an aged and well-intentioned but ineffectual veteran of the Petrograd bureaucracy, a signed order for the dismissal of the Duma. His instructions had been to hold this document in reserve and use it if necessary. Now it was delivered to the assembly, whose members promptly voted to disregard it. In doing so they effectively joined the revolution.

On Monday tens of thousands of soldiers joined it as well. Many simply deserted. Others joined the civilians in a fresh outbreak of rioting. The capital's huge armory was attacked, taken, and pillaged. Thousands of rifles were carried off into every corner of the city and into the hands of every would-be revolutionary. Courthouses and the offices of the secret police were set ablaze. Prisons were broken into, their inmates freed to flee or join the mob.

On Tuesday, March 13, Tsar Nicholas finally left army headquarters and began the five-hundred-mile rail journey back to Petrograd. His progress was slow. In yet another of his endless acts of well-intentioned foolishness, Nicholas had ordered that his train should follow an indirect route so as not to interfere with the flow of troops and matériel to the front. As he drew closer to the capital, he encountered increasing signs of disorder. Finally, with the imperial train still far from its destination, reports of violence along the line ahead made it clear that further progress would be impossible. The locomotive pulling Nicholas and his entourage was shunted into the railyard of the obscure provincial town of Pskov, where it came to a halt.

Telegrams arrived from senior military commanders—one came from Grand Duke Nicholas in the Caucasus—telling the tsar that it had become imperative that he surrender the crown. Nicholas seemed unsurprised. He showed concern only for his wife and children, virtually prisoners since the forty-thousand-man garrison at Tsarskoe Selo had joined the rebellion. All five of the royal children were sick with the measles—no trivial disease in 1917. The tsarina, unable to communicate with her husband, at first found it difficult to believe that any of these things were happening. Soon, however, she recovered. She threw herself into the care of her daughters and twelve-year-old son, and into arranging meals and warm quarters on the ground floor of the palace for the two companies of Cossacks that alone remained loyal. After years of almost insanely self-destructive behavior, she began to display the strength and calm acceptance that would support her family through the months of life that remained to them.

On March 15 two new Russian governments came into existence. One was proclaimed by the Duma, now dominated by the thirty-six-year-old Kerensky, who became minister of justice. Its rival was the Soviet of Soldiers' and Workers' Deputies, made up, as its name indicated, of representatives of army units and industrial laborers. The two set up operations in the same building and agreed that the tsar must abdicate. Members of the cabinet, instead of resisting, presented themselves to the Duma and, pathetically, asked to be arrested for their own protection. A delegation set out from Petrograd to get Nicholas's signature on an act of abdication. By the time its train reached the tsar, he had made up his mind to sign. On one point, however, he refused to cooperate. Asked to pass the crown to his son, he insisted not only on abdicating himself but on doing so on behalf of the boy as well. He understood that the delicate Alexis, his life in almost constant jeopardy because of his hemophilia, would if made tsar be handed over to the care of strangers. This, Nicholas declared, was out of the question.

And so the crown passed to Nicholas's younger brother Michael, a feckless individual who years before had made himself the black sheep of the Romanovs by secretly marrying a twice-divorced commoner with whom he had already had a son. But the new Tsar Michael II, fearing for his life as revolution and chaos spread, abdicated almost immediately. He declared his willingness to resume the crown later, but only if it were offered to him by an assembly of the people's elected representatives. With that, the Romanov dynasty ended. The Duma's provisional government declared its determination to continue the war until victory was achieved. The former Tsar Nicholas, displaying no bitterness, supported the government in this respect without reservation. In a farewell message to the troops, he said that "whoever now dreams of peace, whoever desires it . . . betrays . . . the land of his fathers."

The end of the tsarist regime was soon known to the world. Paris and London, and also those members of the U.S. government who were eager to join the war, received it with something like jubilation. Alliance with the Russian autocracy had from the start been an embarrassment for the French and the British, one that complicated their efforts to depict the war as a conflict between democracy and dictatorship. Now, apparently, Russia too was becoming a democracy—and one no less eager to continue the war than the tsar had been. The Entente was being purified.

In Russia itself the news was tragic for many, a cause of celebration for many more. "God in heaven, it's like a miracle of miracles, it all happened so quickly," a soldier serving as a clerk in a field hospital recorded in his diary. "Such joy, such anxiety that I can't get on with the work. I want to convince all the doubters that these developments are good news and that things will get better for us now. Good Lord, it's so great that Tsar Nicholas and the autocracy no longer exist! Down with all that rubbish, down with all that is old, wicked and loathsome. This is the dawn of a great new Russia, happy and joyful. We soldiers are free men, we are all equal, we are all citizens of Great Russia now! . . . The police are being arrested, their weapons are taken away from them. Please God let it be like this forever."

The tsar's abdication came six weeks after Germany's announcement that it was resuming unrestricted submarine warfare. It immediately made clear just how great a mistake that announcement had been, and that Germany's political system had broken down almost as completely as Russia's. That system, by putting virtually all authority in the hands of a tiny elite with little connection to the nation as a whole, had been creaking badly even before the war. In the best of times it was superficially tidier than Britain's parliamentary monarchy and the French republic with its innumerable changes of government. But even under strong and brilliant leadership (a rare commodity in a political culture as stunted as imperial Germany's), the German system operated in a kind of splendid isolation, with no mechanism for adapting and renewing itself in response to trouble. When its leadership fell as far short of strength and brilliance as it did after Bismarck, it had few outside resources to draw on. Under pressure of war its isolation became pitiable rather than splendid. Thus the Germany of 1917: a civil government unable to control or even compete with the army's high command, and a military inept in politics and diplomacy and blind to its own ineptness. And thus the emergence, more by default than by anyone's design, of a dictatorship led by a man, Erich Ludendorff, who though one of the outstanding generals of German history was devoid of political gifts, experience, or skills.

This dictatorship was quick to produce political disasters equal in magnitude to Ludendorff's military achievements. The first came in October. Like those that followed, it had its roots in Ludendorff's fixation on strengthening the German war machine by every possible means, and in his consequent embrace of what would come to be called "war socialism"—the subordination of every available human being and every particle of the economy to the imperatives of the war. Manpower was in short supply not only in the army but on the home front, and even before Ludendorff's rise to supreme power some thousands of Belgian industrial workers had been forcibly transferred to the factories of Germany. The factory owners wanted more, and almost as soon as he arrived in the west, Ludendorff decided to satisfy them. He set a quota of two hundred thousand transfers. Bethmann, other members of the government, and even the general in command in Belgium all dissented, saying that the program could have little impact on industrial output but would be a propaganda fiasco, a boon for the Entente in its tireless campaign to portray Germany as nothing better than an outlaw nation.

These arguments were swept aside. Late in October Belgian industries that were not contributing directly to the war effort were shut down and mass deportations began. In three months more than sixty thousand Belgians, many of them in bad health, were herded onto cattle cars and transported to Germany under brutal conditions. Ultimately the entire program proved to be as useless as its opponents had warned and had to be brought to an end. By that time, however, it had done terminal damage to Germany's international reputation, ending any possibility that the American public might respond other than with revulsion to the resumption of unrestricted submarine warfare.

A second great blunder came soon afterward. Early in November Germany announced that it intended to create a new Kingdom of Poland out of an unspecified portion of the territories from which the Russians had been expelled in 1915. Like the Belgian deportations, this idea had not originated with Ludendorff, but he had seized upon it and forced it on the government in spite of the reservations of Bethmann Hollweg and others. The underly-ing hope was that the Poles would be so grateful for the gift of a nation of their own after generations of partition and occupation that they would eagerly fight on the side of the Central Powers. The originators of the plan, in selling it to Ludendorff, held out the vision of quickly recruiting five divisions of Polish soldiers—a mil-lion men eventually—to fight against the Russians. Desperate for manpower, incapable of listening to those who knew far more than he about the psychology of the Polish people, Ludendorff lunged at this mirage.

The idea was doomed from the start. Long experience of tsar-ist rule had taught Poland's rural peasantry to hate the very idea of military service. And the promised "kingdom" was far too vague, too obviously false, to tempt anyone to die in the service of Germany. It was not to be created until after the war's end, and its hereditary ruler would be a German rather than a Slavic prince. It was to include only part of the former Russian Poland, other parts of which were to be annexed by Austria or Germany. Some of it was to be not Polish at all but territory stripped from Russia proper. Its army was to be under German command, and the kingdom was to be barred from entering into treaties without German approval.

It was an absurdity, and it produced predictable results. In all of Poland only a few thousand men answered the call to arms, barely enough to make up a few battalions which would be disbanded before the war's end without ever seeing active service. What mat-tered far more—what turned the episode into a disaster—was the impact on Russia. Throughout the summer and autumn of 1916 Bethmann Hollweg had been sending out feelers to Petrograd, ex-ploring the possibility of a separate peace. The response had been ambiguous—Tsar Nicholas had no interest—but not hopelessly negative. This was the period of Boris Stürmer's tenure as prime minister and foreign minister in Petrograd. (Significantly, he was able to hold on to both offices despite being so anti-British and pro-German as to be frequently accused of treason. The Russian court had always included a pro-German faction, and that faction was still in place after two years of war.) But the loss of Poland had been a grievous blow to Russian pride and a profoundly disturbing threat to what the Petrograd government saw as its security needs in Europe. The announcement of a make-believe Polish state amounted to a declaration that Poland could never again belong to Russia. It ended any possibility of a separate peace between Germany and the government of the tsar—a peace that Germany urgently needed. By provoking resentment in every part of Russian society, it ensured that when revolution came and the provisional government succeeded to power, it too would be determined to continue the war. In the longer term, by weakening the provisional government and opening a path to power for the Bolsheviks, it would have even more disastrous consequences for Russia than for Germany. But Ludendorff would misplay that card too.

It has to be said, in fairness to Ludendorff, that his intrusions into diplomacy and politics and even industrial management appear to have been motivated less by a desire to aggrandize himself than by a determination to win the war and by frustration with the inertia and incompetence of the German governing system. "All this is really no business of mine but something must be done," he lamented to Crown Prince Wilhelm. "And if I don't do it nothing will be done."

The greatest blunder was Germany's handling of its relations with the United States during the first three months of 1917. It began with the decision to resume unrestricted submarine warfare, but that set in motion a whole series of subsequent mistakes that proved to have terrible consequences. Those mistakes culminated in an American declaration of war that more competent German leadership might very well have averted.

At the center of the story stands Arthur Zimmermann, who had become head of the German foreign ministry at the end of 1916 after Hindenburg and Ludendorff purged Gottlieb von Jagow for being too inclined to side with Bethmann. Zimmermann was neither inexperienced nor inordinately self-serving; before the war he had declined the foreign ministry because he didn't want to have to deal with the Reichstag and the other chronic headaches that went with the job. A man of considerable charm, he was enjoyed by everyone who knew him, including the American ambassador in Berlin, who was otherwise no admirer of Germany or the Germans. But he was also one of those men capable of believing that they know everything about subjects of which they actually

Arthur Zimmermann
Author of history's most costly telegram.

have no useful experience. Years before the war, upon returning to Germany from the Far East, Zimmermann had crossed the United States by train, spending a few days in San Francisco and New York along the way. Ever afterward he had postured as an authority on all things American, and too many Germans who had never been across the Atlantic accepted his pronouncements. Such Germans were all too willing to ignore the cabled warnings of their own ambassador to the United States, the intelligent and capable Count Johann von Bernstorff, who had been in Washington for eight years and understood that the nation that had fought the American Civil War was not to be trifled with.

In the weeks between the decision to lift restrictions on U-boat operations and the public disclosure of that decision, Zimmermann cast about for ways to exploit it to Germany's advantage. He devised a plan, a scheme for winning new allies—Mexico and Japan, of all the improbable candidates—while at the same time entangling the United States in a war on the North American continent. He began the execution of this scheme by addressing a message to the German ambassador in Mexico City:

WE INTEND TO BEGIN UNRESTRICTED SUBMARINE WARFARE ON THE FIRST OF FEBRUARY. WE SHALL ENDEAVOR IN SPITE OF THIS TO KEEP THE UNITED STATES NEUTRAL. IN THE EVENT OF THIS NOT SUCCEEDING, WE MAKE MEXICO A PROPOSAL OF ALLIANCE ON THE FOLLOWING BASIS: MAKE WAR TOGETHER, MAKE PEACE TOGETHER, GENEROUS

FINANCIAL SUPPORT, AND AN UNDERSTANDING ON
OUR PART THAT MEXICO IS TO RECONQUER THE
LOST TERRITORY IN TEXAS, NEW MEXICO AND ARI-
ZONA. THE SETTLEMENT IN DETAIL IS LEFT TO YOU.

WE WILL INFORM THE PRESIDENT OF THE ABOVE
MOST SECRETLY AS SOON AS THE OUTBREAK OF WAR
WITH THE UNITED STATES IS CERTAIN AND ADD THE
SUGGESTION THAT HE SHOULD, ON HIS OWN INITIA-
TIVE, INVITE JAPAN TO IMMEDIATE ADHERENCE AND
AT THE SAME TIME MEDIATE BETWEEN JAPAN AND
OURSELVES.

PLEASE CALL THE PRESIDENT'S ATTENTION TO
THE FACT THAT THE UNRESTRICTED EMPLOYMENT
OF OUR SUBMARINES NOW OFFERS THE PROSPECT OF
COMPELLING ENGLAND TO MAKE PEACE WITHIN A
FEW MONTHS.

ZIMMERMANN.

Zimmermann originally intended to have his proposal delivered
by hand via a submarine being prepared for a voyage across the
Atlantic. When that venture was canceled, he sent the message
by telegram, and in code, to Bernstorff in Washington, with instructions to relay it to Mexico City. Germany's transatlantic cable having been cut by the British navy early in the war, he used a
British-owned telegraph line that President Wilson had made available to Germany for communications having to do with possible
peace negotiations. Like everyone else in the German government,
Zimmermann was unaware that British naval intelligence had long
since broken the German encryption system and was intercept-
ing virtually every transatlantic message sent by Berlin. Thus the
Royal Navy knew the contents of Zimmermann's telegram almost
as soon as Bernstorff did. Its intelligence chief, as soon as he saw an
incompletely decoded version, understood that the Germans had
bestowed upon the Entente a propaganda weapon of incalculable
power. He also understood, however, that he had a problem: how
to make Zimmermann's proposal known to the Americans without
also revealing to the Germans that their code had been compromised. He locked the message in a safe and kept it secret even from

his own government. There it would remain for more than five weeks, a bomb waiting to be detonated.

On January 22, still ignorant not only of the telegram but of Germany's impending resumption of submarine warfare, President Wilson gave a speech to Congress in which he spoke of the sacredness of freedom of the seas, his vision of a League of Nations that would make future wars impossible, and his hope that the war could end in "peace without victory." The British and French were scornful, furious at Wilson for refusing to say that peace was impossible until Germany had been crushed. Ambassador Bernstorff was barraging Berlin with messages, begging his government to respond to Wilson's request for peace terms and delay its submarine warfare declaration long enough to give Wilson an opportunity to get a conference scheduled. Even if Wilson failed, Bernstorff observed, a display of German willingness to cooperate would have a favorable impact on American opinion. His pleas were ignored. Soon the German admirals were able to say that it was too late for a change of plans—the first of the U-boats had put to sea and could not be recalled.

On January 31, pursuant to his instructions, a disconsolate Bernstorff announced the resumption of unrestricted submarine warfare to U.S. secretary of state Robert Lansing, expressed his regret at having to do so, and withdrew. Foreseeing the outcome, he began preparations for a return to Germany.

On February 2 Wilson met with his cabinet, found that its members were almost unanimously in favor of going to war, and replied that he still had hopes of staying out, of acting as a peacemaker. An American liner, the *Housatonic,* was sunk by a U-boat that day without loss of life.

On February 3 the United States severed diplomatic relations with Germany, giving Bernstorff his passport and inviting him to depart. Cornered by reporters, the ambassador said simply that "I am finished with politics for the rest of my life."

The situation remained static for nearly three weeks, with Republican leaders of the Senate and former president Theodore Roosevelt calling for war and Wilson remaining silent. The ports of the East Coast became gridlocked with loaded merchant ships, their owners afraid to order them to sea. The rail lines leading into those ports began to back up as well, unable to unload the

huge quantities of freight bound for Europe. Farmers and manufacturers, workers and shippers, labor unions and corporations all
began to scream as costs rose, perishable goods began to rot, and
sales and jobs were jeopardized. Everyone looked to the White
House and waited. It began to seem possible, to the astonish-
ment of many and the delight of some, that not even the U-boat
campaign was going to persuade Wilson to make war. The public
remained unsettled where the question of war was concerned.
There was much support in the east, much opposition in other
regions, and millions remained undecided.

But then on February 23, British intelligence having found a
way to disguise the means by which it had learned the contents
of the Zimmermann telegram (this involved pretending that a
copy had been found on an intercepted ship), Foreign Secretary
Arthur Balfour shared its contents with the American ambassador
in London. It was forwarded to Secretary of State Lansing, who
had long been an advocate of war and so was pleased to present it
to Wilson. The president was furious. Lansing persuaded him to
keep the telegram secret until its disclosure could have maximum
impact.

On February 26 Wilson again addressed Congress, this time requesting approval for the arming of American commercial ships
with navy guns and gun crews. The House of Representatives approved his request almost immediately and by an overwhelming
majority. There was no vote in the Senate because of a filibuster organized by the antiwar progressive Robert LaFollette of Wisconsin.
Prowar factions in the Senate and elsewhere were seething, calling
LaFollette and his allies traitors and Wilson a coward.

Late on February 28, with Wilson's approval, Lansing released
the Zimmermann telegram to the press. It made banner headlines
from coast to coast the next morning, stunning the nation. The
story had only one flaw: it was almost too astonishing to be believed. Opponents of war denounced it as a fraud, a British concoc-
tion. Many Americans found this denunciation easier to believe
than that the German government's foreign minister could have
done such a thing.

Then, after days of dispute, Zimmermann again came to the
rescue of the Entente. Questioned by reporters—he was unique
among German officials in his willingness to talk with the press—

he blithely declared that of course the telegram was authentic. *Of course* he had sent it. Why not? he asked innocently. Obviously he had not intended it to be used unless and until the United States declared war.

On March 7 the president went into deep seclusion, refusing to see or confer with anyone. On March 12 he emerged to issue an executive order for the arming of American merchant ships, thereby bypassing the LaFollette filibuster. Then he again withdrew, and the days crept past with the world holding its breath. On March 18 three American ships were sunk by U-boats. Two days later Wilson called his cabinet together and again asked its members for their opinion. To a man, they favored war.

On April 2 Wilson delivered the speech, never to be forgotten, in which he told Congress that war was unavoidable because "the world must be made safe for democracy."

The House approved a War Resolution with 373 members in favor, fifty opposed.

On April 4 the Senate approved the same resolution eighty-two to six.

And on April 6 the United States declared war on Germany.

THE COSSACKS

FOR MANY AMERICANS, GETTING INTO THE EUROPEAN war was a thrilling prospect. It was an opportunity not only to have an adventure, not only to make the world safe for democracy, but to demonstrate to the Old World the superiority of the New.

The Old World, after all, was *old:* tired, benighted, corrupt. The New, by contrast, was the natural habitat of the free and the brave. The inability of the Entente to defeat the forces of evil in more than two years of war was itself an expression of Old World decadence, and it was time for the Yanks to show the British and French how to get it done.

If the Americans had looked for a European people akin to their image of themselves, for a population of rugged, even cowboylike individualists with a history of fighting for their independence, they might have found one in an extremely improbable place. The closest counterparts to the legendary heroes of the Wild West were, ironically, the Cossacks of the Russian steppe—the ultimate symbols of tsarist repression.

No one had been surprised, when Petrograd began to dissolve into chaos, that it was Cossack horsemen who were sent into the streets to restore order. Russians had learned to expect to see Cossacks wherever there was trouble. As often as not, it was Cossacks who *made* the trouble. They were the tsar's enforcers, the scourge of peasants and Jews, a bludgeon used by the Romanov regime to smash whoever seemed to need smashing.

Their very name had become synonymous with despotism. Even today it conjures up images for people who know little of Russian history: rifles and sabers, boots and saddles, mustachioed killers in big shaggy hats. Cossacks had put the first Romanov on the throne in 1613, conquered and settled Siberia, and broken the back of Napoleon's invading army in 1812. They formed the core of Russia's enormous cavalry throughout the Great War.

"Age-old subduers and punishers," Trotsky called them. But that was only part of the story. Tolstoy, who had lived among them in his youth, said that what made them Cossacks was their "love of freedom."

They were unlike any other people in Europe—not exactly Russian but not an entirely distinct tribe, certainly not a military caste like the Junkers of Germany. For centuries their homelands were a kind of melting pot open to anyone brave or desperate enough to enter. There is no better analogy than the gun-toting freebooters of the American West.

Until the fifteenth or even sixteenth century there was no such thing as a Cossack. The Cossacks emerged in the period when the Mongols of Genghis Khan, having forced their way deep into central Europe, controlled an enormous expanse of the fertile open plain, the steppe, that rolls almost without interruption from Hungary to northern China. As the Mongols' expansion ceased and the Great

Cossack fighters
*"Age-old subduers
and punishers."*

Khan's empire was divided into pieces, what is now southern Russia and Ukraine was left in possession of a subgroup called the Tatars. These warlike nomads lived by plunder, constantly raiding the Russian domains centered on Moscow to the north. They carried away not only treasure but thousands of captives to be sold in the slave markets of the Ottoman Empire. To the Russians, the Tatars were a terror, the lands they controlled a dark pit of barbarism.

By the sixteenth century the tsars were consolidating their control of Muscovy and, in the process, reducing the Russian peasants to serfdom—to mere property, a condition not far removed from outright slavery. Not surprisingly, the peasants were less than pleased. Their only choices, however, were to submit, to die, or to flee. There was no place to go except southward into the lands of the Tatars, and those who went were, almost by definition, the boldest and most defiantly self-reliant members of the Russian peasantry. Once beyond the reach of Moscow, they clashed with, learned from, gradually dominated, and finally merged with the Tatars. A new phenomenon among the peoples of the world arose: a community of untamed Orthodox Christian warrior horsemen, of mixed Slavic and East Asian blood, living by the sword and ruled by no one.

The early Cossacks (the origins of the name are shrouded in mystery but apparently have roots meaning both "wanderers" and "free people") created an extraordinary society. Unlike any of the surrounding peoples, they were radically democratic. Even their women were remarkably free. Every member of the community voted, and a leader called the *ataman* was elected for a term of only one year so that power could not be gathered permanently into any single pair of hands. Anyone wishing to join the community—runaway serf, Tatar nomad in search of home and fellowship—had only to declare a wish to do so and accept at least nominally the Orthodox faith. Ethnic or racial origin meant nothing, property was held in common, and there was no such thing as a hereditary elite.

As their numbers and power increased, the Cossacks became both worrisome as a potential threat and attractive as potential allies. For a time the tsars were pleased to have them as a buffer between Russia and its traditional enemies to the south and east. Eventually, however, Moscow attempted to change them from allies into subjects, and that gave rise to conflict. The Cossacks refused to take an oath of loyalty to the tsar, causing much trouble, but Moscow allowed them to keep any territories they conquered (Siberia being one example) so long as those territories became officially part of Russia. In this way the Cossacks came to occupy vast domains. The ambivalence of their relationship with the tsars was never plainer or more painful than during the lifetime of Michael Romanov, the first member of Russia's last dynasty. It was Cossack support, after years of chaos, that allowed Michael to assume the throne. Later, however, when he sent a representative into the Cossack lands to demand submission, the unfortunate emissary was put into a sack and thrown into the River Don.

The seventeenth and eighteenth centuries brought Russian wars on the Cossacks and repeated Cossack rebellions. They ended in defeat for the Cossacks, their absorption into the Russian nation, and the gradual dilution of some of their most distinctive traditions. The *ataman* came to be an appointee of the tsar. Some of the strongest Cossack families seized large estates and established themselves as a landowning aristocracy on the traditional Russian model. Even serfdom was introduced into the Cossack lands. The old traditions were not entirely extinguished, however, and the tradition of every Cossack male being a proudly independent warrior proved to be least extinguishable of all. The price, however, was high. Cossack youths owed the tsar first twenty, then eventually thirty years of military service. Each was required to provide his own horses and equipment, a heavy burden for ordinary families. Sadly, the Cossacks' contempt for outsiders made it easy for the tsars to convert them into instruments of repression, even of genocide. In 1648–49, in just one of the crimes that steep their history in blood, they massacred three hundred thousand Jews. The reward, for a Cossack soldier, was a grant of land at the end of decades of service.

They were never mere murderous robots, however. During the 1905–6 revolution, their arrangement with the Romanovs threatened to break down when Cossack regiments mutinied rather than allow themselves to be used to stamp out rebellion by peasants and workers. A crisis was averted only by the dissolution of the disloyal units. When the Great War came almost a decade later, the Cossacks were once again ready for duty. They were mobilized en masse, boys and middle-aged men alike, creating severe hardships for the families left behind. They made up at least half of the Russian cavalry, and the willingness of the Russian general staff to send them and their horses against German machine guns made the war even more disastrous for them than for most Russians. By 1917, when they were called upon once again to put down popular uprisings, many of them had had enough. They stood aside and allowed the revolution to proceed.

Of all the signs that Nicholas II and his whole system were finished, this was the clearest.

Chapter 10

The Nivelle Offensive

"Do you know what such an action is called?
It is called cowardice."
—General Alfred Micheler

Amazingly, the first three months of 1917 had passed without huge effusions of blood on any of Europe's fronts. Men were still being killed by the hundreds, but not in great offensives. They were dying in what had become merely the routine way. They died every day in the almost absentminded exchanges of artillery and sniper fire that punctuated life in the trenches. They died every night in the dark bloody excursions into no-man's-land that had become so common that almost no one noticed.

On April 6 France's political and military leadership gathered in President Poincaré's railroad car in the forest of Compiègne near Paris. The subject was the impending offensive that would, General Robert Nivelle promised, bring the war to an end. The purpose of the meeting, however, was not to complete the planning of that offensive. It was to settle the question of whether the offensive was going to happen at all. Among those opposed were General Alfred Micheler, a Somme veteran chosen by Nivelle to command the army group that would attack at the Chemin des Dames, and Paul Painlevé, the recently appointed minister of war. The latter had not abandoned his efforts, which began almost the day he took office, to persuade Nivelle to reconsider. By the start of April he was practically begging, promising Nivelle that in light of the German pullback to the Hindenburg Line no one would think less of him if he changed his mind. Painlevé lacked the authority to decide the issue, however. Only Poincaré could do that.

The arguments for not proceeding were almost overwhelming. It was certain that the United States was coming in—its declaration of war became effective, in fact, on the day of the Compiègne meeting. This meant that the French could afford to rest their worn-down armies while waiting for the Americans to arrive. The fall of Nicholas II, which promised democracy in Russia and a restoration of Russian morale, also suggested that 1917 would be a good year for France to husband her strength. What mattered even more was the German withdrawal to the Hindenburg Line; this move, as Painlevé and others pointed out repeatedly, had destroyed many of the premises on which Nivelle's plan had been based from the start. The German defensive line was miles shorter and much stronger than it had been at the turn of the year. Many of the positions that Nivelle had intended to attack were now abandoned. The territory beyond those positions had been left a barren wasteland; Ludendorff, in pulling his forces back, had imitated the scorched earth policy used effectively by the Russians in retreating from Poland in 1915. Every building, every tree, every bit of railway, and every crossroads had been destroyed in the thousand square miles that the Germans gave up, and the Entente was slow to take possession of the resulting desolation. The British and French would have to attack at the two extremities of the Hindenburg Line, with a mixed command under Haig at the western end near Arras and most of the French miles to the east. Neither would be able to support the other directly.

The focal point of the French attack, the Chemin des Dames, could hardly have been a more formidable objective. The German defenses lay atop a high wooded ridge along the base of which the River Aisne followed its east-west course. The roads and railways behind the French lines almost all ran the wrong way, laterally instead of toward the front. Despite the difficulties, Nivelle proposed to overwhelm the Germans with a single crushing blow. When Joffre had first proposed a 1917 offensive, his plan had been to attack on a front of about sixty miles. Nivelle, convinced that the tactics that had worked in the final days of Verdun could

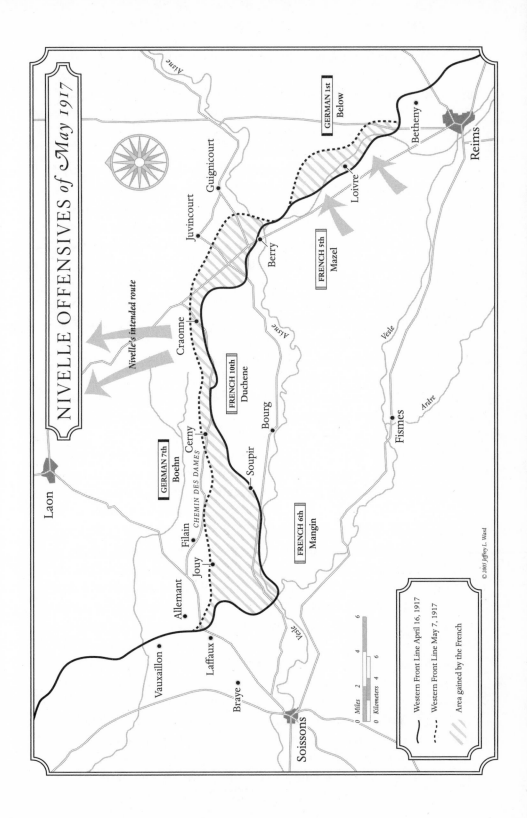

NIVELLE OFFENSIVES *of May 1917*

Laon

GERMAN 7th
Boehn

Nivelle's intended route

Aisne

Guignicourt

Juvincourt

Berry

GERMAN 1st
Below

Betheny

Reims

Loivre

FRENCH 5th
Mazel

Craonne

Aisne

FRENCH 10th
Duchene

Bourg

Cerny
CHEMIN DES DAMES

Soupir

Vesle

Fismes

Ardre

Filain
Jouy

FRENCH 6th
Mangin

Allemant

Vauxaillon

Laffaux

Vesle

Braye

Soissons

Miles   0   2   4   6
Kilometers 0   4   6

——— Western Front Line April 16, 1917
- - - - Western Front Line May 7, 1917
///// Area gained by the French

© 2005 Jeffrey L. Ward

be equally effective on a larger scale, had expanded that to a hundred miles. The Germans meanwhile, aware of what was coming, had increased the number of their divisions on and behind the Chemin des Dames ridge from nine to thirty-eight. Nivelle was undeterred. The more enemy divisions were on the scene, he said, the more he would be able to destroy.

Haig was skeptical, but his doubts were neutralized by Lloyd George's disdain for him and enthusiasm for Nivelle and for his plan. Several of France's most senior generals remained skeptical as well, but because some of them had been passed over when Nivelle was promoted to commander in chief, it was easy to attribute their objections to petty jealousy. Painlevé was so certain that disaster lay ahead that he had tried to resign from the cabinet and been refused. Now, at Compiègne, he explained his fears one final time. Again Nivelle shrugged him off. He said that if he were not allowed to proceed, he would resign. Poincaré, aware that Nivelle's resignation would mean the fall of yet another government, hoping that the offensive would save the Russians and Italians from attack and impressed anew with his new commander's absolute certainty, ended the discussion by telling him to proceed.

The offensive began on April 9 with an attack by four armies, three British and one French, on the northern edge of the old Somme battleground. It was intended partly to draw German reserves away from Chemin des Dames, but it was more than just a diversion. One of the hopes for it was that, if Haig's troops broke through, they could advance to the east and link up with Nivelle's advance. Once combined, the two forces would have enough mass to uproot Crown Prince Wilhelm's army group and drive it out of France. As at the Somme, the British preparations had been on a colossal scale. Their dimensions are apparent in the details: 206 trainloads of crushed rock brought forward to build firm roadways behind the British front, and days of preparatory bombardment by more than twenty-eight hundred cannons and heavy mortars—one for every twelve yards of line.

Haig's Canadians were particularly well prepared and rehearsed. Early on the morning of the attack they moved undetected to within a hundred and fifty yards of the German defenses through a maze of sewers and tunnels that honeycombed the earth under

Arras. Upon emerging they were able to advance under the protection of a perfectly timed creeping barrage. The Germans, their attention fixed on the French buildup at the Chemin des Dames, had not expected anything on this scale. Taken by surprise, within a few hours they were driven off most of Vimy Ridge, which dominates the countryside east of Arras. Thereafter, the advance was slowed by wintry storms and a stiffening of resistance as German reserves came into play.

"We moved forward, but the conditions were terrible," a British artilleryman reported. "The ammunition that had been prepared by our leaders for this great spring offensive had to be brought up with the supplies, over roads which were sometimes up to one's knees in slimy, yellowish-brown mud. The horses were up to their bellies in mud. We'd put them on a picket line between the wagon wheels at night and they'd be sunk in over their fetlocks the next day. We had to shoot quite a number. Rations were so poor that we ate turnips, and I went into the French dugouts, which had been there since 1914, and took biscuits that had been left by troops two years previously. They were all mouldy but I ate them and it didn't do me any harm. We also had crusts of bread that had been flung out of the more fortunate NCOs' mess at a previous date, we scraped black mud from them and ate them. One could make two biscuits last for about three quarters of the day."

Haig continued to attack for weeks, partly to give continued support to Nivelle, partly because the success of the first day had caused him to believe (as he was inclined to do in the middle of all his offensives) that he was on the verge of a breakthrough. But little more was gained. Entente casualties had been fairly light in the early going—almost trivial by the standard of the Somme— but as Haig persisted into mid-May, the total mounted at a rate of four thousand every day. Haig tried as usual to get the cavalry into action, but by the time this was possible the Germans were ready. Machine guns and artillery massacred horses and riders alike.

From a strategic perspective, the results of Arras were ambiguous. Haig had grounds for claiming success: Vimy Ridge was a valuable trophy, the Germans had had to rush in tens of thousands of reinforcements from other points along the front, and in the exhilarating first three days the British had captured fourteen thousand

One of many
Arras Cathedral, destroyed by shelling.

prisoners and one hundred eighty guns. They had also advanced between three and six miles at various points—major gains on the Western Front. On the other hand, they had achieved no break-through and had no hope of linking up with Nivelle. By the time it all ended, the Germans had taken one hundred and eighty thousand casualties, Haig's armies a hundred and fifty-eight thousand. Back in London, Lloyd George was freshly disgusted by the expenditure of so many men for such limited results.

Ludendorff was alarmed. April 9 was his fifty-second birthday, and his staff had prepared a party to observe the occasion, but he withdrew into isolation soon after getting the first reports from Arras. The early British gains, the loss of Vimy Ridge especially, seemed at first to indicate that his new system of defense did not work. "I had looked forward to the expected offensive with confidence, and was now deeply depressed," he would recall. "Was this to be the result of all our care and trouble during the past half-year?" Closer examination, however, revealed that the fault lay in the failure of the German Sixth Army's commander to *use* the system. General Ludwig von Falkenhausen had not followed instructions. Instead he had continued to do the things that he, like all the Western Front veterans on both sides, had been learning to do in two and a half years of trench warfare. He had tried to block the Canadian advance with a heavily manned and continuous front line; instead of falling back when pressed, that line had been ordered to stand its ground and so had been overwhelmed. He had kept his second and third lines close together and near the front, so that like the first they were shattered by the British artillery and overrun. He had positioned his reserves fifteen miles to the rear, too far away to make a difference at the crisis of the attack.

Where the system had been tried, however, it proved its effectiveness. The attackers had been allowed to advance into a killing zone where they were raked with artillery and machine-gun fire and then driven back with counterattacks. German losses had been kept at tolerable levels. As soon as this became clear, Falkenhausen was dismissed. Efforts were redoubled to ensure that the new system would be fully in place at the Chemin des Dames by the time the French attacked there.

Nivelle's attack came at six a.m. on April 16. From start to finish it was a contest between an offensive of the most conventional kind—more than a week of intense artillery preparation, massed formations of infantry slogging in plain view toward their objectives—and the Germans' new defense. Almost immediately it turned into something very like the debacle that Painlevé and so many others had feared. The idea that had governed all of Nivelle's planning—that the tactics he and Mangin had used to retake Forts Douaumont and Vaux at Verdun would work in this different and much larger theater—proved to be totally inadequate to the occasion. (Nor had Nivelle considered that, by the time of his attacks at Verdun, the Germans were quite prepared to abandon ruined fortresses for stronger positions in the rear.) In many places French troops had to cross the Aisne at the start of their advance, then climb a steep hillside obstructed with trees, a ragged network of ravines, and the inevitable German wire. The entire hillside was studded with German machine-gun nests so well dug in and protected with steel and concrete that they had survived the bombardment; they poured fire on the French as they came forward. The German first line was on the reverse slope, beyond the crest of the ridge. Thus most of the French shells had passed harmlessly over it, and those attackers who reached the crest were exposed against the sky. The German reserves were far enough back to be beyond reach of most of Nivelle's batteries (he was undersupplied with long-range guns), but not too far back to enter the battle quickly.

In raw manpower terms, the advantage lay entirely with the French. Nivelle had three armies that among them included fifty-three divisions—at least 1.2 million men—and all three were used in the initial assault. But twenty-seven divisions were held back as the Mass of Maneuver, which was to exploit the breakthrough when it came. To absorb this attack the Germans had twenty-one divisions in position on or near the Chemin des Dames, and another twenty-seven as their counterattack force. They had been in possession of the ridge since September 1914, so that they knew every inch of it and had had more than two and a half years to shape it to their needs. And they were commanded by Crown Prince Wilhelm; he and his staff had become well acquainted with the Nivelle offensive formula at Verdun, and they had had the winter to adapt to it. And of course they held the heights.

One hundred and twenty-eight of France's new tanks participated in the assault but accomplished nothing. As part of the new German tactics, every artillery battery was ordered to direct the fire of one of its guns at any tank that came into view. This tactic proved devastating: fifty-two tanks were blown to bits on the first day, and another twenty-eight broke down. Those that remained either fell into ditches excavated by the Germans or bogged down in mud.

The weather was on the side of the Germans. It had started to rain the night before the attack, and the rain turned to sleet followed by snow—an improbable development at this time of year. At many points the French never got close to their objectives. At others they were able, heroically and at great cost, to advance as much as two and a half miles. "A snow squall swept our position," a French tank officer wrote after observing the opening of the attack. "Our first wounded soldiers were coming in, men from the Eighty-Third Infantry Regiment. We gathered round them, and learned from them that the enemy positions were very strong, the resistance desperate. One battalion did reach the top of the Cornillet—probably the one whose gallant advance we had watched—but it was decimated by fire from intact machine gun positions, and was unable to withstand the enemy's counterattack. One of the wounded men, his arm in a sling and patches of blood on his forehead, shouted while driving by:

" 'The Boches are still holding out in the Grille Wood, but we are attacking them with grenades.'

"A helmetless lieutenant, his clothes disarrayed and with a wound in his chest, walked slowly toward our group:

" 'Ah! If only you [the tanks] had been with us! We found nothing but intact barbed wire! If it hadn't been for that, we'd be far ahead now, instead of killing each other on the spot.'

" 'We just couldn't keep moving,' an alert corporal shouted, while using his rifle as a crutch. 'Too many blasted machine guns, against which there was nothing doing!'

" 'The Boche certainly knew we were going to attack there,' the lieutenant went on, 'their trenches were jammed.' "

Even the French gains were in accord with the German defensive system. By midday the Germans were moving both their reserves and their masses of light artillery forward from the rear. They hit the French after they had been wearied and battered, sending them reeling back toward their starting point. As the day ended, the French had succeeded in moving their line forward approximately six hundred yards on average. (Nivelle had forecast gains of six miles on the first day.) The Mass of Maneuver had had no opportunity to go into action. It was another Somme.

Nivelle attacked again on the second day, this time sending his forces off in two directions in a forking maneuver. One army was to move toward the northeast and try to link up with a French force that was at the same time launching a separate, supporting assault in Champagne. This was a complete failure, first absorbed by the German defenses and then forced back. The other tine of the fork, commanded by Mangin, had some success in pushing to the north and west. It captured three towns of no great importance, but finally even Mangin's relentless aggressiveness could not keep it from bogging down. In the end his men too were driven back. The French were everywhere stymied. Nivelle kept scheduling and canceling and rescheduling attacks by his Mass of Maneuver. The strain of having to prepare again and again to die unnerved the waiting troops.

On April 19 War Minister Painlevé again intervened, trying to get Nivelle to stop. The general, who in demanding approval of his grand plan had promised to call it off if a breakthrough were not achieved within forty-eight hours, refused. The very next day he found to his chagrin, however, that he had no choice but to pause: the divisions at the front were breaking down, both their morale and their supplies of ammunition dangerously low. Late on the day after that, April 21, a new phenomenon appeared. African troops—members of elite units that had often led the assaults of Mangin's army—shocked and embarrassed their officers by shouting *Vive la paix*. "Peace! Down with war! Death to those who are responsible!" Other units were getting drunk en masse and refusing to march to the front.

On April 25, with Paris awash in rumors that put the casualty figures even higher than they actually were, President Poincaré humiliated the commander in chief by ordering an end to the attacks on the Chemin des Dames. Nivelle reacted ignobly. He blamed Mangin for the failure of the offensive and dismissed him from command of the Sixth Army. He then tried to blame Micheler as well. Micheler, who had regarded the offensive as hopeless from the start and had become almost insubordinate in saying so, responded with witheringly wrathful contempt. "What, you try to make me responsible for the mistake, when I never ceased to warn you?" he demanded. "Do you know what such an action is called? It is called cowardice."

By the time the offensive was shut down, it had cost the French two hundred and seventy thousand casualties, including tens of thousands killed. Total German casualties have been estimated at one hundred and sixty-three thousand. These were losses that neither side could afford. Nivelle was destroyed, not so much because of his failure but because he had promised so much. On April 28 Painlevé elevated Pétain to chief of staff of the French army and asked Nivelle to resign as commander in chief (a post distinct from chief of staff). Nivelle, astonishingly, refused. Instead he became increasingly reckless in assigning blame. He completed his self-humiliation by refusing to resign even after Pétain was named commander in chief in his stead. By that time Pétain was faced with an entirely new kind of crisis—an army mutiny so widespread that for a while it appeared possible that France might be unable to stay in the war.

The war had reached a point at which several of the belligerent nations were not only in trouble but in danger of breaking down. The disintegration of the Ottoman Empire was by now well advanced. The Turks, their hard-fighting but weary soldiers chronically low on supplies and reinforcements, had lost the Caucasus to the Russians in 1916. In March 1917 British forces operating out of Egypt had captured the Mesopotamian capital of Baghdad, one of the greatest jewels in the Ottoman crown. The only thing keeping Turkey in the war was the certainty that its empire was doomed if Germany went down to defeat.

Russia's provisional government too was faced with monstrous problems. It was being financed and generously supplied by the British and French but was increasingly unable to keep either its armies intact or its home front under control. On April 11 an All-Russian Conference of Soviets voted to support a continuation of the war, but it also called for negotiations aimed at achieving peace without annexations or indemnities on either side. On April 15 tens of thousands of Russian troops came out of their trenches to join with their German and Austrian adversaries in impromptu and nearly mutinous Easter celebrations. On the following day Lenin arrived in Petrograd from his long exile in Switzerland; Ludendorff, hoping to foment further disruption inside Russia, had approved his travel by rail from Switzerland via Frankfurt, Berlin, Stockholm, and Helsinki. Upon his arrival the Bolshevik leader began maneuvering his followers into an antiwar stance calculated to take advantage of public discontent. The Russians had promised a May 1 attack in support of the Nivelle offensive and had assembled a massive force for the purpose. The offensive proved impossible, however, to carry out. The troops had become ungovernable, and not enough coal could be found to operate the necessary trains. On May 2 Kerensky became leader of the provisional government. He tried to address the army's problems, but everything he did ended up making them worse. When he released all men over age forty-three from military service, a transportation system that was already on the verge of collapse found itself mobbed by middle-aged veterans desperate to get to their homes. When he abolished the death penalty for desertion, a million soldiers threw down their weapons. Many were drawn homeward by the hope of getting a piece of land when the great estates of the aristocracy were distributed to the people. Many were simply sick of war.

Austria-Hungary was a broken and empty shell barely held together by the resentful support of Berlin. Its new emperor, Karl I, not yet thirty, was a pious, earnest, and cultivated idealist who had succeeded to his family's dual thrones after having received no training in politics and no experience in the administration of anything. He desired sincerely not only to hold his empire together but to deliver its people from further carnage. In March he embarked upon one of the most quixotic undertakings of the Great War. He recruited his wife's two young brothers, the Princes Sixtus and Xavier of Bourbon-Parma, both of whom had served as stretcher-bearers in the Belgian army earlier in the war, to be his emissaries in a secret effort to initiate peace discussions with the Entente. This effort was as naïve as it was well intentioned, its naïveté most apparent in Karl's failure to tell the Germans what he was doing. When the inevitable happened and Berlin found out, Karl stood convicted in the eyes of his allies of having attempted to save himself while cutting Germany adrift (something that he does not appear to have intended). When the details of his proposal appeared in the Paris newspapers (the Germans were freshly appalled to learn that Karl was offering Alsace and Lorraine to France), he panicked and denounced the story as a malicious fabrication. This persuaded the French that he was not only a fool but a liar.

His effort had been doomed from the start. At first it generated small sparks of interest, especially in London, but by this point a negotiated peace that did not involve the dismantling of Austria-Hungary was hardly possible. Russia, Italy, and Romania had all been promised great pieces of Karl's patrimony. It was difficult to see how Britain and France could agree to a settlement that did not redeem these pledges. Karl's initiative had been little more than a last gasp of an impotent and dying regime.

If Germany was a tower of strength when contrasted with Turkey, Russia, or Austria-Hungary, serious cracks were appearing in the tower's foundations. The German nation was continuing slowly to starve, and when the flour ration was further reduced in mid-April, workers went on strike in hundreds of factories. As prices continued to rise, workers in steel and munitions plants along with miners by the tens of thousands struck for higher wages and more and better food. Behind this unrest was a deepening weariness with an endless war and with all the tragedy the war had brought. Germany's political parties, which were a barometer of public opinion even if they lacked any role in making policy, began to break apart over how to end the war and how the experience of the war should be translated into reforms. In March the Reichstag created a special committee to study a reform of the German constitution. In April the socialists, echoing their counterparts in Russia, called for peace without annexations or indemnities.

Such ideas were anathema not only to Ludendorff and the rest of the high command but to all the most powerful elements of German society. The Junkers of Prussia, the owners of German industry, and the conservative and center-right parties all were opposed to reforms that might require them to surrender any part of the power that had long belonged to them alone. Nor were they without popular support: ordinary citizens were easily persuaded that any settlement of the war must both repay the nation for its suffering and increase its security through strategic annexations of, for example, Belgium's Liège. In Germany as in all the belligerent countries, propaganda was contributing to making peace impossible. The German public had been taught that the war had been started by an Entente committed to the destruction of their nation, that in prosecuting the war the Entente had flouted international law, and that the armies of the Entente were guilty of unspeakable atrocities. To people who believed these things, it was inconceivable that Germany could accept a peace in which the aggressors were not held to account or were left with the ability to attack again.

Bethmann Hollweg saw things more clearly. Though he exasperated friends and enemies alike with his shifting opinions and pursuit of compromise, the chancellor was consistent in believing that a negotiated peace was Germany's only hope. He also saw constitutional reform—democratization—as necessary to maintain the morale of the nation. By April he was publicly advocating the elimination of Prussia's three-tiered electoral system, which reserved almost all political power to the property-owning classes. Bethmann understood that the war had made such arrangements no longer sustainable: the people were unwilling to tolerate them. In proposing reform, however, he accomplished nothing except a multiplication of his influential enemies. Hindenburg and Ludendorff felt confirmed in their certainty that he was a radical in bureaucrat's clothing and must be removed. The kaiser, himself a waffler and increasingly unable to assert himself, was generally inclined to agree with Bethmann. By repeatedly refusing to replace the chancellor, he made himself an object of contempt among the conservatives and accelerated the process by which he was becoming a marginal figure.

In the near term Germany's problems were almost trivial when compared with those facing the French in the aftermath of the Nivelle offensive. The French army, or a dangerously big part of it, was in open rebellion, refusing to obey orders, assaulting and even killing officers, deserting. Troops were crowding into Paris in a state of extreme disorder. French archives on the mutiny have been sealed since the war and will remain so until 2017, but enough is known to make clear that at its peak it was a threat to the survival of the republic. Within six weeks of its start half of the French divisions on the Western Front were rendered nonfunctional as a result of what one officer called "a sort of moral nihilism, an army without faith." The government, more euphemistically, described the problem as "collective indiscipline."

With minor exceptions, the mutiny was never genuinely revolutionary in impulse—it was not aimed at overthrowing the government or even at ending the war. Rather, it was a kind of spontaneous strike through which the soldiers declared their refusal to continue living in intolerable conditions and dying to no purpose. Thus it was susceptible to being defused with practical remedies aimed at legitimate and manageable grievances. And France, unlike Russia, possessed the means to make the necessary reforms. It had ample food and matériel and money and a reasonably competent government.

For a variety of reasons the Germans remained ignorant of the mutiny and unable to take advantage of it. Had they done so when the rebellion was at its height, they might have met with little resistance in moving on Paris. Before that could happen, however, Henri-Philippe Pétain took up his new responsibilities as commander in chief. His appointment was a stroke of good fortune for the Entente.

Pétain acted as quickly and firmly as he had upon arriving at Verdun in 1916. And he displayed great delicacy of judgment, neither cracking down so hard on the troops as to provoke worse resistance nor allowing the army to drift into deeper confusion. His first moves were aimed at reestablishing discipline. Thousands of soldiers accused of being the mutiny's ringleaders were arrested and brought to trial. Approximately five hundred of them were condemned to death, though fewer than a hundred were actually executed. (The exact numbers will remain uncertain until the records are made public.) Many went to prison, many were exiled to France's colonies, and those returned to active service found themselves subjected to the traditional forms of discipline in undiluted form.

Almost as quickly, however, Pétain also began addressing the abuses that had sparked the mutiny, "not forgetting the fact," he said, "that the mutineers were men who have been with us in the trenches for three years, our soldiers." He promised to provide many of the things that the men demanded—better food, decent shelter when not on the front lines, fairness in such matters as the granting of leave, an end to the pointless offensives that had squandered so many lives. And he saw to it that his promises were kept. Pétain himself visited ninety divisions during the crisis, standing atop his automobile to talk with the troops, listening to questions and complaints, giving straight answers. He had the great advantage of his reputation as a general who had always showed genuine concern for the well-being of the poilus.

It worked. At the height of the crisis, in late May and early June, new outbreaks were occurring at a rate of more than half a dozen every day. There began to be talk of political revolution, of forcing an end to the war. But by mid-July the mutiny was essentially at an end. Pétain had been as good as his word: not only were hundreds of thousands of soldiers given leave, but they received preferential treatment from the railroads in order to get home without delay. Not only were new facilities constructed for units being rested after service at the front, but these facilities were for the first time situated far enough behind the lines to be safe from enemy guns. It was too soon for Pétain to keep his promise that there would be no more insanely wasteful offensives, but the troops had been given reason to trust him and seemed prepared to do so.

Still, even with the crisis behind it, the army was in a badly shaken state. Major new campaigns were out of the question. The Germans too were in fragile condition after Arras and the Chemin des Dames; much of the Russian army had disintegrated; and the Austrians, Turks, and Italians could do little more than flail feebly away on their various fronts. In every case outright collapse appeared to be somewhere between possible and imminent.

Britain seemed in a universe of its own, somewhere above the general calamity. The U-boat campaign was at its height and creating serious problems, sinking more than eight hundred and forty tons of shipping in April, a third more than the campaign's planners had said would be needed monthly to bring the British to their knees. But the solution had emerged. Early in May a first convoy of merchantmen guarded by destroyers set out from Gibraltar and reached England without loss. The British admirals had been reluctant to try the convoy system because it was in a sense counterintuitive, requiring every ship in a formation to proceed at the speed of the slowest. But Lloyd George insisted, and as soon as the idea was tried, any possibility that the U-boats would achieve their objectives disappeared forever. Britain experienced industrial and to a lesser extent political turbulence, with workers striking for better pay and conditions and the socialists demanding peace. But this was nothing compared to what was happening in Russia, Austria-Hungary, and Germany. The BEF had taken substantial losses at Arras, but that problem too was small compared with those of the French.

Britain and its army seemed blessed.

That would be the next thing to change.

THE WAR AND POETRY

HISTORIC EVENTS ARE OFTEN SAID TO HAVE "CHANGED everything." In the case of the Great War this is, for once, true. The war really did change *everything:* not just borders, not just governments and the fate of nations, but the way people have seen the world and themselves ever since. It became a kind of hole in time, leaving the postwar world permanently disconnected from everything that had come before.

As Samuel Hynes details in his brilliant study *War Imagined,* the events of 1914–18 produced "the most important and wide-ranging cultural change in modern English history." To grasp the truth of this—and it does not apply to England only—it is necessary only to look at the literature of the war years, and at the strange way that literature came to a stop, appeared to be dead for a while, and then started up again on an entirely new plane.

The start of the war brought an explosion of writing everywhere. It was the age before radio and television, when poetry still mattered to millions of people, and in August 1914 newspapers were being sent hundreds of poems every day. Almost all of them were amateurish at best, but the subject matter was uniformly lofty: the greatness of this new crusade, the glory of the cause, the heroism of those who had "fallen" on "the field of honor." If poems expressing a less exalted view of the conflict were submitted, few editors in Austria, Britain, France, Germany, or Russia showed any interest in printing them.

Many leading men of letters enlisted their pens in the war effort. In England James Barrie, Arnold Bennett, Robert Bridges, G. K. Chesterton, Arthur Conan Doyle, John Galsworthy, H. Rider Haggard, Thomas Hardy, John Masefield, Arthur Pinero, H. G. Wells—they and many others accepted the Asquith government's invitation to help the nation understand what it was fighting for and why the sacrifices that lay ahead could be embraced with pride. German writers, artists, and intellectuals, stung by stories in Entente newspapers about atrocities committed by Berlin's troops in Belgium and elsewhere, signed and published declarations of the justice of their homeland's cause. The most conspicuous, bearing the signatures of nearly a hundred prominent figures, was addressed "To the Cultured World." Thomas Mann, a future Nobel Prize winner, was among those swept up in the euphoria. The war, he said, was "a purification, a liberation, an enormous hope. The German soul is opposed to the pacifist ideal of civilization, for is not peace an element of civil corruption?"

There were side currents in the flood of patriotic words. The novelist Henry James, an American who had made England his home and would take up British citizenship before his death during the war, was in despair from the beginning. He called the war "this abyss of blood and darkness" and saw the fact that such a thing could happen as a nullification of everything he had believed about Europe, its civilization, and his own work. At the other end of the spectrum were men who, like Mann, wrote of the war as a kind of gift, a purifying fire that would burn away the rotten parts of a sick and effete culture.

The young Rupert Brooke saw it as heroic, beautiful, *and* purifying. He contemplated death in battle and found it pleasing.

> *If I should die, think only this of me:*
> *That there's some corner of a foreign field*
> *That is forever England. There shall be*
> *In that rich dust a richer dust concealed;*
> *A dust whom England bore, shaped, made aware,*
> *Gave, once, her flowers to love, her ways to roam,*
> *A body of England's, breathing English air,*
> *Washed by the rivers, blest by suns of home.*
>
> *And think, this heart, all evil shed away,*
> *A pulse in this eternal mind, no less*
> *Gives somewhere back the thoughts of England given;*
> *Her sights and sounds; dreams happy as her day;*
> *And laughter, learnt of friends; and gentleness,*
> *In hearts at peace, under an English heaven.*

As art this is High Treacle, but to English readers in 1914 it was Shakespearean. Brooke was dead several months after he wrote it.

Of blood poisoning from an infected mosquito bite on a troop ship off Gallipoli. His "corner of a foreign field" is on the Aegean island of Skyros.

As the war wore on without result, the flow of noble feelings set to verse continued unabated. Increasingly, though, it was mere empty verbiage, an unloading of exhausted and irrelevant clichés, poetry done by the numbers. Almost nothing authentic, nothing that expressed the experiences of the men in the trenches or even their families at home, was showing up in print. More and more of the great men of letters were falling silent, as if acknowledging that there was nothing they could say. Those who continued in the old vein began to meet with resentment from men who had been to the front. When a young infantry officer named Roland Leighton received a volume of Brooke's poems from his fiancée, he wrote back in a tone the young lady could not have expected.

"Let him who thinks that War is a glorious golden thing, who loves to roll forth stirring words of exhortation, invoking Honor and Praise and Valour and Love of Country with as thoughtless and fervid a faith as inspired the priests of Baal to call on their own slumbering deity," he wrote, "let him look at a little pile of sodden grey rags that cover half a skull and a shin bone and what might have been its ribs, or at this skeleton lying on its side, resting half-crouching as it fell, supported on one arm, perfect but that it is headless, and with the tattered clothing still draped around it; and let him realize how grand & glorious a thing it is to have distilled all Youth and Joy and Life into a foetid heap of hideous putrescence. Who is there who has known and seen who can say that Victory is worth the death of even one of these?"

Leighton too was soon dead. Killed hours before he was to go home on leave and be married. (His fiancée, Vera Brittain, went on to write a book, *Testament of Youth*, which has remained in print ever since and is among the Great War's classics.)

Literary and artistic life came to be paralyzed by a sense that the established and accepted ways of representing reality—pictures of romantic warriors performing wondrous feats, words about honor and duty and glory—didn't fit with what was happening on the Western Front, and that every effort to make them fit could produce only rubbish. The words died and became hollow, unusable. Something similar was happening in the visual arts, and in fiction and theater; painters and novelists and playwrights, if they were at all serious, seemed not to know what to do. The less serious continued to treat the war as a medieval jousting match, but everything they did was stillborn, irrelevant, even vile. Virginia Woolf attended a concert where "the patriotic sentiment was so revolting that I was nearly sick."

But slowly, finally, in ways that could anger minds that wanted not to be disturbed, new voices began to emerge. A poetry and a kind of painting were born that did not deny reality—new and "ugly" expressions of an ugly thing. The new work came from the only possible source: men who had been there. One such man was the German artist Otto Dix, who had volunteered in 1914 in the expectation that war would bring him "tremendous experiences." Four years of service including fighting in Champagne, the Somme, and Russia changed him and his art profoundly and permanently. "Lice, rats, barbed wire, fleas, shells, bombs, underground caves, corpses, blood, liquor, mice, cats, artillery, filth, bullets, mortars, fire, steel: that is what war is," he wrote. "It is the work of the devil." He survived and spent the rest of his life putting his horror and disillusionment on canvas. Others—poets first, then writers of fiction—did the same in print. Some of them are still famous today. The Englishmen Robert Graves and Siegfried Sassoon. The German Erich Maria Remarque. Henri Barbusse and Guillaume Apollinaire of France.

And Wilfred Owen, a young teacher who had never attended a university, enlisted in 1915 and was wounded three times before being diagnosed with shell shock and sent to a hospital in Scotland. There he met Sassoon, a captain from the landed gentry who had been decorated for heroism and later sent for treatment rather than being court-martialed for declaring his intention never to fight again. Owen showed his early efforts to write verse to Sassoon, who found them conventional and urged him to deal with what he had actually experienced and what he really felt. This is the most famous result:

> *Bent double, like old beggars under sacks,*
> *Knock-kneed, coughing like hags, we cursed through sludge,*
> *Till on the haunting flares we turned our backs,*
> *And towards our distant rest began to trudge.*
> *Men marched asleep. Many had lost their boots*
> *But limped on, blood-shod. All went lame; all blind;*
> *Drunk with fatigue; deaf even to the hoots*
> *Of tired, outstripped Five-Nines that dropped behind.*

Gas! Gas! Quick, boys!—An ecstasy of fumbling,
Fitting the clumsy helmets just in time,
But someone still was yelling out and stumbling
And flound'ring like a man in fire or lime . . .
Dim through the misty panes and thick green light,
As under a green sea, I saw him drowning.

In all my dreams before my helpless sight,
He plunges at me, guttering, choking, drowning.

If in some smothering dreams you too could pace
Behind the wagon that we flung him in,
And watch the white eyes writhing in his face,
His hanging face, like a devil's sick of sin,
If you could hear, at every jolt, the blood
Come gargling from the froth-corrupted lungs
Obscene as cancer, bitter as the cud
Of vile, incurable sores on innocent tongues,—
My friend, you would not tell with such high zest
To children ardent for some desperate glory,
The old lie: Dulce et decorum est
Pro patria mori.

Sweet and fitting it is, to die for one's country. The poems of Lieutenant Wilfred Owen got almost no notice before the war ended. Afterward critics found in them a major voice. Owen never knew. He was killed exactly one week before the war ended, shot while leading his platoon across a canal in Belgium. The telegram reporting his death was delivered to his parents' door as church bells rang in celebration of the armistice.

Chapter 11

Wars Without Guns

"It would be laughable to depart over fantasies."
—Theobald von Bethmann Hollweg

In the aftermath of Russia's March Revolution and the failed offensives at Arras and the Chemin des Dames, struggles for power erupted in Petrograd and London. And although for Germany these events had not been the disasters that they were for the Entente, a struggle of the same kind occurred in Berlin too at exactly the same time. Paris, meanwhile, slipped into a deepening gloom, its leadership demoralized and adrift.

The stakes were perhaps highest in Russia. With the tsar deposed, with the tsar's ministers under arrest and hateful factions battling for control of the provisional government, the Russian nation was faced with the most elemental of political questions. It had to decide not only *who* would govern but *how*. It had to settle on a *form* of government, and on some way of organizing its disintegrating economy. It had to do so in the middle of a war that it was losing, and with few established mechanisms in place. Through the first half of 1917 support for continuing the war remained substantial. Kerensky was saying that the revolution had been in part an angry reaction to rumors that the Romanov government might enter into a separate peace. He and the general staff, though their efforts to mount the offensive promised at Chantilly late in 1916 had ended in chaos, were preparing a more modest campaign for the summer. Resistance, however, was growing, and it was strongest where loyalty was needed most: in the army and the industrial workforce. By late spring more than thirty-five thousand troops were deserting monthly. The home front too remained dangerously turbulent, almost, at times, to the point of anarchy. The recently formed soviets, representing soldiers and sailors and workers, were deeply skeptical of what Kerensky was doing. The Communist Party's Bolshevik faction, with Lenin now in charge, was increasingly bold in stirring up opposition.

The question for Germany was simpler: who was going to be in control? The contest was singularly unequal. On one side were virtually all the dominant elements of German society, united in opposition to reform of any meaningful kind. Their only real opposition was a single man, Chancellor Bethmann Hollweg, with the kaiser floating uncertainly between the two camps. Though his own thinking often coincided with Bethmann's (in 1917 he issued an Easter message endorsing the chancellor's proposals for electoral reform), he knew himself to be disappearing into the shadows cast by Hindenburg and Ludendorff. The two generals blamed Bethmann for everything. His failure to maintain control of domestic politics, they complained, was eroding the loyalty of the Reichstag. His pursuit of peace negotiations was making Germany look weak and encouraging the Entente to fight on. When strikes broke out in Berlin, they too were Bethmann's fault.

The result was a standoff that lasted for months. At an April 23 conference, when Hindenburg and Ludendorff demanded approval of a war aims memorandum that declared Germany's intent to annex large portions of the Balkans as well as parts of Belgium and France, Bethmann did not resist. A week later, however, he placed in the files a note stating that he regarded the memorandum as meaningless because it implied Germany's ability to dictate terms to the Entente—an outcome that seemed worse than improbable at the time. "I have co-signed the protocol," he wrote, "because it would be laughable to depart over fantasies." The ambiguity of his position became public when, in a May 15 speech to the Reichstag, he declared himself to be "in complete accord" with the generals on war aims but also willing to offer Russia a settlement "founded on mutually honorable understanding." This statement was self-defeating. It deepened Ludendorff's hostility while at the same time confusing and alienating the increasing number of Reichstag members who understood that the U-boat campaign was failing, wanted a negotiated settlement, and could have provided the chancellor with a base of public support.

Hindenburg and Ludendorff drew their strength from two sources. One was their record of success in the field—a record that reached back to Tannenberg and had raised them to the stature of demigods. The other was the support they received from the richest, most powerful, most conservative elements of German society—groups convinced that only victory could deflect the general population from demanding reform of the entire system at war's end. This coalition was potent if not entirely stable. But when it pressed for Bethmann's removal, Kaiser Wilhelm showed surprising strength in resisting. He foresaw that any new chancellor was likely to be Ludendorff's tool, and that this would be the end of the Bismarckian system. But the pressure was tremendous. Even the kaiser's wife and Crown Prince Wilhelm were badgering him for the appointment of a new chancellor. And the generals had not played their last card. In contrast to Bethmann and the kaiser, they had the advantage of knowing what they wanted and being willing to do practically anything to get it.

In Britain too the struggle was between the head of the government and the general staff, but beyond that there were few similarities to the situation in Germany. The British political system, being so much more mature than Germany's, made a military challenge to the government's control of policy virtually inconceivable—nothing of the kind arose in the course of the war. The struggle was over control of the BEF only, but was no less intense for being limited. The adversaries were Lloyd George, who had always had strong opinions about how the war should be conducted and now as prime minister was subordinate to no one, and Haig and General Sir William Robertson, based in London as chief of the imperial general staff. At issue, as the summer of 1917 began, was the question of what to do with the BEF, which in two and a half years had grown to be among the most powerful armies in history. Lloyd George, his government now enjoying solid public support after a shaky start, remained scornfully skeptical of the generals' tactics and strategies. Arras and the Chemin des Dames had destroyed whatever inclination he once might have had to leave such matters in the hands of the professionals. He could see no reason to attempt further offensives before American troops were present in large numbers. He continued to push for an Italian offensive while the French and the Russians recovered their strength and the United States translated its potential into an army ready to fight. The generals, inevitably, disagreed.

The importance that Lloyd George attached to the arrival of an American army required, that May, a considerable act of faith. It had not been certain, in the immediate aftermath of Washington's declaration of war, that the United States would be doing more than sending money, equipment, and ships to its new allies. When the chairman of the Senate Appropriations Committee declared that "Congress will not permit American soldiers to be sent to Europe," Wilson quickly proved him wrong, but the president had stunningly little to work with. Until a gradual buildup was authorized in 1916, the U.S. regular army included one hundred and thirty thousand men, which barely put it among the twenty largest armies in the world. It had no tanks, almost no aircraft, and few machine guns in spite of the fact that the machine gun was an American invention. The nation's distrust of military establishments was reflected in a law limiting the general staff to fifty-five officers, no more than twenty-nine of whom could be based in Washington.

The American army also had no divisions; its largest unit was the regiment. A First Division was hurriedly put together and dispatched to France as a demonstration of the seriousness of Washington's intentions. Led by General John J. Pershing, a stern West Pointer who had started his career in the Indian wars, it would march through the streets of Paris on July 4 to an ecstatic reception. It was far too small to make a difference and was not trained for combat, however, and no other divisions were ready to follow it.

The difficulties of creating an army capable of making a difference on the Great War's Western Front are almost impossible to exaggerate. The first draft since the Civil War was put in place, and by mid-1917 every American male between the ages of twenty-one and thirty-one (later this would be raised to forty-five) was registered. Thirty-two training camps, each occupying eight to twelve thousand acres and containing fifteen hundred buildings capable of accommodating forty thousand men, were constructed in sixty days. Nearly every noncom in the old regular army was commissioned, and new schools in every specialty from gunnery to baking were brought into existence up and down the East Coast. The Entente was sending combat veterans across the Atlantic to show green American instructors how to teach even greener inductees the arts of modern war. The French tutors specialized in artillery, liaison, tactics, and fortifications, the British in machine guns, bayonets, mortars, sniping, and gas. Managing all this required

Veteran and newcomer
Ferdinand Foch, left, and John J. Pershing.

expanding and restructuring the War Department and general staff even more rapidly than the new camps were thrown together.

Ambitious as the expansion was, it did not prepare Washington for Pershing's estimate, sent shortly after his arrival in France, of how many troops he was going to require within a year. "It is evident that a force of about one million is the smallest unit which in modern war will be a complete, well-balanced and independent fighting organization," he reported. "Plans for the future should be based . . . on three times this force—i.e., at least three million men."

None of which was of the smallest interest to Douglas Haig, whose attention was focused not a year ahead but on Flanders in 1917 and whose faith centered not on the United States but on his own ability to produce a breakthrough at Ypres. He was supported by the Royal Navy, the leaders of which saw the Belgian coast as a place where their seaborne guns could support infantry operations and as a strategic prize urgently needing to be recovered. The Admiralty had been developing plans for an amphibious invasion since 1915. By the spring of 1917, in cooperation with the army, it had begun the construction of huge floating docks capable of putting ashore infantry and tanks. Haig seized at the opportunity that this appeared to present. He and his staff developed a plan of their own, one that would combine a new offensive out of the Ypres salient with an amphibious landing and unhinge the German position in Belgium. Pressed from two directions, Haig believed, the Germans would have to give up the coast. Without room for maneuver, they might be driven out of Belgium entirely. Then, their flank exposed, they might even be forced back from the Hindenburg Line. At a minimum, the British would capture the ports of Ostend, Zeebrugge, and Blankenberge, thereby depriving the Germans of the ports from which some of their smaller submarines were venturing into the Channel. Such gains would greatly strengthen Britain's position in any peace negotiations.

The amphibious operation was the only novel aspect of the plan. The attack out of Ypres was to be a traditional Western Front offensive: a supposedly overwhelming artillery bombardment followed by a supposedly irresistible infantry attack resulting in a breakthrough that the cavalry could then exploit. The whole thing could not have been better calculated to provoke Lloyd George, who fumed from the moment he learned of it. To him it seemed nothing more than another foredoomed recipe for throwing away thousands of lives and wrecking what remained of the new armies that Britain had been nurturing since 1914. The landing of troops from the sea, genuinely innovative though the idea was, could not be safely attempted until after the main break-through was achieved. To quiet Lloyd George, Haig set down a criterion for the landing. The breakthrough would be counted as real, and the amphibious force sent into action, when the British took possession of the town of Roulers, seven miles inside Ger-man territory. Lloyd George was unimpressed. He was certain that Roulers was out of reach. Haig and Robertson thought it presumptuous of the prime minister to have an opinion on such matters.

Weather, always a factor in war, had to be a particular con-cern for anyone planning operations in western Belgium. Flan-ders is an exceedingly flat geography, one almost devoid of any-thing more notable than scattered farmhouses, sleepy villages, and occasional patches of trees. Today, when visitors search out the battlegrounds around Ypres, they have difficulty identifying the so-called ridges and hills that the Great War made immor-tal; these features are rarely more conspicuous than wrinkles in a tablecloth. Flanders is also an exceptionally low part of northern Europe's great coastal plain, so near to being an extension of the sea that its inhabitants spent centuries installing drains, canals, and dikes to bring it to the point where it could be farmed. Even today it is about as wet as terrain can be without becoming an estuary. Even in what passes for dry weather in Flanders, one has to turn over only a few spadesful of earth before striking water. When it rains—as it almost always does in late summer, and heavily—the whole area turns to mud. The composition of its soil is such that, when saturated, it becomes a bottomless, unmanage-able, uniquely gluey mess.

Haig was warned. The summers of 1915 and 1916 had been unusually dry by Flanders standards, but his staff examined re-cords back to the 1830s and reported that normally "in Flanders the weather broke early each August with the regularity of the Indian monsoon." The retired lieutenant colonel who was military correspondent of the *Times* of London cautioned Robertson against trying to mount a major operation in the low country in late summer. "You can fight in mountains and deserts, but no one can fight in mud and when the water is let out against you," he said. "At the best, you are restricted to the narrow fronts on the higher ground, which are very unfavorable with modern weapons."

"When the water is let out against you": this must have been a reference to what the Belgians had done in the depths of their desperation in 1914, opening the dikes and inundating the countryside east of the River Yser to stop the Germans from breaking through. It was a warning that the Germans might do something similar if in similar jeopardy. It should have brought to mind yet another danger: that heavy bombardment might so wreck the whole region's fragile drainage system as to make flooding inevitable whatever the Germans did. Haig did not brush these warnings aside, but neither did he allow them to deflect him. They made him impatient to get started while Flanders remained dry. As soon as the Arras operation was behind him, he shifted to building up an attack force at Ypres. He proceeded without Lloyd George's approval and even though Pétain had advised him (a warning never communicated to Lloyd George) that his plan had no chance of success.

Haig hoped to prepare by establishing a new strongpoint on the edge of the salient, some piece of relatively high ground that, once reinforced, could serve as an anchor for troops moving forward to pry the Germans out of their defenses. In this connection he was given a magnificent gift by one of his army commanders. General Sir Herbert Plumer, a pear-shaped little man with the bristling white mustache of a cartoon Colonel Blimp, had been commander of the Second Army on the southern edge of the salient for two years—two terrible years during which the fighting at Ypres had accounted for fully one-fourth of all British casualties. In 1915 Plumer had begun a tunneling program aimed at the German positions opposite his line, and in 1916 he expanded it into the most ambitious mining operation of the war. Twenty shafts, some almost half a mile long and many of them more than a hundred feet deep to escape detection and drained by generator-driven pumps, were extended until finally the diggers were beneath the Messines Ridge, from which the German artillery spotters had long enjoyed an unequaled view of the area. One of the mines was discovered and destroyed by the Germans, but by May the other nineteen were finished, packed with explosives, and still unknown to the enemy.

At 3:10 a.m. on June 7, after a week of bombardment by the heaviest concentration of artillery seen on any front up to that time (Plumer had a gun for every seven yards of front), the mines were detonated. All nineteen went off nearly simultaneously, sending the entire ridge into the air. Tremors were felt in London—Lloyd George himself heard a faint boom while working through the night at 10 Downing Street. "When I heard the first deep rumble I turned to the men and shouted, 'Come on, let's go,' " a lieutenant with a British machine gun corps recalled. "A fraction of a second later a terrific roar and the whole earth seemed to rock and sway. The concussion was terrible, several of the men and myself being thrown down violently. It seemed to be several minutes before the earth stood still again though it may not really have been more than a few seconds. Flames rose to a great height—silhouetted against the flames I saw huge blocks of earth that seemed to be as big as houses falling back to the ground. Small chunks and dirt fell all around. I saw a man flung out from behind a huge block of debris silhouetted against the sheet of flame. Presumably

Sir Herbert Plumer
Found the key to Ludendorff's new system.

some poor devil of a Boche. It was awful, a sort of inferno." A
private, a member of a tank crew, got a closer look at the devastation. "We got out of the tank and walked over to this huge crater.
You'd never seen anything like the size of it, you'd never believe
that explosives could do it. I saw about a hundred and fifty Germans lying there dead, all in different positions, some as if throwing a bomb, some still with a gun on their shoulder. The mine had
killed them all. The crew stood there for about five minutes and
looked. It made us think. That mine had won the battle before it
started. We looked at each other as we came away and the sight
of it remained with you always. To see them all lying there with
their eyes open."

Plumer's infantry took possession of the long chain of
seventy-foot-deep craters that now gaped where the ridge had
been. It had been a spectacular success, one that achieved its objectives in minutes at almost no cost in British lives, but it was
also distinctly limited. The British penetration was about two
miles at its farthest point, and no effort was made to push deeper.
Haig, interested in the operation only insofar as it contributed
to his preparations for a main assault that was still more than a
month in the future, had ordered it stopped as soon as the ridge
was taken. His reasons were not trivial: he did not want the Second Army so far forward that his artillery could no longer protect
it, and he did want it to dig in before the Germans could counterattack. Still, for a few hours there had been an opportunity to
cut deeply into and possibly even through the broken German
defenses, and that opportunity was not put to use. Perhaps the
most important consequence of Messines Ridge was the taste it
gave Plumer, a capable commander, of the advantages of a limited attack.

Haig still did not have London's approval for his main offensive, and the success at Messines Ridge (which had, in the end,
left the British still confined inside the old Ypres salient) had
done nothing to ease the prime minister's doubts. Lloyd George
summoned Haig to a June 19 meeting with his recently created
Cabinet Committee on War Policy to explain his plans in detail.
Robertson also attended. Like Lloyd George one of those "only
in America," up-from-nowhere figures who appear in almost every nation in almost every generation, "Wully" Robertson was a

genuinely remarkable individual, especially for the class-bound
society that Britain was a century ago. Born in humble circumstances in 1860, he had joined the army at seventeen. ("I shall
name it to no one for I am ashamed to think of it," his mother
wrote him when she learned of his enlistment. "I would rather
bury you than see you in a red coat.") He did well during ten
years in the ranks, was changed by a commission from the army's youngest sergeant major to its oldest lieutenant, and during
long service in India mastered an array of languages, including
Gurkhali, Hindi, Pashto, Persian, and Urdu. He served with distinction in the Boer War and returned to England to become
both a reform-minded authority on military training and an
expert on the German army. To this day he remains the only
Englishman ever to rise from private soldier to field marshal (a
rank he was given at his retirement, along with a baronetcy),
but throughout his career he never attempted to shed the rough
Lincolnshire accent that made his origins clear to all. From early
in the war he had been committed to victory on the Western
Front (opposing, among other alternatives, the Dardanelles campaign), and since his elevation to the lofty position of chief of the
imperial general staff in December 1915 he had been Haig's most
important supporter. This made him deeply suspect in the eyes
of Lloyd George.

The London conference went on for three days and was a
contest from start to end. Haig laid out his plan and the great
things he expected it to accomplish. Lloyd George peppered him
with questions. He wanted to know why the generals believed a
Flanders offensive could succeed this time, what their estimate
of casualties was, how the enemy's forces were disposed, and
what the consequences of failure might be. He made it plain that
he was not satisfied with the answers. The Royal Navy was called
in and, to no one's surprise, sided with the soldiers. Admiral Jellicoe, the semidiscredited semihero of the Battle of Jutland, raised
Lloyd George's furry eyebrows by asserting that Britain would
be unable to continue the war for much more than another year
unless the Belgian coast was taken. This warning was far-fetched
(only a small number of Germany's smaller submarines was
based in Flemish ports) but so purely speculative that neither
Lloyd George nor anyone else could prove that it was wrong. All

the representatives of the army and navy were impatient with Lloyd George and offended by what they saw as his meddling. The cheek of this craggy Welshman, a man utterly lacking in military training or experience, seemed to them ludicrous and offensive.

In the end the prime minister yielded without having been won over. He gave in to political rather than military realities. After everything had been hashed out and hashed over, he had only one other member of the committee firmly on his side. A third member, the Conservative leader Andrew Bonar Law, also expressed doubt that Haig and Robertson had made their case. But, unknowingly echoing what Bethmann Hollweg had said in Berlin under almost identical circumstances five months earlier, he added that he did not think the committee could "overrule the military and naval authorities on a question of strategy." Lloyd George understood that to countermand Haig and Robertson without broad bipartisan support would leave him exposed and vulnerable in the House of Commons. Also, one of Haig's promises had to be taken into account. In a way reminiscent of what Nivelle had proclaimed when his plans for the Chemin des Dames were challenged, Haig said that if his scheme did not succeed it could quickly be called off. The losses could be ended while still at tolerable levels. Reluctantly and resentfully, certain that he was witnessing Great War stupidity at its worst, Lloyd George told Haig to proceed with his preparations while awaiting final approval.

Thus the meeting ended in a conditional victory for the generals. Viewed in a broader context, however, it had demonstrated the strength of the British system. When Haig and Robertson departed, they took with them not control of strategy but only permission to get ready for one more attack. That permission had been granted by the civil government, the power of which had in no way been diminished. The discussion had happened at the insistence of the prime minister, and the prime minister had the last word. Everyone knew and accepted, if unhappily in some cases, that ultimate authority lay with Lloyd George and his committee. The constitution was intact.

Imperial Germany's constitution was supposed to work in somewhat the same way. Its chancellor was supposed to be in control and in fact had been in control when Bismarck held the office (though even he could have been dismissed by the kaiser at any time and ultimately was). But because the government's leaders had no power base of their own (were not, as in Britain, chosen by the legislature), the strains and uncertainties of a protracted and total war caused control to slip out of the chancellor's hands. The system broke down, finally, and a new one had to be improvised. The improvising could have been done by the one man whom almost the whole German nation trusted, but Hindenburg had no interest. Thus it fell to the one man who both wanted it and seemed able to get Hindenburg to do whatever he wished—Ludendorff, a man elected by no one, a man the kaiser disliked intensely. Thus the war turned Germany into a true military dictatorship, something that it had in fact never before been.

The Russian authorities, meanwhile, were struggling to hold together their forces on the Eastern Front and having distinctly limited success. Among the German troops opposite those forces was a young newly commissioned officer, recently returned to duty after being wounded in action, named Rudolf Hess— the same Hess who in later years would be one of Hitler's top henchmen. "Yesterday we saw heavy fighting," he observed sardonically in a letter to his parents, "but only among the Russians themselves. A Russian officer came over and gave himself up. He spoke perfect German. He was born in Baden but is a Russian citizen. He told us that whole battles are going on behind their lines. Their officers are shooting each other and the soldiers are doing the same. He found it all too ridiculous. They can all get lost as far as he's concerned. We invited him to eat with us and he thanked us. He ate well and drank plenty of tea before going off. There was a lot of noise coming from the Russian side yesterday. They were fighting each other in the trenches. We also heard shots coming from their infantry but they were firing at each other. Charming!"

On July 1, in spite of such disorders and to the delight of Paris and London, Kerensky somehow launched his offensive. Though not nearly as large as what had been promised before the fall of the tsar—not enough troops could be assembled for that—it still involved two hundred thousand men and more than thirteen hundred guns on a thirty-mile front. The mere fact that the Russians were able to take the initiative was cause for happiness, and there seemed to be grounds for optimism. The offensive was under the overall command of General Brusilov, father of the great offensive of 1916 and now commander in chief. It took place in Galicia, where Brusilov had achieved his earlier successes and the Russian forces were in better order, their morale higher, than in the north. They had been superbly equipped by their allies with artillery and aircraft, and nearly half of the defenders were Austrian rather than German troops.

The offensive appeared to go brilliantly at first, with a bombardment that destroyed much of the enemy's forward defenses. The infantry attack that followed swept forward into enemy-held ground. It was all an illusion, however. The Russians were unaware of the new defensive system that Ludendorff had put in place on both fronts and that even the Austrians were using under German direction. The counterattack, when it came, was more than the Russian soldiers were able or willing to endure. They didn't simply retreat, they quit the war on the spot, refusing to obey further orders. Officers who attempted to restore order were shot dead. On July 8 the Russian Eighth Army essentially went out of existence. Ten days after that Brusilov, who had had misgivings from the start but had been ordered to proceed by Kerensky, found himself relieved of command. By July 19 it was the Germans who were on the offensive, driving a disorderly mob of Russians before them. Their commander was the same Max Hoffmann who had been Ludendorff's strategist at Tannenberg and was now chief of staff on the Eastern Front. Wherever the Germans advanced, the Russians fled. When the Austrians joined in, the Russians fled even from them.

It was, for all practical purposes, the end of the war in the east. Russian casualties had been almost trivial by the standards of the preceding three years—only seventeen thousand killed, wounded, or missing—but such numbers were meaningless in the context of a general collapse. The Germans would attack again later, in the north, but by then success would come so easily as to be almost a formality. Russia really was finished this time. It was the end of the provisional government as well. The future belonged to the Bolsheviks.

Hindenburg and Ludendorff, fortified by this success, now settled the question of who was in charge in Berlin. On July 6 the leader of Germany's Catholic Center Party, a moderate and monarchist named Matthias Erzberger, had delivered a speech that shocked the nation. Using information obtained through international contacts made available by the Vatican, Erzberger not only argued but persuasively demonstrated that the submarine campaign had failed. He demanded reform, including a stronger governing role for the Reichstag, and German renunciation of territorial gains in order to secure a "peace of reconciliation." This speech came at a point when the struggle for control over policy was particularly intense (many factions were involved, and their positions were too varied to be dealt with here), and it outraged the conservatives. The Reichstag's annexationists bitterly attacked Bethmann. But in the face of renewed demands for his dismissal, the kaiser continued to support him.

On July 12, with the crisis at its height, there came a new and even greater shock. A telegram from the headquarters of the army high command announced the resignations of both Hindenburg and Ludendorff. It said the resignations of other members of the general staff would soon follow and that the reason was the impossibility of working with Bethmann Hollweg. It was blackmail plain and simple. In Britain or France, the resignation of any general behaving so high-handedly would have been accepted without comment. Kaiser Wilhelm was indignant, but he was also impotent and knew it. He responded by asking Hindenburg and Ludendorff to come to Berlin to see him. Bethmann resigned.

The timing was deeply unfortunate. Monsignor Eugenio Pacelli, the future Pope Pius XII, had called on the chancellor shortly before his resignation and presented an offer by Pope Benedict XV to attempt to mediate an end to the war. The first essential step, Pacelli explained, had to be a declaration of Berlin's intentions with respect to Belgium. It was as clear to the Vatican as to everyone that no peace talks were possible unless Germany demonstrated a willingness to restore Belgium to its prewar status. Even the kaiser, who had long and pompously insisted that Germany's security interests required it to maintain control of at least part of Belgium, had come to understand that such a goal was not realistic. Bethmann had responded encouragingly, telling Pacelli (without seeking the army's agreement, of course) that Germany would agree to Belgium's autonomy if Britain and France would do so as well. He even spoke of resolving the question of Alsace and Lorraine to mutual satisfaction. The Reichstag's increasingly liberal majority almost certainly would have supported Bethmann if given the opportunity. But with Bethmann gone there could be no such opportunity. The papal initiative came to nothing.

After some difficulty in finding a new chancellor (various factions put forth their candidates, who one by one were rejected), the job was given to an obscure bureaucrat named Georg Michaelis. It is a measure of the depths to which Germany had fallen politically that Kaiser Wilhelm had not only never met Michaelis, he had never even heard of him. Michaelis would prove so lacking in experience, judgment, and strength of character that even Ludendorff—whom he was eager to please—was soon disappointed. Ludendorff, a complex and paradoxical character who despite always wanting his way did not really want to become dictator (he scoffed at suggestions that he himself should become chancellor), found himself responsible for everything, with no one of consequence to help on the political and diplomatic side. It hardly needs saying that neither he nor his agents (nor the hapless Michaelis) had any success in bringing the Reichstag under control. On July 19 a substantial majority of its members approved a resolution that offended the conservatives anew. "The Reichstag strives for a peace of understanding and the permanent reconciliation of peoples," the resolution declared. "Forced territorial acquisitions and political, economic or financial oppressions are irreconcilable with such a peace." The German government remained at war with itself.

France was a different case. The Third Republic was, in a sense, *always* at war with itself. It had been so in the days just before the war, when Caillaux with his pacific inclinations would have become prime minister if not for his wife. In the years since then one government after another had fallen, in one case after only days in power. But behind the turmoil France retained the machinery needed to produce coherent political, military, and diplomatic decisions, and that machinery had continued to function. The government, after Joffre's period of total control, had reestablished its authority over military strategy. It had done so in part because the army's high command, divided between republicans and never-quite-trusted Catholics such as Ferdinand Foch, was never a coherent enough force to become a political threat.

In the summer of 1917 France needed only one final ingredient in order to operate effectively. It needed a prime minister as strong and determined and politically savvy as Lloyd George, one capable of making himself master of the nation.

That prime minister had been waiting in the wings all along, and he was about to emerge.

ENTER THE TIGER

BY 1917 GEORGES CLEMENCEAU HAD BEEN A PROMI-
nent figure in French politics and journalism—a magnetic, troubling,
disruptive figure, hated and feared and adored—for half a century.
All four of the governments that had come and gone in Paris since
1914 had kept him on the outside (that was where Clemenceau had
always been happiest, making the insiders squirm), but he remained
a force in public life.

And now his hour had come round at last. The nation, exhausted
and confused, desperately needed new leadership. So many men had
tried and failed that only one possibility remained. It was the man they
called, by no means always affectionately, *Le Tigre.* With many misgivings, seeing no choice but to ignore the savagery with which the
Tiger had been striking at him since the war began, President Poincaré
asked him to form a government. Clemenceau, who throughout most
of his career had been refusing invitations to come inside, accepted
immediately. And immediately everything began to change. France
had found its war leader, its Lloyd George.

Clemenceau was seventy-six years old in 1917, which meant he
had been thirty at the end of the Franco-Prussian War, but he was
still a volcano of energy. He rose at five every morning, wrote and
read for two and a half hours, and then spent half an hour with a
calisthenics coach before going to his office. All through the war he
had been a member of the French Senate. His position on its army
and foreign affairs committees enabled him to know more than most
about how the war was being managed and what was happening behind the scenes, and he used his newspaper to complain about what
he knew. When the war began, the paper was called *L'Homme Libre,*
The Free Man. Before the war was two months old, the government,
offended by its biting criticism, ordered it shut down. One day later
Clemenceau launched a replacement, *L'Homme Enchaîné,* The Man
in Chains. It too was briefly suppressed. When publication resumed,
Clemenceau became somewhat less indiscreet but no less critical.

Premier Georges Clemenceau
"Home policy? I wage war!
Foreign policy? I wage war!"

He regarded it as his mission to raise difficult questions. "The danger of speaking out and the danger of remaining silent," he observed, "balance agonizingly in our minds." His articles were the scourge of the Viviani government, then of the Briand government, then of the governments of Ribot and Painlevé. They also heaped scorn on generals. Clemenceau showed no more deference than Lloyd George to the expertise of military professionals. He admired only two, Foch and Pétain, and deferred not even to them. The poilus loved his paper and bought a hundred thousand copies of every edition.

Not surprisingly, French officialdom regarded him as an impossible man. "So long as victory is possible he is capable of upsetting everything!" Poincaré said early in the war. "A day will perhaps come when I shall add: 'Now that everything seems to be lost, he alone is capable of saving everything.' " It was perhaps the most prophetic statement of the war. It reflected the fact that, regardless of how many enemies Clemenceau had made and how much his enemies resented him, it was impossible to question his patriotism, his ability, his hatred of Germany, or his commitment to victory at any cost.

He had been a singular character from youth, and life had made him more so. The son of a provincial physician who served time in jail for his outspoken criticism of the Second Empire, Clemenceau shaped himself in his father's image: radically republican, antimonarchist, anticlerical, cynical and scornful of the whole French establishment. He completed medical studies but afterward went to the United States, arriving while the Civil War was in progress and remaining for four years. He supported himself as a teacher and correspondent for French newspapers and married a nineteen-year-old American girl named Mary Plummer, who had been his student in Stamford, Connecticut. (The marriage, the only one of Clemenceau's long life, produced three children but ended unhappily after seven years.)

Back in France and living in Paris in 1870, when Napoleon III was captured by the Germans in the Franco-Prussian War, he was already prominent enough in leftist politics to be appointed mayor of the eighteenth arrondissement, working-class Montmartre, after radicals seized control of the city. From there he went on to serve in the Chamber of Deputies, to write for and found radical publications, and to champion such causes as separation of church and state and the rights of miners and industrial workers. Among his passions was one that alienated him from the Jaurès socialists who might otherwise have been his best allies: military preparedness. He regarded the loss of Alsace-Lorraine as an intolerable humiliation and renewed war as not only inevitable but desirable, the only way of putting things right. "One would have to be deliberately blind not to see," he wrote, "that the [German] lust for power, the impact of which makes Europe tremble each day, has fixed as its policy the extermination of France."

Clemenceau gloried in opposition, and for many years he led one of the Chamber's many factions. He regarded the middle classes that dominated French politics, the most respectable people in the country, as enemies of progress and justice. During the years of conflict surrounding the Dreyfus case, in which the leadership of the French army was exposed as having knowingly sentenced an innocent Jewish army captain to a life of penal servitude for allegedly selling state secrets to Germany, Clemenceau led the coalition that broke the power of the conservatives and brought the government and the military under republican control. He had repeatedly refused ministerial appointments, but in 1906, with antagonism between the multitudinous factions causing one government after another to fall in quick succession, Clemenceau consented to become minister of the interior. In this position he surprised and delighted the conservatives by using the army and police to subdue striking miners. Though he continued to advocate the eight-hour day, the right to unionize, accident and old-age insurance for workers, and a progressive income tax, the socialists from that point on regarded him as untouchable. But his unexpected firmness won so much support from the center that later the same year he became premier. His government last- ed almost three years—itself an achievement. It affected the course of the war to come by strengthening France's Entente with Russia (which Clemenceau saw as vital to survival, though he professed to despise the tsarist regime) while laying the foundations of her secret alliance with Britain.

As the Great War became years old and the costs mounted and victory seemed more and more distant, the legislature separated into two irreconcilable camps. On one side were those who believed in the possibility of negotiating an acceptable peace. This group was led by the same Joseph Caillaux who would have become premier in the summer of 1914 if his wife had not chosen that moment to buy and use a pistol. The other, convinced that no peace could be tolerable that was not preceded by the defeat of Germany, lined up behind the Tiger.

The Chamber was so polarized that it became impossible to put together the kind of coalition with which France had been muddling through. War Minister Paul Painlevé became premier in Septem- ber 1917 when the six-month-old Ribot government fell, but within weeks he too was tottering. The socialists were indignant about sud- den food shortages, the conservatives bewailed the state of the army and the war, and in November the Bolshevik takeover in Petrograd shocked everyone. Painlevé, neither experienced nor skillful enough to manage it all, had to go. Poincaré as president had to find someone to form a government. At this point only two men could have done so: Caillaux or Clemenceau. Selection of the former would have meant a search for compromise with the Germans. Clemenceau, by contrast, represented *la guerre à l'outrance,* total war to the end. For Poincaré, the choice was obvious.

The new premier brought many advantages to the job. He knew America, spoke English, and was almost the patron saint of the alli- ance with Britain. Best of all, from the perspective of the conservatives who were now his strongest supporters, his first term as premier had proved beyond doubt that he was no socialist, that under his admin- istration France need not fear Bolshevik contamination, that he would use any means necessary to maintain order. He had become the es- tablishment's Tiger, and from the day he took office he behaved more tigerishly than he ever had in his life. He took charge completely, fill-ing his cabinet with capable but minor figures who lacked a political base from which to challenge his authority. Instead of naming a war minister, he took that position himself and made it plain to the gener-als that he, not they, would have the final word. Ironically in light of his own history, he suppressed publications that questioned govern-ment policy. Dissenters were sent to prison. Stunningly—years later Clemenceau would express some remorse about this—even Caillaux was charged with disloyalty and put behind bars. Clemenceau em-braced the elites—the bankers, the manufacturers, the leaders of the *haute bourgeoisie*—that he had reviled all his life. Talk of limiting or confiscating excess war profits was extinguished as completely as talk of a compromise peace. The moneyed classes could help to win the war, and therefore they were Clemenceau's friends. Anyone express-ing doubt was his enemy.

Making decisions was easy in the Clemenceau government. Whatever could contribute to victory was done. Whatever might make victory more difficult was, whenever possible, stamped out. Anything irrelevant to the war no longer mattered.

"Home policy?" Clemenceau declared when questioned about his plans. "I wage war! Foreign policy? I wage war!"

Chapter 12

Passchendaele

"Blood and mud, blood and mud,
they can think of nothing better."
—David Lloyd George

J uly was exactly half finished when the British began their bombardment in advance of the great offensive that Haig had been waiting so long to undertake at Ypres. In intensity and duration the barrage dwarfed what the Germans had done in opening the Battle of Verdun, dwarfed what the British themselves had done at the Somme almost exactly a year before. Along fifteen miles of front, more than three thousand guns, more than double the density at the Somme, began pouring a day-and-night deluge of high explosives, shrapnel, and gas onto the Germans opposite. During the two weeks ending on July 31 they would fire four million rounds, a hundred thousand of them gas, compared with a mere million during the Somme preparation. These shells had a total weight of sixty-five thousand tons and would inflict thirty thousand casualties on the German Fourth Army even before the British infantry was engaged.

The landscape, already a barren expanse of shell holes and rubble, was rearranged again and again and again, burying the living while excavating the dead. Not incidentally, the rearrangement process destroyed what remained of the area's intricate drainage system. If rain came—and rain was almost certain to come to Flanders at this time of year—there would be no place for the water to go.

Douglas Haig was now in much the same position that Nivelle had put himself in earlier in the year: proceeding in the face of alarmed skepticism (Foch had called Haig's plan "futile, fantastic and dangerous") and refusing to be dissuaded. His goal, once the infantry and the tanks that had been assembled for the offensive went into action, was to drive the Germans back at least three miles on the first day, fifteen miles in eight days. As soon as the railway junction at Roulers had been captured, a meticulously trained division with its own tank force was to be landed on the coast behind the German lines. The Fourth British Army, positioned near where the River Yser enters the sea, was then to move eastward under the protection of the Royal Navy's shipboard guns and link up with the landing force. The Germans, at the end of their strength, would not have enough troops to form a new defensive line once they were forced to withdraw from the coast.

That was the plan. One of its problems—by no means the only problem, but one of the most serious—was that the Germans knew what was coming. Haig appears to have resigned himself to the impossibility of concealing anything except the amphibious landing, which was put under such tight security that the men training for it in the Thames estuary on the north side of the Channel were not allowed to write home. The Germans, from the air and from their observation points on the low ridges circling Ypres, had a clear view of the gathering of the greatest concentration of soldiers and weapons in the history of the British army. And of course they reacted. Fourteen German divisions were transferred to Ypres, four of them from the Eastern Front, while the British were making ready. A week after the Germans were blown off Messines Ridge, Ludendorff sent Fritz von Lossberg, the originator of the new system of flexible defense in depth, to Ypres as chief of staff of the German Fourth Army. This gave Lossberg more than fifty days to prepare. As he did so, the confidence of the German commanders grew. "My mind is quite at rest about the attack, as we have never possessed such strong reserves, so well trained for their part, as on [this] front," Crown Prince Rupprecht of Bavaria, head of the army group in Flanders, observed in his diary.

On July 10 the Germans had launched a preemptive raid on the Yser bridgehead from which the British Fourth Army was to move eastward to join the landing force. This raid, in addition to driving most of the British back to the west side of the river, led to the discovery of a tunnel they had planned to use to blow up key German positions at the start of their advance. The discovery confirmed that something big was being planned for the coast, and the Germans' capture of the high ground (high as such things are measured in Flanders) just east of the Yser left the British in a far less advantageous position.

On both sides the preparations were on the vast scale that industrialized total war was making commonplace. Just the construction of the concrete pillboxes that were Lossberg's first line of defense and the underground bunkers being installed behind the lines to shelter his counterattack troops required a seemingly endless supply of gravel. It was purchased in Holland and carried across Belgium on a stream of trains.

Hanging over everything was the question of whether, his enthusiasm notwithstanding, Haig was preparing anything really different from what the generals of the Entente had been trying without success since the end of the Battle of the Marne. Lloyd George thought not. Winston Churchill thought not as well and said so. Lloyd George had appointed him minister of munitions in July, and though at the insistence of the Conservatives he was not allowed to join any of the government's key war committees, he never hesitated to express himself on policy matters. Pétain, no less than Foch, also thought not. If the immensity of Haig's resources justified his confidence, if his barely concealed contempt for the French made him feel certain that he could succeed where Nivelle had failed, the bloody futility of all previous Western Front offensives provided equal justification for the doubts of the skeptics.

Then there was the weather. It continued to be unusually dry, but this was unlikely to continue, and Haig was determined not to waste time. Tensions rose as one rainless day followed another and the pieces of the plan failed to fall into place. Haig had decided, to the disappointment of older and more senior generals, to assign responsibility for the main part of his offensive to the youngest of his army commanders, the forty-seven-year-old Hubert Gough. Gough was chosen for his boldness, for his eagerness for action, and probably in part for his being, like Haig, a cavalryman by origin. He was also an indifferent executive who had gathered around himself a staff better known for its arrogance than for its ability to perform. At Ypres the ability to manage enormous numbers of men and matériel mattered a good deal more than dash, and difficulties were not slow to appear. On July 7 Gough reported that his preparations were not on schedule and that he was concerned about the readiness of the French forces on his left. He said he needed more time. Haig (who would have been justified in remembering what Napoleon had said to his generals—"ask me for *anything* but time") replied with a flat no. Six days later the two generals met, and again Gough asked for a postponement. He said he needed five days. Haig granted him three, moving the start of the attack from July 25 to July 28. On July 17, with the bombardment under way but fog now impeding preparations, yet another delay of three days was found to be unavoidable. The danger of rain made every one of those days a painful loss, and Haig, increasingly anxious, knew it.

Lloyd George and his War Policy Committee, caught between their fears of what this offensive could turn into and the political risks of forbidding it, seemed paralyzed. Five days into the barrage, they still had not approved the offensive. Finally on July 20, having through their own inaction left themselves with almost no choice, they informed Haig that he was free to proceed. They did so grudgingly at first, warning him that he would have to stop if his attack were not quickly successful and asking him to specify his objectives. Haig was offended, and when he said so he received another message assuring him that he had the committee's "wholehearted support." From that point everything began to move rapidly. On July 22 the barrage was raised to a higher level of intensity. On July 26 seven hundred British and French aircraft took to the air and cleared it of Germans. Two days later came the final stage of the bombardment, a counterbattery barrage intended to knock out the German artillery, which had been inflicting heavy damage on British positions. It came to a premature end as fog returned and made it impossible for the gunners on either side to find their targets. The weather continued to hold. The British would be advancing over terrain that artillery had made a mad jumble of shell holes, but at least the surface was dry. The last two weeks had been punctuated with showers but not to a troublesome extent.

The offensive went off at 3:50 a.m. on July 31, with seventeen Entente divisions advancing and seventeen waiting in the rear. At the northern end were two French divisions whose mission was to protect Gough's flank. At the other end were five divisions of Plumer's Second Army. Their objectives too were modest: to capture a few strongpoints but mainly to stand in place and hold the Messines Ridge as a pivot point for Gough's advance. Ten divisions of Gough's Fifth Army were the battering ram, their assignment to force the Germans back and set the stage for the reserves to come forward. Gough had almost twenty-three hundred guns on his seven-mile section of front, one for every six yards. Together he and Plumer and the French had nearly half a million men.

Waiting for the attack was a hornets' nest of German machine-gun nests arranged in a rough checkerboard pattern. Behind them the Fourth Army's twenty divisions were arranged in four clusters: nine nearest the front, six behind them, two more to their rear, and the last three even farther back. Almost anywhere the British or French succeeded in making a hole, German reserves would be in position to move forward and seal it.

Some things went exactly according to Haig's plan. The troops on Gough's flanks made good progress, advancing to their objectives with comparatively little difficulty. Even in the center, the forward units managed to fight their way through the first German zone (which was, after all, supposed to yield when pressed) and into the second. They penetrated nearly two miles at a few points, no more than half a mile at others. Six thousand German soldiers, shattered by the frenzied final hours of the bombardment, were taken prisoner in a few hours. But by early afternoon, with a light rain sprinkling the field and the leading British units no longer in contact with their artillery, the Germans opened fire with field guns positioned on elevated ground to the north and south of the salient created by the advance. This was artillery that might have been destroyed if not for the fog of the preceding days. The British, taking heavy losses, were forced to pull back. Of the fifty-two tanks that had advanced with Gough's troops, twenty-two broke down and another nineteen were put out of action by German fire. By late afternoon the attack was at a standstill and the drizzle had turned to hard rain. Haig, not aware that twenty-three thousand of his men had been killed or wounded, perhaps drawing a comparison with the first day on the Somme, reported to London that the day's events had been "highly satisfactory and the losses light for so great a battle."

On this same day Pope Benedict XV sent a letter to the governments of the Entente and the Central Powers, offering to mediate a peace of no territorial conquests. As before, a clear response from Berlin, an agreement to give up Belgium, would have been the essential next step. Once again the Germans were unable to respond. A young new foreign minister, Richard von Kühlmann, decided to ignore this latest Vatican initiative and approach London directly instead. He hoped to separate the British from their allies with a private promise to withdraw from Belgium in return for a cessation of hostilities. But the new chancellor, Michaelis, destroyed whatever tiny potential this idea may have had. He yielded to Ludendorff's insistence that Germany must retain effective control not only of most of Belgium but of the coal and iron mines of France's Longwy-Briey district and must be promised extensive portions of Africa as well. There were other clumsy efforts at arranging talks at about this time—Austria and France became involved in various ways at various points—but nothing could come of them because on both sides the people with the power to decide were determined to dictate any final settlement. The performance of Michaelis was so unimpressive through all of it, and like Bethmann Hollweg he came to be so hated in the Reichstag, that he had to resign after only three months in office.

Rain was falling in torrents when Haig resumed his attack on August 2. With the Flanders drainage system in ruins, every hole filled with water and the ground became a soupy morass to a depth that no man's foot could reach. The tanks could not move, the airplanes could not fly, and the German artillery was taking an increasing toll. Still Haig tried to push on. But after two more days, with the rain continuing and the number of French and British casualties up to sixty-eight thousand, he finally ordered a halt until the rain stopped and the ground could dry out.

For the troops, the break in the fighting was something less than deliverance. One British officer would record the experience of waiting day after day in a bunker taken from the Germans. "Inside it was only about five foot high and at the bottom there was about two foot of water. This water was simply horrid, full of refuse, old tins, and even excreta. Whenever shells burst near it the smell was perfectly overpowering. Luckily, there was a sort of concrete shelf the Boche had made about two foot above ground level. It was on this shelf that four officers and six other ranks spent the night. There wasn't room to lie down, there was hardly room to sit upright, and we more or less crouched there. Outside the pillbox was an enormous shell-hole full of water, and the only way out was over a ten-inch plank. Inside the shell-hole was the dead body of a Boche who had been there a very long time and who floated or sank on alternate days according to the atmosphere. The shell-holes were crowded with dead and dying men, the latter crying out for help as they slowly expired."

Haig had to wait until August 10, when at last it became possible to mount a fresh assault aimed mainly at capturing or driving away the German light artillery. This was another limited and costly success. As soon as it ended, Haig began planning for a resumption on August 14. But the rain started again, causing one and then a second postponement of twenty-four hours. When it came, the next attack was more of the same: much death, little to show for it. Haig decided not to give up, which he would have been amply justified in doing and was probably obligated to do under the promises he had made to London. Instead he prepared to change directions.

Thus ended the first phase of the Third Battle of Ypres. In three and a half weeks Haig's troops had advanced two miles—not much more than half of his objective for the first day. The amphibious force remained idle, waiting for the capture of Roulers. As it became clear that Roulers was never going to be captured, that force would be quietly disbanded. On both sides divisions too battered to continue had to be replaced. There were twenty-three such divisions on the German side, fourteen on the British. "Blood and mud, blood and mud," Lloyd George complained back in London, "they can think of nothing better."

The weight of the campaign was now shifted away from Gough to Plumer's Second Army. In two years at Ypres, Plumer had won the loyalty of his troops with a Pétain-like concern for their welfare and a marked unwillingness to waste their lives. The morale of his army was high, the soldiers eager for action. And unlike Gough or Haig, Plumer had paid attention to the Germans' new defensive methods. He devised a countertactic, one possibly inspired by his experience at Messines Ridge, and was given Haig's approval and three weeks to get ready. While he was doing so, Haig was called to London for another meeting with Lloyd George and the War Policy Committee. It was an arid repeat of the earlier discussions. Haig, again supported by Robertson, argued the necessity of continuing to pound away at the Germans until they broke, which he was sure they were about to do. He returned to France with his authority unimpaired, leaving behind a most unhappy prime minister.

At this point Haig had more reason for confidence than he knew. Plumer had in fact found the key to the German defense, one that neutralized its strengths and exploited its inherent weaknesses. Like most truly brilliant military plans, Plumer's approach was elegant in its simplicity and straightforward in its recognition of the facts on the ground. It began with the premise that relatively short gains—gains of a mile or less—had become available almost for the asking as a result of the thinness and elasticity of the Germans' forward positions. Premise number two was that gains of several miles—never mind breakthroughs of the kind that Entente commanders had been seeking since 1914—were now more out of the question than ever because of the Germans' increased ability to counterattack in force. The conclusion was so blindingly obvious that only Plumer and his staff had seen it: the German system could be outsmarted with attacks that stopped upon capturing the easy ground and never went far enough to trigger a counterattack. Cumulatively, a series of such attacks might drive the Germans backward out of their defenses and into a war of maneuver that they lacked the manpower to survive.

Plumer was too good a general to rely on cleverness alone. He used the first three weeks of September—weeks suddenly, blissfully free of rain—to pull together a mass of artillery even more awesome than those of July and August. At the end of his preparations he had one artillery piece for every five yards of front. The Germans would be subjected to five waves of fire, each a zone of destruction two hundred yards deep. The first zone was shrapnel exclusively, the second high explosives, and the third indirect machine-gun fire ("indirect" meaning that the gunners, unable to see their targets, aimed into the air so as to bring the bullets arcing down on the defenders from above). The last two were more high explosives. Every German position would find itself in one zone after another as the entire pattern, half a mile deep from front to back, swept over it in a storm that changed its character every few minutes. Plumer's artillery would fire three and a half million rounds in this way before and on the day of his attack.

Plumer was able to conceal his preparations behind the slightly elevated ground that he had captured first at Messines Ridge and later in moving forward on Gough's flank. When he attacked on September 20, his troops advancing behind a creeping barrage, those Germans who had not been killed by the artillery or pulled back from it were subdued almost with ease. Upon reaching their assigned objectives, the attackers stopped and hurriedly began constructing defenses. The main body of German troops, meanwhile, remained in the rear, waiting for the British to come at them. By the time they realized that the British were finished for the day, it was too late for a counterattack to be effective. The whole operation had been quick and clean, and within the limits of its objectives it had been a complete success. Though it did not come cheaply in the end—British casualties ultimately totaled more than twenty thousand, mainly as a result of German artillery fire after the advance—it was clear to both sides that the game had entered a new phase. The Germans were as alarmed by the results of this Battle of the Menin Road as the British commanders were elated.

The attack had captured not just German ground but part of the German infrastructure—pillboxes and bunkers essential to the new system. This increased the defenders' vulnerability to further attack. Seeing this, Plumer hurried his artillery forward and on September 26 attacked again in what has gone into the chronicles as the Battle of Polygon Wood. The weather remained clear, so that scores of British and French pilots were able to fly low over the German defenders, strafing them and dropping bombs. After another horrendous barrage the infantry

advanced on a front of four miles, dug in after advancing the assigned half-mile, and again left the main German forces looking
on helplessly. The Germans had lost another set of strongpoints.
If this happened several times, they might be left with no infrastructure at all.

Desperate, the Germans gave up on their new system. They
reverted to older tactics, positioning large numbers of troops in a
strong forward line to block the attackers from making easy early
gains. Plumer again had his guns on the move, preparing for another strike. The fates seemed to have turned entirely in his favor:
the meteorological record contained no evidence of a Flanders
September as dry as the last month had been.

But a light drizzle began on October 3, and it was still falling
the next morning when a fresh British assault began the Battle
of Brookseinde. Even more than September 20 and 26, this was
a day of disaster for the Germans. The men in the new forward
line, having had a mere handful of days in which to improvise
their defenses, were slaughtered wholesale by Plumer's barrage.
The reserves, positioned too far forward by generals too eager to
get at the attackers, were caught in the same inferno. The British
troops advanced only seven hundred yards before, maddeningly
for the Germans, stopping as before. In the process they killed
or wounded thirty thousand of the defenders, taking twenty-five
thousand casualties themselves. This rate of loss, painful for the
British, was unsustainable on the German side. And conventional
tactics plainly were incapable of keeping it from happening again.

At his headquarters, alarmed by the dispatches arriving from
Flanders, Ludendorff cast about for some way to launch an offensive that would draw British troops away from Ypres. No such
thing was possible. The necessary troops were not available, in
part because Pétain was now launching holding attacks at Verdun and elsewhere with French divisions sufficiently recovered
to be trusted in action. Ludendorff ordered the Sixth Army to
shift back to the new system. At least this would keep most of the
troops out of reach of the British artillery. Beyond that there was
nothing for the Germans to do but hope for deliverance. "The
fighting on the Western Front became more severe and costly
than any the German Army had yet experienced," Ludendorff
would recall of this period. "I myself was put to a terrible strain.

Man and beast, together in war
A German rider and his mounts, prepared to encounter gas.

The state of affairs in the West appeared to prevent the execution of our plans elsewhere. Our wastage had been so high as to cause grave misgivings, and had exceeded all expectations."

Deliverance came literally from the heavens. The drizzle that had started on October 3 turned to a steady rain, and after a few days more it became a downpour that went on and on. Flanders was turning into an enormous shallow lake, every shell hole and piece of low ground filled to the brim. It would have been a sensible time to wrap up Third Ypres, and when the British commanders met on October 7, Plumer and Gough both were in favor of doing so. Haig would not hear of it. Plumer's advance had left his troops deployed along a line that would be difficult to hold without exceptional hardship through the coming winter. One remedy would have been to pull back to slightly higher and dryer ground—a horrifying prospect for Haig in light of the price paid for his gains and what was sure to be Lloyd George's reaction. The only acceptable course, Haig declared, was to push forward to the capture of Passchendaele Ridge, the northern extension of the same snakelike strip of high ground of which Messines Ridge was also a part. Virtually every British division in the Ypres salient having been reduced to tatters, the lead role was to be played by divisions from the Commonwealth—from Australia, New Zealand, and Canada.

The first attack at Passchendaele, the Valley of the Passion, went off in the rain on October 9 under conditions that were not merely difficult but impossible. Standing water covered almost everything, and what was not under water (the men included) was covered with mud that seemed to go down and down forever. It was impossible to find a foothold, impossible to move the artillery or set it firmly in place where it was, nearly impossible even for men on foot to move. Big guns sank out of sight. So did an entire light railway. The only way to bring shells forward was by pack mule, but many of the mules sank and drowned. When fired, the shells disappeared without exploding because the surface, even the mud beneath the water, had become too soft to activate their fuses. Somehow the Australians and New Zealanders at the center of the attack managed to fight their way forward, but their progress served only to expose them to machine-gun fire from three directions instead of one. Finally they had no choice but to struggle back to where they had begun. The wounded, unavoidably left behind, disappeared into the muck.

"The slope," said an Australian officer of a scene he came upon while on reconnaissance, "was littered with dead, both theirs and ours. I got to one pillbox to find it just a mass of dead, and so I passed on carefully to the one ahead. Here I found about fifty men alive, of the Manchesters. Never have I seen men so broken or demoralized. They were huddled up close behind the box in the last stages of exhaustion and fear. Fritz had been sniping them off all day, and had accounted for fifty-seven that day—the dead and dying lay in piles. The wounded were numerous—unattended and weak, they groaned and moaned all over the place . . . Some had been there four days already." Moving on again, he came upon another bunker with "twenty-four wounded men inside, two dead Huns and six outside, in various stages of decomposition. The stench was dreadful . . . When day broke I looked over the position. Over forty dead lay within twenty yards of where I stood and the whole valley was full of them."

When the Canadians were selected to lead the next assault, their commander, Sir Arthur Currie, expressed his reservations. He predicted that taking Passchendaele would cost him sixteen thousand men. He did not, however, refuse. When his men attacked on October 26, they took heavy casualties, inflicted equally severe losses on the Germans, and were brought to a halt well short of Passchendaele Ridge and the sorry assortment of low rubble that had once been Passchendaele village. The Canadians tried again four days later, and the results were no different. A shortage of drinking water, ironically, added to the torment of the men. Bringing water forward was as difficult as hauling shells, and the swamp that extended in all directions had been poisoned by human waste and the rotting cadavers of animals and men.

Another of Europe's battlegrounds was now fully ablaze—the Italian front this time, where the bloodletting that had marked Italy's entry into the war in the summer of 1915 suddenly soared to new heights. The Italian commander in chief, Luigi Cadorna, had launched two more Battles of the Isonzo earlier in the year, in May and August, and these two fights had cost his armies more than two hundred and eighty thousand casualties. The Austrians too had suffered hideously, and when the two battles were over, both sides were begging their allies for help. The monstrous Cadorna, a kind of savage in uniform who seriously advocated the shooting of every tenth man in units that failed to perform to his satisfaction, feared that the collapse of Russia was going to free Austria-Hungary to send all of its armies against Italy. He turned to the British and French for reinforcements, but found them willing to do no more than continue to send artillery. Austria-Hungary's young Emperor Karl, warned by his general staff (no longer headed by Conrad, who had been demoted) that the Austrians were unlikely to survive another of Cadorna's assaults, asked Ludendorff for help. Rebuffed, he appealed directly

General Sir Arthur Currie
*Foretold the cost of
taking Passchendaele.*

to Kaiser Wilhelm, who intervened. When a general sent to eval-
uate the Italian front reported that the Austrians were indeed at
the end of their strength, Ludendorff reluctantly created a new
German Fourteenth Army out of infantry, artillery, and aircraft
taken from the Baltic, Romania, and Alsace-Lorraine. He sent
this army southward under the veteran Otto von Below with orders to stabilize the Italian front with the shortest, most limited
campaign possible.

The resulting Battle of Caporetto—also known, inevitably, as
the Twelfth Battle of the Isonzo—began on October 24 with a
joint German-Austrian attack that quickly developed into an unexpectedly far-reaching success. The Germans and Austrians, whose
thirty-three divisions faced forty-one divisions of Italians, advanced
more than ten miles on the first day, and the retreat that Cadorna attempted to organize soon degenerated into headlong flight
and the surrender of hundreds of thousands of his troops. Below's
orders were to proceed no farther than the River Tagliamento,
which flows southward into the Adriatic west of the Isonzo, but his
forces reached that objective so quickly that they pushed on in hot
pursuit. The government in Rome fell, Cadorna was sacked, and
the Italian forces continued to run until they were on the banks of
the River Piave twenty miles beyond the Tagliamento. There they
were able to make a stand. They were helped in doing so by the
exhaustion of the pursuing Germans and the onset of winter rains.

Below had advanced eighty miles in seventy days, shortening the southern front by a crucial two hundred miles. Italian casualties totaled three hundred and twenty thousand during the retreat to the Piave, including two hundred and sixty-five thousand men taken prisoner, and the stand on the Piave had claimed another one hundred and forty thousand. Tactically, Caporetto had been one of the war's most spectacularly successful campaigns, and when it ended the war on the southern front seemed almost over. But it was not conclusive. The upheavals that it generated brought the government in Rome and its army under more capable leadership. The gross mistreatment that had destroyed the morale of the Italian troops ended. All this would work to the detriment of the Central Powers.

Not until November 6, under nightmarish conditions, did fresh Canadian troops finally drive the Germans off a large enough portion of Passchendaele Ridge for Haig to claim victory. The price had been almost exactly what Currie had predicted: nearly sixteen thousand men. A final attack four days later allowed the Canadians to consolidate their new positions and brought the Third Battle of Ypres to an end. In three months and one week the forces of the Entente had advanced all of four and a half miles, taking ground that Haig described as a splendid starting point for further fighting in 1918 but that less ecstatic generals dismissed as worthless. The British, Canadians, Anzacs, and French between them had taken a quarter of a million casualties, the Germans nearly as many. The Germans had used—and in many cases used up—118 divisions. The British, whose divisions were considerably larger than their German counterparts at this point, had used forty-three, the French six. Both sides were exhausted, the BEF nearly as broken as the French army had been after the Chemin des Dames.

Haig, however, was not satisfied. On November 20, near Cambrai east of the old Arras battlefield, he sent nineteen divisions and the largest force of tanks yet assembled into an attack on a thinly defended section of the Hindenburg Line. Like Caporetto, this was a tremendous success for the attackers from the start, but unlike Caporetto the success was short-lived and soon reversed. Of the 216 new Mark IV tanks used in the initial assault, seventy-one broke down mechanically, sixty-five were destroyed by enemy

Not invincible
Burnt skeleton of a British tank, in German hands.

fire, and forty-three bogged down. Some of them, however, bulled their way through the forward defenses, terrifying the Germans and putting them to flight. But Haig had intended Cambrai as a mere demonstration, a year-ending morale-booster. No follow-through had been planned, and none was attempted. The British found themselves with enemies on three sides—always the curse that followed success on a narrow front—and on November 30 a counterattack by twenty German divisions recovered almost all the lost ground.

A German lieutenant at Cambrai left a record of how he and his comrades learned to cope with Haig's tanks. "When the first tanks passed the first line, we thought we would be compelled to retreat towards Berlin," he wrote. "I remember one tank, by the name of Hyena, which advanced very far and suddenly stopped about 1,000 yards from my little dugout. Some of the boys soon discovered they could stop the tanks by throwing a hand grenade into the manhole on the top. Once this was known, the boys realized that there was a blind spot—that the machine guns couldn't reach every point around the tank, and these points were very important in the defense.

"I was shocked and felt very sorry for those fellows in the

tanks, because there was no escape for them. Once a man was on top of the tank it was doomed to failure, and the poor fellows were not able to escape. The fuel would start to burn and after an hour and a half or two hours we saw only burning tanks in front and behind us. Then the approaching troops behind the tanks still had to overcome the machine guns of our infantry. These were still effective because the British artillery had to stop shooting as the tanks were advancing, and naturally some of our machine gun nests were still in full action.

"Anyhow, the attack came to a standstill and we waited for several regiments of cavalry to sweep up and drive us towards Berlin. But this didn't happen, much to our surprise. When new troops were pulled together near this break-in of the British tanks, the situation settled down, we were formed anew, and afterwards we could clearly see the spot where the British tanks had driven into the German lines. Then after a few days we made a counterattack. It didn't succeed on the first or the second day, but on the third day we were finally successful."

Yet another British offensive had been for nothing. It had not, however, been without meaning. Generals on both sides saw that the new tanks, if properly used, could have produced very different results—that Cambrai was a sign of things to come.

And so ended 1917. On the Western Front, the year had taken the lives of two hundred and twenty-six thousand British, one hundred and thirty-six thousand French, and one hundred and twenty-one thousand German soldiers. And still the stalemate continued.

Between them, Arras, the Nivelle offensive, Third Ypres, and Cambrai had rendered the French and the British incapable of mounting a major offensive at the end of the approaching winter.

At the same time they had destroyed the Germans' confidence in their defensive system.

These two facts would shape the year ahead. They would put the conflict on the road to its end at last.

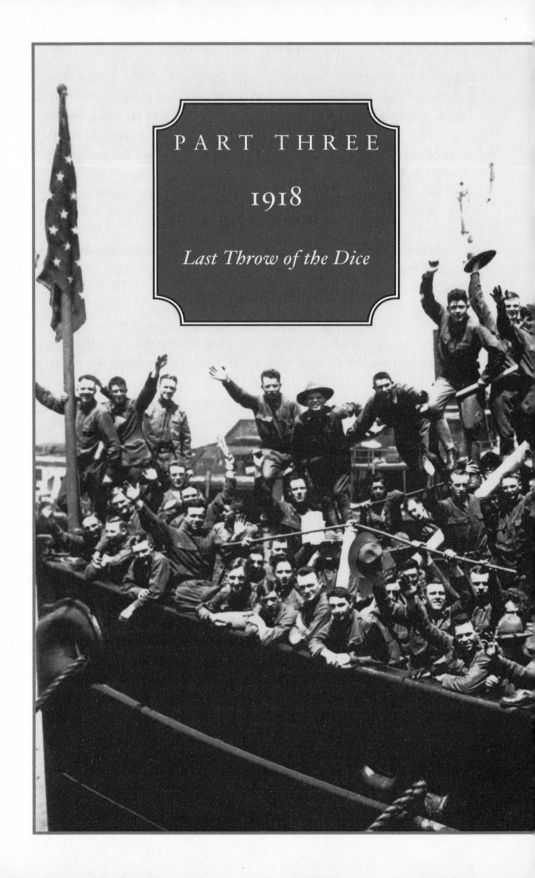

Doughboys: American soldiers embark for France.

Chapter 13

Going for Broke

"We make a hole, and the rest will take care of itself."
—Erich Ludendorff

The Europe that settled in for the war's fourth winter was beginning to give evidence of being a dying civilization. Russia, often hailed before the war as the European nation with the most brilliant future, was in ruins. Tsar Nicholas and his wife and children were prisoners, Kerensky's potentially democratic government was gone, and Lenin and his Bolsheviks were taking control of the wreckage. The people were sunk in destitution, without security or stability, millions of them so sick of the war as to be unwilling to participate in it. Lenin, accordingly, was almost desperately eager to give them peace.

Conditions were less terrible elsewhere, but not always a great deal less. Even in France and Great Britain, where access to the riches of the New World had prevented discomfort from deepening into general deprivation, there was weariness with the war and the heartbreak it had brought. There was also weariness, unmeasurable because harshly suppressed, with governments committed to fighting on no matter what the cost. Everyday life had become dark. The "democracies" allowed little in the way of liberty to citizens not fully in favor of the war, information not bent to the purposes of propaganda was difficult to find, and there seemed no reason to expect anything except more of the same, conceivably for years to come.

For Germany and even more for Austria-Hungary, strangled by a blockade that there was now no hope of breaking, the fate of Russia was a warning of what could lie ahead. Here there was no mere discomfort but widespread malnutrition and the prospect of another winter without heat or light or enough food to sustain health or even life. Here was the despair of watching one's children starve. Life had become tragic—unlivable, even—in the most elemental terms. The possibility of rebellion against the war and the people responsible for continuing it was becoming real.

As winter brought with it the usual suspension of major military operations, the general staffs began once again to make their plans for the year ahead. On both sides, this annual ritual was becoming more difficult. The failure of one campaign after another to deliver what the generals promised—the failure of *every* offensive on the Western Front, from the initial German drive on Paris to Passchendaele—made it hard to believe that the next great scheme could have any chance of success. The armies on both sides were in deplorable condition.

Although Russia had not surrendered or made peace, the two-front war was at an end. Until American troops could be mustered in sufficient numbers and adequately trained—no such thing was expected for another half-year at best—Britain and France would have to fight the Germans alone. There were the Italians, of course, but in the aftermath of Caporetto little could be expected of them.

And Italy's losses seemed almost unimportant compared with those of Britain and France. The latter's casualties totaled three million by late 1917; they had occurred at an average of forty thousand per month throughout that murderous year, and replacements were hard to find. General Pétain, the commander in chief, forecast that he would need 1.02 million troops on the Western Front in 1918 but would have only 85 percent of that number. (As things worked out, he never had 75 percent.) Under Pétain's ministrations the army had largely recovered from the mutiny of 1917. It had fought off more than a hundred German attacks from June through August and had attacked successfully at Verdun and the Chemin des Dames, capturing ground and taking prisoners. However, Prime Minister Clemenceau and his principal military adviser, Ferdinand Foch, had limited regard for Pétain's achievement.

In their opinion his caution was excessive, and his determination to carry the fight to the enemy much too qualified.

With its larger population, its global empire from which to draw manpower, and "only" two million casualties since the start of the war, Britain should have been in a better position than France. But in fact it was not, at least in the view of its commanders. The problem was not, strictly speaking, a shortage of soldiers. Rather it was Prime Minister David Lloyd George's refusal to let the commander of the BEF, Douglas Haig, have enough divisions for a repetition of the Somme or Passchendaele. Some four hundred and fifty thousand fit and ready combat troops were being held at home at Lloyd George's insistence, and only labor units that were neither trained nor armed for battle were allowed to cross the Channel. Haig was so short of replacements that he reduced the number of battalions per brigade from four to three to avoid having to dissolve whole divisions. This gave rise to organizational confusion that would be far from resolved when the British found themselves once again in heavy fighting.

In terms of the matériel needed to support their populations and troops, however, Britain and France were entirely out of danger. The American cornucopia was disgorging itself across the Atlantic, overwhelming the German U-boats as they tried to stem the flow. Virtually everything needed by the Entente, money included, was being generously provided. British production of ammunition had been increased by nearly 3,000 percent during the two years beginning in March 1915, when Lloyd George became minister of munitions. It underwent a further quadrupling in the nine months after Winston Churchill, exonerated by a commission investigating the Gallipoli disaster, took charge of production. By late 1917 a quarter of a million tons of shells was being shipped across the Channel monthly, and this was less than a third of the tonnage of supplies arriving at BEF bases on the north coast of France. The problem, for the Entente, was management. After three years of war there was still no effective mechanism for coordinating British and French operations.

In November 1917, shortly after the Battle of Caporetto, the Entente's leaders had met at Rapallo in Italy and agreed on the creation of a grandly titled Inter-Allied Supreme War Council. This body included the heads of the governments and representatives of their general staffs. The United States, though not involved at first, soon joined. Lloyd George welcomed the council as a counterweight to his own general staff—to Haig and "Wully" Robertson. Lloyd George had regarded Haig as an unfit commander of the BEF since before he became prime minister. He had never stopped wanting to remove Haig, but doing so had remained impossible.

The Supreme War Council proved to have value, but principally in improving administration. It was effective in coordinating the various national transportation systems, and in allocating matériel and, to a limited extent, manpower. It even, before the end of 1917, satisfied Lloyd George's highest aspirations for it by rejecting Haig's proposal of another offensive in Flanders. At its second meeting, in December at Versailles, the council decided that there should be no great offensives anywhere in 1918. Where the active direction of military operations was concerned, however, the council was useless. Neither Haig nor Pétain wanted to surrender control to an international authority, and neither cooperated with efforts to get them to do so. Early in 1918 King George V underscored Haig's untouchability—the strength of his support in high places—by promoting him to field marshal. At almost the same time, ironically, South African General Jan Smuts was on the continent on Lloyd George's behalf, secretly trying to identify a replacement for Haig. Both Herbert Plumer and Henry Rawlinson were regarded as possibilities.

The Central Powers had no comparable problems of coordination; Germany no longer had allies substantial enough to require much coordination with. Turkey, in her northern theaters, had been saved by Russia's collapse. But she was exhausted and overextended. To the south she was in increasing peril from British forces pushing eastward out of Egypt and a British-supported Arab revolt. Falkenhayn was in the Middle East now, as was Otto Liman von Sanders, the onetime commander at Gallipoli. Their assignment was to help the Turks, but they had neither the troops nor the matériel to make a decisive difference. Bulgaria was safe enough, for the time being, but unable to do more than help in the Balkans. It was unsettled by domestic opposition to the regime that had taken it to war on the side of the Central Powers.

That left Austria-Hungary, now little more than an empty

shell. In 1917 Vienna conscripted into its tattered armies the hundred and sixty thousand eligible men—boys, really—born in 1900. That left it with no remaining sources of manpower except for whatever wounded veterans and repatriated prisoners of war (four hundred thousand of these would be recovered from Russia early in 1918) could be returned to combat duty. The Austrians were dangerously short of coal, iron, oil, guns, ammunition, and food for men and animals. The horses needed to move artillery were dying by the tens of thousands because there was no fodder. The 1917 potato harvest, one of the few substantial sources of new food, would be exhausted by spring. Monthly rifle production was plummeting from one hundred and thirteen thousand in March 1917 to nine thousand the following February. Production of heavy shells, which exceeded four hundred thousand per month in the autumn of 1917, would be down to a third of that less than a year later. Bandages were being made of paper because there was no cotton. Paper underwear was being issued to the troops. For soldiers and civilians alike, life had become a degrading struggle for survival.

In November the Austro-Hungarian general staff, in reviewing its options, was forced to the conclusion that its armies would be incapable of mounting offensive operations in 1918. It still had forty-four divisions on the now-quiet Russian front and thirty-seven in Italy, but these were so depleted of men and equipment, typically including between five and eight thousand troops each, as to be barely worthy of being called divisions. Desertion was epidemic, those troops who did not desert were displaying an increasing inclination to revolt (this was especially true of returning prisoners of war), and in rural areas life was reverting to a kind of Dark Ages barbarism. Deserters formed themselves into bandit gangs and preyed on local populations.

Conrad had been displaced as chief of staff but commanded an army on the Italian front. And evidently he had learned nothing in three years of mounting grand campaigns beyond the capabilities of his forces. He began hatching plans for an offensive southward out of the Tyrolean Alps onto the plains northwest of Venice—yet another scheme for punishing the despised Italians, made more attractive this time by the hope of capturing as much territory as possible before the hoped-for German victory. Soon Conrad was peddling his ideas in Vienna. His superiors did their best to ignore him.

All of which left Germany on her own. Even so, the situation seemed far from hopeless. In spite of another year of heavy casualties, in spite too of shortages of many essentials, the end of the war in the east was making it possible to bring Berlin's military might fully to bear on the Western Front. And if the German armies were no longer what they had been two or three years earlier, they were no more badly damaged than those of Britain and France. If they were wretchedly ill equipped in comparison with their enemies—even Germany's front-line troops could be given small rations of meat only three or four times weekly, and their trucks and wagons had no rubber tires—in other ways they enjoyed significant advantages.

High on the list of such advantages was the strength of the German defenses in Belgium and France. At all points except where the difficulties of the terrain made enemy attack improbable, these defenses had been improved beyond recognition since 1914. They were massive, sophisticated, ten-mile-deep systems of interconnected and mutually supportive machine-gun pillboxes, moatlike traps for infantry and tanks, and artillery-proof bunkers, all of it guarded by shoals of barbed and razor wire. Hundreds of thousands of laborers, many of them prisoners of war and civilians from captured territory, had been engaged in building this system since the start of the stalemate. The result was a barricade that, once reinforced with troops from the east, promised to be all but impregnable.

In the second half of 1917, first on the northeastern front and then at Caporetto and Cambrai, the Germans had introduced a new offensive system to complement their defenses. Called the "Hutier method" because it was first used by a cousin of Ludendorff's named General Oskar von Hutier, this system promised to be a way of breaking the deadlock in the West. It involved a new kind of assault unit made up of detachments of only six or eight men, so-called storm troops trained not to try to overwhelm the enemy's defenses with sheer mass but to make use of whatever cover the terrain afforded, slip around and past the strongest positions (instead of stopping to destroy them), and so move deep into

General Oskar von Hutier, at left
First to employ the new offensive doctrine.

enemy territory with unprecedented speed. The bypassed strong-points would later be reduced by larger, more heavily armed units following in a second wave. Though such tactics had been tried on only a modest scale on the Western Front, there seemed no reason why they should not prove effective in much larger operations—*if* the Germans took the offensive.

That was the question facing the high command: whether to attack or stand on the defensive as in 1915 and 1917. The decision was Ludendorff's, and from the start he favored the offensive. He was influenced in that direction by what Plumer had achieved with his limited attacks at Ypres late in 1917, but what decided him was the U.S. army. American troops were arriving in France by the scores of thousands every month (the number would grow to a quarter of a million monthly by mid-1918). Though almost all were still in training, they would soon be a force of overwhelming size. Green though they were, the Yanks were well fed, enthusiastic, and equipped with the best of everything. Still unbloodied, they displayed a kind of innocent eagerness that was no longer possible for the British, French, or Germans.

Ludendorff calculated that the Americans could not be a problem until the middle of 1918, but that thereafter they would tip the scales conclusively. If Germany was to win the war in the west, it had only the first half of the year in which to do so. It was with this in mind that a new booklet, "The Attack in Trench Warfare," a treatise explaining the Hutier method and how to use it, was distributed to the armies of Germany. Selected officers were pulled out of the line for an eight-day retraining course that was soon expanded to four weeks. The best German divisions in the east, along with soldiers under age thirty-five culled from less capable units, were loaded onto trains and moved back to Germany for rest, refitting, and instruction. The goal was to create forty-two elite mobile divisions made up of the best soldiers Germany still had—fit young fighters skilled in the use of grenades, light machine guns, flamethrowers, and trench mortars and schooled in the new system. After years of standing in a defensive posture that offered no chance of victory, after ordeals like Passchendaele, these men wanted to attack. They "pined for the offensive," Ludendorff said, "and after Russia's collapse expected it with relief." Something similar was true of the home front. People not only wanted an end to the war but expected—had been taught to expect by German propaganda—that the end would come soon and in the form of an unambiguous victory.

The remaining question was where to attack. That came down to a question of *whom* to attack—the British or the French? To explore it, on November 11 Ludendorff met with Generals Friedrich von der Schulenburg, chief of staff of Crown Prince Wilhelm's army group, and Hermann von Kuhl, chief of staff of the army group commanded by Crown Prince Rupprecht of Bavaria. Both were seasoned commanders (Kuhl had been Kluck's chief of staff during the 1914 drive on Paris), and both had strong opinions. Schulenburg urged an attack on both sides of the Verdun salient—not as ridiculous an idea as it might at first seem, the French having drastically reduced their defenses in that sector. He saw a possibility of shattering the line around Verdun and driving the French back toward Paris. Kuhl pushed for Flanders, arguing that it was the only place where strategic objectives could be achieved. If the BEF's line could be pierced, the British would have their backs against the sea and might be destroyed or forced to escape to England. Ludendorff himself laid out a number of other possibilities, giving particular attention to the point near St. Quentin where the British and French lines met. He declared that no offensive could go forward unless three conditions were met. The Russians and Italians must continue to pose no threat. The attack must come at the earliest possible time—in March at the latest, in February if possible. Wherever it came, even if against the French, the objective must be the defeat of the British. The BEF, so tiny at the start of the war, was now the dominant element in the Entente's strength. If it could be eliminated, the French would be unable to continue. If it could be eliminated by midyear, the Americans would not matter.

Fifteen days later any lingering worries about a possible revival of the war on the Eastern Front were put to rest when three Russian soldiers waving a white flag approached the German line in Courland in the far north. They said they had been sent by General Kirilenko, a new chief of staff appointed by the Bolsheviks. Their mission was to communicate their government's wish for a negotiated peace. Within days German and Russian delegates, among them Max Hoffmann and German foreign minister Richard von Kühlmann (who had succeeded Arthur Zimmermann), were gathering in the city of Brest-Litovsk.

Many peace feelers were being put forward at about this time, usually secretly and with tangled motives, and the leaders on both sides were speaking publicly about their willingness to make peace on reasonable terms. The Entente was trying to arrange a separate peace with Vienna, which would have been fatal to Germany in the east. The Germans were using intermediaries to see if one member of the Entente or another—now London, now Paris, now Petrograd—might be ready to talk. And the pope,

who had regarded the war as madness from the start, continued
to rouse the ire of Italian nationalists by looking for some common ground upon which an armistice might be arranged. The
story of these pronouncements and initiatives, some of them sin-
cere and others cynical, is complicated, interesting, and at points
amusing or sad. But there was never much chance of working out
a general peace.

The only conceivable peace, as long as the deadlock continued,
was a return to the status quo ante. But at this stage only Russia and Austria-Hungary would have embraced such an idea, and
they were willing to do so only because they had failed. Berlin and
London and Paris and Rome still saw victory as possible or even
likely in the long run, and none would settle for less. In a sense,
all were *unable* to settle for less. Having told their peoples that this
was a fight of good against evil, they would have found a decision
to reconcile with the enemy (not to mention everything sacrificed
in fighting that enemy) awkward to explain.

Germany's leaders were more divided than those of the Entente on the question of war aims. Hindenburg and Ludendorff
still expected to win, and therefore they had no interest in peace
terms not dictated by Berlin. By contrast, Count Georg von
Hertling, the aged Bavarian Catholic and former professor of
philosophy who had become chancellor on November 1 after Michaelis resigned, said he wanted a place in history as the "reconciliation chancellor." But even for him reconciliation meant a peace
that brought gains to Germany—Luxembourg and Liège, perhaps,
as well as France's Longwy-Briey basin with its rich deposits of
coal and iron. In this he was supported by Richard von Kühlmann,
who pursued negotiations in many directions so energetically and
ingeniously that Hindenburg and Ludendorff came to regard him
as another of their problems. But he never did so with the intention of ending the fighting; his objective was to get any one member of the Entente to drop out of the war, freeing the generals to
finish off the others.

If Kühlmann's activities were less disastrous than Zimmermann's had been, they were sterile nevertheless. With Lloyd
George secure as prime minister in Britain and Clemenceau totally dominant in Paris, separating their two countries was impossible. Both men understood that Europe could not possibly be

returned to what it had been at the start of the war. The Russia that had been France's most important ally in 1914 no longer existed. Postwar Russia, broken and reduced, would be little better than a satellite of Germany—unless Germany too were broken. More than at the beginning, this was now an all-or-nothing war.

It was all or nothing for Ludendorff too. On December 27 he met again with Schulenburg and Kuhl. (It is revealing of Ludendorff's power that he was free to settle momentous questions without involving the two crown princes to whom Schulenburg and Kuhl formally reported, or Hindenburg or the kaiser, or any member of the government.) Schulenburg continued to want an offensive at Verdun, and Kuhl still favored Flanders. Undecided, Ludendorff instructed army and army group staffs all along the front to develop plans for possible offensives: not only at Verdun and in Flanders but at St. Quentin, Arras, Champagne, and even the all-but-impenetrable Vosges Mountains west of Strasbourg. He feared that an attack at Verdun could be answered and undone by a British response in Flanders. Though he agreed with Kuhl that Flanders was ideal strategically, he feared that the ground there would be dangerously muddy so early in the year. He continued to show particular interest in the St. Quentin option, but his colleagues were not enthusiastic. Kuhl had already sent him a memorandum arguing that although a breakthrough might be fairly easy at St. Quentin, exploiting it would require defeating the British while simultaneously blocking the French from coming to their aid. This, he said, was likely to be asking

Georg von Hertling
Aspired to be
"the reconciliation chancellor."

too much of the troops. Ludendorff's own operations chief, Major Georg Wetzell, expressed his own fears that the St. Quentin option was too ambitious and that either Flanders or Verdun would be preferable. There was of course nothing unhealthy in open disagreement over such questions; the debate reflected Ludendorff's ingrained willingness to consider the opinions of those military (as opposed to his civilian) associates whom he trusted. But the fact that he remained undecided about the location of an attack that he wanted to take place within ten or twelve weeks is suggestive of a lack of strategic clarity.

Fresh good news came from the Eastern Front: by Christmas the Germans and Russians had agreed to a thirty-day armistice during which negotiations would proceed, and Bolshevik leader Leon Trotsky arrived at Brest-Litovsk to take charge of the Russian delegation. But this development was balanced by trouble behind the lines. On January 14 cuts in bread and flour rations ignited strikes across Austria. Seven hundred and fifty thousand workers went out, including hundreds of thousands in Vienna, and they demanded not just food but peace. The disorder spread to warships in Austria-Hungary's Adriatic ports and to Germany's Kiel naval base, where authorities apprehended the protest leaders and inducted them into the army. The intensity of the discontent, and the extent to which the dissidents were organized, became clear when the executive committee of a Workers Council issued a January 27 call for a general strike and as many as a million German workers (exact numbers, in these matters, remain impossible to establish) went out the next day. Many of the strikers were munitions workers, which made the walkout intolerable to the military authorities. Equally intolerable—and deeply troubling—was the political content of the strikers' rhetoric. The Workers Council, echoing its allies in the Reichstag, called for "the speedy conclusion of peace without annexations and indemnities, on the basis of self-determination of peoples." After a week of street violence in which a number of people were killed, the strike was not settled but crushed by the army. Forty thousand strikers, supporters, and family members were arrested. Between thirty-five hundred and six thousand of the leaders were inducted into military service and told they were bound for the front. In the eyes of conservatives and even moderate elements of the German public,

Leon Trotsky
*Gave up on negotiations
with Germany.*

Ludendorff and the army had preserved law and order. The episode heightened Ludendorff's sense that the home front was dangerously unstable, that the war had to be won before the urban rabble became absolutely unmanageable and the nation's resolve was destroyed.

He found additional reason for concern when, on February 11, liberal members of the Reichstag issued a statement calling for a *political* offensive against Great Britain—emphatically not a *military* offensive—"including an unequivocal declaration of the sovereignty and integrity of Belgium." This statement served as a highly unofficial (and officially repudiated) response to a January speech in which Lloyd George had suggested a willingness to accept a negotiated settlement. Lloyd George had not been looking for a response—the purpose of his speech was not to get negotiations started but to persuade the British labor unions that responsibility for the continuation of the war lay with Berlin—and Ludendorff was not wrong in regarding the whole affair as meaningless. He remained confident that Germany could come out of the war as master of Belgium and more *if* his domestic adversaries were not permitted to deflect him from the victories that lay ahead.

On January 21, after a tour of the Western Front, Ludendorff announced his decision. The attack would be at St. Quentin, in Picardy east of the old Somme battleground at the juncture of the British and French lines. This was not the attack he really wanted—

that would have been farther north. But Flanders would have to wait until it was sure to be dry enough not to suck the Germans into another Passchendaele. St. Quentin presented no such danger. It would be code-named "St. Michael" after the sword-bearing archangel who was patron saint of the German Reich. By forcing Haig to shift his reserves southward it would, according to Ludendorff's plan, set the British up for a later pair of Flanders offensives, St. George One and Two.

Crown Prince Rupprecht of Bavaria was puzzled by the Michael plan (the "St." prefix was soon abandoned). An intelligent and skillful army group commander, a descendant through his mother of the Stuart kings of England, he asked what its strategic objective was supposed to be. "We make a hole and the rest will take care of itself," Ludendorff replied. "That's how we did it in Russia." It was not an answer that many strategists, thinking calmly, would have found satisfactory.

Wetzell had offered a word of caution before the question was closed. If Michael went ahead, he suggested, it should be kept within strict limits. If the troops succeeded in breaking through, the generals should be content to allow the resulting threat to draw the British reserves down from Flanders. The advance should *not* continue into the tangled wasteland that the Battle of the Somme had created and that the Germans had made worse with their scorched-earth withdrawal to the Hindenburg Line.

Ludendorff disregarded this advice.

KAISER WILHELM II

ALTHOUGH WILHELM II HAD ACTUALLY *DONE* VERY little to ignite the war (his biggest contribution was a careless failure to restrain the Austrians at the outset, and he tried to reverse course as soon as he understood the danger), the war might never have happened if not for what he *was.*

That was the story of his life. In the quarter of a century between his becoming emperor and the outbreak of hostilities, he had accomplished almost nothing. If Germany flourished in almost every sphere from economics to the arts, its success was not his doing. But his personality had cast an unsettling shadow across Europe all the same, alienating powerful neighbors, increasing Germany's isolation, and worsening the tangle of ambition and fear that finally drew all the Great Powers into the abyss.

To take a word from *Wilhelm II and the Germans,* a penetrating psychoanalytic study by Professor Thomas A. Kohut of Williams College, the kaiser's personality was "fractured." It made him an immensely complicated, dangerously unstable, deeply damaged public figure, sometimes appealing but more often offensive, full of bluster and swagger but terribly insecure, intelligent but only in superficial and unreflective ways, made up of parts that never formed a coherent whole. He was "one of those strange figures in history whose personalities have had more effect on the course of affairs than their deeds."

The kaiser's complexities rose partly out of his ancestry. The grandson on the paternal side of modern Germany's first emperor, on the maternal side of the majestic Victoria who was Queen of Great Britain and Ireland and Empress of India, he was heir to two awesome and radically different traditions. Britain at the time of his birth was not quite a democracy by today's standards, but it was a distinctly liberal society in which most political power resided in Parliament and the monarch was well along the path to becoming a revered figurehead. Hohenzollern Prussia on the other hand, and the empire that Prussia created when Wilhelm was still a boy, were autocracies that concentrated nearly all power in the crown. England had long been the richest country on the planet and the center of the world's greatest empire, and it possessed all the assurance that came from generations of dominance. Germany by contrast, after centuries of fragmentation and weakness, was a newcomer to the world stage. Like an overgrown adolescent it was both surprised by and overly proud of its new strength, unsure of itself, often unsure of how to behave. It had an inferiority complex that made it quick to respond resentfully to trivial, even imaginary, slights.

All this was made personal for the boy Wilhelm by his parents, the character of their marriage, and their unhappy destinies. Princess Victoria of Britain (Queen Victoria's eldest child) and Crown Prince Friedrich of Prussia and Germany were an attractive, intelligent, and well-intentioned couple who unquestionably loved each other and their many children. Despite the immense advantages with which they began, however, their lives and careers were tragic. Vicky, as she was known in the family, was a strong-willed and opinionated young woman who had been raised by her parents—especially by her adored father Prince Albert, who had begun life as a member of provincial German royalty—to regard English culture and England's liberal political traditions as pinnacles of human achievement. When she went to Berlin as Fritz's teenage bride, she did so with a self-imposed mission: to transform the backward Germans and their feudal politics into a mirror image of enlightened Britain. She made little effort to conceal her disdain for her new home, making herself an object of distrust not only to the Junker establishment but to her in-laws.

It was part of Fritz's tragedy that, though he played a distinguished part in Prussia's victories over Austria and France, he not only accepted his wife's attitudes and aspirations but allowed himself to be so completely dominated by her as to become an object of contempt in official Berlin, a male-chauvinist society if ever there has been such a thing. He lost the confidence of his father, the king-emperor, and of Chancellor Bismarck, who came to see him as the mere instrument of his wife's dangerous notions. The couple's first son, Willy, was therefore from earliest childhood pulled in two directions. His mother wanted desperately for him to become another Prince Albert, an English gentleman of German origin, a progressive and reformist liberal. But the world in which he was raised—his grandfather the emperor most definitely included—was equally determined to ensure that he grew up to become a worthy heir to the long line of Prussian warrior-kings. The court looked to him to display a proper Hohenzollern hatred for anything tainted with such decadent abominations as liberalism or, even worse, an even quasi-democratic sharing of power.

The difficulties of the child's situation were made worse by serious physical disabilities. He nearly died during a horrendously difficult breech birth from which he emerged with the muscles, tendons, and nerves of his left shoulder nearly destroyed. His arm and hand were paralyzed, and his upper torso and neck were affected to such an extent that in early childhood he could neither walk normally nor hold his head consistently upright. Throughout his life he would be incapable of dressing himself or cutting his food. It is possible though not provable that he suffered minor brain damage as a result of oxygen deprivation during the birth ordeal.

Little Willy's deformities made him an object of concern for the Hohenzollern family and court. For his mother, they were a nightmare. The princess was laden with guilt over having produced so defective an heir. Still a teenager when her son was born, she was unable to conceal her horror from the child. "He would really be so pretty," she wrote mournfully to her mother in England, "if not for [the birth damage]." Inevitably if unintentionally, she implanted in him the conviction that he was not what he should be. This message was reinforced by the Hohenzollern inner circle. A great-uncle declared sternly that "a one-armed man should never be king of Prussia."

His mother hoped desperately to make the boy whole. He underwent years of treatment that, however well intentioned, was not far from torture. His limp left arm was regularly wrapped in the body of a freshly killed hare to warm it. Electric current was applied in an effort to stimulate muscle growth. For an hour each day he was locked into a brace that forced his head upright against the resistance of stiffening muscles and tendons. Ultimately, tendons on one side of his neck had to be severed to correct his distorted posture and facial expressions.

The child was unable to stay atop a horse—an inconceivable failing in a Hohenzollern heir. And so, weeping, he was forced to mount and fall and remount and fall again until finally, after weeks of agony and humiliation, he became the skilled and confident horse-man that he would be throughout his reign. It was a splendid achieve-ment for a small boy, but he does not appear to have received praise for it. The same iron discipline was applied in all his early training: his education had been entrusted to a taskmaster, the cold and distant Herr Hinzpeter, who not only demanded a round-the-clock Spartan regimen but believed that praise corrupted the soul. Thus Willy's hun-ger for approval, for assurance that he was not a misfit, remained totally unsatisfied. Out of that hunger there grew a habit of covering his self-doubts with bravado and responding with wrath to even the appearance of rejection.

Freudians will argue that young Willy, in order to have a chance of establishing his own identity, was bound to rebel against his moth-er, against her anxieties and her frustrated efforts to mold him into a replica of her father. (She was always disappointed in his academic performance.) Be that as it may, rebel he did. As he approached manhood, he broke with his parents, moving in the one direction certain to appall them: toward his grandfather the emperor, toward Bismarck, toward the whole reactionary Junker ethos including what his grandmother in England called "that terrible Prussian pride and ambition." As he took up a commission in one of the elite regiments, he said that he found there his first real home. He married a girl who could scarcely have been less like his mother—a dull, unquestioning German girl who in short order bestowed on him six sons in whom he took little interest and a daughter on whom he doted. His approv-ing grandfather began to send him on diplomatic missions that should rightfully have been given to his father, humiliating poor Fritz and dividing the family into two openly warring camps.

All this history went into the making of the man who in 1888—the year his grandfather and his cancer-stricken father both died—became at twenty-seven the master and All-High Warlord of the most powerful nation on the European continent. Wilhelm II's youthful impetuous-ness, compulsive self-aggrandizement, and painstakingly concealed insecurity so perfectly mirrored the nation he led that throughout the early years of his reign he and his brilliant uniforms and his theatri-cal displays of self met with public adulation. He was a precociously modern figure in his obsession with how he was covered in the press, an early and for a time successful practitioner of the dubious art of public relations. But it could not last. Wilhelm himself was psychologically too fragile to hold together the image, the facade, that he had worked long and hard to create. In his need to prove himself master of everything, he dismissed the mighty Bismarck two years after taking the throne. He intruded constantly into domestic and international affairs that he had neither the knowledge nor the skill to manage. "The emperor is like a balloon," Bismarck had said. "If one did not hold him fast on a string, he would go no one knows whither." With Bismarck no longer holding the string—Wilhelm could tolerate no underlings except those who made obsequious displays of submission—he soon went out of control. The last ten years of peace were punctuated with scandals and sometimes outlandish political and diplomatic blunders. He suffered a series of nervous breakdowns, the first of which, interestingly, occurred when his one close friend was revealed to be homosexual. He emerged from each setback and collapse more depressed than ever, more obviously a hollow man swollen with pretense, less able to function as a real—as opposed to a make-believe—ruler.

And through it all like a dark thread there ran his immensely complicated relationship with his mother's homeland. He admired and even loved, craved the approval of but also envied and resented, the grandmother, uncle, and cousin who successively reigned in Britain. He built a fabulously expensive navy in the improbable hope that somehow this would cause Britain to want Germany's friendship. "Nothing will change," he said, "until we are so strong on the seas that we become valuable allies." When the result was exactly the opposite of what he had hoped—when Britain felt so threatened that she was driven to friendship with Russia and even her ancient enemy France— Wilhelm reacted with angry, bitterly uncomprehending complaints of betrayal.

What he was, finally, was a weak and often foolish man who nevertheless managed to persuade much of the world that he was a monster and a danger. By 1914 he was only marginally capable of heading his government and even less prepared to direct Germany's massive military machine. By 1918 he was little more than a figurehead in whom the real leaders of Germany had no confidence. By autumn his story would be very nearly finished.

Chapter 14

Entangling Misalliances

"I am sick of this d—d life."
—General Sir William Robertson

The British and the French, once they agreed that no large-scale offensives should be attempted in the new year, were left with much to guess at where German intentions were concerned. They had to try to figure out where (if anywhere) the Germans were likely to attack, and to settle on tactics and how to deploy their troops.

It was not easy to agree on any of these matters. The possibilities were too numerous for comfort. At the end of 1917 the Western Front still ran in the old zigs and zags from the Belgian coast down to Picardy in France, from there westward to Verdun, and then southward again to Switzerland. The eighteen miles nearest the English Channel were defended by thirteen Belgian divisions and, more decisively, by the broad shallow lakes created when the coastal dikes were opened in 1914. This flooding made the northern end of the front impregnable—essentially took it out of the war. Nearly as impregnable were the 150 miles at the southern end, where the steep pine forests of the Vosges Mountains, the heights looming over the River Meuse, and France's mighty chain of fortresses formed a formidable wall.

That left hundreds of miles of potential battleground. German initiatives were feasible everywhere from the start of the British line at a Belgian stream called the Coverbeeck to south of Verdun.

Flanders, Picardy, Champagne, the Argonne, the big German salient at St. Mihiel—all remained in play. The known fact that the Germans were now transferring large numbers of troops to the west made it probable not only that an attack was coming but that it would be on a bigger scale than what had been seen thus far.

Lloyd George's miserliness with replacements notwithstanding, Douglas Haig had an immense army under his command. Fifty-seven British, Indian, Australia–New Zealand, and Canadian divisions, along with two unhappy Portuguese divisions that their government had tossed into the war as a gesture of friendship with England, held a hundred and twenty-five miles of front on a line running north-south from Flanders to the Somme. The BEF had held much of this ground exactly as long as the Germans opposite, but they had been far less conscientious about improving their defenses. Like his French allies, Haig had always been focused on the offensive, and so he had always regarded his position less as a fortress to be secured than as a series of launching points for attacks. He had encouraged his subordinates to think likewise, with the result that his front line was not what it could have been and his rear defenses were in many places rudimentary. These weaknesses could not be blamed on Lloyd George. While withholding infantry, the prime minister had dispatched more than a hundred thousand laborers to the continent. But as 1917 ended, only seventeen hundred of these men were at work on the British defenses. Even the following March, with Ludendorff's blow known to be coming, only twenty-seven hundred would be so employed.

There was also a problem with how Haig's forces were deployed. Passchendaele had been a drive out of the Ypres salient toward the north and west. The success of that drive, meager though it was, had drawn the British forward into a tight pocket between Ypres and the sea. Haig had kept his heaviest troop concentrations in and near this pocket, where there was little room for maneuver. He did so in part to protect the ports through which the BEF's lifeline ran from England. His doing so was also a function of his belief, which revolted Lloyd George, that the ground taken at such cost at the end of 1917 could be an ideal starting point for a resumed offensive in the new year.

Another problem was the approach to defensive warfare taken

by most of Haig's army commanders. All but the savvy Plumer adhered to the old practice of packing large numbers of infantry into the line nearest to the Germans. They also left their second line within reach of enemy guns.

Lloyd George and the generals continued to be at loggerheads. At the turn of the year the prime minister forced Haig to replace his chief of staff, deputy chief of staff, and heads of intelligence, engineering, and medical services. Haig was not pleased. The new men were not drawn from the cavalry fraternity he favored, and having them imposed upon him was an embarrassment—the closest Lloyd George could come to replacing Haig himself. But they proved markedly more competent than their predecessors (Haig's original chief of intelligence had been reviled and ridiculed for an optimism untroubled by facts), and so ultimately the changes would work to Haig's advantage. As a further affront, Lloyd George appointed one of Haig's rivals and critics, the venomously charming Henry Wilson, to be Britain's military representative on the Supreme War Council.

Little more harmony was evident in the French camp, or in relations between the British and the French. Pétain, who commanded the army groups that would have to deal with any German attacks between Picardy and Verdun, was becoming an isolated figure. Only he among the French appeared to see the implications of what the Germans had achieved with their new assault tactics, and to understand that these innovations required a new kind of response. When on January 8 he promulgated his Directive No. 4, which offered such a response, his army commanders received it with indifference or poorly concealed scorn. Clemenceau, who understood what Pétain had achieved at Verdun and in dealing with the mutiny, saw also that the general no longer showed much confidence that the war could be won. This troubled him and contributed to his rejection of Pétain's idea for a 1918 offensive in Alsace. Its purpose was to have been limited: a capture of coveted ground that would improve France's bargaining position if peace talks began. That was not nearly enough for Clemenceau. For inspiration—for a professional's assurances that victory could be achieved—the prime minister looked not to Pétain but to Foch. But instead of putting Foch in Pétain's place, he held him in reserve. He was convinced that the Entente needed a supreme military commander. He was determined to put a French general in that post, and to see that Foch got the job.

And so Pétain remained the commander in chief, if not a greatly appreciated one. His Directive No. 4 offered badly needed changes. It drew on the lessons of the chess game that Plumer and the Germans had played in Flanders, and of the German counteroffensive at Cambrai, in calling for a thinly manned and flexible front line. This amounted to a revolution in French tactical thinking, an abandonment of the old idea, long since abandoned by the Germans, of holding every foot of ground at all costs. It was heresy to most of the army group, army, corps, and divisional commanders. Some of them protested. When Pétain did not withdraw his directive, they united in ignoring it. For support they had to look no farther than to Foch, who had never stopped worshiping at the altar of *offensive à l'outrance* and was known to have Clemenceau's ear.

But it was Pétain who, with little support from above or below, had to get on with the job of preparing for a German offensive. He had ninety-nine divisions with which to do so, sixty of them spread along the front and the others in reserve. (There were also more than a hundred thousand American troops in France by this time—four oversize U.S. divisions—but Pershing did not regard them as ready to play an active role at the front. Nor was he willing to put them at the service of British or French commanders.)

They seemed immense, the forces at Pétain's disposal, until one took into account the amount of territory they had to defend and the number of German divisions being brought from the east. He had only four divisions in reserve at the northern end of his line, not nearly enough for safety. In the hope of freeing more troops, late in 1917 he asked Haig to extend the British line fifty-five miles to the south, so that it would reach to and even beyond St. Quentin. Haig had no interest in doing anything of the kind.

Both Pétain's request and the broader question of how to create an adequate reserve force in Picardy—precisely the place, as it happened, that Ludendorff chose for his attack—were still unresolved when, on January 24, the senior British, French, and American generals gathered at Compiègne. When the idea of creating a general reserve out of divisions contributed by Haig and Pétain was proposed, both men backed away from it with all possible haste. United only in their determination to continue operating independently of each other, they insisted that they had no troops to spare for such experiments. The conference ended without result.

Six days later the third meeting of the Supreme War Council brought the generals together with Lloyd George and Clemenceau. This meeting went on for four days and was contentious. Lloyd George made the last of his many efforts to shift the focus of the war away from the Western Front, trying to persuade the others to make Turkey the primary target in 1918. The idea was not without potential—the Turkish army was little better than a wreck, and taking it out of the war could have exposed Austria-Hungary's eastern flank, and created tremendous problems for Germany in the Balkans and beyond. But the others were not interested. Clemenceau was absolutely opposed; nothing mattered to him so much as driving the Germans out of France. When Robertson supported Clemenceau instead of his own prime minister, his name went to the top of Lloyd George's unwritten list of nuisances to be eliminated.

Inevitably, the reserve issue came up again. Lloyd George, by prior arrangement with Clemenceau, nominated Foch to be chairman of an executive committee responsible for establishing a general reserve. For him it was another way of keeping Haig in shackles, for Clemenceau a first step toward giving Foch authority over Pétain and Haig. As before, these two generals wanted nothing to do with any such proposal. Though unable to block the creation of the new committee or Foch's appointment as its head, they regarded the whole exercise as unnecessary and unimportant. They had already agreed that, if either was seriously threatened, the other would send as many as six divisions to the rescue. This agreement seemed sufficient to them.

Haig, abandoning his hopes for an offensive in Flanders, agreed to extend his right wing far enough to the south to take over twenty-five miles of French line. This was less than half of what Pétain had requested, but it would allow him to shift two corps, at least four and possibly six divisions, to his reserve. It did not, however, prevent Foch from requesting that Britain, France, and Italy between them contribute thirty divisions to the new general reserve, which otherwise would exist only on paper. Haig, who had been obliged to send five divisions to Italy in November and now had only eight in reserve, declared that he would resign rather than comply.

A dispute broke out within the British camp over the role of Henry Wilson and, by implication, of Robertson. Wilson, a French-speaking Francophile, had long been the French general staff's favorite Englishman. (He was a passionate Ulsterman, actually, and would be assassinated in Ireland after the war.) As London's principal agent in the secret prewar sessions that had first brought the staffs of the two armies together for joint planning, he had developed such an admiration for Foch that some who did not share his enthusiasm referred to him as Foch's lapdog. He made little effort to conceal his disdain for Haig and Robertson, which won him favor in the eyes of Lloyd George. The new trouble erupted over the question of whether Wilson, in his new position as Britain's military representative on the Supreme War Council, should report to Robertson as chief of the imperial general staff or to the government—to Lloyd George. Wilson wanted to report to the prime minister. Robertson's position was that Wilson, being a general representing the army, must report to him directly and only through the chain of command to the gov-

"Wully" Robertson
Targeted by Lloyd George.

ernment. Lloyd George, weary of Robertson's insistence that the war had to be won on the Western Front and his unwavering support of Haig, no doubt saw in the situation an opportunity to rid himself of a problem. He therefore supported Wilson. Robertson, demonstrating that he was standing on principle rather than trying to aggrandize himself, offered to serve in either position, as chief of the imperial general staff or as council member, so long as the latter reported to the former. When Lloyd George refused, Robertson resigned.

Lloyd George added insult to injury, and made the entire disagreement seem contrived from the start, by appointing Wilson to replace Robertson as chief of the imperial general staff. (The job was first offered to Herbert Plumer, whose refusal may have stemmed from indignation at how Robertson had been treated.) Wilson completed the farce by replacing himself on the council with a junior general whom he was easily able to control. Robertson was consigned to the British home forces. Thus was neutralized one of the most capable and respected generals to serve in the British army during the Great War. Robertson himself appeared to have few regrets. As he had written to Haig, "I am sick of this d—d life."

Haig extended his line to the south in the simplest possible way: by ordering the commander of the army that formed his right wing, Hubert Gough, to spread out his troops to cover the additional twenty-five miles. The advantage of this approach was that it required no thinning of Haig's left, where he continued to expect the enemy to attack. Such an expectation was not foolish. Haig knew at least as well as Ludendorff that the proximity of the sea put his left in an awkward position, and that the loss of the port towns of northeastern France would be a disaster from which recovery might not be possible. What he failed to anticipate was Ludendorff's decision to strike elsewhere first because of the weather factor. The problem for Gough—one that he recognized and quickly reported—was that the thinning of his line made him alarmingly vulnerable. The frontline defenses that he had inherited from the French were in a poor state of preparedness, and in some places rear defenses barely existed.

Gough, whose Fifth Army was the smallest in the BEF, was being asked to cover forty-two miles of front with fourteen divisions. The two armies immediately to his north had sixteen divisions each and together had to defend only sixty-one miles. Gough complained, asking for more troops and for labor units with which to improve his position. He got no response. Haig believed, evidently, that in the unlikely event of an attack on his right, Gough would have ample room to pull back to the east and north while Pétain moved French troops from the south to fill any gaps. He is not known to have been aware that Pétain was under instructions, in case of an emergency, not to support the British but to fall back to a position from which he could protect Paris.

The Germans too remained tangled in disagreement and uncertainty. The preparations for the Michael offensive were moving forward efficiently enough—Ludendorff decided that the attack would begin on March 21, the earliest practicable date—but the generals and politicians were divided over how, and on what terms, to shut down the war in the east. This led to a breach between Ludendorff and certainly the cleverest, possibly the most brilliant general officer in the German army, the recently promoted Major General Max Hoffmann. On New Year's Day, when Hoffmann returned from the peace talks in Brest-Litovsk for a meeting of the kaiser's Crown Council, Foreign Minister Kühlmann invited him to lunch. Kaiser Wilhelm invited himself to join them. He asked Hoffmann for his views on what Germany should claim as the spoils due to it as the victor in the east. Hoffmann, mindful that Ludendorff had forbidden all officers to talk with the kaiser without first consulting him, tried to avoid answering. When Wilhelm insisted—he was, after all, the monarch to whom every German officer swore obedience—Hoffmann had little choice except to comply. He explained, knowing that everything he said was in direct opposition to Ludendorff's thinking, that in his opinion it would make no sense to take permanent control of large expanses of territory in the east. Adjustments along the frontier with Poland could have military value, he said, but absorbing substantial non-German populations would bring only trouble.

After lunch Hoffmann attempted to telephone Ludendorff and explain what had happened. He was unable to reach him: Ludendorff was in transit, en route to the next day's council session. When that meeting began, the kaiser launched into a lecture about the inadvisability of demanding too much from the Rus-

General Max Hoffmann
*Master tactitian of
the Eastern Front.*

sians. Then, with the astounding lack of judgment of which he was capable, Wilhelm proudly declared that he was supported in this matter by a general of unquestioned ability: Max Hoffmann. Ludendorff was almost apoplectic. Soon he was demanding Hoffmann's dismissal.

Ludendorff was blind where the settlement with Russia was concerned. He could see only that Russia was no longer capable of defending herself, and he took this as Germany's opportunity to become master of everything east of Berlin. What he did not see, or more likely did not care about, was that stripping Russia bare would persuade the surviving members of the Entente that there was no possibility of negotiating an acceptable end to the war. It would convince them that Germany wanted nothing less than the destruction of her enemies and dominance of all Europe. Such worries had no meaning for Ludendorff. He *did* want the destruction of Germany's enemies—the European ones, at any rate—and he intended to achieve exactly that. He was opposed not only by Hoffmann but by Kühlmann and Chancellor Hertling, both of whom urged restraint. Kühlmann in particular understood that if Ludendorff's demands were satisfied, Germany and Russia could never be other than enemies. He wanted to lay the groundwork for postwar friendship—albeit with a Russia that had been seriously weakened. He hoped that at least a gesture in the direction of generosity would encourage Britain to enter into negotiations.

A week after the Crown Council meeting, Woodrow Wilson delivered an address to Congress in which he unveiled his famous Fourteen Points. These were a loftily idealistic expression of what America sought to achieve in the war: self-determination for all peoples, open covenants openly arrived at, and other fine notions that would prove to be entirely unachievable when put to the test. Characteristically, the president had not deigned to consult with his allies in preparing his speech. Though they were pleased with some of his words (a call for the restoration of Belgium, a suggestion that Alsace-Lorraine should be returned to France and that Austria-Hungary's Italian possessions should be surrendered), they were surprised and confused by others and not much inclined to take them seriously. When news of the speech reached Berlin, it strengthened Ludendorff. Wilson the would-be peacemaker, by indicating that such fraught questions as Belgium and perhaps even Alsace-Lorraine might not even be open to discussion, had given Ludendorff new ammunition to use in insisting that the war had to be fought to a conclusion.

The mercurial Kaiser Wilhelm had altered his thinking on an eastern settlement by the time the Crown Council next met on February 13. Ludendorff was aggressive as always, urging not only that Estonia, Livonia, Finland, and Ukraine should be taken from Russia but that the German army should continue driving eastward until they had overthrown the Bolsheviks. The kaiser went even further. He proposed breaking what had been the Romanov empire into four separate entities: a truncated Russia proper, Ukraine, Siberia, and a Union of the South East. Such skeptics as Hoffmann, Kühlmann, and Hertling were not only powerless but by now essentially voiceless.

The Russians were shocked by what was demanded of them in the aftermath of this meeting. Trotsky threw up his hands, telling the Germans that he would never agree to what they wanted and urging Lenin to adopt a "no war, no peace" policy in which Russia would neither continue to fight nor agree to Germany's terms. When the negotiations broke down completely, the Germans swiftly put fifty divisions back into motion along the Eastern Front. The Russians were so helpless that the Germans, though their best men and equipment were now in France, advanced a hundred and fifty miles in five days. The Turks, also unimpeded, advanced through the Caucasus to oil-rich Baku in Azerbaijan. The Ukrainian capital of Kiev fell to the Germans on March 1. Trotsky, furious, said that Russia should rejoin the Entente and resume the war. Lenin, fearing the capture of Petrograd and the destruction of his fledgling regime, moved his government to Moscow and said no.

On March 3 the Russian delegation, with Trotsky no longer participating, signed at Brest-Litovsk one of the most punitive peace treaties in history. Russia relinquished (not to Germany but to puppet regimes to be put in place by Germany) Courland, Estonia, Finland, Latvia, Lithuania, Livonia, Poland, Ukraine, and White Russia (or Belarus). With these territories went something on the order of fifty million people, a third of the old empire's population, and hundreds of thousands of square miles. Russia also lost a third of its rail system and agricultural land, more than half of its industry, three-fourths of its iron ore, and nine-tenths of its coal mines. The Russians agreed to demobilize what remained of their armies.

The Russian delegation treated the settlement as a bad joke. The delegation's chief refused even to read the document that he signed, dismissing its contents as meaningless. There was no possibility that the Russian nation, regardless of who governed it, ever would accept such a settlement as anything other than an act of coercion without a trace of legitimacy. The settlement was precisely the opposite of what Bismarck had done after Prussia's nineteenth-century victory over Austria-Hungary, taking no territory at all to avoid embittering a humiliated foe. Brest-Litovsk guaranteed that there could be no reconciliation—no true peace—between Russia and Germany.

Even in the short term, the treaty was a greater misfortune for Germany than for Russia. The Bolsheviks gave away little—what they surrendered was beyond their power to hold. The Germans got a liability of enormous dimensions. At a time when they needed every available man and gun and locomotive in the west, they took on a new, ramshackle, unmanageable, and doomed eastern empire, the occupation of which would require one and a half million troops. They had to send soldiers to subdue Finland, Romania, Odessa, Georgia, Azerbaijan—an almost endless list of distant places with little relevance to the outcome of the war. Ukraine alone soaked up four hundred thousand German and a quarter of a million Austro-Hungarian troops. And for what? The payoff never came. Ukraine was supposed to become a bread basket for the starving populations of the Central Powers. But the troops sent there consumed thirty rail cars of food daily. The grain that eventually reached the German and Austrian home fronts was never more than 10 percent of what had been hoped for. The situation would continue to deteriorate, compounding the problems of the Germans, as civil war erupted in Russia and its former possessions.

Even this outcome was overshadowed by the impact that Brest-Litovsk had on Germany's principal enemies. The draconian treatment of Russia was taken as a stern lesson in what had to be expected if imperial Germany was not broken. Those leaders most determined to fight on—Lloyd George for one, Clemenceau for another—could claim to have been vindicated. On both sides of the Western Front, potential peacemakers were left without influence.

Ludendorff could scarcely have cared less. He basked in the satisfaction of having achieved a triumph as complete and world-changing as any in history. In the west he was assembling an astoundingly powerful force—191 divisions, three and a half million men—trained in new tactics and eager to put them to work.

He was within days of bringing down on his enemies the greatest series of hammer blows in the annals of war. If he could succeed this one last time, Germany would be master of east and west.

LAWRENCE OF ARABIA

BY THIS TIME A WHOLE OTHER WAR, ONE BETWEEN the British and the Turks (but with Arabs doing much of the fighting and dying), was growing up from small beginnings on the fringes of the Sinai Desert east of Suez and west of Palestine. Even at its height it would be a tiny war compared to what was happening in Europe, and viewed from a sufficient distance it could seem a wonderfully exotic affair.

It was also more fertile ground than the battlefields of Europe for the emergence of heroes. Trenches and massed artillery and machine guns had a way of putting would-be heroes underground before they properly got started. But in the desert, men wearing burnooses rode camels into battle. Even an *Englishman* could do so. Out of that possibility grew the greatest romantic story of the Great War, the legend of Lawrence of Arabia, the man the Bedouins called El Aurens.

The story began in the Egyptian capital of Cairo in September 1916, with the preparations of a British diplomat named Ronald Storrs to travel into the Hejaz region east of the Red Sea. Storrs wanted to make contact with the followers of Sherif Hussein, Arab emir of the sacred city of Mecca. The British had earlier duped and bribed Hussein, making promises they had no intention of keeping, to get him to raise a rebellion against the Ottoman Empire. He had done so, and the Turks had responded. In February and again in August, Turkish troops led by German officers had unsuccessfully attacked the Suez Canal, which ran north and south along the western edge of the Sinai and was the jugular through which Britain maintained contact with India and the Far East. Though thrown back, the Turks were threatening to take Mecca from the Arab rebels and crush Hussein's small force of warrior-tribesmen.

A young and very junior lieutenant, Thomas Edward Lawrence, requested permission to accompany Storrs. Still in his twenties, a deskbound intelligence officer with no military experience or training, Lawrence was on the staff of a recently created entity called the

Arab Bureau, which was to develop policies to guide British relations with the Arabs. Lawrence said he wanted to gather information about how the Arab troops were organized, and to identify competent, dependable Arab leaders. His superiors granted his request; evidently he was not popular among the Cairo officer corps, so that "no one was anxious to detain him."

It was a perfect meeting of man and situation. One of five sons of a baronet named Chapman and the governess with whom he had run away from his first family—creating such a scandal that they had adopted a new family name—he already had extraordinary knowledge of the Arabs and their world. As a student at Oxford he had become fascinated with medieval military fortifications, and while still an undergraduate he traveled through Ottoman Syria and Palestine studying castles constructed by the crusaders. The resulting thesis, later published in book form, led to a degree with highest honors and a traveling fellowship. From 1911 to early 1914 Lawrence worked on archaeological digs and broadened his knowledge of Arabia, its people, and their language and culture.

In England when the Great War began, he joined the war office in London and was put to work making maps. Before the end of the year he was given a commission and sent to Cairo. Though he looked utterly unlike the Peter O'Toole who would one day play him on the screen (Lawrence was short and lantern-jawed), he had exceptional intellectual gifts and made himself valuable during a year spent questioning prisoners, analyzing information procured from secret agents, and continuing to make maps. His appreciation of the magnitude of the war on the far-off Western Front was no doubt strengthened by the death of two of his brothers there in 1915.

Though his background and peculiarities (which included a powerful masochistic bent) meant that Lawrence had a limited future at best in the regular army, from the start of the Storrs mission his liabilities became assets. Instead of returning to Cairo with the rest of the mission, Lawrence went deeper into the Arabian desert, traveling by camel and adopting Arab garb (the only sensible way to dress in that uniquely inhospitable environment). South of the city of Medina he met one of Hussein's sons, Prince Feisal. The two quickly formed a bond. When Lawrence returned to Cairo, he told his superiors that the Arab revolt had the potential to seriously weaken the Turks everywhere from Syria southward, that Feisal was the man to lead it, and that he should be given money and equipment. Lawrence was sent back into the desert to become Britain's liaison and to deliver promises of support.

This eccentric academic intellectual turned out to be a guerrilla fighter of almost incredible courage, a shrewd military strategist, an absolutely brilliant tactician, and an inspiring leader of Arabs. Having won the confidence of Feisal, he was able to open a new, miniature, but important, front. It became a war of his own creation, it kept the Turks constantly off balance, and ultimately it would protect the flank of a conventional British force moving out of Cairo to the conquest of a Sinai, Palestine, and Syria. Coming at the same time as the collapse of Bulgaria, which opened Constantinople to attack out of the Balkans, the advance into Syria would help make it impossible for Turkey to continue the war. By then young Lawrence was a lieutenant colonel and holder of one of Britain's highest military decorations, the Distinguished Service Order or DSO.

Lawrence's approach was to probe into enemy territory with the smallest, most mobile force possible, hitting hard and escaping quickly. He led the raids that he planned, taking the Turks by surprise by approaching across murderously hot and waterless wastes, blowing up bridges and railways, then disappearing back into the desert. He was engaged in countless gun battles, was wounded several times, and was once captured while on a spying mission by Turks who didn't know who he was but beat him severely before letting him go. Probably he was sexually assaulted during this episode, though in later years he was evasive on the few occasions he made reference to it. The war in the desert was a savage affair in which terrible atrocities were committed by both sides. At the same time that Lawrence's activities made him an international hero (an American journalist named Lowell Thomas brought his exploits to the world's attention), they left him physically and emotionally exhausted and psychologically damaged.

The traumatic effects of the war were worsened, for Lawrence, by the knowledge that Britain was deceiving Hussein, Feisal, and the Arabs generally. Britain and France had signed but kept secret the Sykes-Picot Agreement, according to which, after the war, the southern parts of the Ottoman Empire were to be divided between the two. Britain was to get southern Mesopotamia (Iraq to us) and ports on the Mediterranean. Lebanon and Syria were promised to France. The

Arabian Peninsula was to be divided into spheres of influence that, if nominally autonomous, would be dominated by the Europeans.

Sykes-Picot could not be reconciled with what the Arabs had been promised: autonomy across their homeland, from the southern tip of the peninsula up through Lebanon and Syria. Lawrence revealed much of the true situation to Feisal, urging him to strengthen the Arabs' bargaining position by capturing as much territory as possible before the war ended. Though his credibility with the Arabs was enhanced when the Bolsheviks published the details of the Sykes-Picot deal in 1917, his position remained difficult all the same. When it became certain, after Damascus fell to the Allies, that the pledges made to the Arabs were not going to be redeemed, Lawrence departed for London without waiting for the war to end.

His postwar life would be as improbable as his wartime career, though in a radically different way. He refused a knighthood and promotion to brigadier general, resigning his commission instead. He went to the Versailles Peace Conference, where he appeared in Arab headdress and robes and lobbied in vain on behalf of the Arabs. Thereafter, offered lofty academic positions and high office by Colonial Secretary Winston Churchill, he joined the Royal Air Force as a private under the name Ross. When this was discovered and became a sensation in the press, he was discharged. With the help of influential friends, he became a private in the Royal Tank Corps, this time using the name Shaw. In the years that followed he kept this identity but simultaneously produced books that are today minor classics, maintaining friendships with some of the important literary and political figures of the day. He retired from the RAF in 1935, moved to a cottage in the countryside, and died, forever mysterious, in a motorcycle accident.

Chapter 15

Michael

*"There must be no rigid adherence
to plans made beforehand."*
—German infantry manual

Ludendorff's hammer came down on the British through an
impenetrable fog early on the morning of Thursday, March
21, shattering everything it struck. For a long breathless moment,
the fate of Europe hung in the balance.

The force of the blow was magnified by surprise. In spite of
the immensity of their preparations—building up huge ammunition dumps, concentrating sixty-nine divisions and more than
sixty-four hundred guns between Arras to the north and St.
Quentin to the south—the Germans had managed to keep their
intentions secret. By early March Haig and Pétain knew that an
offensive was coming: troop movements on such a scale could
not be concealed and could not be without purpose. But the
Germans had been in motion all along the front that winter as Ludendorff, unable to decide where to attack, ordered his generals
to be ready everywhere. It was impossible to know which movements actually mattered. The final placement of the guns did not
begin until March 11. The assault divisions did not start for the
front until five days after that, and even then they marched only
by night, staying under camouflage by day. Between February
15 and March 20 ten thousand trains hauled supplies forward, but
they too moved by night. Early in March Ludendorff moved his

headquarters to Spa, in southeastern Belgium. On March 19 he moved again, to Avesnes in France.

Ludendorff had had 150 divisions in the west in November. By mid-March the total was 190—three million men, with more on the way. And to the extent that after years of slaughter there was still cream at the top of the German army, Ludendorff had drawn it together for this operation. He had refined it with a winter of training. The results were at the front in the predawn fog of March 21: forty-four divisions of storm troops, young men at the peak of preparation, equipped with the best mobile weapons that German industry could produce. Many of these soldiers were veterans of the eastern war, experienced in movement and accustomed to winning. They brimmed with confidence. Told that they were opening the campaign that would end the war, they were eager to believe.

Many of them, when they attacked, would not even be using their rifles, which would be slung behind them across their backs. They would be on the run, in the tiny groups that the new doctrine prescribed. They would make use of whatever cover they could find, scrambling to keep pace with the creeping barrage that was their shield. When they encountered enemy troops, they would hurl grenades or lay down a field of fire with the light machine guns that some of them carried—whatever it took to keep moving. They had colored flares with which to signal success or trouble, a need for artillery support or for the artillery to stop firing. They were to pay no attention to whether their flanks were exposed or enemy troops remained in place behind them. The pace was to be set by whoever could move fastest, and there was to be no such thing as a continuous line. When they had advanced so far that they could no longer be protected by friendly artillery, the junior and noncommissioned officers were to make their own decisions about what to do next. Everything would depend on initiative, boldness, flexibility, and the ability to adapt to whatever developed. The main rule was that the old rules no longer applied. "The objective of the first day must be at least the enemy's artillery," said a newly issued pamphlet. "The objective of the second day depends on what is achieved on the front; there must be no rigid adherence to plans made beforehand . . . The

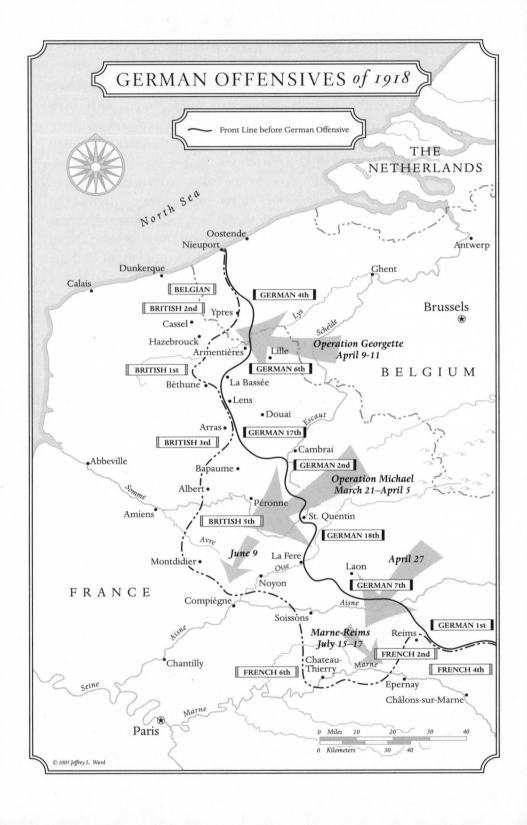

GERMAN OFFENSIVES *of 1918*

Front Line before German Offensive

THE NETHERLANDS

North Sea

Oostende
Nieuport
Antwerp
Dunkerque
Ghent
Calais
Brussels

BELGIAN
BRITISH 2nd
Ypres
Cassel
Hazebrouck
Armentières
Lille
Operation Georgette
April 9-11
GERMAN 4th
GERMAN 6th
Lys
Schelde
BELGIUM

BRITISH 1st
Béthune
La Bassée
Lens
Douai
Escaut
Arras
BRITISH 3rd
GERMAN 17th
Cambrai
GERMAN 2nd

Abbeville
Bapaume
Albert
Péronne
Operation Michael
March 21–April 5
Somme
Amiens
St. Quentin
BRITISH 5th
Avre
GERMAN 18th

June 9
La Fere
Laon
April 27
Montdidier
Oise
GERMAN 7th
Noyon
FRANCE
Compiègne
Aisne
GERMAN 1st
Soissons
Aisne
Marne-Reims
July 15–17
Reims
FRENCH 2nd
Chantilly
Chateau-
Thierry
Marne
FRENCH 6th
FRENCH 4th
Seine
Marne
Epernay
Châlons-sur-Marne
Paris

0   Miles   10   20   30   40
0   Kilometers   30   40

© 2005 Jeffrey L. Ward

reserves must be put in where the attack is progressing, not where it is held up."

Behind this assault force would follow a wave of "battle unit" divisions bringing forward heavier machine guns, flamethrowers, field artillery with ammunition, and engineering equipment. Their job was twofold: to reduce the strongpoints bypassed by the storm troops, and to throw together defensive works from which to hold off counterattacks. To their rear, manned by the third-best divisions, lay the Hindenburg Line, a home base to which everyone could withdraw in case of disaster. Farther back still were the reserves, ready to go wherever they were sent.

None of this could work, could produce more than another Verdun or Somme or Passchendaele, unless the storm troops got through the enemy's front line with their fighting power intact. To ensure that they did, the Germans had something new to show the British. That something was a man: Georg Bruchmüller, the one true artillery genius of a war dominated by artillery, the same retirement-age lieutenant colonel (throughout the war he was never promoted) whom Hoffmann had nicknamed "Breakthrough-müller" for his dazzling accomplishments in the east. The Germans had never indulged in the weeks-long bombardments with which the British had so often tried and failed to annihilate their enemies before attacks, but Bruchmüller was the first on either side to fully grasp the futility of such tactics. Heavy barrages told defenders that an attack was coming and where. When they went on for days, they created opportunities for defenders to adapt either by digging in deeper or, as happened more and more commonly, by pulling back out of range. The damage they caused rarely proved to be enough to make a decisive difference.

The Bruchmüller answer was as complex and sophisticated as a twenty-first-century Fourth of July fireworks display. It lasted for hours instead of days, preserving the element of surprise, and involved a constant back-and-forth shifting between front-line and rear targets, high explosives and shrapnel and gas. When it was properly executed, the surprise was total, because there had been no preliminary registration of the guns on their targets. Instead, every gun was registered on firing ranges before being brought to the front. Then it was locked onto its targets silently, by mathematical calculations including adjustments for atmospheric conditions.

Bruchmüller barrages concluded with an overwhelming concentration of high explosives on frontline positions, throwing any survivors into shock before the appearance of the storm troops. Beyond the first line, heavy reliance on gas avoided the cratering of the ground over which the infantry would have to advance. Bruchmüller had been with Hutier in the northeast, where his methods had made possible the rapid conquest of strong Russian defenses. A month later those same methods produced similar results at Caporetto. Ludendorff had brought Bruchmüller to the west. He was, in all likelihood, the most valuable individual in the entire German army during the great climax of 1918.

There was a way for the enemy to deal with a Bruchmüller bombardment, as the Germans themselves had demonstrated at Ypres in 1917. It required giving up the idea of a strong, solid front line, leaving only a screen of machine-gunners in forward positions and moving most of the troops far enough back to be out of reach of the guns. Pétain understood this, but he was not Ludendorff's target. The British commanders who would be hit by Michael showed no understanding at all.

Those commanders were Henry Horne, whose First Army defended Arras at the northern end of the attack zone, Julian Byng and his Third Army immediately to Horne's south, and Gough with the Fifth Army on the right, centered on St. Quentin. Among them the three had almost fifty divisions, with the strongest concentration in the north and Gough's line the longest and thinnest, much of it recently inherited from the French. Byng and Gough had fully a third of their troops in forward positions, and most of the remainder were no more than two or three miles in the rear. Haig's main reserve was fifteen miles behind the front, too far back to be able to go into action quickly.

As March unfolded, Haig remained certain that the BEF would be the target. But he thought the attack would come in Flanders, where he was strongest—which gave him confidence. "I was only afraid," he wrote in his diary after an inspection of his northern line, "that the enemy would find our front so very strong that he will hesitate to commit his Army to the attack with the almost certainty of losing very heavily." In fairness to Haig, the reports he received from his intelligence staff were sometimes woefully wrong and cumulatively confusing. "There are strong indications," one such report stated on March 2, "that the enemy intends to attack on the Third and Fifth Army fronts, with the object of cutting off the Cambrai salient [also known, in its abbreviated 1918 form, as the Flesquières salient] and drawing in our reserves." This was a virtually letter-perfect account not only of what Ludendorff was planning but why, and it was confirmed by another report a week later. Nothing was done in response, perhaps because other intelligence pointed in other directions. On March 16 Haig was assured that there was no evidence of a German buildup south of the line running from Cambrai to Bapaume, the sector that included the Flesquières salient. This report, though correct in its facts, was dangerously wrong in its conclusion that there was no reason to fear an attack south of Cambrai-Bapaume. The German attack force had indeed not yet arrived in the area by March 16, but forty-seven of its divisions were moving in that direction and were only a few nights' march from the front.

Every new day brought fresh indications that *something* big was coming—and soon. On March 11 the Germans changed their codes, always a sure sign of impending action.

By March 20 the fourteen divisions and twenty-two hundred guns of the German Seventeenth Army were in position on nine and a half miles of front opposite Horne and Byng. This army was to be the cutting edge of the offensive. Commanded by Otto von Below, the victor of Caporetto, it was to break through Horne's line, push westward past Arras, and then swing to the right. By threatening to circle around behind the British, it was supposed to force Haig to shift his reserves to block Below's path, weaken his forces in Flanders, and so accomplish Michael's primary objective.

On Below's left was the German Second Army under Georg von der Marwitz, who had directed the 1917 counteroffensive at Cambrai and earlier was chief of staff of the army that cleared the Russians out of Galicia. He was to advance in step with Below, broadening the penetration of the British line. Immediately to the south of Marwitz, on his left, was the Eighteenth Army, commanded by Hutier himself, freshly arrived from the east. Little was expected of Hutier in this campaign. His army was to provide an anchor for Below and Marwitz as they swept forward. It included twenty-one divisions and more than twenty-six hundred guns; that was expected to be enough to block any French forces coming up from the south. Hutier's artillery was directed personally by Bruchmüller. Together, Below, Marwitz, and Hutier had a million men—an avalanche of infantry.

At about two a.m. on March 21 the kind of thick fog that is common in Picardy at that time of day and year came up out of the ground and reduced visibility to a few yards. Shortly before five, after some hesitation about whether the wind would blow the gas in the right direction, the bombardment began. Along a line of more than forty miles between the Sensée and Oise Rivers, 6,473 pieces of artillery began pouring out fire and steel and gas. Heavy and light cannon and howitzers alternated ammunition and angles of fire according to Bruchmüller's symphonically intricate schedule. At eight-fifteen all the guns came together in a final convulsion of maximum-rate fire concentrated on the defenders' front line. This went on and on, the explosions coming too rapidly to be distinguished, until after eighty minutes it climaxed in a five-minute crescendo surpassing everything that had come before. Then, with shocking abruptness, there came five minutes of silence during which the guns were adjusted for their next task: a creeping barrage that drew the storm troops out of their trenches and led them toward the west. The fog had not lifted. This was a problem for the Germans, who could barely see where they were going and easily lost their sense of direction. But it created far worse problems for the British who had survived the barrage. They were able to see and fire only at whichever attackers happened to stumble directly onto them as they advanced through the murk.

The fog, the soul-shattering power of the artillery, and the speed with which the storm troops followed the creeping barrage—all of it combined to produce a rout. The first lines of defense were quickly overrun, the troops in them killed or captured or put to flight. In the center, units of Byng's army hung on stubbornly in the Flesquières salient, the little bulge that was all that remained to the British of the ground they had won in the Battle of Cambrai the previous fall. But with Gough's troops falling back on their right, the men in the salient were in danger of being cut off. Gough's army, driven not only out of its first line but out of its second as well, could find no place to make a stand. "It was flamethrowers forward," a young storm trooper later wrote home. "The English dugouts were smoked out and we took our first prisoners. They were trembling all over. Now we went forward without resistance. The next dugouts were passed, and we came to the railway. There the English had dug a field post in a declivity, and before it were corrugated iron huts. Here they had their kitchen, canteen, etc. The kitchen was naturally stormed immediately. I was astonished at what the English still had. The stove was still lit, bacon was sizzling, a side of beef lay on the table . . . We stuffed our knapsacks. Each man took an English iron ration. In the next hut, a canteen, we found English cigarettes in great supply. Each man lit up . . . On the entrance to the village we found a machine gun nest. We made an effort to take it, but there was much barbed wire in front, and it would have cost many lives. It was very hazy still, and our artillery could not help us. We let it go and went on."

To the extent that Gough's army could maintain the semblance of a continuous line, the retreat was making that line longer by the hour; by day's end it would be stretched a harrowing five miles. By then Hutier's troops had taken possession of Gough's entire battle zone, including its artillery line. After dark, to save his army, Gough ordered a ten-mile withdrawal to the only natural defense available to him, the River Somme at a point where its meandering course runs north-south and connects to the Crozat Canal.

The Germans had captured hundreds of Gough's guns and achieved something almost never before seen on the Western Front: a breakthrough into open territory beyond the enemy's lines. But that breakthrough had been achieved only in the south—the one place where Ludendorff neither expected nor particularly wanted any such thing. That night, in considering his next steps, Ludendorff found himself confronted with something more complicated than clear-cut success or failure. Though some things had gone brilliantly, nothing had gone according to plan. On the German right, where the deepest penetration had been expected and Below's army was supposed to punch through toward Arras, nothing of the kind had happened. The fog had been lightest on the right and had burned off more quickly than elsewhere, the bombardment had been less effective there than where Bruchmüller was in charge, and the advance had been fought to a standstill at the British second line. Marwitz in the center had done better but not dramatically so. All the drama was on the left, where Hutier and Bruchmüller had been on the scene to implement the tactics bearing their names and had done so with impressive efficiency.

Ludendorff had limited numbers of storm troops in reserve. One of the questions facing him was how to use them to best effect. Staying with his original plan would have required reinforcing Below and trying again to break through on the right. That would have been a Haig-like or Falkenhayn-like decision, another in the long series of attempts to turn failure into success by increasing the amount of force being applied. Ludendorff decided to do otherwise. He sent six of his best divisions to Hutier and none to Below. This was consistent with the Germans' new doctrine, a reinforcement of success rather than of failure, but it also reflected Ludendorff's worsening lack of focus. If Hutier continued to advance, his troops would be moving into territory that had been turned into a barren obstacle course by the Battle of the Somme and by the Germans' own scorched-earth withdrawal to the Hindenburg Line. It would be a difficult advance at best, exhausting the men who undertook it. It was precisely what Ludendorff's operations chief had urged him to avoid.

No one including Ludendorff himself could have said at that point what the purpose of a continued Hutier advance was supposed to be. Below and Marwitz had had a clear mission from the start, but there had never been a comparable goal for Hutier. His astonishing progress gave rise to a question: progress toward *what*? What actually was the *value* of the ground he had taken and the great expanses of territory that lay open in front of him? The absence of an answer exposed the emptiness of the Michael operation after the first day's failure on the right. "We tear a hole in the enemy line," Ludendorff had said when challenged, "and everything else follows." Now he had his hole—though not the hole he had wanted—and his next step was going to be to jump into it. Whatever his decision should be called, it was not strategy. It was more like an act of faith—of Micawberish blind hope that something, somehow, would turn up.

On Friday morning all three German armies returned to the attack. There could be no surprise this time, and because the troops on both sides were in new positions and the fog had returned to blind the gunners, there could be no Bruchmüller barrage. Below's troops, running head-on into reserves sent forward by Byng, got nowhere. Marwitz managed to inch forward on both sides of the Flesquières salient, but the salient itself, which Ludendorff had expected to crush on the first day, again refused to fall. Again almost all progress was on the German left, where Hutier's men continued to advance almost as fast as their legs could carry them. They got across the Somme and the Crozat Canal—the British had failed to blow the bridges—and forced Gough to resume his retreat.

Gough's efforts to find a foothold became increasingly desperate. Military police stopped fleeing troops at gunpoint and forced them into whatever defenses could be found or thrown together. Officers stood in the rear, pistols in hand, to keep the men at their posts. None of it was enough, and the retreat always resumed. Haig sent an appeal to Pétain, asking him to send help. By the time this message arrived, Pétain already had seven divisions on the way—one more than he and Haig had promised to send if either came under attack.

By nightfall on March 22 the Germans had again accomplished something new to the Western Front: they had kept a major offensive moving forward through a second day. Also again, their success had been limited to the left wing. Ludendorff's plan had been completely overtaken by events. As he tried to adapt, his difficulties mounted. His supply system, positioned for an advance in the north, was not prepared to follow Hutier's army. That army, weary after two days of rapid pursuit over difficult ground, was running out of essentials as basic as water. French and British reserves, meanwhile, were racing to intercept it.

Dawn on Saturday, March 23, found the British on the verge of ruin. Not only Hutier's army but even Marwitz's advance units were now fifteen miles beyond their starting points. Gough's army was ceasing to be a coherent fighting force. Eight of the divisions with which Gough had begun the battle were in shambles. Hutier's troops were west of the Somme, gobbling up mile after mile. As it disintegrated, Gough's left wing had lost contact with Byng's right. Byng's flank was exposed, and the line he had to defend grew longer. Haig asked Pétain for an additional twenty divisions. Pétain replied that this was impossible—he was expecting an attack in Champagne. He did, however, send another six divisions. This was in addition to the seven sent earlier—divisions that were now reaching the battlefield but finding it impossible to get around behind Gough's fast-fleeing troops and into the path of the Germans. Pétain had done far more than he had ever promised. His doing so has to be considered a magnanimous act, especially in light of the fact that he was right about Champagne: the Germans *were* preparing an attack there. Haig, however, was not satisfied. To the contrary, he was resentful of Pétain.

On the third day the Germans' advance put them within reach of a bona fide strategic prize. Directly ahead, due west of St. Quentin, was the city of Amiens, the importance of which can be made clear even today by a glance at an ordinary road map. Almost all the highways in the region run into Amiens, which sits at their center like the hub of a great wheel. In 1918 all the railways ran through Amiens too, creating a transport center very near to where the British sector ended and the French began. The town was vital to the British, to the French, and to their ability to maintain contact. On March 23 it was thinly defended. If Ludendorff had ordered it taken, he could have separated the two allies so completely that it might then have become possible to destroy their armies one by one.

Instead, turning away from a vital target that the enemy was unprepared to defend, Ludendorff sent his armies in three directions, each of which had comparatively minor potential. Below, once again bogged down, was given reserves and told to turn farther toward the north. Marwitz was to push westward on a trajectory that would carry him not to Arras, not to Amiens, but to a point between the two. Hutier was directed southward toward the town of Noyon in the direction of Paris.

Perhaps Ludendorff thought he could finish both of his enemies with one master stroke, a great combination of separating and enveloping movements that would simultaneously destroy the British on his right and the French on his left. If that was the idea—no alternative explanation seems equally plausible—it was beyond the capabilities of the German forces. It brings to mind the campaigns of Conrad von Hötzendorf, who had wrecked the Austro-Hungarian armies with theoretically brilliant but unrealistic lunges at instant glory. The March 24 orders issued by Ludendorff—a Ludendorff alienated from the Max Hoffmann whose brains had so often been so useful, and increasingly remote from his own staff and the commanders of his armies—provide early evidence that he was breaking down under the strain with which he had been living for nearly four years.

On this same day an explosion mysteriously occurred in the heart of Paris. People searched the sky for enemy aircraft but found nothing. Then came another explosion, and another. Finally the mystery was solved: this was the work of artillery. An enormous new cannon called the Kaiser Wilhelm gun was firing eight-inch shells from freshly conquered territory more than seventy-five miles from the capital. Between its March debut and August, it would fire 283 rounds into Paris, killing civilians and destroying property at random, accomplishing absolutely nothing.

Kaiser Wilhelm himself was exceptionally active on this day. Rocketing about in his private train, declaring victory to everyone within earshot, he ordered the schools of Germany closed in celebration. He had champagne served at dinner. "If an English delegation came to sue for peace," he pronounced, exposing the childishness of his daydreams, "it must kneel before the German standard."

Also on March 23 a young German pilot was shot down behind the British lines—the second of Ludendorff's beloved stepsons to die in this way.

Early on the morning of Sunday, March 24, the commanders of the six British battalions clinging to the Flesquières salient agreed that, with their position rapidly deteriorating, their choice was to withdraw or to be destroyed. They ordered a retreat that left the British center without its anchor. The entire British line was now pulling back, the Germans advancing everywhere. Even Below was making slow progress. Hutier continued to encounter almost no resistance, though his army was running down badly. Looting and drunkenness were breaking out wherever tired, hungry German troops came upon some of the enormous stores abandoned by the British. Not as malnourished as their families back home but chronically ill-fed nonetheless, they were astonished to find the enemy so abundantly provided with food, liquor, and good wool and cotton clothing—things almost unavailable in Germany. They had been told that the Entente was suffering as severely as they were. They saw that this was untrue.

The greatest weakness of Ludendorff's attack force had come fully into play: he had no pursuit capability with which to run down and destroy the defeated British divisions. What remained of the German cavalry was in the east, where vast open spaces afforded scope for operations of a kind not possible in the west. Ludendorff had neither tanks nor enough armored cars to make a difference. Germany being without access to rubber, its few motor vehicles were fitted with steel tires that destroyed whatever roads they used. Hutier could advance no faster than his men could walk, and those men had been walking and fighting for four days. They ended Sunday's march eight miles short of their assigned objective. Farther north the Germans took possession of Bapaume but also did not reach their goal.

This was no consolation to Haig and Pétain. The Germans were not only continuing to advance but positioned to drive a wedge between them. Relations between the two commanders were badly strained, Haig unimpressed with the two hundred thousand troops that Pétain had sent to his aid. Haig understood the importance of maintaining the connection between his line and that of the French—"our Army's existence in France depends

Without access to rubber, the Germans equipped their vehicles with steel tires

on keeping the British and French armies united," he declared—
but somehow he regarded this as Pétain's responsibility. When
the two generals met on Sunday night, Haig learned that if the
German advance continued, the French intended to fall back toward the south. His reaction appears to have been a mixture of
rage and panic. He blamed Pétain, who had no choice in the matter: his orders, direct from the French cabinet, were to defend
Paris at all costs and to the exclusion of other priorities. Pétain
sent a telegram asking his government to get the British to stay far
enough to the south that he would not be required to overextend
himself in order to maintain contact.

The crisis produced in Haig an abrupt change of mind on the
subject of a supreme commander for the Entente armies. Knowing that such an assignment was sure to go to Foch, judging that
Foch was likely to be far more willing than Pétain to advance to
the north rather than withdraw, Haig that night sent a telegram to
Lloyd George asking him to reopen the question. It happened that
just hours earlier Clemenceau, prodded by Foch, had sent a wire
of his own to London suggesting the same thing. Lloyd George
dispatched Lord Alfred Milner, the war minister, to France to make
it happen.

On Monday Ludendorff awoke at last to the importance of
Amiens. With French and British reserves now pouring into the
front lines, Below was once again blocked, his objectives hopelessly out of reach. But Amiens, if captured, could justify the entire campaign. Ludendorff ordered Marwitz to link his left wing
with Hutier and move to take the city. The head of the French
rail system, meanwhile, was begging Foch to "save Amiens or everything's lost—it's the center of all our communications." Foch,
Pétain, and Clemenceau met at Compiègne, trying to figure out
how to balance Haig's appeals for more help with the defense
of Paris. Haig was meeting with his army commanders—all but
Gough, who had more pressing concerns—at Doullens, not a
great distance away from Compiègne. When Clemenceau offered
to join them the next day, the British readily agreed.

On March 26, with the Germans sixteen miles from Amiens and
still advancing, the French leaders arrived at Doullens. They were
a formidable group: President Poincaré, Clemenceau, Pétain, and
Foch, who was delighting the premier with talk of shifting over to

the offensive. On hand to greet them were Haig and his generals plus, from London, Wilson, the new chief of the imperial general staff, and Lord Milner. Haig was, for once, eager to cooperate. In response to a question from Clemenceau, he declared his determination to stand and fight at Amiens rather than pull back to the north. It was Milner who brought up the matter that had brought all of them together. He proposed that Foch be named "coordinator" of the Entente forces "around Amiens." The French, of course, assented, all but Pétain enthusiastically. Haig, of all people, objected that Foch must be given more authority than Milner's words implied. His motives were obvious. Foch's new role would permit a more thorough and systematic sharing of reserves, and under current circumstances that could only benefit the British. The wording was changed, accordingly, to extend Foch's responsibilities to the entire Western Front. Haig's diary entry of this date reveals his thinking. "In my opinion," he wrote, "it was essential that Foch should control Pétain."

To the extent that Foch's elevation was an implicit criticism of Pétain's response to the German offensive, it was undeserved and unnecessary. By March 26 the offensive was essentially at an end, in large measure because Pétain had stripped so many troops from his own line and reserves that twenty-four French divisions were now assembling in the path of Hutier's and Marwitz's armies. As more arrived and the tide began to turn, Foch would win much credit—less because of anything he had done than because of the timing of his appointment. Still, the appointment was important. A step had been taken toward unified command.

Foch, immediately after his promotion, complained of having been given the task of winning a battle that was already lost. Something closer to the opposite was true. The Michael offensive was losing its force and coherence, deteriorating at times into a kind of blind and almost random lashing out at the defenders. Hutier's worn-down troops continued, where they were confronted only by the remains of Gough's army, to move forward at a pace that would have seemed incredible except that the British were not even trying to resist.

Hutier moved forward nine miles on March 26, ten on the day following. The character of the campaign was becoming almost farcical, with the British retreating at an easy walk and Germans following at the same pace. When the British stopped to rest, the Germans would stop as well, keeping a safe distance. They had left behind most of their artillery and were short of almost everything. Their officers were unable to prevent them from looting whenever an opportunity arose. "Today the advance of our infantry stopped near Albert," a German captain observed. "Nobody could understand why. Our airmen had reported no enemy between Albert and Amiens. The enemy's guns were only firing now and again on the very edge of affairs. Our way seemed entirely clear. I jumped into a car with orders to find out what was causing the stoppage in front . . . As soon as I got near the town I began to see curious sights. Strange figures, who looked very little like soldiers, and certainly showed no signs of advancing, were making their way back . . . There were men driving cows before them on a line; others who carried a hen under one arm and a box of notepaper under the other. Men carrying a bottle of wine under their arm and another one open in their hand. Men who had torn a silk drawing-room curtain off its rod and were dragging it to the rear as a useful piece of loot. Men with writing paper and colored notebooks. Evidently they had found it desirable to sack a stationer's shop. Men dressed up in comic disguise. Men with top hats on their heads. Men staggering. Men who could hardly walk . . . When I got into the town the streets were running with wine. Out of a cellar came a lieutenant of the Second Marine Division, helpless and in despair. I asked him, 'What is going to happen?' It was essential for them to get forward immediately. He replied, solemnly and emphatically, 'I cannot get my men out of this cellar without bloodshed.'"

The retreat continued everywhere except at Amiens, where the British straggled onto the high ground east of the city and found themselves welcomed by French and British reserve divisions already in place there. They prepared to make a stand. The Germans stopped opposite them and waited for their guns to catch up.

Although the meaning of Michael had come down to the fate of Amiens, on March 28 Below's army was launched on another attack on Arras. It lacked enough troops to do the job, there was no fog that morning, and because Byng had pulled back most of his troops, the opening bombardment fell on empty trenches.

The result was a slaughter of the attackers and a decision by Ludendorff not to try again. No possibility remained except Amiens.

Recently so vulnerable, the city was now heavily defended and growing stronger by the day. Ludendorff sent nine of Below's divisions to reinforce Marwitz's army for an assault, but the shift came too late. The French Fifth Army, detached from Champagne by Pétain, arrived on the scene. This was the third army that Pétain had moved into the British sector, and it settled the issue. Soon, with the Germans no longer able to advance anywhere, both sides were digging in for a resumption of trench warfare. By April 5, sixteen days after it began, Michael was at an end. Gough, the scapegoat, was sent home and never granted the official review of his actions that he demanded. Haig would have been sacked as well, but Lloyd George remained unable to find a politically acceptable replacement.

The Germans had captured twelve hundred square miles, ninety thousand prisoners, more than a thousand guns, and mountains of supplies. They had inflicted more than one hundred and sixty thousand casualties on the British (the men taken prisoner included) and seventy thousand on the French. But one hundred sixty thousand of their own best troops had been killed or wounded as well, and seventy thousand had been taken prisoner. And all the ground they had won was worthless or less than worthless. It included not a single place of true strategic value. The German line had been lengthened by fifty miles at the same time that the number of troops available to defend that line had been significantly reduced. In moving forward into a huge and worthless new salient, the Germans had left behind the best defensive infrastructure on the Western Front. They had to start from scratch on ground where they had no finished defenses, no support system, no anything.

Ludendorff had driven his enemies to make changes that would have momentous consequences in the months ahead. Not only were the rudiments of a system of unified command now in Foch's energetic hands, but the Americans were involved as never before. Until Michael, Pershing had been jealously husbanding his growing force, concentrating on getting it ready to make war in 1919. But Michael changed his thinking. "The Allies are very weak and we must come to their relief this year," he told Washington in asking for an acceleration in the shipment of troops to France. "The year after may be too late. It is very doubtful if they can hold on until 1919 unless we give a lot of support this year." On March 28, having no way of knowing that the emergency was coming under control, he had gone to see Foch and invited him to use the American troops in any way he wished. From that day the Americans were in the fight.

LUDENDORFF

THINGS HAD NEVER GONE SO BADLY FOR ERICH Ludendorff, or gone badly in so many ways over such a long period, as they did in 1918. As his problems mounted, he grew visibly fragile.

All his life he had displayed an insatiable appetite for work, but now his staff noticed him slipping away from headquarters without explanation. A member of the medical staff, writing of Ludendorff, would recall that at this juncture "there were reports of occasional crying episodes."

Officers who served him became concerned for him personally and about his ability to function. Quietly, with considerable trepidation, they arranged for a psychiatrist who knew Ludendorff, a Dr. Hocheimer, to visit and see what might be done.

Everyone was on pins and needles the day Hocheimer arrived, wondering how he was going to approach Ludendorff and how the general was going to react. Ludendorff was a stiff, distant man with no visible sense of humor and firm control over all emotion except the rage that could break out in moments of intense stress. An ugly explosion was by no means out of the question. What happened was more unexpected than that. It revealed the depth of Ludendorff's neediness.

He was predictably impatient at being interrupted but consented to see the doctor. "I talked earnestly, urgently and warmly, and said that I had noticed with great sadness that for years he had given no consideration to one matter—his own spirit," Hocheimer recalled afterward. "Always only work, worry, straining his body and mind. No recreation, no joy, rushing his food, not breathing, not laughing, not seeing anything of nature and art, not hearing the rustle of the forest, nor the splashing of the brook."

Ludendorff sat for a long time without answering. "You're right in everything," he said at last. "I've felt it for a long time. But what shall I do?"

The High Command, posing for the camera
From left: Hindenburg, Kaiser Wilhelm, and Ludendorff.

Hocheimer urged a move from Ludendorff's cramped quarters at Avesnes back to the more pleasant accommodations at Spa in Belgium. He recommended walks, breathing exercises, and a change in routine calculated to induce relaxation and the ability to sleep. Ludendorff followed these instructions conscientiously, even eagerly. As long as he continued to do so, his torments eased.

He and Hocheimer continued to confer. The doctor's ultimate diagnosis: "The man is utterly lonely."

Utterly lonely: the theme of Ludendorff's life. He had spent his first four and a half decades in a terrible solitude. Then, suddenly and unexpectedly, he had found an escape. And now the solitude was closing in on him again. That is almost certainly part of what he meant when, upon receiving heartbreaking news not long before Hocheimer's visit, he said that "the war has spared me nothing."

The third of six children in a respectable family of very limited means (his mother's family was of aristocratic origin but impoverished), Ludendorff in childhood was notable for three things. He was so obsessed with cleanliness that he spurned games that might dirty his shoes. He was a diligent and talented student, especially in mathematics. And he had no capacity for making friends. He was drawn to a military career—his father had been a cavalry captain—and when he took the entrance examination for cadet school he did so well that he was not only admitted but advanced to a class of boys two years older than himself. His performance remained exceptional in everything except gymnastics—he was without physical grace, another thing that separated him from his classmates. The age difference and his extreme fastidiousness (he never showed the slightest interest in the adventures and misadventures to which schoolboys and junior officers are naturally drawn) kept him always on the outside. He was a drudge and a grind, if an able one.

After receiving his commission, he went through the usual rotation of assignments, distinguishing himself at every step. In his late twenties he was selected for study at the War Academy, an honor reserved for only the most promising young officers. The commandant there, observing his intelligence and performance, singled him out for the ultimate recognition: eventual assignment to general staff headquarters. By age forty he was in Berlin, a major working closely with the chief of the general staff, the fabled Field Marshal Alfred von Schlieffen, whom he came to regard as "one of the greatest generals who ever lived." After Schlieffen's retirement, Ludendorff was promoted to lieutenant colonel and became a protégé of the new chief, Moltke the younger. He assisted Moltke in translating Schlieffen's secret scheme for an overwhelming envelopment of the French army into settled German policy.

But he was still alone.

Then one evening when he was forty-four and apparently consigned to permanent bachelorhood, he noticed a woman stranded in the rain as he was walking home after one of his long days of work. He offered to share his umbrella, and the woman gratefully accepted. She was Margarethe Pernet, beautiful, lively, the mother of three young sons and a daughter, unhappily married. Somehow—it seems miraculous for a man as sealed up inside himself as Ludendorff—the two connected. They were married as soon as Margarethe could divorce her husband.

A new life, a new world, opened for Ludendorff. He delighted in his new family, and the children worshiped him. He remained addicted to a rigid routine, always departing for work no later than seven A.M. and expecting meals to be served not a minute early or a minute late. But now a new dimension was added, a connection, thanks to his ready-made family, to a wider and cheerier range of experience. All the evidence indicates that the marriage was genuinely intimate and happy, and Ludendorff's career flourished. He became an influential member of Moltke's planning staff, winning important admirers and powerful enemies as he pushed hard (much too hard, his enemies said) for an expansion of the army in anticipation of war. He was promoted to colonel in 1911, to command of a Düsseldorf regiment in 1913, and to one-star general in charge of a brigade less than a year after that. The outbreak of the war brought an immediate second star and assignment as chief of staff of the Second Army as it prepared to join the invasion of France. Before he could take up this new position, he was detached for temporary duty with the special force created to capture Liège; the plans for attacking the Belgian fortifications were largely his work. This led to his first taste of glory, to his receiving Germany's highest military honor, and to his reassignment with Hindenburg to the East Prussian front.

His stepsons, all of whom emulated Ludendorff and had been preparing for military careers, went eagerly to war. The eldest, Franz, a promising youngster almost as gifted academically as his stepfather and far more popular with his peers, suffered such serious grenade wounds in 1914 that, after being awarded the Iron Cross, he was declared unfit for further duty. He began to apply for the Flying Corps and finally was accepted, possibly with Ludendorff's help. His brothers followed his example, and soon all three were pilots flying combat missions on the Eastern Front. Franz suffered a concussion and broken hip in a crash landing, but as soon as he recovered he went back into action. In September 1917 he was shot down over the English Channel and killed. When Ludendorff learned of this, he hurried to Berlin to break the news to his wife. He was stricken, and perhaps guilty at having made the boy's flying career possible. Margarethe was shattered.

Ludendorff was especially close to the youngest of his stepsons, who happened to share his first name. In March 1918 he received word that young Erich, still a teenager, had been shot down behind British lines, his fate uncertain. Not long afterward, with German troops advancing across France in the Michael offensive, Ludendorff was told of the discovery of a fresh grave. Its marker said, in English, "Here rest two German pilots." He went to the grave and had the bodies dug up. One was Erich's. It was temporarily reburied at Avesnes while arrangements were made for its transfer to Berlin.

That was where Ludendorff was going when he began to disappear from headquarters: to brood at Erich's grave. That was also when an army doctor heard "reports of occasional crying."

Nothing could ever be the same. Margarethe was broken, permanently in the grip of depression, grief, and fear. Ludendorff, in his own words, felt that the war had taken everything.

Chapter 16

An Impossibly Complex Game

"With our backs to the wall and believing in the justice of our cause, each man must fight to the end."

—Sir Douglas Haig

I n departing from his plan for Michael, in pursuing Hutier's breakthrough all the way to Amiens, Ludendorff had used up the resources needed for the next stage of his campaign. Ninety German divisions had been thrown into the fight, and many emerged with only a few thousand of their men alive and unwounded. The scale of the losses, and the fact that he now had a huge new salient to defend, left Ludendorff with only eleven intact assault divisions to commit to Flanders—barely a third of the number originally planned. Nothing that he had originally intended was now feasible in the near term. The dream of winning the war by midyear was losing whatever grounding in reality it might have had at the start.

Probably what should have come next was a diplomatic initiative. The Germans were not in a weak position from which to offer to open negotiations. Brest-Litovsk had sealed their success in the east, and Michael had been if nothing else a persuasive demonstration of their power in the west. Germany could have offered to relinquish vast amounts of what it had won and still, possibly, have emerged from the war with gains. Even if it gave up all of its conquests, the war would still have demonstrated that Germany was at least as powerful as all its European enemies combined. No one could have denied its claim to world power status.

France, meanwhile, had reached a point where it could no longer replace its battlefield losses; it had almost no eligible recruits except those reaching the age for induction. Britain was not notably better off. In the spring of 1918 the Lloyd George government abandoned a pledge never to send boys under eighteen to the front, and it was considering conscription in Ireland. Neither Lloyd George nor Clemenceau had any interest in a peace that would leave Germany undefeated, but if Berlin had addressed the most abrasive issues—agreeing to give up Belgium and to reverse the draconian provisions of Brest-Litovsk—the Entente's hawks might have been forced to compromise. Certainly they would have been pressured to do so by a public hungry for peace. If improbable, such an outcome was not impossible.

There continued to be Germans in high places, even influential members of the military, who wanted to make peace. Early in 1918 Max Hoffmann had agreed with the idea of trying for a military decision in the west, but when Michael produced nothing but gains of useless territory, he decided that a change of course was necessary. He would write later that the high command, faced with the hard fact "that it could not take Amiens, in other words, that the breakthrough had not succeeded . . . should also have realized that decisive victory on the Western Front was no longer within reach . . . It was its bounden duty to tell the government that the time had come to begin negotiations."

Ludendorff saw no such duty. He was a man for whom, in the words of a longtime member of his staff, "all political questions were military questions." He had settled the political questions of eastern Europe with his victories, and Michael's disappointing conclusion did nothing to deflect him from wanting to do the same in the west. It is by no means clear that in the aftermath of Michael he remained an entirely rational man. He became not only bent on but obsessed with victory, impervious to the promptings of reason and reality alike.

Speed—haste—continued to be essential to Ludendorff's plans. The number of American troops in France was growing explosively. If they or the British and French were given an opportunity to take the offensive, the Germans might never regain the initiative. If the St. George One operation that Ludendorff had planned for Flanders was no longer feasible and St. George Two could go forward only on a reduced scale, Ludendorff would settle for that. The British, after all, had also been weakened by Michael. They had been forced to reduce their reserves in the north to stop the German advance. By late March, even before the end of Michael, Ludendorff was shifting troops and artillery to Flanders. Arrangements were hurriedly made for a scaled-down operation to which Ludendorff's staff gave the almost derisory name Georgette. It was a feeble substitute for the showdown toward which all of Ludendorff's changing plans continued to be aimed, but he embraced it as a step in that direction.

While Michael was limping to its close and preparations for Georgette were just getting started, Lloyd George traveled to France for an April 3 meeting at which, with the Americans participating, the Allies agreed to strengthen the authority earlier conferred on Foch. He was given "all powers necessary" for "the strategic direction of military operations" on the Western Front. Haig had by now lost interest in this idea. With the French taking over part of his line and fresh British troops arriving from Egypt and Mesopotamia (Iraq), he no longer saw any need to be strategically directed by anyone. His reluctance fueled Lloyd George's enthusiasm. His chagrin would reach its peak, as would Lloyd George's satisfaction, when on April 14 Foch was given the title of General in Chief of the Allied Armies. In terms impossible to mistake, this made the Frenchman Haig's commanding officer.

Georgette (sometimes called the Battle of Lys, or Fourth Ypres) opened modestly on April 9 with an attack by nine German divisions on an eleven-mile front. As at the start of Michael, there was heavy predawn fog. Again Bruchmüller preceded the advance of the storm troops with a five-hour barrage of crushing intensity, and again the Germans made startling early gains. The British were taken by surprise; Haig's intelligence specialists, having observed German artillery moving to the north, guessed wrongly that the attack would come at Vimy Ridge. The worst of the barrage fell on the pair of Portuguese divisions that had been more or less donated to the Entente by a Lisbon government, since fallen, friendly to England. The morale of the Portuguese troops was low—they had been left in the trenches far too long and had never understood what they were doing in this war in the first place—and they were to have been rotated out of the line and sent home later that very morning. When Bruchmüller's fire came down on them, they broke and ran. The storm troops advanced three and a half miles, running into resistance toward the end of the day and beginning to take heavy losses. It happened to be Ludendorff's fifty-third birthday, and the kaiser was at German headquarters. He gave a little speech celebrating this latest triumph—so he saw it—and extolling Ludendorff's brilliance. He honored the general by presenting him with a little metal statuette of—Kaiser Wilhelm II!

Georgette's main objective was Hazebrouck, a railway junction from which, if they captured it, the Germans would be able to disrupt the BEF's supply lines and shell the Channel ports. The defenders, through the first two days of fighting, were Horne and his British First Army. But by the second night, the Germans having torn a thirty-mile hole in his line, Haig was asking for French assistance and sending in the Second Army under Herbert Plumer, who had just returned from helping to stop the Germans' Caporetto campaign in Italy. The fighting was ferocious and costly to both sides, and as day followed day it continued to be inconclusive. On April 11 Haig issued an order of the day that would be derided in the trenches and celebrated at home: "Every position must be held to the last man. There must be no retirement. With our backs to the wall and believing in the justice of our cause, each man must fight to the end." These words were marvelous theater, grist for the propaganda mills of London, but otherwise empty. Many of the troops greeted them with sarcasm. The part about holding every position was tactically deplorable, as Plumer would soon demonstrate. As for the BEF having its back to the wall, Haig knew very well that there were doors in that wall, and he was not unwilling to use them. At the time he issued his order, he was discussing with General Wilson a possible removal of his armies from France via the Channel ports.

On April 12 Ludendorff attacked again with an increased number of divisions. This new effort got to within five miles of Hazebrouck but then petered out. On the following day, probing for weak spots, the Germans attacked on the northern edge of the Ypres salient, where Plumer's defenses were thin. To avoid having his line shattered and his troops overrun, Plumer disregarded Haig's order of April 11 and began to pull back, abandoning all the ground for which Haig had paid a quarter of a million casualties in 1917. Lloyd George, when he learned of this, sourly rejoiced. He felt vindicated in his criticism of the assault on Passchendaele. "The conquest was a nightmare," he said. "The relinquishment of it was a relief and inspiration." He was right on both counts. By shortening his line, Plumer strengthened it enough to make a German breakthrough impossible. Once again he demonstrated to his men that he would not sacrifice their lives in pointlessly heroic gestures.

Through two long weeks Plumer slowly fell back and back, giving up ground but inflicting heavy casualties on the attackers and relieving the pressure that otherwise would have broken his line. French help was beginning to arrive—infantry and dismounted cavalry that Foch had taken from Pétain, whose own lines were left even weaker than they had been at the end of Michael. The Germans noted these movements. Ludendorff ordered Crown Prince Wilhelm, whose army group faced Pétain's forces in Champagne, to complete his preparations for an offensive there. The game was becoming almost impossibly complex.

Meanwhile Ludendorff had no more to show for Georgette than he did for Michael—nothing but more casualties and another salient that increased his vulnerability without providing anything of value in return. He had told the kaiser that he could end the war in 1918, cautioning that it would be "a gigantic struggle beginning in one place, continuing in another, and demanding much time" but promising victory all the same. After so much futile action he needed to capture something, some specific *thing,* that actually mattered. His troops stood just short of Amiens, just short of Hazebrouck, and not far from a pair of high points called Mont Kemmel and Mont des Cats that, if taken, could allow him to dominate Ypres and everything around it. Any one of these would have been a great prize. Instead of making a choice, Ludendorff decided, as at the Michael crisis, to do everything at once.

On April 24 nine divisions of Marwitz's Second Army attacked on a narrow front in the direction of Amiens. It was a rare instance of the Germans using tanks; Marwitz had thirteen of Germany's monstrous and cumbersome new A.7.V tanks, each carrying a crew of eighteen. They routed the British until the BEF's smaller, more agile Whippet tanks met and routed them. The Germans made progress that day, though at high cost, but after nightfall a fierce counterattack by Australian and French troops drove them back to their starting point. Ludendorff gave up on Amiens. The forward edge of the Michael salient became static once again, this time permanently.

The next day, at the edge of the Georgette salient, French troops who had just relieved the British on Mont Kemmel (being in Flanders, this was less a real "mount" than part of a long, low ridge) were beginning a Foch-ordered attack when they were hit by a Bruchmüller barrage followed as always by an infantry advance. Many of the French survivors were put to flight, and those who tried to resist were soon overwhelmed. "Gray-blue figures

Shock troops
German soldiers advance over ground pocked with shell holes.

out of the half-buried entrances of the dugouts spring up and try to pull machine guns after them," one of the attackers observed. "Once they bring one into position, but the hand grenades of our first wave destroy weapon and crew before it can be used. Most of the defenders think no more about resistance; then the firestorm has passed over them, the German shock troops are already before them, and it is better to raise one's hands. Ever more frequently come the blue figures creeping out of the ground, smeared with mud, with fixed, bewildered eyes."

By ten a.m. the Germans had possession of the high ground. They had not only captured Mont Kemmel but swept the defenders away, creating a wide hole in the line. Mont des Cats, a more valuable objective, lay directly ahead and completely open. But

Ludendorff, having grown wary of unexpected successes that drew his troops too far into worthless terrain, had ordered the attack force to stop upon reaching Mont Kemmel and wait there for instructions. All that day the Germans remained in place, doing nothing to exploit one of the best opportunities to fall within their grasp during all of 1918. Toward the end of the day a British reserve division arrived from the rear and began filling the gap. It was followed by others, until a resumption of the German advance became impossible. It was a repeat of the earlier failure to make a timely move against Amiens. General von Kuhl, chief of staff of the army group in that sector, said afterward that if the Germans had taken Mont des Cats, the British would have found themselves threatened from their rear and forced to abandon not only Ypres but their positions along the River Yser nearby. Much of what Ludendorff hoped to accomplish in Flanders could have been achieved with that one move. Instead, his troops were once again short of their goal and blocked.

He made one more try. On April 29, again in the Lys valley, he sent his Fourth Army with all available reserves into an attack aimed at taking Cassel, a town overlooking the port of Dunkirk. It was another bloody fight, it gained nothing, and the Germans' failure brought Georgette to an end.

Ludendorff's situation was now worse than it had been at the start of Michael. He still regarded the destruction of the BEF in Flanders as both possible and the key to everything, but because Georgette had brought French and British reserves streaming back northward, he again needed to draw those reserves away before delivering the conclusive blow. To accomplish this, he decided to attack the French where the movement of their reserves had left them weakest, along Pétain's thinned-out line in the Champagne country around Reims. Bruchmüller's artillery and all available infantry divisions were loaded onto trains and sent to join in an offensive that Crown Prince Wilhelm's army group had long been preparing east of the Michael battleground.

But Ludendorff no longer had the army with which he had begun the year. His casualties since the start of Michael now totaled nearly three hundred and fifty thousand, one of every ten German soldiers in the western theater. More than fifty thousand of his best troops had been killed, and replacements of comparable quality did not exist. More than a hundred of his divisions, nearly all of the elite assault units among them, had seen action, often suffering mightily. "The absence of our old peace-trained corps of officers was most severely felt," Ludendorff would observe in his *War Memoirs*. "They had been the repository of the moral strength of the country." He was writing euphemistically. In using the word "absence," he was speaking of annihilation.

Many of the surviving troops were demoralized by the failure of their ordeal to produce the promised victory. Though French and British losses had been comparably horrendous, Americans were now arriving in France in army-size numbers: eighty thousand in March, one hundred and eighteen thousand in April, two hundred and forty-five thousand in May. Though they had seen no action of consequence, their best-trained divisions were now part of Foch's reserve and available for use.

Making them available had been a stupendous challenge. In 1916 the U.S. army was smaller than the number of British casualties in the Battle of the Somme, smaller than the French or German losses at Verdun. It had so few senior officers that, after the American declaration of war, the volunteers and draftees were organized into divisions of twenty-seven thousand men each—nearly twice the size of European divisions, so that only half as many commanders and staffs were required.

After hurrying the First Division to France, the War Department kept the rest of its army at home for months of training. As troops began to cross the Atlantic in serious numbers, arguments arose over how to deploy them. The Entente commanders, the British especially, wanted to absorb them into their own armies piecemeal, as they arrived. "Black Jack" Pershing, whose taciturn dignity was at variance with the Europeans' image of Americans, refused absolutely. The American Expeditionary Force, he made clear, would go into action only when it was ready. It would do so as an autonomous entity, operating separately from the British and the French. First, however, he was going to put it through considerably more training behind the front.

The next question was where to put the AEF. The northern part of the front was British home ground and out of the question. The Champagne region, blocking the way to Paris, belonged to Pétain and the French. That left the east, the region just south of

Taken prisoner
French troops being marched to the rear by their German captors.

Verdun. This was agreeable to Pershing: a breakthrough there, if it captured the rail center at Metz, could hurt the Germans badly. He established his headquarters at the town of Chaumont in Lorraine. The First Division went into training nearby, and as more troops arrived a Second Division was assembled. The men were quartered in barns, the officers wherever French families had bedrooms to spare. At the midlevel of Pershing's officer corps were

men who would be giants of another, later war: Douglas MacArthur, George Marshall, and George Patton.

Pershing himself had much to learn about combat on the Western Front, and though a capable executive, he was not a military genius. He refused to follow the advice of his allies and give first priority to the disciplines of trench warfare. With the confidence of a newcomer, he insisted that what lay ahead was a war of movement, of breakthrough and advance. Blind to the impact of the machine gun on infantry operations (his troops would pay a high price for this blindness), he saw skill with the rifle as the key to success.

There was no greater challenge than supplying the AEF as it took shape not only far from home but far from France's coasts. Three Atlantic ports were given over to the use of the Americans and were expanded to permit the unloading of a swelling stream of ships. The French were reluctant to give up control of rail lines connecting the ports with the American theater of operations, but they were won over with a kind of bribe. France was given three hundred American locomotives, and the Americans got hundreds of miles of track.

Millions of tons of matériel had to be moved from the coast, along with hundreds of thousands of men. An office was established in Paris under a friend of Pershing's, the Chicago banker and newly minted Brigadier General Charles G. Dawes (a future vice president of the United States), to manage the purchase of still more matériel—12 million tons by the end of the war, more than was shipped from America. The management of all these supplies had to be improvised on a day-by-day basis, and for a time the whole system teetered on the brink of chaos. Its magnitude is apparent in the details—in what was required, for example, just to provide the AEF with telephone communications. The Americans would install twenty-two thousand miles of phone lines and lease an additional twelve thousand from the French. The War Department, in response to a request from Pershing, found, recruited, and sent several hundred American telephone operators who were fluent in French.

As May began, however, little of the American presence was visible to the people of Britain or even France. In London, Lloyd George's government was under pressure to send more men to the continent and, at the same time, to demonstrate to a restive public that it was not ignoring opportunities for bringing the war to an end. It responded in two ways. It broadened conscription, drafting fifty thousand coal miners and men in other occupations that were previously off-limits. On May 15 Foreign Secretary Arthur Balfour declared in the House of Commons that Britain was prepared to enter into negotiations. There was one condition, and it was no surprise to anyone: Germany must declare her willingness to restore Belgium to her prewar autonomy and neutrality. This was an opportunity for the Germans. But the men who might have responded positively—Chancellor Hertling, Foreign Minister Kühlmann—continued to be overshadowed by Ludendorff and his unbending rejection of compromise. Just a week earlier, on May 7, Ludendorff's domination of German policy had manifested itself in a settlement with Romania. Nearly as shortsightedly greedy as Brest-Litovsk, the Treaty of Bucharest made Romania permanently subject to Berlin. It gave Germany a majority interest in the Romanian oil fields (Vienna was given 24 percent) under a lease of ninety-nine years.

What Ludendorff planned now was a pair of offensives in rapid sequence: first at the Chemin des Dames line and then, farther west, across the little River Matz between the towns of Montdidier and Noyon less than sixty miles from Paris. The defenders, in both cases, would be Pétain's troops. The immediate objective was a familiar one: to so threaten the French line (and also Paris) that Foch would be forced to shift his (and Haig's) northern reserves to the south. The ultimate objective was equally familiar: to set the stage for a death blow in Flanders.

Preparing for the new attacks would require a month. The artillery needed for Bruchmüller's fireworks show, and all the necessary ammunition, had to be moved yet again. Many divisions of infantry—tired, disheartened troops—had to be moved as well. The French would have plenty of time to prepare.

The French had 103 divisions on their home soil. (Others were in other places, such as Italy, Salonika, and the Middle East.) But of this total, forty-five were north of the River Oise. Even if some of these divisions were moved quickly to the southeast, Pétain could have no more than sixty with which to defend everything from the Oise to beyond Verdun. This at a time when Ludendorff had more than two hundred divisions—albeit badly battered divisions—in the west. Verdun, supposedly France's most sacred citadel after Paris itself, was now almost undefended. Preparations for German initiatives all along Pétain's line had been obvious for months, but determining where an attack might come had remained impossible. The challenge of responding to these difficulties was one of the greatest faced by Pétain during the war. His difficulties were magnified by the recurrent need to share whole armies with Haig.

Pétain's problems were further deepened by opposition, at almost every step, from Foch and other generals. These men continued to believe that the only way to wage war was to attack and attack again almost regardless of the circumstances, and that when the enemy attacked the only acceptable response was to stand in place and die rather than retreat. They saw Pétain's openness to other tactics, his willingness to learn the lessons of the past year, as weakness bordering on cowardice. When Pétain repeated his order for the implementation of Directive No. 4, which called for an elastic defense-in-depth, he was again ignored. Foch, in his new capacity as supreme commander, explicitly undercut him by issuing, on May 4, an order of his own to the effect that when attacked the French commanders were not to consider even temporary withdrawal.

The line along the Chemin des Dames was commanded by General Denis Duchesne, a former chief of staff to Foch and one of the new generalissimo's most ardent disciples. His force, though mainly French, included three British divisions that after being severely mauled in the Michael fighting had been sent to this long-quiet area to recover. Contemptuous of Pétain and his directive, encouraged in his insubordination by Foch's example, Duchesne crowded his troops into poorly prepared entrenchments up on the front line. His entire array of defensive positions, artillery included, was five miles deep at most. And all of it was north of the River Aisne, so that the defenders would have to fight with water at their backs. The whole arrangement was magnificently bold and ripe for disaster.

General Hamilton Gordon, commander of Duchesne's British corps, questioned the French general about his arrangements. *"J'ai dit,"* Duchesne haughtily replied. *I have spoken.* The troops were to stay where they were. If attacked, they were to yield nothing.

As before Michael, and despite the fact that their preparations filled four weeks with the movement of men and guns, the Germans were almost miraculously successful in maintaining secrecy. More than twenty divisions were assembled opposite

Corporal Hitler, seated at left: Winner of two Iron Crosses

Duchesne, and more than three hundred thousand shells were stockpiled for each corps of two or three divisions. And yet as late as May 26, when the British reported signs of imminent trouble, Duchesne was unconcerned. "There is no indication," he said, "that the enemy has made preparations which would enable him to attack the Chemin des Dames tomorrow." He then departed for Paris and an assignation with his mistress.

Hours later, at one a.m. on May 27, four thousand German guns and four thousand mortars began their work of devastation. The barrage fell mainly on the unfortunate British, whose worst fears suddenly became real. At four a.m. fourteen divisions of storm troops with seven more in close support attacked behind a wall-solid creeping barrage. They found the defenders either dead or in shocked disarray. Discovering a gap between the French and the British, they pushed through. By midday they had advanced five miles and (the British and French having failed to destroy the bridges) were across the Aisne. Corporal Adolf Hitler, armed only with a pistol and operating alone, captured twelve French soldiers during the advance. For this action he was given an Iron Cross First Class, complementing the Iron Cross Second Class he had received almost four years earlier.

By nightfall the Germans were across a second river, the Vesle, and still moving. Once again, however, their lack of cavalry or armored motor vehicles deprived them of the means to overtake the fleeing French and British. In an effort to compensate, the commander of the German Seventh Army ordered that the advance continue all night—a thing that proved to be physically impossible. By the time exhaustion made a halt imperative, the lead German units had moved forward twelve miles across twenty-five miles of front. It was a spectacular achievement, comparable to what Hutier had done at the start of Michael.

All was not well, though. On the German left, near the city of Reims where the French defenses were stronger and had been more intelligently arranged, the offensive had failed. This compromised all the gains at the center and on the right, leaving the advancing units with an exposed flank. To support his offensive as it moved south, Ludendorff needed the rail centers of Soissons and Reims, the former at the western end of the entry to the new salient, the latter to the east. German troops would enter Soissons on the second day of the battle but, bizarrely, be ordered out again, apparently because their looting went out of control and their commander feared a collapse of discipline. Ludendorff, upon learning of this, would order them to go back in and stay. Soissons was not enough, however. Until Reims fell, the Germans would be advancing into a kind of sack that, while growing bigger at the bottom, had a dangerously narrow mouth and only one vulnerable lifeline.

Pétain and Foch were surprised that Ludendorff had attacked in such force at the Chemin des Dames. As the attack resumed on May 28 and continued to progress, they puzzled over how he was sustaining his momentum, not knowing how many troops he had taken from the north. For once they were in agreement: Reims must be held, along with a wooded plateau just beyond Soissons. This would keep the mouth of the new salient from opening wider. Neither general thought Paris was in danger. To threaten the capital, the Germans would have to shift their attack toward the west. If they did so, the French Tenth Army that was part of

Foch's reserve was in position to fall on their flank. Pétain ordered one of the armies north of the Oise to come south. He also asked Foch to send reserves but was refused. Clemenceau, never one to leave military operations in the hands of the generals, traveled to Foch's headquarters and was surprised to learn of this refusal. When Foch explained that he believed the new offensive to be intended not to capture Paris but to drain the Flanders reserve, Clemenceau declined to interfere.

By the end of the second day, the Germans were in possession of high, easily defended ground south of the Vesle. They had reached nearly all the objectives that Ludendorff had set for their offensive, and in doing so they had captured huge quantities of desperately needed supplies. The familiar pattern was once again emerging. At one end of their line, around Soissons, the Germans had succeeded more easily and completely than they had expected. But at the other end, in the attempt to take Reims, they had failed. As before, the question was what to do next—whether to push on where the troops had been so successful, or try again where they had failed, or simply call the whole thing off. German intelligence was watching keenly for evidence that Entente reserves were moving out of Flanders. Thanks to Foch, no such evidence existed: the reserves were staying put. The entire effort had to be judged a failure. At an evening meeting at Crown Prince Wilhelm's headquarters, all the generals in attendance, Ludendorff among them, agreed that the offensive had to continue. Once again losing sight of what he had originally intended, Ludendorff ordered seven of the divisions being saved for Flanders to be brought south to join in the attack. He was like a roulette player trying to recoup his losses by putting chips on more and more numbers.

THE WOMEN

ONE OF THE STAPLES OF GREAT WAR PROPAGANDA was the poster showing a nurse (always beautiful and composed, always immaculate) bending over a handsome young soldier (calm and alert, seriously but not mortally wounded, never injured in ways unpleasant to the eye) who gazes up at her in gratitude and admiration.

Such art had always been a fantasy, and by the war's climax it was an affront to truth. Many thousands of female nurses were doing heroic service near the front lines in the summer and autumn of 1918, but there was nothing romantic about their experience. The avalanche of casualties on both sides had turned field hospitals into places of horror.

"Hundreds upon hundreds of wounded poured in like a rushing torrent," an American nurse remembered. "The crowded, twisted bodies, the screams and groans, made one think of Dante's *Inferno.*" Men came in with parts of their faces missing, with their sexual organs gone, with limbs reduced to dripping shreds.

Things were even more terrible on the other side. "We are supposed to care for up to three hundred wounded here, but there are absolutely no supplies!" a German nurse recorded in her diary. "In the morning helpful soldiers found us some mattress ticking. We began by tearing it up for bandages, since there was no material for dressings. Later we took down the curtains and made bandages of them. Our charges are starving, and all we can give them is dry army bread."

There was the stink of gangrene, and the pathetic shell-shock cases. Dying boys cried out for their mothers, and, in the second half of 1918, more and more fevered men were dying of influenza.

More than fifteen thousand women were with the American Expeditionary Force and auxiliary organizations such as the Red Cross by that time. (Ten thousand American nurses had volunteered to serve with the Entente forces before the end of 1914.) The BEF had twenty-three thousand nurses and fifteen thousand nurses' aides, the armies of France sixty-three thousand, the Germans ninety-one thousand. They performed magnificently—a hundred and twenty American nurses died in Europe, and two hundred were decorated for bravery under fire—but they were only a tiny percentage of the women whose lives were affected by four years of war.

The start of the conflict, and the outburst of patriotism to which it gave rise, had brought out masses of women volunteers in all the belligerent nations. At first their governments scarcely knew what to do with them. Women had few rights in those days. (New Zealand had granted them the vote in 1893, but two decades later it remained almost alone.) Women of "good" family had little access to careers and almost none to the world of public affairs. Nurses were obviously essential and quickly put to work, but in other respects things continued—for a time—in the old familiar ways. The volunteer associations of women that sprang into existence in Britain, France, and Germany were not only dominated but monopolized by the upper and middle classes. If working-class women had been accepted, many would not have been able to afford the required uniforms.

But soon, with so many millions of men at the front, women were needed badly. The volunteers were put to work as clerks, cooks, drivers, canteen workers, telephone operators—in nearly any job, as time passed, where they could free a man for combat. The British would ultimately have a hundred thousand women in service in this way—all carefully screened to ensure that they came from the right kind of background. For young women who had expected the future to be limited to marriage and childbearing, it all could be wonderfully thrilling. "For the first time I was going to be someone," said a French girl. "I would count in the world."

For the women of the lower classes, millions of whom were employed before the war began, more than adventure was involved. The pay of common soldiers was minuscule, allowances for dependents not sufficient to sustain life. (The allowance for a wife was one and a quarter francs per day in France, nothing for a dependent mother or sister.) And ironically, the war destroyed many women's jobs. In France 85 percent of women in industry when the war began were employed in textile manufacturing. As many of the factories were shut down, 60 percent of those women were thrown out of

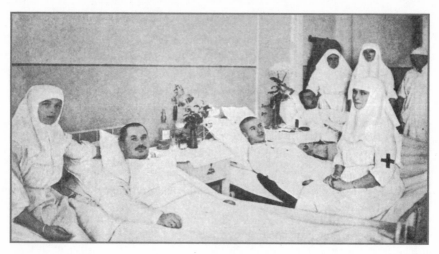

Russia's Tsarina Alexandra, seated at right, in a hospital far from the front

work. Sixty-seven percent of garment industry jobs disappeared. In France and elsewhere many of the women who went into the munitions factories were no doubt motivated by patriotism. But for many it was also a matter of survival.

The resulting changes were dramatic. In Germany more than five million women entered the labor force, rising from 35 to 55 percent of the total employed. In Britain the comparable total was more than one and a half million, with seven hundred and fifty thousand women taking jobs previously held by men, three hundred and fifty thousand moving into new war-related positions, and almost a quarter of a million becoming agricultural laborers. In France, whose population was more heavily rural than Britain's or Germany's, food production became increasingly the work of women. Female employment in French munitions factories rose from fifteen thousand early in 1915 to six hundred and eighty-four thousand in 1917. The French railways, which had employed six thousand women before the war, had fifty-seven thousand on their payrolls by the end. Female employment in the Paris subways rose from 124 to more than three thousand.

Neither France nor Germany integrated women into its armed forces, though the Germans were preparing to do so late in 1918. The British were pioneers, creating women's branches of their army, navy, and air force in 1917. Female officers were called "administrators" rather than given military rank. Noncommissioned officers were "forewomen," the privates "workers." In what was a bold in-

Members of Britain's Auxiliary Ambulance Corps
making a morning milk delivery

novation by British standards, the army began to accept women from
the working class. Traditionalists were shocked. A letter to an English
newspaper complained of women "making themselves and, what is
more important, the King's uniform, ridiculous."

The Americans followed Britain's example and soon went further.
As early as March 1917 the U.S. Navy was enlisting female clerks as
"yeomanettes," who were barred from sea duty but given formal naval rank. In the summer of 1918 the Marine Corps advertised for female volunteers, got two thousand responses just in New York City,
and eventually accepted three hundred.

All this took place against a background of vast suffering for the
women of Europe. In Germany alone more than a million and a half
soldiers were dead by late 1918, and nearly a third of them had been
married. Widows, many of them living in severe deprivation and
struggling to support children, had become a significant element of
every country's population. Little better off were the families of prisoners of war. Hundreds of thousands of unmarried young women
would never find husbands.

In western Europe the new roles assumed by women proved to
be surprisingly short-lived. Women's suffrage movements had been

gaining strength up to 1914—had appeared to be on the verge of success in places—but the war brought them to an end. In January 1918
Britain granted the vote to women, but only to women who owned
property. Later in the year, in an odd twist, it allowed women to hold
elective office while continuing to deny them the vote. Women who
had expected to be given the vote and other rights in return for their
service and sacrifice learned that they were mistaken.

The changes wrought by the war proved to be most permanent
in the most improbable places. In Turkey, before the war, women
had been virtually excluded not only from employment but from
education and even social life beyond the walls of their homes. The
lynching of women deemed to be of bad moral character was accepted practice. The war turned Turkey's women into office workers,
organizers of charities, teachers, nurses, and even transporters of
ammunition. The veil was abolished, and schools for girls appeared
in surprising numbers. Things later reverted to the traditional pattern
in rural areas, but in Constantinople the changes stuck.

Change was most dramatic in revolutionary Russia. Huge numbers of women had gone to work in war factories where conditions
were even more abominable than in the West. This and the severe
deprivations of the long conflict—never enough food or fuel, vast
numbers of men killed—radicalized the women of Russia's cities.
They figured importantly in the uprisings that brought down the tsar.
When the Bolsheviks took power late in 1917, equal pay and rights
for women became the law of the land. The final irony is that civil
rights in Russia soon became once again meaningless for women as
well as for men.

Chapter 17

The Black Day of the German Army

*"The scale and nature of operations required
a 'big business' type of commander, a great constructing and organizing brain."*
—Basil H. Liddell Hart

On a morning at the end of May, for the first time in more
than three and a half years, German soldiers stood on the
banks of the River Marne barely fifty miles from Paris. They were
bone-weary and threadbare, and in days of moving south some
had made themselves sick gorging on captured enemy stores. Still,
the return to this place must have felt like triumph. Since the start
of the Chemin des Dames offensive, they had rolled over or swept
aside every enemy unit in their path. They had wrecked seven
French and British divisions, taken fifty thousand prisoners, and
advanced thirty miles. And the way ahead looked clear: the troops
retreating before them were thin on the ground, almost without
artillery, and unable to find a place to stop and turn and fight. The
Germans must have felt that, if they found the strength, they could
keeping on walking to the Eiffel Tower.

It is unlikely that many of them understood how empty their
triumph was. Their advance was creating an enormous salient,
the biggest yet, a kind of sack with a narrow mouth. They were
inside the sack, and every step they took made it deeper or wider.
But the mouth was not growing at all. It was in danger of becoming smaller. If it were closed altogether—if the French held on to
Reims and retook Soissons—the German assault troops would be
trapped.

The Allied side too (with the Americans in the fight, the term *Allies* becomes appropriate as a substitute for *Entente*) had little appreciation of how vulnerable the Germans were. They had taken Soissons, they appeared to be on the brink of taking Reims, they had advanced so far between the two cities that they were starting to cross the Marne, and they appeared to be unstoppable. The crisis bore all the earmarks of a disaster, and a contagion of panic set in. At the eastern end of the front, south of St. Mihiel, French General Castelnau began laying out a plan for a withdrawal to the west—for abandoning the fortresses that had long made his sector all but impregnable. To the north Haig's staff was dusting off its plans for an evacuation back to England. Even the irrepressible Foch was infected. He suggested that Clemenceau prepare the government to leave Paris, whose citizens were fleeing by the hundreds of thousands, and talked of fighting all the way to the Pyrenees. Franchet d'Esperey, the "Desperate Frankie" of 1914 fame, ordered the French Fifth Army to give up Reims. Lloyd George, having returned to Versailles, yielded at last to Foch's appeals for more troops from England. (They were desperately needed; Haig was disbanding 145 battalions to replenish those that remained.) Only Pétain, the supposedly overcautious pessimist, remained untroubled. He felt certain that the Germans had fatally overextended themselves and that their ruin was inevitable if the Allies just held on.

But then, just as everything seemed to be unraveling for the Allies, the situation began to turn around. Two of Pershing's big divisions, ordered to converge where the Germans were crossing the Marne, linked up with French units and met the enemy at Château-Thierry. It was the Americans' first major engagement, and it brought the German advance to a stop. The commander at Reims disobeyed Franchet d'Esperey, stayed in place, and stopped the Germans there as well. When the Germans pulled themselves together for another assault on Reims, they had to do so without storm troops or Bruchmüller's artillery and failed miserably.

Ludendorff, thwarted again, turned to the next phase of his plan: the attack at the River Matz west of Soissons. The goal here—it had become an urgent need—was to broaden the mouth of the salient at its western end, pushing the Allies far enough back that they could no longer threaten the one rail line carrying German supplies and troops southward toward the Marne. The attack was to begin on June 9, with Hutier's army taking the lead. Everything had to be done so hurriedly that secrecy was impossible. As the preparations proceeded, American Marines launched an attack at Belleau Wood to block one of the Germans' approaches to Paris. They did so artlessly, advancing shoulder to shoulder in a way rarely seen since the slaughter of the British at the Somme in 1916, but their high morale and the sheer weight of their numbers kept them inching forward. It would take them almost three weeks and many casualties to secure the wood, but the process consumed German troops that Ludendorff could ill afford to lose.

Hutier's preparations at the Matz were so rushed and unconcealed that the French began to suspect a German ruse designed to draw their attention away from some other, more secret operation elsewhere. German deserters even told the French the exact times when the bombardment and the infantry's advance would come. Nevertheless, when the attack began—another Bruchmüller barrage, a forward rush by experienced troops who had been allowed to rest since Michael—it was a complete success, and for the least excusable of reasons. Once again the defenders were commanded by a Foch disciple who had scorned Pétain's instructions and put his main force on or near the forward line, where the German artillery devoured it. Hutier's troops advanced six miles that day, demolishing three French divisions and taking eight thousand prisoners.

But then on June 11, as if from out of nowhere, the French counterattacked west of Soissons. Their advance was directed by Charles Mangin, "the Butcher," the almost maniacally aggressive French general who throughout the war had alternately been glorified for his ferocious offensives and censured, even removed from command, for carrying things too far. Thanks to Foch, he was back in command of a corps, and he was unquestionably the right man for the job at hand. This time it was the French who were concealed by fog. Rushing eastward, they caught Hutier's troops on open ground without prepared defenses. The Germans were thrown back with such shocking force that Ludendorff immediately called off the Matz operation.

There followed a month of comparative quiet that the armies on both sides used to catch their breath and pull themselves together. Not only the Germans but now the French as well were preparing fresh attacks. Something new made its appearance on the Western Front during this period: the first cases of the Spanish influenza that would spread around the world and in eleven months kill more people than the war itself. All the armies were affected, but chronic malnutrition made the problem worse on the German side. Thousands of men all along the front became too sick for duty—as many as two thousand per German division. By the end one hundred and eighty-six thousand German soldiers would die of the disease along with four hundred thousand German civilians.

The quiet was interrupted on July 4 by the Battle of Hamel, one of the most remarkable (if largely forgotten, perhaps because comparatively bloodless) operations of the war. It took place near Amiens, its aim was to clear away the German threat to that city, and it was planned and executed by John Monash, who in April had been knighted by King George, promoted to lieutenant general, and made the first non-English commander of the BEF's Australia–New Zealand Corps.

Monash himself was one of the war's most fascinating figures and arguably the most effective commander on either side. Raised on the Australian outback by Jewish shopkeeper parents who had emigrated from Prussia (the Monasch family home—that was the original spelling of the name—had been not far from Ludendorff's birthplace), he had risen from humble beginnings to take degrees in engineering, liberal arts, and law, to become an accomplished musician and linguist, and to found a consulting firm that directed the construction of bridges and railways all across Australia. Along with all these accomplishments, almost as a kind of avocation, Monash distinguished himself as a reserve officer in Australia's tiny army, designed a breech-loading cannon, and became popular as a lecturer on tactics and military technology. He was given command of one of Australia's first brigades at the start of the war and spent 1915 at Gallipoli, where his brigade went ashore with the first invasion and stayed until the end. He contributed significantly to Plumer's success at

Messines Ridge in 1917 and, as a major general, commanded a division at Third Ypres and Passchendaele.

Powerful people in Australia had tried to keep Monash out of the war, and powerful people in Europe later tried to obstruct his advancement. Eyebrows went up, in 1918, at the thought of giving a third star and command of two hundred thousand Anzac troops to a man who was not only an amateur soldier, not only a colonial, but a Jew whose parents had come from Germany. He survived only because every general who served with him became his admirer and defender, and because the king came to respect him.

It was at Hamel that Monash showed what he could do. He used his organizational genius and experience in the management of huge projects to integrate as never before all the terrible new machinery of war: machine guns, artillery, aircraft, and tanks. Executing Monash's plan of attack, his troops needed only ninety-three minutes to reach all their objectives, capturing thousands of enemy soldiers and suffering only light casualties, making Amiens secure and opening a way for further Allied offensives. Their success explains why Captain Basil Liddell Hart, a veteran of the Great War who spent the rest of his life writing its history, said that Monash "had probably the greatest capacity for command in modern war among all who held command." It was a kind of capacity, Liddell Hart continued, that abandoned the old-school dash and flair of the British and French professionals and "fulfilled the idea that gradually developed in the war—that the scale and nature of operations required a 'big business' type of commander, a great constructing and organizing brain."

Hamel has been called the first truly modern battle. It became the model for later British operations; a brochure describing Monash's tactics was distributed to every officer in the BEF. It set the stage for the Anzacs, often operating jointly with the Canadians, to serve as Britain's shock troops for much of the rest of the war.

Eleven days after Hamel—one wonders how such things continued to be possible—forty-nine divisions of Crown Prince Wilhelm's army group made yet another attack on Reims. It was intended as the climax of Ludendorff's Chemin des Dames operation. It was to open a second rail line into the Marne salient and prepare the way for the long-awaited push in Flanders, which was to follow in just five days. But again things did not go according to plan. Pétain, with patient argument, had won the commander of the French Fourth Army over to his way of thinking, so that an effective system of defense in depth was put in place east of Reims. The result validated Pétain's ideas: the German attack on that side of the city got nowhere. On the west side, where the Foch school still prevailed, the Germans achieved a quick and deep penetration in spite of a total lack of surprise. By the second day, it was clear that the German failure east of the city had left the advancing troops to the west dangerously exposed. Ludendorff called the attack off. He left to meet with Crown Prince Rupprecht at Tournai in the north. It was time to finalize preparations for Flanders. Bruchmüller's guns were already heading there on trains.

After four months of struggle and sacrifice, the German situation in Flanders was not remotely as good as Ludendorff had hoped to make it. Haig had greatly improved his defenses—his hundred thousand laborers were fully employed at last, building new fortifications and laying out miles of wire—and powerful reserves remained nearby, thanks to Foch's refusal to release them for the Marne. But Flanders was the last card left to Ludendorff, and he was determined to play it. He and the Bavarian crown prince were deep into their discussion when shocking news arrived. The Germans south and west of Soissons had been hit by a massive French offensive and were in retreat.

This was another of Mangin's surprises, and again it had come out of the forest west of the Chemin des Dames. Twenty-three divisions, four of them American, had followed five hundred tanks in an eastward attack aimed at recapturing Soissons and sealing off the salient. By nine-thirty a.m., with Ludendorff speeding south by train, the Americans and French had overrun three German lines. The American First and Second Divisions were at the center of the attacking force, and the fighting was ferocious. "Machine guns raved everywhere; there was a crackling din of rifles, and the coughing roar of hand grenades," one soldier would recall. "Company and platoon commanders lost control—their men were committed to the fight—and so thick was the going that anything like formation was impossible. It was every man for himself, an irregular, broken line, clawing through the tangles, climbing over fallen trees, plunging heavily into Boche rifle pits. Here and there a well-fought Maxim gun held its front until somebody—officer, non-com, or private—got a few men together and, crawling to left or right, gained a flank and silenced it. And some guns were silenced by blind, furious rushes that left a trail of writhing khaki figures, but always carried two or three frenzied Marines with bayonets into the emplacement; from whence would come shooting and screaming and other clotted unpleasant sounds, and then silence."

Eventually arriving German reserves stopped the advance, and field artillery firing at point-blank range destroyed most of Mangin's tanks. By day's end the Germans had managed to cobble together a defensive line some five miles back from where they had started, but fifteen thousand of them had been taken prisoner, and they had lost four hundred guns. They had stopped Mangin short of Soissons, but he continued to pose a mortal threat. With all hope of taking Reims gone and Soissons in increasing danger, the Marne salient had become untenable. Ludendorff was left with no choice but to postpone Flanders indefinitely.

He dispatched an army to the defense of Soissons. Late in the day he met with Kaiser Wilhelm and told him that, as in 1914, it was necessary to withdraw from the Marne. Preparations began for getting the troops and as many guns and supplies as possible—much would have to be left behind—out of the salient and up through Soissons to safety.

The balance of power had shifted. In March the Germans had had three hundred thousand more troops than the Allies, but between the start of Michael and the end of July more than a million of those troops, a large proportion of them the prime young men trained as storm troops, had been killed, wounded, or captured. The British and French lost half a million men each, and the French, like the Germans, had almost no replacements. But the Americans were continuing to arrive in France at a rate of more than a quarter of a million a month, and they were going into action. Now the Allies had two hundred thousand more troops than the Germans, and the difference was widening daily. Though the Allies still had fewer divisions, that statistic has little meaning. The German divisions were ravaged. More than a hundred were classified as unfit for use on the offensive.

All the force that Ludendorff had expended in driving his troops south to the Marne had gone for nothing. The men who had fought their way across the Marne were being destroyed at a horrendous rate by the Allied armies now opposing them, and the only remaining question was whether they could be got back out of the salient before their escape was cut off. "Midnight," a German soldier remembered of the start of the withdrawal. "Time to leave, to escape the annihilating fire at daybreak. The Sixth Company remains behind to cover the retreat. The first group starts off, ten minutes later the second, and then after a few rifle salvoes the rest. We leave the ruined glade, climbing over the numerous shell holes in the underbrush. Here and there rises a sandy mound in which a rifle is stuck, a steel helmet over its butt. There they lie buried, those who would never come back from the battle of the Marne . . . Along the road back to Romigny the column passes rattling artillery, the riders in the blowing rain bent over in their saddles, the cannoneers hanging on the limbers of the guns. Between slouch the dispersed fragments of infantry, the remnants of companies, guns slung round necks, tarpaulins over heads against the rain, the knapsacks underneath bulging with the effect of a line of comic hunchbacks . . . The long lines of infantry file in the gray morning out of the woods, over the open field, without haste . . . Behind us thunder the engineers' demolitions. The engineers soon come running down the slope, followed by the infantry rearguard . . . Only our dead remain behind."

The great Flanders offensive that was supposed to be the point of everything the Germans had done was overdue and unlikely ever to take place. Ludendorff himself was in obvious torment—self-isolated, distracted, easily enraged, on the edge of collapse. To all the weight of his military problems was added the fear of what would happen when the German public, still assured daily that its armies were victorious in the field, awoke to the magnitude of his failure.

The fighting was not only bloody and continuous but extended over huge sections of front. Allied troops, at Foch's prodding, were attacking all around the edges of the Marne salient, which shrank rapidly as the Germans hurried to extricate themselves from it. On July 24 Foch, Haig, Pershing, and Pétain met and agreed, with some difficulty, on a coordinated series of major offensives. Haig was to attack eastward out of Amiens (Monash's success at Hamel had made this possible), Pétain northward across the Marne. Pershing, who was demanding the return to his sector of the divisions that had been scattered to help deal with the German offensives, would advance on the old St. Mihiel salient south of Verdun. The objective in each case was to capture rail lines that were essential to the Germans and that, if taken, would tremendously improve the Allies' ability to move their troops and supplies. The fact that the Allies were able to make plans on such a tremendous scale demonstrates the extent to which they now had the initiative, while Ludendorff could only react.

Nevertheless, the next day Ludendorff made a final, desperate effort to encircle Reims. It was another complete failure; his armies no longer had real offensive punch. The retreat back toward Soissons proceeded in orderly fashion in spite of continuous attacks from three directions; it was punctuated with counterattacks that kept the Allies from getting too close. When Pétain attacked along the Marne, his troops made little headway against a thin but tenacious rear guard. His attack drew in additional German troops, however, thereby preparing the way for the next French blow. It came on August 1, when Mangin advanced from the west in a renewed attempt to take Soissons. It was a near-triumph. Mangin's combined French-American force pushed the Germans back five miles in a day and captured the high ground south of the Vesle, from which they could train their guns on Soissons. By the tiniest of margins, however, the attack had come too late. The Germans slipped safely out of the salient and took up new positions north of its mouth. They gave up Soissons, and the French moved in behind them, with scarcely a shot being fired.

It had all been weirdly like 1914. Once again the Germans had reached and crossed the Marne, had been unable to sustain their advance, and had recovered their footing along the Aisne after a hurried withdrawal. But the German army of August 1918 was not what it had been in September 1914. It faced bigger and stronger enemies, and it had fewer resources with which to establish a defensive line. Ludendorff, strangely, could not accept or perhaps even see this. As late as August 2, in a communication to his army commanders, he spoke of an imminent return to the offensive. Nothing of the kind was even remotely possible.

Reality came crashing in on August 8, remembered ever since by the name Ludendorff conferred upon it: the Black Day of the German Army. It arrived in the form of the British attack east of Amiens. This too was planned, organized, and executed by Monash, whose corps had become part of a new army created to replace Gough's broken Fifth. The attack had been put together hurriedly in order to deny the Germans any opportunity to regroup after their race back from the Marne, but it proceeded flawlessly. With six hundred tanks and Monash's Anzac troops in the lead, it took the Germans by surprise and scattered them in all directions. Their organization collapsed as completely as their morale. The Anzacs advanced six miles by ten-thirty a.m., nine miles by noon. What was new and shocking was the refusal of the German troops to respond to orders, even to attempt to stop and fight. Reinforcements coming up from the rear were taunted as "scabs" and "strikebreakers." The Germans lost more than six hundred and fifty officers and twenty-six thousand troops that day. Two-thirds of them surrendered. They did so willingly, eagerly, often in large and well-armed groups.

Almost as surprising as the Germans' initial disintegration was Marwitz's success in bringing the situation under control. He sealed the hole in his line with reserves and organized a counterattack that shrank the British gain to a few miles. Not all his troops were out of fight, obviously, and those willing to continue were learning that the Allied tanks were not invincible. Many tanks would break down after an hour or two in action. Others overturned or became stuck in muddy, shell-pocked terrain, and the rest could be perforated by heavy machine guns or blown apart with field artillery. The Germans were also helped by the British and French infantry's lack of experience on the offensive. As black as August 8 may have been for the Germans, as clearly as it showed the extent of their decline, it showed too that finishing them was likely to be a slow and costly process.

August was a hard and bitter month across Europe. On the

Western Front the initiative lay entirely with the Allies. With Foch in command, the British, French, and Americans were constantly either attacking or preparing to do so. The Germans recovered their cohesion and defended effectively under conditions that Ludendorff was making unnecessarily difficult. Though his own staff and the army group commanders begged him to order a pullback to the Hindenburg Line and other redoubts left behind by his offensives, he refused to do so, perhaps finding it impossible to acknowledge that his gains were worth nothing and in fact were barely defensible. The weakness of the positions he was requiring his divisions to hold was increasing their losses and making things easier for the enemy.

At meetings of the German leadership, it came to be generally acknowledged, even by Ludendorff, that military victory was now out of the question. Somehow, however, no one did anything to try to get negotiations started. At one point Kaiser Wilhelm instructed Foreign Minister Kühlmann to approach the Queen of the Netherlands about acting as an intermediary, but Kühlmann did nothing to follow up. He and the others clung to the hope that, by restabilizing the front and returning it to stalemate, Germany would be able to initiate peace talks from a position of strength. It was a vacuous hope. The troops were in such a sorry state, many of them rebellious and undependable, that Ludendorff had ordered deserters to be summarily executed and whatever property they possessed confiscated by the state. This was another sign of desperation: throughout the war, up to this point, the German army had been far more restrained than either the British or the French in its use of the death penalty for cowardice and desertion.

The Western Front was far from Germany's only problem. If any embers of life and force had continued to glow inside Austria-Hungary, they were extinguished in mid-June in an offensive out of the Tyrolean Alps. The architect of this final disaster was, inevitably, Conrad von Hötzendorf, long since replaced as Vienna's chief of staff but now in a field command. In May he had bullied the young and thoroughly demoralized Emperor Karl into approving his scheme. Actually, the emperor did worse than simply allow Conrad to proceed—he suggested expanding the offensive into a two-pronged affair, making it doubly certain that at no point would the Austrians have enough strength to succeed. Originally planned for May 28, the operation was delayed by problems with Austria's barely functional transport and supply systems. When they finally attacked on June 15, the Austrians managed to push the Italians back and cross the River Piave. This gave Ludendorff a moment of hope that, with continued progress, they might cause a diversion of American troops to Italy. But then the Austrians ran into a British-French rear guard and were abruptly brought to a stop. On the second day they were driven back to their starting line with a loss of forty-six thousand men. By June 25 their losses were ruinous: one hundred and forty-two thousand men, of whom eleven thousand had been killed and tens of thousands had surrendered. Those not yet dead, wounded, captured, or absent without leave found themselves without food or ammunition.

This campaign left the armies of Austria-Hungary incapable of maintaining a credible defense. On July 25 Conrad was relieved of command and elevated from baron to count, presumably for some reason other than his contributions to the destruction of the Hapsburg empire. Desertions were accelerating, the armies melting with the Alpine snows. Soon Vienna was informing Berlin that it could not continue. If Germany would not join it in seeking peace, Austria would do so alone. When it attempted to approach the Allies, however, it was rebuffed. It had acted too late to save itself.

Farther to the east, the folly that had been Brest-Litovsk was continuing to draw German troops into a military, political, and economic quagmire. They had to occupy the city of Kharkov deep inside Ukraine to maintain some vestige of control and any hope of extracting grain from that distant and unmanageable corner of their new eastern domains. They had to move into the Donets Basin, which since the start of the war had been Petrograd's primary source of coal, in search of fuel for the decrepit railways taken from the Russians. They had to stretch their lines of communication into the Crimea to discourage an Allied advance from the Middle East. The Turks, meanwhile, had overextended themselves in the Caucasus by advancing in the aftermath of Russia's collapse, and elsewhere they were entering a state of disintegration almost as advanced as that which had overcome the Austrians. They were being outmaneuvered and outfought by British and Arab forces in the crumbling southern reaches of their dying empire.

All was not hope and glory on the Allied side, either. The end of the German threat to Paris had ended also any possibility that the Clemenceau government would fall, a development that might have brought to power a government willing to negotiate with the Germans. But Britain and France alike were staggering under the weight of 1918's cascade of casualties; the British were drafting fifty-year-old men, while the French were organizing combat units made up almost entirely of men over forty. Economic dislocations also were taking a toll. Workers at ammunition factories in Birmingham and Coventry went out on strike, returning only when Lloyd George threatened to draft them into the army. In August Britain's police declared a one-day strike in protest of inflation's ruinous impact on their wages. This was followed by a railway strike in several regions. Strikes were even more widespread in France, and the strikers were often at least as intent on pressuring the government to make peace as on winning financial concessions.

Such unrest reflected the fact that, to the uninformed eye, 1918 could still have the appearance of a year of German gains. The map continued to show Germany in possession both of eastern Europe and of more of France and Flanders than it had held at the beginning of March. The breakdown of the German army was not readily apparent behind the front lines as its remnants continued to put up a stubborn defense, hold the Allied advance to a glacial pace, and kill British, French, and Americans.

The German forces too were paying heavily, of course, and the relentlessness of the Allied attacks gave them no chance to rest, reorganize, or throw together adequate defenses. Their casualties in August alone totaled two hundred and twenty-eight thousand. Of this total, a hundred and ten thousand men were listed as missing, a gentle way of saying that many had deserted. German soldiers were celebrating when they managed to surrender without being killed. When newly captured troops arrived at the holding pens created by the Allies for their growing hordes of prisoners, those already inside welcomed them with cheers. By September the number of German divisions on the Western

Front would be down to 125, and only forty-seven of those were considered capable of combat. The Allies by then were up to more than two hundred divisions, increasing numbers of them fresh and double-sized American units.

The impossibility of a German victory had become clear to all the senior commanders on the Allied side and to most of their German counterparts. Germany's only hope, if any hope remained, was to take action on the diplomatic front before it, like Austria-Hungary, had nothing left to offer.

THE GARDENERS OF SALONIKA

THERE IS A NICE SYMMETRY TO THE FACT THAT, AS August 1918 arrived and the war became four years old, a huge multinational army lay bottled up in the Greek port city of Salonika under the command of French General Louis-Félix-Marie-François Franchet d'Esperey.

The idea of establishing an Entente base in Salonika had originated with Franchet d'Esperey as early as October 1914, when he was commanding the French Fifth Army on the Western Front and had already been nicknamed "Desperate Frankie" by his British allies. He suggested it to President Poincaré, who was interested enough to ask him to draw up a detailed proposal. Franchet d'Esperey did so, explaining that by opening a front in the southern Balkans, France could protect Serbia and drain off German and Austrian troops from other places. But by the time the proposal was ready for consideration, the attention of the French and British was focused on the Dardanelles.

The possibility remained dormant for almost a year. Then, with the Gallipoli campaign in ruins and the Russians driven out of Galicia by the Gorlice-Tarnow offensive, Erich von Falkenhayn decided that the time had come to take possession of Serbia and secure an overland route to Constantinople. In October 1915, facing an invasion, the Serbs appealed for help. Paris was eager to respond. It wanted not only to keep Serbia intact but to win over Greece and Romania through a show of force. It also saw an opportunity to give France a strong presence in the Balkans—one that could be valuable after the war. Britain's leaders, with the exception of David Lloyd George, were skeptical. But they agreed to send one battered division from Gallipoli as junior partner to a much larger French contingent.

The expedition was put under the command not of Franchet d'Esperey, who by then commanded an army group in the west, but of Maurice Sarrail, an able but notoriously political officer who had recently been relieved by Joffre after a German offensive in the

Ardennes caught his Third Army off guard. Uniquely among senior French generals, Sarrail was closely affiliated with the socialists in the National Assembly. He had become popular with critics of Joffre's management of the war. His dismissal created an outcry, the leftists accusing Joffre of trying to eliminate a potential successor. The Salonika assignment was a convenient way of restoring him to command while getting him as far away from Paris as possible.

The first troops arrived at Salonika on October 5, and in short order Sarrail had them on the march toward Belgrade. They had only one single-track railroad to make use of, and the troops had to advance over some of the roughest, most barren hill country in Europe. They were met by Bulgarian troops who had recently been drawn into the war by German promises of rich territorial concessions—everything Bulgaria had lost in the Second Balkan War and more. They were still a hundred miles from Serbia when word arrived that the Serbs had been defeated and were fleeing for the coast through Albania. Sarrail could do nothing to help them. By late November he was pulling his troops back to their starting point.

He began building defenses that turned Salonika into a miniature Western Front, practically impregnable. The British wanted out. Even Lloyd George had changed his mind, and Prime Minister Asquith was describing Salonika as "dangerous and likely to lead to a great disaster." But France, Russia, and Italy all demanded that they not only remain but send more divisions. London complied for the sake of harmony.

Sarrail's Army of the Orient grew rapidly. It included one hundred and sixty thousand men by January 1916, three hundred thousand by May. French, British, Italian, and Russian troops were gradually absorbed into it, along with Serbs who had been refitted on the island of Corfu. Sarrail involved himself so deeply in Greek politics (which were indescribably confused, with King Constantine leaning toward his brother-in-law the kaiser while leading politicians favored the Entente) that Britain and Russia became suspicious of French ambitions in the Balkans. Rumors circulated to the effect that Sarrail wanted to establish a kind of crusader kingdom in the region with himself as potentate.

The next complication was Romania, which both sides had been courting since the start of the war. When the Romanians agreed to join the Entente on condition that Sarrail attack the Bulgarians, the

French government ordered him to proceed. It wanted to expand its reach in the Balkans and to draw German troops away from Verdun. Sarrail was preparing his offensive when the Bulgarians, as part of their role in Germany's campaign against Romania, seized the initiative and attacked him first. Sarrail counterattacked in September (allowing the Serbs to take the lead and sacrifice a fifth of their army in the process) and took the Serbian city of Monastir before being stopped. Stalemate was restored, and civil war broke out in Greece. Sarrail was actively supporting the king's political rivals.

The deadlock continued through 1917. The Entente had more than half a million men in Salonika by early that year, and in Europe the enterprise came to be regarded as a bad joke. German generals called Salonika their largest internment camp. Clemenceau, in his newspaper, called Sarrail's troops "the gardeners of Salonika," a waste of manpower needed on the Western Front. The place was far from a rural idyll, however. It was humid, swampy, and filled with pestilence. Hundreds of thousands of soldiers were stricken with a virulent strain of malaria. The city of Salonika, which had belonged to the Ottoman Empire until four years earlier, was a hellhole. Refugees from the Balkan wars were crowded together in makeshift slums, and unsavory entrepreneurs grew rich by providing amusement for restless Entente troops. Venereal disease was epidemic, and a French division that had not had leave in more than a year briefly mutinied.

Sarrail tried an offensive in the spring of 1917, but it quickly failed. The Serbian army became embroiled in rumors of a plot to replace Serbia's king with a military dictatorship. Colonel Dragutin Dmitrijevic, the same "Apis" whose Black Hand had plotted the assassination of Franz Ferdinand three years earlier, was arrested, convicted of conspiracy, and executed on June 26. That same day King Constantine of Greece was forced to abdicate and move to Switzerland. A provisional government that Sarrail had been fostering in exile took power in Athens, and Greece declared war on the Central Powers. Everything was in confusion, and Sarrail was widely despised.

When Clemenceau became premier, he sent Sarrail into retirement. The new commander was General Adolphe Marie Guillaumat, a veteran of France's colonial wars and a Western Front army commander who offered the advantage of being determinedly apolitical.

Guillaumat began making preparations for a 1918 attack on the Bulgarians; it was to be a limited operation with modest objectives. The Germans, meanwhile, were pulling their troops out of the Balkans for use in Ludendorff's coming offensive in the west. Even the British generals in Salonika grew optimistic. The Bulgarians, left on their own, seemed unlikely to stand their ground if seriously threatened.

In June 1918, with the Western Front in crisis, Guillaumat was called home to become military governor of Paris. (There was more to this appointment than met the eye. Clemenceau and Foch, their minds made up to sack Pétain if conditions in France continued to deteriorate, had selected Guillaumat as his replacement.) It happened that Franchet d'Esperey was out of work at the time. In May, after the German breakthrough at the Chemin des Dames, Clemenceau had half-apologetically offered him up as a scapegoat to politicians demanding change. ("I bear you no ill-will," he had told the general in dismissing him.) Franchet d'Esperey had been offered the Salonika command late in 1917, before Guillaumat. He had turned it down out of fear that, because he was known to be one of the army's Catholic, even quasi-royalist conservatives, his appointment would outrage the leftists. Invited to succeed Guillaumat rather than Sarrail, however, he felt free to accept.

Almost as soon as he arrived in Greece, he began expanding Guillaumat's plans. "I expect from you savage vigor," he told the generals who greeted him when he landed. Two hundred and fifty thousand Greek troops had become available as a supplement to his army, and soon he was cabling Paris, demanding permission for a major campaign. Clemenceau was in favor. With the Germans on the defensive in Belgium and France and masses of Americans in action, there was no longer a need for more troops in the west, and with Austria nearly defenseless southeastern Europe seemed to offer rich opportunities. He got London and Rome to agree.

In September the Army of the Orient began moving north. This was its last chance to show that the whole thing had not been a tragic waste.

Chapter 18

The Sign of the Defeated

"No no no! . . . You do not finish wars like this! . . .
It is a fatal error and France will pay for it!"
—General Charles Mangin

Forced to accept the impossibility of victory in the west, Ludendorff clung to the hope that he could deny victory to the Allies. He persisted in believing that Germany could emerge from the war in possession of part of Belgium and of France's Longwy-Briey basin. "The man could escape even now," Foch said of him on August 28, marveling at his stubbornness, "if he would make up his mind to leave behind his baggage."

That Ludendorff was living in a fantasy was soon made plain. The British were readying an offensive out of Arras, and Foch was demanding that the Americans contribute divisions to it. Pershing, variously described by frustrated French commanders as "tactless" and even "obtuse," would not agree. He wanted to concentrate his troops on his own sector of the front, where he could use them to pursue his own objectives. Foch was indignant. Pétain brokered a resolution of the dispute that provided French support for the attack that Pershing was preparing at St. Mihiel. This attack would have three objectives: to drive the Germans out of their salient; to cut the rail line running laterally behind the salient; and to threaten Longwy-Briey. It was to take place in just five days. The Allies were doing everything in a rush now, thinking for the first time that it might be possible to finish the war before the onset of winter.

The push at Arras, with Canadian troops in the lead, was another success for the Allies; they broke through everywhere they attacked. The defense proved so porous that Ludendorff agreed at last to a pullback to the Hindenburg Line—to the surrender, finally, of everything taken in the year's offensives. His decision came too late, however, for an orderly retreat to be possible. On the British part of the front alone, during the two weeks of the withdrawal, the Germans lost one hundred and fifteen thousand men, four hundred and seventy guns, and stores that they had no means of replacing.

The war had come down to a rapid succession of hard Allied blows that the Germans could only do their diminishing best to contain. A disproportionately large number of these blows were being delivered by the Anzac and Canadian corps, which after four years of hard fighting remained so potent that Haig turned to them repeatedly as a battering ram with which to smash the German line. A strong case can be made that these were the best fighters of the war, their divisions the most effective on either side. This was made possible partly by John Monash, partly by his Canadian counterpart, Lieutenant General Sir Arthur Currie.

Currie, like Monash, came from a background that set him apart from almost all the other BEF generals. He had grown up a farm boy in British Columbia, wanting to become a lawyer but obliged after his father's death to settle for schoolteaching instead. From there he went into insurance, then into real estate speculation. At twenty-one he joined the Canadian Garrison Artillery, a weekend-warrior operation, as a lowly gunner. A combination of competence and amiability opened the doors to advancement: he was commissioned at twenty-five, promoted to captain a year later, and at thirty-three became a lieutenant colonel commanding a regiment.

He had been keenly disappointed when medical problems kept him out of the Boer War, and when the Great War came he was eager to go. He was as well qualified as it was possible for a Canadian soldier to be at that time and was put in command of one of Canada's first four brigades. Trouble, however, pursued him. A real estate bubble had burst early in 1914, leaving him deep in debt. He borrowed regimental funds to stave off bankruptcy and might have been charged with embezzlement if not for the intervention of friends. To the end of the war he would be haunted by the obligations he had left behind. In sending $10,000 to a creditor in 1917, he wrote that "for nearly three years the last thing I thought of at night and the first thing in the morning was this"—the money he owed.

By then, however, he was one of the BEF's most respected commanders. In April 1915 the courage and tenacity of his brigade in holding off a German attack on the village of St. Julien had kept Second Ypres from turning into a disaster for the British. A year later the brilliance with which his Canadian First Division captured Vimy Ridge provoked General Henry Horne to declare it "the pride and wonder of the British Army." But in June 1917, when the British selected Currie to become the first Canadian commander of the Canadian Corps, politicians back home complained of not having been consulted and proposed other candidates. They urged Currie's creditors to demand payment in full. His promotion was changed to "temporary" and seemed likely to be rescinded. He had always been a kind of alien among the BEF's generals; even the Australian Monash was a model of gentlemanly refinement by comparison. "He had a tremendous command of profanity," his own son would recall. "He didn't swear without a cause. But boy, when he cut loose he could go for about a minute without repetition."

Currie was saved—and knighted—when two of his officers advanced him $6,000, and when the veneration in which he was held by Canada's troops made it clear that his removal would spark protests. At the end of the summer of 1918 those troops were keeping intact a record that is nothing less than astonishing in the context of the Great War. They never once failed to capture an objective, never were driven out of a position they had an opportunity to consolidate, and never lost a gun.

At the beginning of September, Ludendorff's worst headache was not the Canadians or the Anzacs but the huge numbers of Americans assembling near Verdun. Anticipating an attack, temporarily free of his obsessive determination to hold his ground everywhere, he ordered the abandonment of the two-hundred-square-mile, thirteen-miles-deep St. Mihiel salient. This timely move would disappoint Pershing, who had originally planned to attack at St. Mihiel on September 7 but was forced to delay by difficulties in getting French artillery into position. He wanted not only to capture the salient but to destroy its defenders, and he had the resources to do so: a million U.S. and a hundred and ten thousand French troops, three thousand artillery pieces, absolute air superiority, and unlimited ammunition.

The attack began on September 12 with a four-hour barrage, but when the infantry went in, it encountered not dug-in resistance but merely a rear guard shielding the escape of eight shabby, undermanned German divisions. The entire salient fell in a single day. Fifteen thousand German troops succeeded in getting themselves captured, handing over four hundred and fifty guns in doing so. Pershing and his staff immediately began preparations for another attack in an area bordered by the heights of the River Meuse and the Argonne Forest. Here the Germans would be waiting with a twelve-miles-deep defensive system nearly as formidable as the Hindenburg Line. But Pershing had eight hundred and twenty thousand men to throw against them, six hundred thousand of them Americans, plus four thousand guns and enough shells for those guns to fire at their maximum rate until their barrels burned out. The staff was given fourteen days to get everything ready.

The rest of the world was falling apart for the Germans. The Serbian, British, French, Greek and Italian troops of Franchet d'Esperey's Army of the Orient, though weakened by malaria and influenza, unleashed their attack on strong Bulgarian and German entrenchments outside Salonika. For several days the defenders held their ground so successfully that yet another effort to break out of Salonika seemed doomed to end in failure. But then, their confidence flagging because of shortages of ammunition and supplies, the Bulgarians attempted a limited retreat aimed at drawing the attackers into an ambush. It proved a fatal mistake: Franchet d'Esperey's aircraft began to attack almost as soon as the Bulgarians were out of their defenses. The withdrawal turned into a rout. The Bulgarian troops, weary of a long war that had accomplished nothing and disaffected from the king who had consigned them to the Central Powers, abandoned the fight. Franchet d'Esperey's advance units reached a position from which the Hungarian interior lay open to them. German troops were dispatched to salvage the situation, but they had no real hope of doing so. "We could not answer every single cry for help," Ludendorff would lament later. "We had to insist that Bulgaria must do something for herself, for otherwise we, too, were lost." On September 25 the Bulgarians asked for an armistice; it was granted five days later. The Turks, having been defeated by an Allied force under British General Edmund Allenby in Palestine, were in retreat toward Damascus and could do nothing about Bulgaria without leaving Constantinople unprotected. The war in the Balkans was over.

On September 28, meeting at their headquarters at Spa, Ludendorff and Hindenburg abandoned their illusions. They admitted to each other that not only the Balkans but the war itself was lost. A few days later Hindenburg would write that this admission had been made unavoidable in large part "as a result of the collapse of our Macedonian front" and Germany's consequent exposure to attack from the east. In the long story of the war, there are few greater ironies than the fact that this was accomplished, after years of disease-ridden idleness, by the gardeners of Salonika.

Ludendorff, all options exhausted, sent his army group commanders a message of desperation. He told them (it is unlikely that they were comforted by his words) that there would be no more withdrawals in the west. Once again he was demanding that every position be held, even against impossible odds. He told his staff that something called pneumonic plague had broken out in the French army—he had heard a rumor of such a development and, he would recall, "clung to that news like a drowning man to a straw." It was nonsense.

The BEF and the French were attacking the Hindenburg Line, capturing soldiers by the thousands and guns by the hundreds, and the Americans and French were attacking on a forty-mile front in the Meuse-Argonne. The war had rarely been bloodier—the British took a hundred and eighty thousand casualties between August 28 and September 26, and the Americans would have twenty-six thousand killed and ninety-five thousand wounded in approximately the same period. But for the Allies such losses were made bearable by the hope that a satisfactory end was coming within sight. Obviously the Germans could not possibly stand up against all the blows being directed at them without collapsing eventually. "I have seen prisoners coming from the Battle of the Somme, Mons and Messines and along the road to Menin," a British sergeant wrote home.

"Then they had an expression of hard defiance on their faces; their eyes were saying: 'You've had the better of me; but there are many others like me still to carry on the fight, and in the end we shall crush you.' Now their soldiers are no more than a pitiful crowd. Exhaustion of the spirit which always accompanies exhaustion of the body. They are marked with the sign of the defeated."

The end of the story is as much a tale of politics as of combat. The fighting continued on its immense scale, with the dominance of the Allies increasingly undeniable. Though the best of the surviving German units continued to resist with a determination that at times almost defies belief, they were obviously sacrificing themselves in a lost cause. The Allies now had six million men in the west, but as their artillery and tank advantage became overwhelming and the tactics pioneered by Monash were widely adopted, not all those men were needed. Guns, tanks, and aircraft rather than the bodies of the troops became the hammers with which the Germans were destroyed and driven back. The French now had nearly 40 percent of their army—more than a million men—assigned to the artillery. They had nearly six thousand medium and heavy guns, compared with three hundred in 1914. When the Canadians finally broke through the Hindenburg Line on September 28 and 29, they were able to do so in large part by firing almost nine hundred and forty-four thousand artillery rounds in those two days. Early in October twelve thousand *tons* of munitions were being fired every twenty-four hours. France's 75mm light field guns were firing two hundred and eighty thousand rounds daily. To be a German soldier on or near the front was to live under a round-the-clock Bruchmüller barrage.

Though the German line was being punctured with increasing regularity—on October 5 each of Haig's four armies broke through the Hindenburg Line at one or more points—none of these successes turned into a rout. Low on food and ammunition, never able to get a day's rest, the hard core of the German army continued to give up its ground grudgingly, to take a heavy toll of the advancing Allied troops, and even to counterattack at critical junctures. In some places the German line was manned only by officers with machine guns, but still it never dissolved. Amazingly, the number of British, French, and American troops being killed in combat continued to exceed German fatalities.

Almost 90 percent of the men in an American Marine battalion were killed or wounded in an ultimately successful effort to drive the Germans off a hill in Champagne—a region, as one of the attackers would recall, that years of fighting had reduced to "blackened, branchless stumps, upthrust through the churned earth . . . naked, leprous chalk . . . a wilderness of craters, large and small, wherein no yard of earth lay untouched." This same Marine left a vivid account of how horrifically difficult it could be to advance against the German defenders even at this late and, for them, hopeless stage in the war: "All along the extended line the saffron shrapnel flowered, flinging death and mutilation down. Singing balls and jagged bits of steel spattered on the hard ground like sheets of hail; the line writhed and staggered, steadied and went on, closing toward the center as the shells bit into it. High-explosive shells came with the shrapnel, and where they fell geysers of torn earth and black smoke roared up to mingle with the devilish yellow in the air. A foul murky cloud of dust and smoke formed and went with the thinning companies, a cloud lit with red flashes and full of howling death. The silent ridge to the left awoke with machine guns and rifles, and sibilant rushing flights of nickel-coated missiles from Maxim and Mauser struck down where the shells spared. An increasing trail of crumpled brown figures lay behind the battalion as it went. The raw smell of blood was in men's nostrils."

Heavy autumn rains also slowed the Allied advance. So did the difficulty of the terrain and the strength of the remaining German infrastructure, especially along the eastern sections of the front where the Americans were attacking. Still another problem was the sheer size of the Allied forces—the difficulties of keeping so many men and guns deployed, supplied, and in motion. Things became so complicated in the Argonne that Pershing suspended his offensive for most of a week to get them sorted out.

In the immediate aftermath of the Salonika disaster, Ludendorff met with Admiral Paul von Hintze, who had become foreign minister after the forced resignation of Kühlmann. Ludendorff, echoing what he had already acknowledged to Hindenburg, outlined the truth of the situation. He said an armistice was not only advisable but needed immediately. Hintze was shocked to discover that Ludendorff thought a cease-fire could be secured within a few days. More astonishingly, he wanted an agreement that would allow the German armies to pull back to their own border, rest their troops and build their defenses, and later resume the fight if they chose to do so. The conversation was not a calm exchange of views; at one point Ludendorff, in one of his rages, collapsed to the floor.

Hintze's objectives were to save Germany and the Hohenzollern dynasty. To this end, once he and Ludendorff had agreed to approach Woodrow Wilson about an armistice based on his Fourteen Points, he made a surprising proposal. He suggested something that he called "revolution from above." This was to be a transformation of the German political system that would demonstrate to the Allies that Germany was now under progressive, even democratic leadership, and that the change had been accomplished by, rather than in spite of, Kaiser Wilhelm. Actually, the plan was far from revolutionary; its most radical innovation was giving representatives of the Reichstag a place in the cabinet. This made it possible for Ludendorff, and later the kaiser, to assent. Modest as the changes were, however, in the context of Prussian and Hohenzollern history and in the eyes of the conservatives they were a shocking violation of tradition. Even Hertling, not a Prussian, resigned the chancellorship rather than accept what Hintze proposed. On September 27 the kaiser—a "broken and suddenly aged man," according to one officer, but doing everything possible to salvage something of his inheritance—signed a proclamation of parliamentary government, a thing that, as he knew, every one of his forebears except his own father would have considered an abomination. His signature was the strongest imaginable evidence of how desperate the German leaders now understood their situation to be. It was also, sadly, a way of maneuvering the liberals and socialists in the Reichstag into taking a share of the blame for the disaster that was unfolding.

Hintze insisted that, to demonstrate that the proclamation was not mere empty rhetoric, he must join Hertling in resigning. The kaiser and Ludendorff tried to dissuade him but failed. The situation was unraveling rapidly. On September 30 a member of Ludendorff's staff, a mere major, was dispatched to Berlin to inform the Reichstag of what was happening on the Western Front. The truth so totally contradicted everything that the Reichstag deputies (and the public) had been told previously that it dealt a mortal blow to the credibility of government and military alike. Three days later "the one prominent royalist liberal in the empire," Prince Max of Baden, succeeded Hertling as chancellor and was charged with arranging a peace. He was a man of ability though in poor health, and the fact that he was well known within the German establishment for reformist sympathies was supposed to show the Allies that a new kind of government, one with which the democracies could come to terms, was in place in Berlin. The Allies saw only the elevation of a man who was both a relative of the kaiser's and a member of Baden's royal house. The choice of Prince Max was ill conceived not because of who he was but because of how he appeared to Germany's enemies: as simply more of the same.

On the day he took office the prince signed a note that had been drafted by Hintze and was addressed to Woodrow Wilson. It requested an immediate armistice, accepting the peace terms that the president had been issuing through the course of 1918. Wilson replied promptly and in firm but almost friendly terms, advising the Germans to confirm their acceptance of the Fourteen Points and their willingness to withdraw from all occupied territory. Prince Max's government, encouraged, signaled its agreement. The Allied armies, meanwhile—this was the second week of October—were briefly stymied on the Western Front. The Americans were finally clearing the Argonne (a dashing young brigadier general named Douglas MacArthur constantly exposed himself to enemy fire), but they had taken heavy casualties during a hard, protracted fight at the end of which they found themselves facing still stronger defenses farther east. Ludendorff found new straws to clutch at. He began to talk of line-shortening measures that could, he insisted, enable the Germans to hold out through the approaching winter, wear down the Allies through attrition, and extract acceptable terms.

But Wilson was under pressure at home. The American public, after a year and a half of propaganda and patriotic oratory, had become so passionately anti-German as to be in a state resembling mass hysteria. Members of Congress responded in ways calculated to enhance their own popularity. The president had been severely criticized for what was seen as the gentle tenor of his re-

Brigadier General Douglas MacArthur
A dashing—and risk-taking—young division commander.

sponse to the German request, his party had only a thin majority in both houses of Congress, and the midterm elections scheduled for November 5 threatened to give control to his Republican foes. Everything and everyone, the French and British not least, were pushing him to take a harder line.

Then on October 12 a young U-boat commander fired two torpedoes into the hull of the steamer *Leinster* as it plied its usual course between Ireland and the west coast of England. Almost four hundred and fifty people perished, a hundred and thirty-five women and children among them. Once again the war was repeating itself. It was the *Lusitania* revisited, though this time with even more devastating political consequences. All the Allies seized the opportunity to toughen the peace terms that they had proposed earlier, when the outcome of the war had been less certain. Wilson extricated himself from his domestic problems by sending a new note to Berlin. He not only demanded an end to submarine warfare but adopted an entirely new tone. He made reference to the "arbitrary" power of Germany's military elite and the threat it posed for the world. He declared that any armistice terms must be settled not with him, not even with the Allied governments acting jointly, but with the commanders in the field. With this he took himself off the hook.

Ludendorff's talk of holding the line in the west, meanwhile, was being rendered meaningless by events in the east. Hungary had separated itself from the Austro-Hungarian empire, declaring itself an autonomous nation. Emperor Karl, attempting to save something from the wreckage, issued a manifesto that transformed what remained of the empire into a federation in which all the members, even nationalities as obscure as the Ruthenians, would have their own national councils. No one paid attention. All the pieces of Karl's empire were going their own ways. The remnants of his army were breaking up as well. Various non-Austrian units—Croatian, Czech, Magyar, Romanian, and others—were marching home. The road to central Europe lay open to Franchet d'Esperey's Army of the Orient. Romania, the source of oil supplies without which the Germans could not have continued the war beyond several months, was his for the taking.

October 17 brought a gathering of the German Council of War—Kaiser Wilhelm, Hindenburg, Ludendorff, and the new government's leading officials. Ludendorff was at his least rational, not only repeating his determination to hold out through the winter (that very night he would learn that the British had made a new breakthrough and were again advancing) but threatening to resign if other generals were allowed even to express their opinions. He demanded that the pointless submarine campaign be continued in defiance of Wilson. The kaiser, somehow, found it possible to agree. Prince Max alone dissented. He adopted Ludendorff's old tactic, threatening to resign if Wilson's terms were not accepted in every detail. He carried the day—letting him go so soon after attaching such importance to the creation of his "liberal" government was impossible. In so doing, he broke Ludendorff's power at a single stroke.

Crown Prince Rupprecht of Bavaria, still commanding the German army group in the north, sent a warning (no longer to Ludendorff, significantly, but to Prince Max) that if an armistice were not arranged soon the enemy could not be kept from invading Germany. General Wilhelm Gröner, who had started the war as head of the German railway system and held other important positions since, finding himself at odds with Ludendorff along the way, reported that at least two hundred thousand troops, possibly as many as a million and a half (it was no longer possible to keep track), were missing, many of them having deserted.

The blood continued to flow—one hundred and thirty-three thousand French troops were killed, wounded, or reported missing in October—but always the Allies were attacking and always

Crown Prince
Rupprecht of Bavaria
*Descendant of English kings,
left by the war without a
home to return to.*

the Germans were slipping deeper into disorder. The Germans were without replacements, almost without reserves, while the Allies had grown so rich in manpower that they were able to pull the Anzac Corps out of the line. Monash's troops were near the breaking point. Monash himself had adopted the habit of keeping his left hand pocketed because he could not keep it from trembling.

On October 22 Admiral Franz von Hipper, newly appointed chief of the German High Seas Fleet, tried to execute what he called Operation Plan 19, according to which his ships were to put to sea and engage the British and American fleets in a final, suicidal *Götter-dämmerung.* Learning of this plan, the crews of three dreadnoughts mutinied at Kiel and ran red banners of revolution up their masts. The Kiel army garrison joined the revolt, which quickly spread, and the kaiser's prized fleet ceased to exist even as a potential fighting force.

On October 23 the Germans were shocked to receive a third note from Wilson, who was now only two weeks from the congressional elections. "If the Government of the United States must deal with the military masters and monarchical autocrats of Germany," the president declared, ". . . it must demand not peace negotiations but surrender." Wilson's harsh new tone provoked a message to the German troops, written by Ludendorff and signed by him and Hindenburg. "Our enemies merely pay lip service to the idea of a just peace in order to deceive us and break our resistance," it said. "For us soldiers Wilson's reply can therefore only constitute a challenge to continue resisting to the limit of our strength." Ludendorff traveled from his headquarters to Berlin, where his purpose was to terminate Prince Max's dialogue with Washington. Upon arrival he found that his message had created a furor. It had aroused the indignation of a public hungry for peace, of a large part of the Reichstag, of Prince Max, and even of the military. It had provoked so many protests from the army's field commanders that it had to be withdrawn—a fresh humiliation for Ludendorff. Members of the Reichstag were demanding his removal. Some were saying that if peace was impossible as long as Kaiser Wilhelm remained on the throne, then Wilhelm too must go.

Every day, almost every hour, brought word of new disasters.

In Italy an Allied force of fifty-six divisions, three of them British and two French, was attacking northward in what would be known as the Battle of Vittorio Veneto, an effort by the Italians to seize as much territory as possible before the fighting ended. The Austrians, rather than resisting, rose up in revolt. Half a million of them surrendered. Their generals, helpless, sent a delegation to Trieste to beg for an armistice.

Ludendorff in Berlin began talking of upholding something that he termed "soldier's honor" through a mustering of the entire German nation for a final Wagnerian fight to the death. The deputy chancellor, after listening to the general's rant, replied simply and poignantly. "I am a plain ordinary citizen and civilian," he said. "All I can see is people who are starving." On October 26 Hindenburg and Ludendorff met privately with the kaiser. Ludendorff, understanding that his position had become impossible, coldly offered his resignation. When the kaiser offered him transfer to a field command, he refused and asked to be relieved. This time the kaiser accepted. Hindenburg too asked to be relieved. "You will stay," Wilhelm told him curtly. Hindenburg bowed in acquiescence. For the rest of his life Ludendorff would regard Hindenburg's obedience as an unforgivable betrayal.

When news of Ludendorff's departure was announced in Berlin movie houses, audiences cheered. Germany had become so dangerous for him that he slipped away in disguise and soon was in exile in Sweden.

On October 27 a fourth German note went to President Wilson. It was a capitulation, stating almost abjectly that Germany "looked forward to proposals for an armistice that would usher in a peace of justice as outlined by the President." In other words, the Germans were now prepared to have the president tell them what the terms of peace would be, though they assumed that those terms would correspond to the Fourteen Points. For nine long days Wilson did not deign to reply. While Berlin waited, the Americans captured the city of Sedan and severed the Germans' last north-south rail line in France. Turkey and Austria surrendered, and even Bavaria began to explore a separate peace. Revolution broke out in nearly every provincial capital. In Munich a republic was declared, the king fled, and Crown Prince Rupprecht found himself without a home to return to.

On October 28 the commanders in chief of the Allied armies met to decide on the armistice terms to be offered the Germans. The discussion was not amiable. Haig had the easiest expectations, proposing that the Germans be required to withdraw from Belgium and France and surrender Alsace-Lorraine. Pétain was tougher, demanding that the Germans withdraw east of the Rhine even north of Alsace-Lorraine and so hand over large areas of their homeland to the Allies. Pershing was even more demanding, laying out terms far more punitive than anything suggested by the others.

A new dynamic came into play: the desire of the British and French to end the war as quickly as possible out of fear that, if it continued, the Americans would become so dominant that they could dictate the peace. Such fears were not irrational; they had begun with Wilson's earlier failure even to consult with the Entente while communicating with the Germans. And serious issues divided the Allies. Lloyd George had very different ideas from Wilson's on how such questions as postwar trade, freedom of the seas, and the German colonies should be decided. When the president's Fourteen Points were introduced into the discussion, the generals had to send out for a copy. None of them could say just what it was that the president had proposed.

On November 1 Kaiser Wilhelm was asked to abdicate. He refused and talked of leading the armies back to Germany to put down the spreading revolt. General Gröner, having been appointed quartermaster general in Ludendorff's place, asked the most senior generals on the Western Front if their troops would follow the kaiser home and participate in suppressing the population. An able and decent man who in future years would twice save a fledgling German democracy from collapse, becoming an enemy of Hitler's by doing so, Gröner had little doubt about what the answer would be. He received thirty-nine replies. One said yes, fifteen said possibly, and twenty-three said no. Soon after being informed of this, told by Hindenburg that his safety could no longer be assured, Wilhelm abdicated. He crossed the border into Holland, where the queen had agreed to accept him.

On November 8 a German delegation led by Matthias Erzberger, head of the Catholic Center Party, arrived at Allied headquarters in Compiègne. The Berlin government, faced with civil war and fearful of a Communist takeover, had instructed Erzberger to accept whatever terms were offered. Foch, after making it clear that there would be no discussion of terms, presented the conditions under which the Allied commanders would agree to a thirty-day armistice. These included German withdrawal to east of the Rhine within fourteen days; repudiation of the Treaty of Brest-Litovsk and withdrawal to the eastern borders of August 1, 1914; the handover of five thousand artillery pieces, three thousand mortars, thirty thousand machine guns, and two thousand aircraft; and the surrender of Germany's possessions in Africa. The Allied naval blockade would continue—alarming news for the representatives of a nation desperate for food. The Germans were given three days to decide—take it or leave it. Eventually a few minor adjustments were permitted: the Allies too feared a Communist revolution in Germany and so reduced the number of machine guns to be surrendered in order to give the German authorities means with which to restore order. Erzberger, who would later be assassinated for his "betrayal" of the Fatherland, led his fellow delegates in signing.

It was over. The armistice went into effect at eleven a.m. on November 11. Not everyone on the Allied side was pleased. "No no no!" Mangin exclaimed when he learned of the terms. "We must go right into the heart of Germany. The armistice should be signed there. The Germans will not admit that they are beaten. You do not finish wars like this . . . It is a fatal error and France will pay for it!"

THE FATE OF MEN AND NATIONS

WHATEVER IT WAS THAT FOLLOWED THE ARMISTICE of November 11, 1918, it was not peace.

Something on the order of 9.5 million men were dead: four million from the Central Powers, almost a million more than that on the Allies' side. Among them were 1.8 million Russians, nearly 1.4 million French, eight hundred thousand Turks, seven hundred twenty-three thousand British, five hundred seventy-eight thousand Italians, and one hundred fourteen thousand Americans. (Romania and Serbia each lost more than twice as many men as the United States.)

The tally was two million dead for Germany, one million for Austria-Hungary. Germany had lost fifty-five men for every hour, thirteen hundred thirty for every day, of the fifty-two months of the war. One in every fifty citizens of the Hapsburg empire had been killed.

These numbers do not include the more than fifteen million men wounded, or the nearly nine million who had become prisoners of war. Nor do they include the numberless millions of civilians who had died in every imaginable way.

Whatever else it did, the armistice did not end the killing. Life in Europe had become too deranged, too many things remained unsettled, and too many young men who knew nothing but war found that there was nothing for them to go home to, for that to be possible.

Russia proceeded almost seamlessly to an enormous civil war that would go on for years, kill more of its people than the Great War, draw in troops from western Europe and the United States, and end with the Communists in firm control. Just weeks after the armistice, an uprising aimed at establishing something like a Bolshevik regime in Germany erupted in Berlin and was bloodily suppressed not by the civil authorities but by rough paramilitary "Free Corps" made up of demobilized German soldiers unwilling to lay down their arms. Communist governments briefly seized power in Budapest and Munich. Fighting over territory erupted in the newborn nations of Poland and Czechoslovakia, in Transylvania, in Ukraine, in the Caucasus, and in the disputed borderland between Turkey and Greece. "Central Europe is aflame with anarchy," American Secretary of State Lansing wrote in April 1919. "The people see no hope."

The disorder was beyond anyone's power to control, and the soldiers who had won the war had little interest in trying. They wanted to go home. When troops based near Folkestone in Britain learned of plans to send them to Russia, they mutinied. Crews of French ships in the Black Sea did the same thing for the same reason.

This was the state of affairs as the victors gathered in Paris in January 1919 to remake the world. Dozens of nations were invited to attend, but from the start it was clear that all decisions would be made by a very small number of them. At first the proceedings were dominated by a Council of Ten, the heads of government and foreign ministers of Britain, France, Italy, Japan, and the United States. Eventually even this group was found to be too large for secrecy to be maintained, and the foreign ministers were excluded. Japan interested itself only in issues related to Asia and the Pacific, Italy eventually walked out in indignation over not getting everything it wanted, and in the end the conference was dominated by three men: Georges Clemenceau, David Lloyd George, and Woodrow Wilson.

The Moscow government of V. I. Lenin was absent because its former allies not only feared and refused to recognize it but were supporting its White Russian enemies. In a radical departure from historical practice (a tradition that had given France, for example, a prominent part in the Treaty of Vienna after the final defeat of Napoleon), Germany was excluded as an outlaw nation. The Austro-Hungarian and Ottoman empires had ceased to exist, and Austria and Turkey hardly seemed to matter. Out of the ruins new countries were emerging almost overnight: Czechoslovakia, Finland, Hungary, Lithuania, Poland, and the Yugoslavia that had coalesced around Serbia. They and others that would soon emerge—Estonia and Latvia in the Baltic, Lebanon and Syria in the Middle East—could only wait on the sidelines (often fighting with their neighbors as they did so) while the great powers decided their fates.

Those powers assembled in Paris with very different agendas. By the end of the war Britain had already achieved its primary objectives. Belgium was saved, the German naval threat was eliminated, and the British army had made spectacular conquests in the Middle East, where the collapse of Russia had eliminated a longtime rival.

Lloyd George, his coalition government having been resoundingly returned to office in a December election, had few major aspirations beyond protecting the British Empire's gains, restoring some kind of balance of power on the continent, and satisfying popular demand for the punishment of Germany. The public's hunger for revenge, white-hot after four years of suffering and anti-German propaganda, had somehow to be balanced against the desirability of maintaining Germany as a buffer against Communist Russia and as a future trading partner.

It was very different with Clemenceau. Germany, though defeated, remained larger and more populous than France, which no longer had a Russian ally to even the scales. Clemenceau's vision, one shared by the French nation, was of a Germany either dismantled or so permanently disabled as to be incapable of posing a threat.

And then there was Wilson, who fancied himself a disinterested mediator free of the cynical and selfish calculations of the Old World. He arrived in Paris aspiring to end not only the Great War but all war through the creation of a League of Nations, and to make the world "safe for democracy" through the implementation of his Fourteen Points (in which he would gradually lose interest). In light of the strict secrecy with which he and his allies undertook to redraw the map of the world, there is irony in his first point's demand for "open covenants of peace, openly arrived at." The irony is deepened by the contrast between Wilson's preachments about the right of national self-determination and the haste with which Britain, France, Italy, and Japan were gobbling up whole regions all around the world without pausing to consider what the peoples affected might want. Irish Americans were outraged by Wilson's refusal to support Ireland's demands for separation from Britain. Other ethnic groups felt similarly betrayed.

Eventually, probably in an effort to maintain some degree of influence with Clemenceau and Lloyd George, Wilson abandoned even the pretense of championing the Fourteen Points. He became as vengeful toward Germany as Clemenceau, accusing Americans who questioned his ideas for the League of Nations of being "pro-German."

A further irony is that Italy and Japan, neither of which had contributed greatly to the defeat of Germany (Japan had contributed essentially nothing), achieved more at Paris than any other country and yet came away not only unhappy but alienated. Italy was given even more territory than it had been promised by the 1915 Treaty of London (Wilson consented while complaining that the United States had not signed that agreement and was not bound by it), absorbing Alpine regions inhabited by hundreds of thousands of ethnically German Austrians. But when it was refused Fiume in Croatia, its delegates indignantly packed up and returned to Rome. For centuries Italy had been dominated by Vienna. Now, its empire gone, Austria was an almost negligible little country of seven million, a poor and landlocked place so alone that it petitioned to be absorbed into Germany. Italy found itself stronger than at any time since the fall of the Roman Empire and with no neighbors dangerous enough to be feared. It saw little need to remain on friendly terms with Britain or France and chose to be aggrieved. Its young democracy had been badly compromised by wartime struggles for power in Rome, and the way was cleared for the emergence of Benito Mussolini.

Japan had prospered during the war, selling industrial products and raw materials to the West. It emerged in possession of Germany's North Pacific colonies, in control of China's Shantung Province (China protested, but to no effect), and with big ambitions on the Asian mainland. At Paris, their conquests ratified, the Japanese asked for one thing more: inclusion in the covenant of the new League of Nations of an "equality clause" that would declare discrimination on the basis of race to be unacceptable. No enforcement provisions were demanded; for the Japanese this was a symbolic issue, an assurance that they were accepted as equals by Europe and America. When Wilson offered no support (the United States excluded Asian immigrants, and the western states were determined to continue doing so) and the Australians objected vehemently for similar reasons, the Japanese washed their hands of the West. Dominant in East Asia, they like Italy saw no need to seek the approval of their onetime allies before pursuing their next objectives.

Turkey was quietly accepting the loss of its empire until, at the insistence of a French government seeking to strengthen its position in the Balkans, the Aegean port city of Smyrna was given to Greece. This sparked anger in Constantinople, the rise of a Turkish nationalist movement under Mustafa Kemal, the hero of Gallipoli, and a war that would continue until Smyrna was taken from the Greeks. To the south, Britain and France came into conflict over how to divide their

Middle Eastern spoils. Britain took Palestine, opening it to emigration by European Jews under the Balfour Declaration. After suppressing a rebellion in Mesopotamia, it threw Kurdish, Sunni, and Shia populations together in a new puppet kingdom called Iraq. France was allowed to have Lebanon and, despite deep reluctance on Britain's part, Syria.

Every one of these developments planted seeds for generations of discord. All of them were peripheral, however, to the great central question of Germany. Clemenceau proposed breaking it up—separatist movements had appeared in Bavaria and the Rhineland, and he was eager to exploit them—but Lloyd George would have none of it. Clemenceau then suggested turning Germany's Rhineland regions into an independent ministate that would in practical terms be a French dependency. This too went nowhere. While such questions were being debated, the naval blockade was kept in place, needlessly causing the death from starvation and disease of perhaps a quarter of a million Germans, many of them children. Future president Herbert Hoover, in charge of European relief operations, begged for permission to send food to Germany and was rebuffed even by Wilson. Those Germans who did not die were left deeply, and justifiably, bitter.

The complications were endless. The Allies refused to be bound by the terms of the November armistice, and Clemenceau and Lloyd George (neither of whom liked or respected Wilson) happily joined the American president in forgetting the Fourteen Points. The question of reparations moved to center stage. Britain and France had hoped that the loans they had received from the United States would be forgiven after the war. When Wilson refused, both men looked to German reparations as the solution to their financial problems. Colossal amounts were suggested—sums sufficient to cover not only all damage to Belgian and French property but the costs incurred by the Allies in fighting the war and the pensions due to their veterans. The question of how much to demand, and when to require payment, became impossibly tangled. Lloyd George worried that, if Germany were pushed too hard, it would fall to the Communists. Clemenceau feared that, if the wrecked German economy was not drained white, it would fuel a military resurgence. Both, as a kind of sidelight, wanted to put the former kaiser on trial for war crimes, but the Queen of Holland refused to hand him over. Wilson, once the

advocate of peace without victory, now regarded Germany as unde-
serving of the slightest consideration. Neither he nor Lloyd George
nor Clemenceau considered the possibility that, Berlin's imperial regime having been removed, welcoming the new Weimar Republic
into the family of nations might have been a sensible next step.

Not until May was the Weimar government directed to send a delegation to Paris. Upon arrival, the delegates were confined behind
barbed wire and allowed no contact with anyone. On June 7 they
were summoned to appear before the Allies and presented with what
would be called the Treaty of Versailles. The terms included:

German acknowledgment that it was solely and entirely responsible for the war.

Germany's exclusion from the League of Nations, the creation of
which was embedded in the treaty.

The return of Alsace and Lorraine to France without a plebiscite
in either province.

The surrender of small amounts of German territory to Belgium.

French occupation of Germany's coal-rich Saar for fifteen years,
after which the region's disposition was to be determined by plebiscite.

Allied occupation of all German territory west of the Rhine for
fifteen years.

No union of Austria and Germany.

The award of the Sudetenland, a region whose population was
overwhelmingly German, to Czechoslovakia.

The award of German port cities on the Baltic to the new nation of
Poland, creating a "Polish corridor" that would separate East Prussia
from the rest of Germany.

The surrender of Upper Silesia, long part of Germany, to Poland.

The surrender of northern Schleswig to Denmark.

The limitation of the German army to one hundred thousand volunteer troops, the dissolution of the general staff and the air force,
and the destruction of all U-boats and all but six of Germany's battleships.

Germany was to pay reparations, but the amount and the time
over which they were to be paid remained unspecified. This was to
Clemenceau's liking. He hoped that Germany would be unable or
unwilling to pay, that its noncompliance would allow France to stay

on the Rhine indefinitely, and that the people of the occupied territories might eventually choose to become part of France.

The head of the German delegation, when he saw what was in the treaty, summed up his interpretation of it in four words. "Germany," he said, "renounces its existence."

The terms of the treaty united the warring factions of German society. Officials in Weimar complained that Germany had been deceived and betrayed, that it had accepted an armistice under the Fourteen Points, and that the Allies were now ignoring both the terms of that armistice and the Wilson formula. But Germany was continuing to starve, and it was incapable of defending itself. When the Allies threatened to invade, the government had little choice but to sign.

It did so in much the same spirit in which the Russians had accepted Brest-Litovsk, conscious of being coerced, convinced that Germany had no moral obligation to comply. A further source of poison was the fact that the Allies had chosen to deal with the Weimar government exclusively, leaving the German army uninvolved. The ground was prepared for claims that the army, never having surrendered and still in possession of vast conquered territories at the time of the armistice, had been "stabbed in the back" by cowardly and traitorous liberal politicians. Germans were given an excuse to despise their new government.

By the time the Treaty of Versailles was signed, several of the characters in the drama of the war's beginnings were dead. Tsar Nicholas and his wife and their five children had been executed by their Bolshevik captors in Siberia. István Tisza, the Hungarian prime minister who in July 1914 tried to slow Vienna's rush to war, was assassinated by Communists as Hungary began to disintegrate in October 1918. Gavrilo Princip, the killer of Franz Ferdinand, had died in jail of tuberculosis in April 1918, regretting nothing except the inadvertent shooting of the archduke's innocent wife.

Others didn't last long.

Theobald von Bethmann Hollweg, whose son had been killed in the war, died in retirement in 1921.

Henry Wilson, who left the British army to become a member of Parliament from Ulster, was shot to death by Irish Republican army gunmen on the doorstep of his home.

Karl I, deposed as the last Hapsburg emperor but refusing to abdicate, died of pneumonia in exile, barely thirty-five years old.

Woodrow Wilson, his League of Nations rejected by the U.S. Senate, left the White House in poor health in 1921 and died in 1924.

President Wilson's end was paralleled by that of Lenin, who was also disabled by cerebral hemorrhages and also died in 1924.

Many of the old soldiers faded slowly away.

Robert Nivelle finished his career in North Africa and was heard of no more.

William Robertson commanded the British occupation troops in the Rhineland in 1919 and 1920, was made a field marshal and baronet, and went into retirement.

Alexei Brusilov served the Bolsheviks until 1924.

Ferdinand Foch was made a Marshal of France and heaped with honors. Then, like Joseph Joffre and Erich von Falkenhayn, he withdrew from the world stage.

Luigi Cadorna, in disgrace after his calamitous failure at Caporetto, would be rehabilitated by Mussolini and made a field marshal in 1924.

Franz Conrad von Hötzendorf moved to Germany and, like many others, devoted the twilight of his life to writing self-serving memoirs of limited historical value.

Douglas Haig, though made an earl and voted a gift of £100,000 by Parliament at the end of the war, was too controversial and too hated by Lloyd George to be made chief of the imperial general staff. He devoted himself to raising money for needy veterans until his death in 1928.

John Monash, the brilliant commander of the Anzac Corps, stayed in Europe long enough to oversee the return of his troops and establish educational programs to help prepare them for civilian careers. He was an Australian national idol after the war, and a university was named for him.

The comparably brilliant Arthur Currie of the Canadian Corps had a much different postwar career. The shadows that had pursued him to Europe followed him home, and he was given an insultingly chilly welcome by Canada's political leaders. He filed suit when a journalist charged him in print of squandering the lives of his troops at Passchendaele. When his accuser was found guilty, Currie was put in a carriage and paraded through the streets by crowds of cheering veterans. He found employment as vice chancellor of McGill University and faded into inexplicably deep obscurity. His name does not appear in *The Macmillan Dictionary of the First World War*, a hefty volume that gives substantial attention to the likes of Admiral Alexander Kolchak and Ante Trumbic of Croatia. Nor is it listed in the 834-page *Harper Encyclopedia of Military Biography*.

The only senior Great War general who played a genuinely major role in the postwar world was Mustafa Kemal. Taking the name Atatürk (father of the people), he became president of the Turkish republic in 1924 and began turning it into a secular, westernized state.

Kaiser Wilhelm lived quietly on a small estate in Holland until 1940, putting pins in maps, at the end, to mark the progress of Germany's armies in a new war.

His cousin George V died four years before Wilhelm, his last years troubled only by the refusal of his eldest son and heir to break off a scandalous relationship with an American divorcée named Wallis Simpson.

Georges Clemenceau, who had already been in his late seventies when he became Premier of France in 1917, lived on to have probably the fullest postwar years of any of the heads of government. Resented by many French politicians for the way he had monopolized the management of the war in its last year and the negotiations that followed, he ran for president in 1920, lost, and resigned as premier. He then traveled the world, hunting tigers in India, wrote books, and made a tour of the United States to warn of the dangers of American indifference to affairs in Europe before dying at eighty-eight. His hatred of Germany never waned.

Some of the war's great figures lived too long. David Lloyd George lost his place as prime minister in 1922, when the Conservative Party left his coalition and took power independently. His own Liberal Party had withered by then, and Labour had become Britain's most important opposition party. Lloyd George remained in Parliament for more than two decades, a sadly marginal figure without a power base. He never again held office.

Erich Ludendorff, upon returning from exile in Sweden, associated himself with the darkest elements in German politics. He became involved in efforts to overthrow the Weimar Republic in 1920 and 1923 (the second time in affiliation with Adolf Hitler), ran unsuccessfully for president of the republic in 1925, and divorced his wife Margarethe. His second wife encouraged him in a crackpot cultish campaign to rid Germany of Christians, Jews, and Freemasons—of almost the entire population, in short. Ludendorff thus isolated himself not only from everything progressive but even from the Nazis and the Junker officer corps. In the months before his death in 1937, when in a return to something like sanity he began to raise the alarm about the dangers of the Hitler dictatorship, no one was listening.

The most brilliant and dynamic of the Bolsheviks, Leon Trotsky, lost out in a power struggle with Joseph Stalin in the years after Lenin's death. He was expelled from the Russian Communist Party in 1927, exiled to Central Asia in 1928, and expelled from the Soviet Union altogether in 1929. Endlessly pursued by Stalin's agents, he moved on to Turkey, to France, to Norway, and finally in 1936 to Mexico. He was murdered four years later, killed by an ax blow delivered to the back of his skull.

Paul von Hindenburg retired from the German army after the war, already in his seventies. Despite being an avowed monarchist with no respect for the new republic, he consented to run for president in 1925 and, still a national hero, was elected. In 1932, in his eighties and an even more passive figurehead than he had been during the war, he ran for reelection because there seemed to be no alternative to Hitler. Again he was successful. A year later he was persuaded to name Hitler to the chancellorship by associates who assured him that, once in office, Hitler would be easily contained. He was still alive, if barely, as the Nazis began the reign of terror with which they seized control of the government and the country.

An even more melancholy story is that of Henri-Philippe Pétain, who at the start of the Great War had been an aging colonel near retirement and at its end was a Marshal of France and commander in chief of the armies of his nation. In his sixties in 1918, he remained on active duty and moved from one exalted position to another. Eighty-four when Germany invaded France in 1940, he was asked to form a government. When the Germans conquered two-thirds of France, Pétain arranged an armistice and was named chief of state with nearly unlimited powers by a new government based at Vichy. His performance during the German occupation was ambiguous at worst—he remained in office out of fear that his departure would lead to worse Nazi outrages, and attempted in many ways to obstruct the occupiers—but after liberation he was put on trial by the new French government and condemned to death. The sentence was reduced to life imprisonment by Pétain's onetime protégé Charles de Gaulle. He died in confinement on an island off France's Atlantic coast in 1951, aged ninety-five.

One of the war's youngest leading figures also appeared to live too long. Winston Churchill's career prospered in the decade after the Treaty of Versailles. He served as secretary of state for war from 1919 to 1921, as colonial secretary in 1921 and 1922, and as chancellor of the exchequer from 1924 to 1929. Along the way he left the Liberals to return to the Conservative Party, where he had begun a quarter century earlier, but the Conservatives despised him for his old apostasy and distrusted him deeply. From 1929 on he was consigned to what he called "the political wilderness," a has-been issuing warnings about the rearmament of Nazi Germany that few were prepared to take seriously.

But that is another story.

Notes

PART FOUR

1916: *Bleeding to Death*

An enormous literature on the great battles of 1916 has grown up over nine decades. In approaching the Battle of Verdun, the author found two works to be particularly helpful as overall guides: *The Price of Glory: Verdun 1916* by Alistair Horne, and *The Road to Verdun* by Ian Ousby. A volume requiring special acknowledgment in connection with the Battle of the Somme is *The First Day on the Somme* by Martin Middlebrook. Both battles are dealt with helpfully in *Attrition: The Great War on the Western Front, 1916,* by Robin Neillands, and the year's diplomatic background is illuminated by *Divide and Conquer: German Efforts to Conclude a Separate Peace, 1914–1918,* by L. L. Farrar, Jr. In connection with 1916 as well as other years, Stone's *The Eastern Front* and Herwig's *The First World War: Germany and Austria* are rich in information about the war in the east.

Page

3   More than twelve hundred guns: The size of the German bombardment at the start of the Battle of Verdun is, like so many aspects of the Great War, a question to which there appears to be no conclusive answer. Stevenson, on page 132 of *Cataclysm*, says the Germans had 1,220 guns. Divergent numbers in other recent histories are 1,300 (Clayton, 100), "about 1,200 . . . over half of them heavy caliber" (Ousby, 63), "1,521 heavy guns" (Herwig, 183), and "850 heavy guns" (Gilbert, *First World War*, 231).

3   All through the morning: Asprey, *German High Command*, 222.

3   "Thousands of projectiles": Austin, 4:54.

4   Nine divisions came forward: Stevenson, *Cataclysm,* 132.

5   In the Gorlice-Tarnow campaign: Casualty figures and the Falken-hayn quote are in Herwig, 179.

5   Three hundred and thirty-five thousand: Ousby, 7.

5   This had brought to two million: Mosier, 18, puts French casualties by the end of 1915 at 2,478,000 with 941,000 dead or missing. Neillands gives comparable totals of 1,932,051 and 1,001,271 respectively.

5   Some two hundred thousand British were dead: Neillands, 36.

5   Italy's entry into the war: Isonzo casualty figures are in Banks, 201.

6   By the start of 1916 the British: Mosier, 34, gives a total of 987,000.

7   The Germans had generally been far more careful: The success of the Germans in keeping their casualties below Entente levels is examined and discussed at length in several parts of Mosier and Ferguson.

7   They also understood, however: The German and Entente division totals are in Herwig, 178. Clayton, 196, says the Entente had ninety-five French, thirty-eight British, and six Belgian divisions versus 117 German.

8   Forty French divisions: The number of divisions that Joffre originally planned for the Somme offensive is in Clayton, 96.

8   "the Russian armies have not been completely": Neillands, 60.

9   "She is staking everything on a war": Ibid.

9   Since then, however, his pessimism: The assurances of the German naval leaders are in Asprey, *German High Command,* 219.

9   "There can be no justification": Ibid.

9   "We should ruthlessly employ every weapon": Neillands, 66.

9   "cannot intervene decisively": Herwig, 181.

10   "France has arrived almost at the end": Goodspeed, 176.

10   His thoughts were focused: An exceptionally illuminating explanation of Falkenhayn's Verdun strategy and the thinking behind it is in Farrar, *Divide and Conquer,* 49–56.

10   "the forces of France will bleed": Ousby, 52.

13   "Should our front line be overrun": Ibid., 74.

13   "In the morning, Council of Ministers": Mosier, 188.

13   "I consider that nothing justifies": Ibid., 189.

13   "I cannot permit soldiers under": Ousby, 75.

14   On the east bank of the Meuse: Manpower data are in ibid., 76.

14 Though he had more than nine hundred: Ibid. Horne, *Price,* 55, says the French had only 270 artillery pieces at Verdun at the start of the battle; this total differs greatly from other sources.

15 No fewer than five new railway lines: Marshall, 170.

15 In a seven-week period between late December: Stevenson, *Cataclysm,* 132.

15 In the sky above all this was: details of the German air umbrella are in Clayton, 100, and Mosier, 208.

17 "an offensive in the direction of Verdun": Asprey, *German High Command,* 221.

17 When night fell, nothing was left: Driant's surviving force on the night of February 21 is in ibid., 221.

20 By the outbreak of the war: Clayton, 99.

20 Ultimately 80 percent of its artillery: Neillands, 73.

21 The behavior of the Prussians seemed: Conflicts between German authorities and residents of Alsace-Lorraine are described in Alan Kramer, "*Wackes* at War: Alsace-Lorraine and the Failure of German Mobilization, 1914–18" in Horne, *State,* 110–20.

23 During the first day's bombardment: Keegan, *Illustrated History,* 257.

23 Casualties on the German side were as light: Numbers are in Mosier, 213–14.

26 They advanced three and a half miles: Falls, 189.

26 "It wouldn't take anything": Ousby, 100.

28 Those men, however, numbered only sixty: Ibid., 108.

29 Four hundred and fifty thousand shells: Herwig, 190.

31 Pétain's staff could find only seven hundred: Data about truck traffic are in Keegan, *Illustrated History,* 262; Clayton, 106; and Ousby, 146.

32 In time three-fourths of the entire French army: Ousby, 128.

32 Between February 24 and March 6: Asprey, *German High Command,* 190.

34 "not to defeat but to annihilate France": Ibid., 184.

35 By December British doctors: Shephard, 21.

35 Their German counterparts would record: Ibid., 98.

35 But the number of men unable: Ibid., 38.

38 "a singularly ill-chosen term": Ibid., 31.

38 Further confirmation came: Ibid., 75.

39 This is an area in which data: British and German totals are in

Stevenson, *Cataclysm,* 170.

39   Sixteen thousand cases were reported: Shephard, 41.

39   Fifteen percent of all the British: Ibid., 144.

39   In 1922, four years after: Ibid., 158.

40   Pétain, anticipating a German advance: French west bank troop deployments are in Neillands, 175.

43   In the north, in the sector: German and Russian troop strength in the three main sectors of the Eastern Front is in Stone, 227.

44   They began Verdun-style: Information about shells expended, and the five-to-one troop margin, is in Rutherford, 188.

44   Twelve thousand unwounded Russians: Gilbert, *First World War,* 237.

45   "One must have lived through": [Story], 10:2881.

46   And the losses were mounting: Ibid.

46   "a vigorous and powerful offensive": Mosier, 218.

47   "Verdun was the mill on the Meuse": Neillands, 197.

48   "Tell me . . . when was the war over?" Gilbert, *First World War,* 257.

48   "I shall sleep in peace": Rutherford, 193.

50   In the two fights at Lake Naroch: Stone, 231, says Russian casualties totaled one hundred thousand. Rutherford, 191, says the total was between one hundred ten and one hundred twenty thousand.

52   "a useless and expensive fad": Neillands, 82.

52   "good for sport but not for war": Ibid.

52   Though both France and Germany: Details about prewar aircraft development and numbers of planes acquired by the Great Powers up to 1914 are in Herrmann, 140–42 and 201–06.

53   "We literally thought of": Marshall, 316.

54   Even so, the Eindeckers: Michael Spick, "The Fokker Menace," in Cowley, 261.

55   "steam tractors with small": Gilbert, *Churchill,* 3:535.

55   It was a mother indeed: The specifications of the first tank are in Cooper, 26.

56   "These were the happiest days of my life": Jamie H. Cockfield, "Brusilov's Immortal Days," in Cowley, 227.

56   By the end of April: Mosier, 108.

56   To that purpose he assembled: Horne, *Price,* 170.

57   The Germans captured Côte 304: Neillands, 211.

57   Whatever the cause: Ousby, 275.

58   He and Falkenhayn were encouraged: Horne, *Price,* 229.

58   "if Main Headquarters order it": Ibid.

59   "Dago dogs": Herwig, 204.

59   Six of the divisions committed to the Trentino: Conrad's removal of six prime divisions from Galicia is in Herwig, 205.

60   Their cumulative result: Austria-Hungary's 1915 casualty figures are in ibid., 204.

61   When the Austrians finally attacked: Initial Austrian and Italian troop strength is in ibid., 206.

61   By the end of May: Numbers of soldiers and guns captured by the Austrians are in Stone, 246.

61   "Even the wounded refuse": Austin, 4:224.

62   In the five days preceding: Bombardment details are in Horne, *Price,* 236.

62   The failure had been so complete: French casualty figures are in Ousby, 267.

62   "You did your duty": Ibid.

62   He was reluctant in spite of: Cockfield, "Brusilov's Immortal Days," in Cowley, 225.

62   "the French Army could cease": Horne, *Price,* 293.

65   The Austro-Hungarian Fourth Army: Casualty figures are in Herwig, 213.

65   It was the same almost everywhere: Prisoner-of-war totals are in ibid., 209.

65   Before the end of the first week: Stone, 254.

66   "the crisis would probably have developed": in Rutherford, 204.

68   "This town today is a veritable maelstrom": [*Story*], 9:2668.

69   "not the monkey our caricaturists": Horne, *Price,* 264.

70   The last of Falkenhayn's reserves: Data on the force attacking Fort Souville are in ibid., 284.

70   "Our heads are buzzing": Lewis, 209.

71   Joffre's view of the situation: Horne, *Price,* 289.

74   From 1885 to 1914 not one Jew: This history, and the associated data, are in Christhard Hoffmann, "Between Integration and Rejection: The Jewish Community in Germany, 1914–1918," in Horne, *State,* 96–104.

74   "the curse of my country": MacDonogh, 439.

74   "A war after the war stands before us": Horne, *State,* 100.

78   Seven thousand miles of telephone lines: Johnson, 60.

78   Ten squadrons of aircraft: Middlebrook, 66.

79   Haig had eighteen divisions on the Somme: Falls, 198. Different historians give divergent numbers of British, French, and German divisions at the start of the Battle of the Somme, perhaps because of the frequency with which divisions were being shifted from place to place during the multiple crises of mid-1916.

79   He had fifteen hundred pieces of artillery: Middlebrook, 68.

79   Between them the British and French: Artillery totals are in Herwig, 199.

80   "You will be able to go over the top": Middlebrook, 78.

80   The French had one corps: Johnson, 57. Here again different writers give different numbers in describing the French forces on the Somme. For example, Johnson says the French had two divisions in reserve in addition to those on the front line, while Herwig, 199, says they had six.

80   Below had only seven divisions: Mosier, 233, and Herwig, 199, give this number, while Falls, 198, says the total is six.

81   By the time the troops went over the top: Shell numbers are variously in Cowley, 321; Herwig, 199; and Johnson, 61.

82   "Shall I live till morning": Macdonald, *Somme,* 49.

82   Nearly seven thousand of them died: Tim Travers, "July 1, 1916: The Reason Why," in Cowley, 327.

83   "The ground where I stood": Johnson, 67.

88   "The attack must be made in waves": Travers, "July 1," in Cowley, 329.

88   "Fancy advancing against heavy fire": Ibid., 321.

88   "We were surprised to see them walking": Mosier, 235.

88   "The infantry rushed forward":Lewis, 215.

89   the Thirty-fourth Division: Middlebrook, 248.

89   At Beaumont-Hamel: Casualty figures are in Travers, "July 1," in Cowley, 326.

89   The number of casualties: Numbers are in Middlebrook, 244. The following casualty figures from Waterloo and Normandy are in Middlebrook, 246.

89   German losses for the first day: Travers, "July 1," in Cowley, 327.

90   It had torn open the defenses: Ibid., 324.

90   "speed, dash and tactical brains": Falls, 200.

90   "no serious advance is to be made": Johnson, 63.

95   "Tsar of the land of Russia": Massie, *Nicholas and Alexandra,* 374.

95   "Whatever pride I had": Cowley, 354.

97   On July 2 Haig: Middlebrook, 225.

98   Evert had a thousand guns: Artillery numbers and the Russian and German casualties that follow are in Stone, 260–61.

98   In four days he took: Ibid., 261.

98   On July 10, in a final lunge: Horne, *Price,* 296.

98   "Those who went outside were killed": Austin, 4:247.

99   His plan this time was to send: The size of Rawlinson's attack force and the German defense is in Liddell Hart, *Real War,* 240.

100   "Although most Australian soldiers were optimists": Ibid., 244.

100   He struck at the Turkish Third Army: Falls, 248.

100   Three months earlier the Germans: Numbers of German divisions in the East and West in May and August 1916 are in Mosier, 252.

101   The Austrians were on the defensive: Casualties for the Sixth Battle of the Isonzo are in Banks, 201.

101   To complete the picture, French General Sarrail: Mosier, 255.

102   On August 27 Romania issued a declaration: The size of the Romanian force invading Transylvania and of the Austrian forces defending is in Stone, 274, and Liddell Hart, *Real War,* 264.

102   The addition to the Entente of Romania: The size of Romania's military forces is in Mosier, 254. Stone, 264, says Romania had six hundred and twenty thousand soldiers.

103   It was untrained and disorganized: The Romanian makeup order is in Stone, 265.

104   Whole armies were being hurried: Train numbers are in ibid.

104   The commander of this fortress: The Turtukai episode is in ibid., 276.

105   "this will be our Verdun": Ibid., 277.

105   Only sixty of the new machines: Liddell Hart, *Real War,* 245.

105   "My poor 'land battleships' ": Gilbert, *Churchill,* 3:810.

106   The Guards, a hundred and thirty-four thousand of the best: Details of the Kovel offensive are in Rutherford, 213–15, and Stone, 261–63.

106   It burned out of control: the Tavannes Tunnel disaster and its casualties are in Horne, *Price,* 305–7.

106 Again Haig used his tanks: Neillands, 285.

107 On October 19, satisfied: French artillery preparations are in Horne, *Price,* 308 and 314.

108 Nor was Haig quite finished: Isonzo casualties for 1917 are in Banks, 201.

108 On November 13 the British detonated: The number of British divisions is in Liddell Hart, *Real War,* 247; the number of German prisoners is in Falls, 206.

108 Casualties on the Somme totaled: The facts about British, French, and German casualties are explored at length in Mosier, 241.

109 "The first principle in position warfare": Cowley, 350.

110 Since their government's declaration: Casualties of the Romanian campaign are in Mosier, 260.

110 Over the next year and a half: Amounts of materials extracted from Romania in 1917 and 1918 are in Stone, 265.

111 Meaningless as it was: The story of the bleating French troops is in Horne, *Price,* 318.

PART FIVE

1917: *Things Fall Apart*

Three books with suggestively divergent subtitles— *Ludendorff, Genius of World War I* by D. J. Goodspeed, *Ludendorff, The Tragedy of a Military Mind* by Karl Tschuppik, and *Tormented Warrior: Ludendorff and the Supreme Command* by Roger Parkinson—become increasingly valuable as the war enters 1917 and their subject emerges as something very like a military dictator of Germany. In dealing with the Western Front in 1917, the author found much of value in *The Defeat of Imperial Germany, 1917–1918* by Rod Paschall and *In Flanders Fields: The 1917 Campaign* by Leon Wolff. *Paths of Glory: The French Army 1914–1918* by Anthony Clayton is a helpful guide to its subject at this stage in the war, *The War to End All Wars* by Edward M. Coffman and *Illusion of Victory* by Thomas Fleming to America's entry into the conflict.

Page

115 "victory over the military powers": Gleichen, 117.

116 "put our trust rather": Gilbert, *First World War,* 303.

116 "economic, military and political": Parkinson, 114.

116 "a likeness between the two": Gleichen, 278.

117 "the reorganization of Europe": Woodward, 237.

118 "Our position was extremely difficult": Ludendorff's words are in Tschuppik, 66.

118 Almost the only general inconvenience: Data on lost coal production are in Ferguson, 250.

118 Problems had arisen, inevitably: Heyman, 199.

119 The situation was worse in Britain: Ibid., 197.

120 A decline in nutrition manifested itself: Tuberculosis data are in Ferguson, 277.

120 Russia was increasingly unsuccessful: Refugee numbers are in Stevenson, *Cataclysm,* 234.

120 The infant mortality rate doubled: Hours spent by women working and standing in line, and the numbers that follow on strikes in January and February 1917, are in ibid., 249.

121 As early as October 1914 ten thousand horses: Herwig, 274.

121 Nine million animals perished: Ferguson, 276.

121 Before the war Germany had been importing: Herwig, 272.

121 As this input dwindled: The decline in German grain production is in Ferguson, 251.

121 Food prices rose 130 percent: The Berlin percentage increase is in Herwig, 286, the Vienna increase in Herwig, 276.

121 Even for industrial workers: German wage increase percentage is in Stevenson, *Cataclysm,* 305.

122 The chief physician at one of Berlin's: The doctor's estimate is in a report by an American journalist excerpted in Thoumin, 274.

122 The average daily adult intake: Asprey, *German High Command,* 314.

122 Deaths from lung disease increased: Ferguson, 277.

122 "One of the most terrible": Wolff, 22.

122 A German who was a schoolboy: Arthur, 200.

123 Even the expected bounty: Percentage increase from Romanian exports is in Wolff, 251.

124 "I will give Your Majesty my word": Gilbert, *First World War,* 306.

124 "the only means of carrying the war": Parkinson, 123.

124 "I declared myself incompetent": Tschuppik, 87.

125 Holtzendorff estimated that the submarines: Stevenson, *Cataclysm,* 213.

125 Even in January, while still allowing: Gilbert, *First World War,*

306.

125   The lifting of restrictions became effective: Tons of merchant shipping sunk February through June 1917 are in Stevenson, *Cataclysm,* 264.

127   Under prodding from Erich Ludendorff: Details of the Auxiliary Service Law are in Herwig, 263; the increases in gunpowder and weapons production are in the same work, 260.

128   "not fighting, but famine": Ferguson, 9.

128   "socially and economically futile": Angell, 72.

129   "As long as there are goods and labor": Keynes's words are in Strachan, *First World War,* 817.

129   By 1917 the German government's expenditures: British, French, and German government spending as a percent of net national product is in Stevenson, *Cataclysm,* 179. The percentages of Britain's and the German federal government's budgets covered by tax revenues are in *Cataclysm,* 180.

129   Eventually it borrowed £568 million: Strachan, *First World War,* 956.

130   This accomplished nothing: The percentage of Russia's prewar tax revenue provided by the vodka monopoly is in Stevenson, *Cataclysm,* 181.

131   Germany issued war bonds twice: Ibid., 182.

131   By April 1917 the British were spending: Strachan, *First World War,* 975.

131   It is estimated that the war ultimately cost: numbers are in Stevenson, *Cataclysm,* 183.

133   Though the extent of the withdrawal: The dimensions of the withdrawal are in Johnson, 96, and Parkinson, 126.

134   Three hundred and seventy thousand men: The numbers of men and trains used to construct the new line are in Herwig, 250.

134   "The decision to retreat": Parkinson, 127.

135   The army itself was restructured: The number of newly created divisions is in Mosier, 269.

135   The Hindenburg Line would be twenty-five miles: The number of miles the front was shortened is in Johnson, 96; the number of divisions and batteries freed is in Herwig, 250.

135   At the start of 1917 the Germans had: The number of men is in Liddell Hart, *Real War,* 298; the number of divisions in Herwig, 247.

136   It was to be yet another massive offensive: The number of divisions planned for the Entente attack is in Paschall, 29.

137 This trench was almost ten feet deep: a physical description of the new defenses is in Herwig, 251.

137 They agreed also that they would wait until May: British generals (most importantly Haig and Robertson) would later claim that the plan approved at Chantilly called for the attack to begin in February 1917, which would have made the German withdrawal to the Hindenburg Line impossible and allowed the subsequent Flanders attack to take place before the onset of seasonal rains. This version of events has been accepted by historians ever since. Denis Winter, however, using documents not available until half a century after the war, offers persuasive evidence that the Chantilly conference ended in agreement to launch the joint offensives in May. The examination of this issue is in Winter, *Haig's Command,* 70–84.

138 "legacy of inevitable disaster": Lloyd George's words are in Wolff, 37.

139 "cur": Ibid., 40.

140 The death blow would be delivered: The number of divisions planned for Nivelle's Mass of Maneuver is in Johnson, 92.

141 The only difficulty was the question of timing: The difficulties over when to start the Nivelle offensive, and the final compromise, are in Winter, *Haig's Command,* 76.

141 "The French put forward a terrible scheme": Ibid., 83. Haig's letters are important as one part of Winter's demonstration that Lloyd George did not propose the appointment of a French supreme commander as Haig would later claim.

142 "This is a plan for the army": Clayton, 125.

143 "However the world pretends": Haste, 81.

144 London alone had sixteen daily papers: Ibid., 29.

144 Germany had four thousand: Welch, 29.

144 "a war in which we risk everything": Ferguson, 216.

144 "an anti-German frame of mind": Haste, 5.

145 "of such a nature as is calculated": Ibid., 83.

146 "the new philosophy of Germany": Ibid.

147 The unprecedented sum of £240,000: Ibid., 40.

147 "Good propaganda must keep well ahead": Welch, 195.

149 When Joffre fell and was succeeded: The number of Russian divisions to be involved in the 1917 joint offensive is in Rutherford, 235.

149 General Sir Henry Wilson, a senior member: Massie, *Nicholas and Alexandra,* 388.

150 "by terrorist methods if there is": Taylor, *Dynasties*, 257.

152 "Lovy, be firm": Radzinsky, 174.

152 "I order that the disorders": Nicholas's message is in Massie, *Nicholas and Alexandra*, 400.

153 He showed concern only for his wife: The size of the rebelling garrison is in Radzinsky, 180.

154 "whoever now dreams of peace": Taylor, *Dynasties*, 290.

155 "God in heaven, it's like": Palmer and Wallis, 290.

156 He set a quota of two hundred thousand transfers: The size of the quota, and the number of Belgians deported, are in Asprey, *German High Command*, 317.

157 The originators of the plan: The numbers are in Goodspeed, 197.

158 "All this is really no business of mine": Parkinson, 119.

159 we intend to begin unrestricted: Tuchman, *Zimmermann Telegram*, 146.

161 "I am finished with politics": Ibid., 149.

163 The House approved a War Resolution: The vote totals are in Ferrell, 2.

164 "Age-old subduers and punishers": Taylor, *Dynasties*, 262.

165 "love of freedom": Tolstoy, 46.

171 The Germans meanwhile, aware: The number of German divisions is in Paschall, 46.

172 The offensive began on April 9: The number of attacking armies is in Clayton, 128.

172 Their dimensions are apparent in the details: The trainloads of rock are in Paschall, 33, and the number of guns and heavy mortars in Paschall, 38.

173 "We moved forward, but the conditions": Arthur, 206.

173 Entente casualties had been fairly light: The average of four thousand per day is in Johnson, 119.

173 Haig had grounds for claiming success: Prisoner and captured gun numbers are in Wolff, 62.

174 By the time it all ended: Casualty figures are in Evans, *Battles*, 35.

175 "I had looked forward": Parkinson, 129.

176 Nivelle had three armies that among them: Division and troop totals are in Herwig, 327.

176 But twenty-seven divisions were held back: The size of the Mass of Maneuver is in Paschall, 33, and the number of German line and reserve divisions in Paschall, 46.

176 One hundred and twenty-eight: Tank numbers are in Clayton, 129.

177 "A snow squall swept our position": Lewis, 286.

178 "Peace! Down with war!": Herwig, 329.

178 "What, you try to make me responsible": Marshall, 211.

178 By the time the offensive: French and German casualty figures are in Herwig, 329.

182 Within six weeks of its start: The words of the unnamed officer are in Clayton, 130.

182 Approximately five hundred of them: Various writers give exact but widely differing numbers. For example, Clayton, 134, says 499 were condemned and twenty-seven were executed; the corresponding numbers in Herwig are "between 500 and 600" and "perhaps as many as 75."

183 "not forgetting the fact": Clayton, 134.

184 The U-boat campaign was at its height: Tons of shipping sunk in April 1917 is in Herwig, 318.

186 "the most important and wide-ranging": Hynes, 11.

187 "a purification, a liberation": Tuchman, *Guns of August,* 311.

187 "this abyss of blood and darkness": Ibid., 3.

187 *"If I should die, think only this of me"*: Silkin, 81.

188 "Let him who thinks that War is a glorious": Hynes, 112.

189 "the patriotic sentiment was so revolting": Ibid., 36.

189 "tremendous experiences": Winter, *Sites of Memory,* 160.

189 *"Bent double, like old beggars under sacks"*: Ward, 21.

192 By late spring: Rutherford, 248.

192 "I have co-signed the protocol": Feldman, 34.

192 "in complete accord": Farrar, *Divide and Conquer,* 80.

194 "Congress will not permit": Coffman, 8.

194 Until a gradual buildup was authorized: 1916 troop totals and the provisions of the National Defense Act are in Eisenhower, 22 and 23.

194 The nation's distrust of military establishments: Ibid., 22.

195 Thirty-two training camps: Coffman, 30.

196 "It is evident that a force": Ibid., 127.

197 "in Flanders the weather broke early": Wolff, 81.

198 "You can fight in mountains": Ibid., 79.

198 General Sir Herbert Plumer: Ypres as the scene of one-fourth of BEF casualties 1914–16 is in ibid., 83.

199 One of the mines was discovered: Paschall, 62, says five hundred

tons of explosives were placed under the ridge. Herwig, 330, and Liddell Hart, *Real War,* 331, both put the total at six hundred tons. Johnson, 126, gives a total of "nearly four hundred tons," and Wolff, 90, gives a most improbable figure of one million tons.

199 "When I heard the first deep rumble": Lewis, 292.

200 "We got out of the tank": Arthur, 217.

200 Plumer's infantry took possession: The number of Germans killed is estimated at ten thousand to twenty thousand in various sources. Mosier, 281, offers evidence that the total is not likely to have been as high as ten thousand.

201 "I shall name it to no one": Bonham-Carter, 5.

202 "overrule the military and naval authorities": Wolff, 118.

203 "Yesterday we saw heavy fighting": Palmer and Wallis, 292.

203 Though not nearly as large as what: The numbers are in Rutherford, 250.

204 Russian casualties had been almost trivial: Ibid., 254.

206 "The Reichstag strives": Feldman, 42.

209 "The danger of speaking out": Bruun, 121.

209 "So long as victory is possible": Jackson, Clemenceau, 120.

310 "One would have to be deliberately blind": Bruun, 116.

212 "Home policy?": Jackson, Clemenceau, 126.

213 Along fifteen miles of front: Evans, *Battles,* 40, and Wolff, 124, give 3,091 as the number of British guns. The comparison with the Somme is in Johnson, 139.

213 During the two weeks ending: The number of shells fired is in Evans, *Battles,* 40.

213 These shells had a total weight: The weight of the shells fired is in Paschall, 66, and the German casualties are in Paschall, 69.

214 "futile, fantastic and dangerous": These words are actually General Sir Henry Wilson's, in a diary entry presumably paraphrasing what Foch had said to him, in Wolff, 79.

214 Fourteen German divisions: Paschall, 69.

214 "My mind is quite at rest": Wolff, 135.

216 "ask me for *anything* but time": Ibid., 122.

216 "wholehearted support": Ibid., 124.

217 The offensive went off: Division numbers are in Groom, 185.

217 They penetrated nearly two miles: Paschall, 67.

217 Of the fifty-two tanks: Ibid., 67.

218 Haig, not aware that twenty-three: Haig's words are in ibid., 69.

218 But after two more days, with the rain: casualty figures are in ibid., 71.

219 "Inside it was only about five foot": Arthur, 229.

219 There were twenty-three such divisions: Paschall, 71.

219 "Blood and mud": Wolff, 165.

221 At the end of his preparations: One gun for five yards of front is in Paschall, 73.

221 Plumer's artillery would fire three and a half million: Wolff, 171.

221 Though it did not come cheaply: Casualty numbers are in Paschall, 73.

222 In the process they killed: Casualty figures are in ibid., 75.

222 "The fighting on the Western Front": Parkinson, 137.

224 "The slope," said an Australian: Wolff, 239.

225 The Italian commander in chief: Casualty figures for Tenth and Eleventh Isonzo are in Banks, 201.

226 The Germans and Austrians, whose thirty-three divisions: The numbers of divisions are in Mosier, 292.

227 Italian casualties totaled three hundred and twenty thousand: The numbers are in Evans, *Battles,* 43.

227 The price had been almost exactly: Paschall, 77.

227 The British, Canadians, Anzacs, and French: Casualty figures for Third Ypres are in Evans, *Battles,* 41, and Paschall, 79.

227 On November 20, near Cambrai: The numbers are in Mosier, 290.

227 Of the 216 new Mark IV tanks: The numbers are in Paschall, 126.

228 The British found themselves: The number of divisions is in Mosier, 298.

229 On the Western Front, the year had taken: Numbers of soldiers killed on the Western Front in 1917 are in ibid., 284 and 299.

PART SIX
1918: *Last Throw of the Dice*

Several books previously credited for their usefulness in earlier parts of this book were also particularly helpful in connection with 1918. Among them are L. L. Farrar's *Arrogance and Anxiety* (illuminating in connection with diplomacy), Holger H. Herwig's *The First World War,* and the fourth volume of Gerhard Ritter's *The Sword and the Sceptre.* The author is also indebted to Corelli Barnett for the final section of *The Swordbearers,* to Roger Parkinson's *Tormented Warrior: Ludendorff and the Supreme*

Command, to Alan Palmer's *The Gardeners of Salonika,* and to the following works dealing with 1918 exclusively: *The Battle for Europe 1918* by H. Essame; *Crisis 1918* by Joseph Gies; *1918: The Last Act* by Barrie Pitt; and *To Win a War* by John Terraine.

Page

234   The latter's casualties totaled: King, *Generals and Politicians,* 194.

234   General Pétain, the commander in chief: Clayton, 161.

234   It had fought off more than: Details of the French operations are in Terraine, *To Win a War,* 11.

235   With its larger population: British casualty figures are in King, *Generals and Politicians,* 194.

235   Some four hundred and fifty thousand fit and ready: Essame, 32.

235   British production of ammunition: Tonnage of shells and total British shipments to the continent are in ibid., 23.

236   Lloyd George had regarded Haig: Haig's pledge to the Conservatives not to replace Haig and Robertson is in Pitt, 33.

237   In 1917 Vienna conscripted: Herwig, 353.

237   That left it with no remaining: Ibid., 366.

237   Monthly rifle production was plummeting: Weapons production figures are in Herwig, 357.

237   It still had forty-four divisions: Numbers of divisions are in Herwig, 366.

240   "The Attack in Trench Warfare": Pitt, 44.

240   The goal was to create: Herwig, 395.

240   "pined for the offensive": Barnett, 280.

241   He declared that no offensive: Ludendorff's conditions are in Pitt, 42.

242   "reconciliation chancellor": Gies, 17.

242   Kühlmann, who pursued negotiations: Kühlmann's diplomatic objectives, and the divide-and-conquer objectives of German diplomacy generally, are the subject of Farrar, *Divide and Conquer.*

244   Seven hundred and fifty thousand: Herwig, 362.

244   The intensity of the discontent: Pitt, 39.

244   "the speedy conclusion of peace": Parkinson, 159.

244   Forty thousand strikers: Pitt, 39.

244   Between thirty-five hundred and six thousand: Herwig, 381.

245   "including an unequivocal declaration": Gies, 66.

246   "We make a hole": Asprey, *German High Command,* 367.

247   "fractured": Kohut, 47.

247   "one of those strange figures": Steinberg, 26.

249   "He would really be so pretty": Kohut, 47.

249   "a one-armed man should": Ibid., 43.

251   "The emperor is like a balloon": Ponsonby, 363.

251   "Nothing will change": Kohut, 214.

253   Fifty-seven British, Indian: Essame, 26.

253   While withholding infantry: The numbers of laborers sent, and the numbers put to work, are in ibid., 15.

255   He had ninety-nine divisions: Pitt, 62.

256   This was less than half: The number of corps to be shifted is in Gies, 75.

256   Haig, who had been obliged: King, *Generals and Politicians,* 47.

258   "I am sick of this d—d life": Terraine, *To Win a War,* 37.

258   Gough, whose Fifth Army: Miles and division totals are in Gies, 76.

261   Ludendorff was aggressive as always: The positions of Ludendorff and Kaiser Wilhelm at this meeting are in Herwig, 383.

261   "no war, no peace": Terraine, *To Win a War,* 21.

262   The Russians were now so helpless: German gains are in Stevenson, *Cataclysm,* 321.

262   Russia relinquished: Details of what Russia signed over at Brest-Litovsk are in Pitt, 45; Terraine, *To Win a War, 22;* and Asprey, *German High Command,* 360.

262   The delegation's chief refused: Goodspeed, 239.

262   At a time when they needed: The number of occupation troops that Germany required is in Ritter, 4:116.

263   Ukraine alone soaked up: Herwig, 386.

263   In the west he was assembling: The number of German troops is in Stevenson, *Cataclysm,* 325; the number of divisions in *Cataclysm,* 326.

265   "no one was anxious to detain him": Bruce, 60.

268   In spite of the immensity: The numbers are in Pitt, 45.

268   Between February 15 and March 20: Herwig, 392.

269   Ludendorff had had 150 divisions: Terraine, *To Win a War,* 22.

269   The results were at the front: The number of divisions is in Herwig, 395.

269   "The objective of the first day": Barnett, 291.

272   Among them the three had almost: Division numbers are in

Gies, 76.

272 Byng and Gough had fully a third: The deployment of troops is described in Barnett, 291.

272 "I was only afraid": Pitt, 57.

272 "There are strong indications": Barnett, 300.

273 The German attack force: Division and gun numbers are in Palmer, *Victory 1918,* 167.

273 By March 20 the fourteen divisions: Barnett, 293.

273 It included twenty-one divisions: Ibid., 293.

274 Along a line of more than: Pitt, 71.

274 "It was flamethrowers forward": Gies, 82.

275 To the extent that Gough's army could maintain the semblance: The extension of Gough's line is in Barnett, 307.

276 He sent six of his best divisions: Ibid., 311.

277 By the time this message arrived: Ibid., 312.

277 Eight of the divisions with which Gough: Ibid.

277 Haig asked Pétain for an additional: Haig's request, and the number of divisions sent by Pétain, are in Pitt, 95.

279 An enormous new cannon: Asprey, *German High Command,* 383.

279 "If an English delegation came": Herwig, 406.

279 Early on the morning of Sunday, March 24: Pitt, 93.

280 They ended Sunday's march: Parkinson, 157.

280 Haig understood the importance: Terraine, *To Win a War,* 46.

281 "save Amiens or everything's lost": Gies, 99.

281 "In my opinion . . . it was essential": Barnett, 326.

282 By March 26 the offensive was essentially: Pitt, 100.

283 "Today the advance of our infantry": Terraine, *To Win a War,* 48.

284 The Germans had captured twelve: Pitt, 109.

284 They had inflicted more than: Casualty and prisoner numbers are in Asprey, *German High Command,* 391.

285 "The Allies are very weak": Freidel, 85.

286 "there were reports of occasional": Parkinson, 174.

286 "I talked earnestly, urgently": Hocheimer's treatment of Ludendorff is described in ibid., 176.

287 "the war has spared me": Ibid., 157.

289 He was promoted to colonel: In their biographies Goodspeed, Parkinson, and Tschuppik all explore the meaning of Luden-

dorff's transfer away from the high command headquarters.

291 Ninety German divisions had been thrown: Herwig, 408.

291 The scale of the losses: Essame, 48.

292 Britain was not notably better off: Pitt, 111.

292 "that it could not take Amiens": Ritter, 4:233.

292 "all political questions were": Barnett, 278.

293 "all powers necessary": Pitt, 111.

293 Georgette . . . opened modestly: Details are in ibid., 120.

294 "Every position must be held": Essame, 48.

295 "The conquest was a nightmare": Gies, 118.

295 "a gigantic struggle beginning": Parkinson, 149.

295 On April 24 nine divisions: Keegan, *Illustrated History*, 374.

296 "Gray-blue figures out of the half-buried": Gies, 121.

298 General von Kuhl, chief of staff: Kuhl's view of the consequences of the failure are in Pitt, 130.

298 His casualties since the start of Michael: Numbers are in Barnett, 331.

299 "The absence of our old": Terraine, *To Win a War*, 53.

299 Though French and British losses: Numbers of arriving American troops are in Palmer, *Victory 1918*, 177.

302 An office was established in Paris: The 12-million–ton figure is in Freidel, 73.

302 The Americans would install: Eisenhower, 57.

302 It broadened conscription, drafting: Gies, 124.

303 The French had 103 divisions: Ibid., 143.

304 *"J'ai dit"*: Essame, 58.

304 More than twenty divisions were assembled: The numbers and the words in quotes are in Essame, 59.

308 "Hundreds upon hundreds of wounded": Heyman, 122.

308 "We are supposed to care": Ibid., 124.

308 More than fifteen thousand women: Ibid., 120–21.

309 "For the first time I was going": Ibid., 122.

309 In France 85 percent of women: The data are in Steven C. Hause, "More Minerva than Mars: the French Women's Rights Campaign and the First World War," in Higonnet et al., 106.

310 In Germany more than five million: Ferguson, 267–68.

310 Female employment in French munitions factories: Hause, "More Minerva," in Higonnet et al., 104.

311   In Germany alone more than a million and a half: The data are in Karin Hausen: "The German Nation's Obligation to the Heroes' Widows of World War I," in Higonnet et al., 128.

315   Hutier's troops advanced: German gains are in Essame, 72.

316   By the end one hundred and eighty-six thousand German: Terraine, *To Win a War*, 150.

317   "had probably the greatest capacity": Serle, 377.

317   Eleven days after Hamel—one wonders how: Pitt, 179.

318   Twenty-three divisions, four of them American: Gies, 229.

319   "Machine guns raved everywhere": Terraine, *To Win a War*, 78.

320   In March the Germans had had three hundred thousand: The numbers in this paragraph are in Essame, 101.

320   "Midnight," a German soldier: Gies, 248.

322   The Germans lost more than six hundred and fifty officers: Ibid., 131.

323   The troops were in such a sorry state: Parkinson, 164.

324   On the second day they were driven back: Herwig, 370.

325   But Britain and France alike: Drafting of fifty-year-old Britons is in Paschall, 165.

325   Workers at ammunition factories: British labor troubles are in Terraine, *To Win a War*, 126.

325   Their casualties in August alone: German casualties, and the following sentence on the declining number of divisions, are in Herwig, 424.

328   "dangerous and likely to lead": Palmer, *Gardeners of Salonika*, 49.

328   It included one hundred and sixty thousand men: Troop numbers are in ibid.; the January 1916 total on 52, the May total on 63.

328   Rumors circulated to the effect that: Ibid., 95.

329   The Entente had more than half a million: Pope and Wheal, 418.

329   "the gardeners of Salonika": Palmer, *Gardeners of Salonika*, 71.

330   "I bear you no ill-will": Ibid., 183.

330   "I expect from you savage vigor": Ibid., 186.

330   Two hundred and fifty thousand Greek: Pope and Wheal, 418.

331   "The man could escape even now": Parkinson, 175.

332   On the British part of the front: Essame, 149.

333   "for nearly three years the last": Swettenham, 33.

333   "the pride and wonder of the British": Ibid., 171.

333   "He had a tremendous command of profanity": Dancocks, 18.

333   They never once failed: Ibid., 174.

334   He wanted not only to capture: Essame, 155.

334   Fifteen thousand German troops: Ibid., 158.

334   But Pershing had eight hundred and twenty thousand men: Ibid., 157.

334   "We could not answer every single cry": Terraine, *To Win a War*, 131.

335   "as a result of the collapse": Palmer, *Gardeners of Salonika*, 228.

335   Ludendorff, all options exhausted: Ritter, 4:339.

335   "clung to that news like a drowning": Ibid., 4:340.

335   The war had rarely been bloodier: Terraine, *To Win a War*, 224.

335   "I have seen prisoners coming": Ibid., 129.

336   The French now had nearly 40 percent: Clayton, 163.

336   When the Canadians finally broke through: Terraine, *To Win a War*, 166.

336   Almost 90 percent of the men: Terraine, *To Win a War*, 163.

338   "revolution from above": Ritter, 4:342.

338   "broken and suddenly aged man": Terraine, *To Win a War*, 158.

339   "the one prominent royalist liberal": Palmer, *Victory 1918*, 234.

342   General Wilhelm Gröner: Gröner's report on missing troops is in Herwig, 442.

342   The blood continued to flow: French casualties are in Clayton, 162.

343   "If the Government of the United States": Parkinson, 181.

343   "Our enemies merely pay": Ritter, 4:365.

344   In Italy an Allied force of fifty-six divisions: division numbers are in Herwig, 436.

344   "soldier's honor": Ritter, 4:366.

344   "I am a plain ordinary citizen": Ibid., 367.

344   "You will stay": Ibid., 368.

344   "looking forward to proposals": Ibid., 369.

345   He received thirty-nine replies: Herwig, 445.

346   These included German withdrawal: The terms of the Treaty of Versailles are examined clearly and in detail in Sharp, 102–29.

346   "No no no!": Essame, 205.

347   Something on the order of 9.5 million men: Overall casualty figures are in Ferguson, 295.

348   "Central Europe is aflame": Sharp, 130.

Bibliography

Allen, Kenneth. *Big Guns of the Twentieth Century and Their Part in Great Battles.* Hove, England: Firefly, 1976.

Angell, Norman. *The Great Illusion.* London: William Heinemann, 1910.

Arthur, Max. *Forgotten Voices of the Great War.* Guilford, Conn.: Lyons Press, 2002.

Asprey, Robert B. *The First Battle of the Marne.* Philadelphia and New York: J. B. Lippincott, 1962.

———. *The German High Command at War.* New York: William Morrow, 1991.

Audoin-Rouzeau, Stephane, and Annette Becker. *1914–1918: Understanding the Great War.* New York: Hill and Wang, 2000.

Austin, Walter F., ed. *Source Records of the Great War.* [no city given]: National Alumni, 1923.

Bach, H. I. *The German Jew.* London: Oxford University Press, 1984.

Balakian, Peter. *The Burning Tigris.* New York: HarperCollins, 2003.

Banks, Arthur. *A Military Atlas of the First World War.* Barnsley, South Yorkshire: Leo Cooper, 1997.

Barber, Noel. *The Sultans.* News York: Simon and Schuster, 1973.

Barnett, Corelli. *The Swordbearers.* New York: Signet, 1965.

Barrie, Alexander. *War Underground: The Tunnelers of the Great War.* Staplehurst, Kent: Spellmount, 2000.

Berenson, Edward. *The Trial of Madame Caillaux.* Berkeley: University of California Press, 1992.

Berghahn, V. R. *Germany and the Approach of War in 1914.* New York: St. Martin's Press, 1973.

Bismarck, Otto von. *The Kaiser vs. Bismarck: Suppressed Letters.* New York: Harper & Brothers, 1920.

Blond, Georges. *The Marne.* Harrisburg, Pa.: Stackpole Books, 1965.

Bonham-Carter, Victor. *The Strategy of Victory, 1914–1918.* New York: Holt, Rinehart and Winston, 1964.

Brandenburg, Erich. *From Bismarck to the World War.* London: Oxford University Press, 1933.

Bruce, Anthony. *The Last Crusade: The Palestine Campaign in the First World War.* London: John Murray, 2002.

Bruun, Geoffrey. *Clemenceau.* Cambridge, Mass.: Harvard University Press, 1943.

Buchan, John. *The Battle of the Somme.* New York: George H. Doran, 1917.

Buehr, Walter. *Firearms.* New York: Thomas Y. Crowell, 1967.

Caffrey, Kate. *Farewell, Leicester Square: The Old Contemptibles 12 August–20 November 1914.* London: André Deutsch, 1980.

Cameron, James. *1914.* New York: Rinehart & Co., 1959.

Carew, Tim. *The Vanished Army: The British Expeditionary Force 1914–1915.* London: William Kimber, 1914.

Carsten, F. L. *The Origins of Prussia.* Oxford: Clarendon, 1954.

Cassels, Lavender. *The Archduke and the Assassin.* New York: Stein & Day, 1985.

Chickering, Roger. *Imperial Germany and the Great War, 1914–1918.* Cambridge: Cambridge University Press, 1999.

Churchill, Winston S. *The Unknown War, The Eastern Front.* New York: Scribner's, 1931.

———. *The World Crisis, 1916–1918.* New York: Charles Scribner's Sons, 1927.

Clark, Alan. *The Donkeys.* London: Pimlico, 1998.

Clark, Christopher M. *Kaiser Wilhelm II.* London: Longman, 2000.

Clayton, Anthony. *Paths of Glory: The French Army 1914–1918.* London: Cassell, 2003.

Coetzee, Frans, and Marilyn Shevin-Coetzee, eds. *Authority, Identity and Social History of the Great War.* Providence, R.I.: Berghahn, 1995.

Coffman, Edward M. *The War to End All Wars.* New York: Oxford University Press, 1968.

Cooper, Bryan. *The Ironclads of Cambrai.* London: Cassell, 1967.

Cowles, Virginia. *The Kaiser.* New York: Harper & Row, 1963.

Cowley, Robert, ed. *The Great War.* New York: Random House, 2003.

Craig, Gordon A. *The Politics of the Prussian Army 1640–1945.* New York: Oxford University Press, 1972.

Crankshaw, Edward. *The Shadow of the Winter Palace.* New York: Viking, 1976.

Cruttwell, C.R.M.F. *A History of the Great War 1914–1918.* 2nd ed. Chicago: Academy Chicago Publishers, 1991.

Dallas, Gregor. *At the Heart of a Tiger: Clemenceau and His World 1841–1929.* New York: Carroll & Graf, 1993.

———. *1918: War and Peace.* London: Pimlico, 2002.

Dancocks, Daniel G. *Sir Arthur Currie.* Toronto: Methuen, 1985.

Darrow, Margaret H. *French Women and the First World War.* Oxford: Berg, 2000.

David, Daniel. *The 1914 Campaign.* New York: Military Press, 1987.

Dedijer, Vladimir. *The Road to Sarajevo.* New York: Simon & Schuster, 1966.

De Groot, Gerard J. *Blighty: British Society in the Era of the Great War.* London: Longman, 1996.

Dupuy, Trevor N., Curt Johnson, and David L. Bongard. *The Harper Encyclopedia of Military Biography.* Edison, N.J.: Castle Books, 1995.

Edwards, Cecil. *John Monash.* Melbourne: State Electricity Commission of Victoria, 1970.

Eisenhower, John S. D. *Yanks.* New York: Free Press, 2001.

Eksteins, Modris. *Rites of Spring: The Great War and the Birth of the Modern Age.* New York: Doubleday, 1990.

Ellis, John. *The Social History of the Machine Gun.* Baltimore: Johns Hopkins University Press, 1975.

Enock, Arthur Guy. *This War Business.* London: Bodley Head, 1951.

Essame, H. *The Battle for Europe 1918.* New York: Charles Scribner's Sons, 1972.

Eubank, Keith. *The Summit Conferences 1919–1960.* Norman: University of Oklahoma Press, 1966.

Evans, Martin Marix. *Battles of World War I.* Marlborough, Wiltshire: Airlife, 2004.

Evans, R. J. W., and Pogge von Strandmann, eds. *The Coming of the First World War.* Oxford: Clarendon Press, 1988.

Eversley, Lord. *The Turkish Empire from 1288 to 1914.* New York: Howard Fertig, 1969.

Falls, Cyril. *The Great War, 1914–1918.* New York: Putnam's, 1959.

Farrar, L. L., Jr. *Arrogance and Anxiety: The Ambivalence of German Power, 1848–1914.* Iowa City: University of Iowa Press, 1981.

———. *Divide and Conquer: German Efforts to Conclude a Separate Peace, 1914–1918.* Boulder, Colo.: East European Quarterly, 1978.

Farrar-Hockley, Anthony. *Death of an Army*. Ware, Hertfordshire: Wordsworth Editions, 1998.

Farwell, Byron. *Over There: The United States in the Great War*. New York: W. W. Norton, 1999.

Fay, Sidney Bradshaw. *After Sarajevo: The Origins of the World War*. New York: Free Press, 1966.

Feldman, Gerald D., ed. *German Imperialism, 1914–1918*. New York: John Wiley & Sons, 1972.

Ferguson, Niall. *The Pity of War*. New York: Basic Books, 1999.

Ferrell, Robert H. *Woodrow Wilson and World War I*. New York: Harper & Row, 1985.

Ferro, Marc. *The Great War 1914–1918*. Boston: Routledge & Kegan Paul, 1982.

Fleming, Thomas. *The Illusion of Victory: America in World War I*. New York: Basic Books, 2003.

Ford, Roger. *The Grim Reaper: Machine Guns and Machine Gunners*. New York: Sarpedon, 1996.

Freidel, Frank. *Over There: The American Experience in World War I*. Short Hills, N.J.: Burford Books, 1964.

French, John Denton Pinkstone. *1914*. Boston: Houghton Mifflin, 1919.

Friedrich, Otto. *Blood and Iron*. New York: HarperCollins, 1995.

Fromkin, David. *Europe's Last Summer*. New York: Alfred A. Knopf, 2004.

Fussell, Paul. *The Great War and Modern Memory*. New York: Oxford University Press, 1975.

Geiss, Imanuel, ed. *July 1914: The Outbreak of the First World War: Selected Documents*. New York: Charles Scribner's Sons, 1967.

Gies, Joseph. *Crisis 1918*. New York: W. W. Norton, 1974.

Gilbert, Martin. *The First World War*. New York: Henry Holt, 1994.

———. *Winston S. Churchill*. Boston: Houghton Mifflin, 1971.

Gleichen, Lord Edward, ed. *Chronology of the Great War, 1914–1918*. London: Greenhill Books, 2000.

Goemans, H. E. *War and Punishment: The Causes of War Termination and the First World War*. Princeton, N.J.: Princeton University Press, 2000.

Goerlitz, Walter. *History of the German General Staff, 1657–1945*. New York: Frederick A. Praeger, 1960.

Goldberg, Harvey. *The Life of Jean Jaurès*. Madison: University of Wisconsin Press, 1968.

Goodspeed, D. J. *Ludendorff: Genius of World War I*. Boston: Houghton

Mifflin, 1966.

Griffiths, Richard. *Pétain.* Garden City, N.Y.: Doubleday, 1972.

Groom, Winston. *A Storm in Flanders: The Ypres Salient, 1914–1918.* New York: Atlantic Monthly Press, 2002.

Guinn, Paul. *British Strategy and Politics, 1914–1918.* Oxford: Oxford University Press, 1965.

Haber, L. F. *The Poisonous Cloud: Chemical Warfare in the First World War.* Oxford: Clarendon, 1986.

Hall, Richard C. *The Balkan Wars 1912–1913.* London: Routledge, 2002.

Halperin, John. *Eminent Georgians.* New York: St. Martin's, 1995.

Haste, Cate. *Keep the Home Fires Burning: Propaganda in the First World War.* London: Penguin, 1977.

Hayward, James. *Myths and Legends of the First World War.* Stroud, Gloucestershire: Sutton, 2002.

Hazelhurst, Cameron. *Politicians at War, July 1914 to May 1915.* New York: Alfred A. Knopf, 1971.

Herrmann, David G. *The Arming of Europe and the Making of the First World War.* Princeton, N.J.: Princeton University Press, 1996.

Herwig, Holger H. *The First World War: Germany and Austria 1914–1918.* London: Arnold, 1997.

Heyman, Neil M. *Daily Life During World War I.* Westport, Conn: Greenwood Press, 2002.

Higgins, Trumbull. *Winston Churchill and the Dardanelles.* New York: Macmillan, 1963.

Higonnet, Margaret Randolph et al., eds. *Behind the Lines: Gender and the Two World Wars.* New Haven, Conn.: Yale University Press, 1987.

Hoehling, A. A. *The Great War at Sea.* New York: Barnes & Noble, 1965.

Horne, Alistair. *The Price of Glory: Verdun 1916.* New York: St. Martin's, 1963.

Horne, John, ed. *State, Society and Mobilization in Europe During the First World War.* Cambridge: Cambridge University Press, 1997.

Hough, Richard. *The Great War at Sea.* Oxford: Oxford University Press, 1983.

Hynes, Samuel. *A War Imagined: The First World War and English Culture.* New York: Atheneum, 1991.

Isselin, Henri. *The Battle of the Marne.* Garden City, N.J.: Doubleday, 1966.

Jackson, J. Hampden. *Clemenceau and the Third Republic.* New York: Collier, 1962.

———. *Jean Jaurès.* London: George Allen & Unwin, 1943.

James, Robert Rhodes. *Gallipoli.* New York: Macmillan, 1965.

Jannen, Jr., William. *The Lions of July.* Novato, Calif.: Presidio Press, 1997.

Jenkins, Roy. *Asquith.* New York: Chilmark, 1964.

Johnson, J. H. *Stalemate! Great Trench Warfare Battles.* London: Rigel, 2004.

Joll, James. *The Origins of the First World War.* London: Longman, 1984.

Keegan, John. *A History of Warfare.* New York: Vintage Books, 1994.

————. *An Illustrated History of the First World War.* New York: Alfred A. Knopf, 2001.

Keiger, John F. V. *France and the Origins of the First World War.* New York: St. Martin's, 1983.

Kennedy, Paul M., ed. *The War Plans of the Great Powers, 1880–1914.* Boston: Allen & Unwin, 1979.

Kent, George O. *Bismarck and His Times.* Carbondale, Ill.: Southern Illinois Press, 1978.

King, Jere Clemens, ed. *The First World War: Selected Documents.* London: Macmillan, 1972.

————. *Generals and Politicians.* Berkeley: University of California Press, 1951.

Kitchen, Martin. *The German Offensives of 1918.* Stroud, Gloucestershire: Tempus, 2001.

Kluck, Alexander von. *The March on Paris and the Battle of the Marne.* London: Edward Arnold, 1920.

Kohut, Thomas A. *Wilhelm II and the Germans.* New York: Oxford University Press, 1991.

Kraft, Barbara S. *The Peace Ship.* New York: Macmillan, 1978.

Lacouture, Jean. *De Gaulle: The Rebel 1890–1944.* New York: W. W. Norton, 1990.

Lafore, Laurence. *The Long Fuse.* Prospect Heights, Ill.: Waveland Press, 1971.

Lauret, René. *France and Germany.* Chicago: Henry Regnery, 1964.

Lederer, Ivo J., ed. *The Versailles Settlement.* Boston: D. C. Heath, 1960.

Leed, Eric J. *No Man's Land: Combat and Identity in World War I.* Cambridge: Cambridge University Press, 1979.

Leese, Peter. *Shell Shock: Traumatic Neurosis and the British Soldiers of the First World War.* New York: Palgrave Macmillan, 2002.

Lewis, Jon E., ed. *The Mammoth Book of Eyewitness World War I.* New York: Carroll & Graf, 2003.

Liddell Hart, B. H. *The Real War 1914–1918*. Boston: Little, Brown, 1930.

———. *Reputations. Ten Years After*. Boston: Little, Brown, 1928.

Lincoln, W. Bruce. *In War's Dark Shadow*. New York: Oxford University Press, 1994.

Listowel, Judith. *A Hapsburg Tragedy*. New York: Dorset, 1986.

Lomas, David. *First Ypres 1914*. New York: St. Martin's, 1963.

Ludendorff, Erich von. *Ludendorff's Own Story*. New York: Harper & Brothers, 1919.

Lutz, Ralph Haswell, ed. *The Causes of the German Collapse in 1918*. Archon Books, 1969.

Macdonald, Lyn. *1914*. New York: Atheneum, 1988.

———. *1915, The Death of Innocence*. New York: Henry Holt, 1993.

———. *Somme*. London: Michael Joseph, 1983.

MacDonogh, Giles. *The Last Kaiser*. New York: St. Martin's, 2000.

Macdougall, A. K., ed. *War Letters of General Monash*. Sydney: Duffy & Snellgrove, 2002.

Macmillian, Margaret. *Paris 1919*. New York: Random House, 2002.

Magnus, Philip. *Kitchener*. New York: Dutton, 1968.

Mann, Golo. *The History of Germany Since 1789*. New York: Frederick A. Praeger, 1968.

Marshall, S. L. A. *The American Heritage History of World War I*. [no city given]: American Heritage, 1964.

Marwick, Arthur, ed. *Total War and Social Change*. New York: St. Martin's, 1988.

Massie, Robert K. *Castles of Steel*. New York: Random House, 2003.

———. *Nicholas and Alexandra*. New York: Atheneum, 1967.

May, Arthur. *The Passing of the Hapsburg Monarchy 1914–1918*. Philadelphia: University of Pennsylvania Press, 1966.

Mayeur, Jean-Marie, and Madeleine Reberieux. *The Third Republic from Its Origins to the Great War, 1871–1914*. Cambridge: Cambridge University Press, 1987.

McDougall, Walter A. *France's Rhineland Diplomacy, 1914–1924*. Princeton, N.J.: Princeton University Press, 1978.

Middlebrook, Martin. *The First Day on the Somme*. New York: W. W. Norton, 1972.

Miller, Steven E., Sean M. Lynn-Jones, and Stephan Van Evera, eds. *Military Strategy and the Origins of the First World War*. Princeton, N.J.: Princeton University Press, 1991.

Millis, Walter. *Road to War, America 1914–1917*. Boston: Houghton

Mifflin, 1935.

Mitchell, David. *Monstrous Regiment: The Story of the Women of the First World War.* New York: Macmillan, 1965.

Mombauer, Annika. *Helmuth von Moltke and the Origins of the First World War.* Cambridge: Cambridge University Press, 2001.

Mommsen, Wolfgang J. *Imperial Germany, 1867–1918.* London: Arnold, 1990.

Moore, William. *The Thin Yellow Line.* Ware, Hertfordshire: Wordsworth, 1974.

Moorehead, Alan. *Gallipoli.* New York: Perennial Classics, 2002.

Mosier, John. *The Myth of the Great War.* New York: HarperCollins, 2001.

Muncy, Lysbeth Walker. *The Junker in the Prussian Administration under Wilhelm II, 1888–1914.* New York: Howard Fertig, 1970.

Neiberg, Michael S. *Fighting the Great War.* Cambridge: Harvard University Press, 2005.

Neillands, Robin. *Attrition: The Great War on the Western Front, 1916.* London: Robson, 2001.

Nomikos, Eugenia, and Robert C. North. *International Crisis: The Outbreak of World War I.* Montreal: McGill–Queen's University Press, 1976.

Ousby, Ian. *The Road to Verdun.* New York: Anchor, 2003.

Palmer, Alan. *The Gardeners of Salonika.* New York: Simon & Schuster, 1965.

———. *Twilight of the Hapsburgs.* New York: Grove, 1995.

———. *Victory 1918.* New York: Atlantic Monthly Press, 1998.

Palmer, Svetlana, and Sarah Wallis. *Intimate Voices from the First World War.* New York: Perennial, 2005.

Panichas, George A., ed. *Promise of Greatness: The War of 1914–1918.* New York: John Day, 1968.

Parkinson, Roger. *Tormented Warrior: Ludendorff and the Supreme Command.* New York: Stein & Day, 1979.

Paschall, Rod. *The Defeat of Imperial Germany, 1917–1918.* Chapel Hill, N.C.: Algonquin Books, 1989.

Passingham, Ian. *All the Kaiser's Men.* Stroud, Gloucestershire: Sutton, 2003.

Pedersen, P. A. *Monash as Military Commander.* Carlton, Victoria: Melbourne University Press, 1985.

Perry, Roland. *Monash: The Outsider Who Won a War.* Sydney: Random House Australia, 2004.

Philpott, William James. *Anglo-French Relations and Strategy on the*

Western Front, 1914–1918. New York: St. Martin's, 1996.

Pitt, Barrie. *1918: The Last Act.* New York: Norton, 1963.

Ponsonby, Frederick, ed. *The Letters of Empress Frederick.* London: Macmillan, 1929.

Pontig, Clive. *Thirteen Days: The Road to the First World War.* London: Chatto & Windus, 2002.

Pope, Stephen, and Elizabeth-Anne Wheal. *The Macmillan Dictionary of the First World War.* London: Macmillan, 1997.

Pound, Reginald. *The Lost Generation of 1914.* New York: Coward-McCann, 1964.

Preston, Diana. *Lusitania.* New York: Walker, 2002.

Rachamimov, Alon. *POWs and the Great War: Captivity on the Eastern Front.* Oxford: Berg, 2002.

Radzinsky, Edvard. *The Last Tsar.* New York: Doubleday, 1992.

Read, James Morgan. *Atrocity Propaganda 1914–1919.* New Haven: Yale University Press, 1941.

Remak, Joachim. *Sarajevo.* New York: Criterion Books, 1959.

Renouvin, Pierre. *The Immediate Origins of the War.* New York: Howard Fertig, 1969.

Reynolds, Francis J. *The Story of the Great War.* New York: P. F. Collier & Son, 1916.

Ripley, Tim. *Bayonet Battle: Bayonet Warfare in the Twentieth Century.* London: Sidgwick & Jackson, 1999.

Ritter, Gerhard. *The Sword and the Scepter; The Problem of Militarism in Germany.* Coral Gables, Fla.: University of Miami Press, 1970.

Röhl, John. *1914—Delusion or Design?* New York: St. Martin's, 1973.

Rutherford, Ward. *The Russian Army in World War I.* London: Gordon Cremonesi, 1975.

Schmitt, Bernadotte E., and Harold C. Vedeler. *The World in the Crucible, 1914–1919.* New York: Harper & Row, 1984.

Schulz, Gerhard. *Revolutions and Peace Treaties 1917–1920.* London: Methuen, 1967.

Schwink, Otto. *Ypres 1914* [An Official Account Published by Order of the German General Staff]. London: Constable & Co., 1919.

Serle, Geoffrey. *John Monash.* Melbourne: Melbourne University Press, 1982.

Seton-Watson, R. W. *Sarajevo.* London: Hutchinson, 1926.

Sharp, Alan. *The Versailles Settlement.* New York: St. Martin's, 1991.

Sheehan, James J., ed. *Imperial Germany.* New York: New Viewpoints,

1976.

Shephard, Ben. *A War of Nerves.* Cambridge, Mass.: Harvard, 2001.

Silkin, Jon. *The Penguin Book of First World War Poetry.* London: Penguin, 1996.

Simpson, Andy. *Hot Blood and Cold Steel.* London: Tom Donovan, 1993.

Sked, Alan. *The Decline and Fall of the Hapsburg Empire 1815–1918.* London: Longman, 2001.

Smithers, A. J. *Sir John Monash.* London: Leo Cooper, 1973.

Spears, Major General Sir Edward. *Liaison 1914.* New York: Stein and Day, 1968.

Steinberg, Jonathan. *Yesterday's Deterrent: Tirpitz and the Birth of the German Battle Fleet.* London: Ashgate, 1965.

Stevenson, David. *Cataclysm: The First World War as Political Tragedy.* New York: Basic Books, 2004.

———. *The First World War and International Politics.* New York: Oxford University Press, 1988.

———. *French War Aims Against Germany.* Oxford: Clarendon Press, 1982.

Stone, Norman. *The Eastern Front, 1914–1917.* New York: Scribner's, 1975.

Strachan, Hew. *The First World War,* vol. 1, *To Arms.* Oxford: Oxford University Press, 2001.

Strachan, Hew, ed. *World War I, A History.* Oxford: Oxford University Press, 1998.

Sweetman, John. *Tannenberg 1914.* London: Cassell, 2002.

Swettenham, John. *To Seize the Victory: The Canadian Corps in World War I.* Toronto: Ryerson, 1965.

Taylor, A.J.P. *The First World War: An Illustrated History.* New York: Penguin, 1972.

Taylor, Edmond. *The Fall of the Dynasties.* Garden City, N.Y.: Doubleday & Co., 1963.

Terraine, John. *The Western Front 1914–1918.* Philadelphia and New York: Lippincott, 1965.

———. *To Win a War.* Garden City, N.Y.: Doubleday & Co., 1981.

Thoumin, General Richard. *The First World War.* New York: G. P. Putnam's Sons, 1964.

Tolstoy, Leo. *The Cossacks.* Boston: Houghton Mifflin, 1932.

Tschuppik, Karl. *Ludendorff: The Tragedy of a Military Mind.* Boston: Houghton Mifflin, 1932.

Tuchman, Barbara W. *The Guns of August.* New York: Macmillan, 1962.

——. *The Proud Tower.* New York: Macmillan, 1966.

——. *The Zimmermann Telegram.* New York: Macmillan, 1966.

Tucker, Spencer C. *The European Powers in the First World War, An Encyclopedia.* New York: Garland, 1996.

——. *The Great War 1914–18.* Bloomington: Indiana University Press, 1998.

Vincent, C. Paul. *The Politics of Hunger: The Allied Blockade of Germany 1915–1919.* Athens: Ohio University Press, 1985.

Ward, Candace, ed. *World War One British Poets.* Mineola, N.Y.: Dover Publications, 1997.

Weintraub, Stanley. *Silent Night.* New York: Free Press, 2000.

Welch, David. *Germany: Propaganda and Total War, 1914–1918.* New Brunswick, N.J.: Rutgers University Press, 2000.

Williamson, Samuel R., Jr. "The Origins of the War." In *World War I: A History,* edited by Hew Strachan. New York: Oxford University Press, 1998.

Winter, Denis. *Haig's Command.* New York: Viking, 1991.

Winter, Jay. *Sites of Memory, Sites of Mourning.* Cambridge: Cambridge University Press, 1995.

Winter, Jay, and Jean-Louis Robert. *Capital Cities at War: Paris, London, Berlin 1914–1919.* Cambridge: Cambridge University Press, 1997.

Winter, Jay, Geoffrey Park, and Mary R. Habeck, eds. *The Great War and the Twentieth Century.* New Haven, Conn.: Yale University Press, 2000.

Wolff, Leon. *In Flanders Fields: The 1917 Campaign.* New York: Viking, 1958.

Woodward, Sir Llewellyn. *Great Britain and the War of 1914–1918.* London: Methuen, 1967.

Zeman, Z.A.B. *The Gentlemen Negotiators: A Diplomatic History of the First World War.* New York: Macmillan, 1971.

Zuckerman, Larry. *The Rape of Belgium.* New York: New York University Press, 2004.

Index

About the Author

G. J. Meyer is the author of four popular works of history, *The World Remade: America in World War I, The Borgias, The Tudors,* and *A World Undone: The Story of the Great War,* as well as *Executive Blues* and *The Memphis Murders.* He received an M.A. from the University of Minnesota, where he was a Woodrow Wilson Fellow, and later was awarded Harvard University's Nieman Fellowship in Journalism. He has taught at colleges in Des Moines, St. Louis, and New York, and now lives in Wiltshire, England.